West from Fort Bridger

—*Charles Kelly photo, Utah State Historical Society*

OLD EMIGRANT TRAIL ON THE SALT DESERT

Floating Island to the left; Silver Island in the distance. Note the trail of the emigrant wagons preserved in the salt and part of the running gears of an abandoned wagon.

West from Fort Bridger

The Pioneering of the Immigrant Trails across Utah
1846–1850

Original Diaries and Journals Edited and with Introductions by
J. Roderic Korns and Dale L. Morgan

Revised and Updated by
Will Bagley and Harold Schindler

Utah State University Press
Logan, Utah
1994

To the Memory of J. Roderic Korns and Dale L. Morgan

First edition published as Volume XIX of the *Utah Historical Quarterly*. Revised and reprinted by arrangement with the Utah State Historical Society.

Second Printing, January 1995.

Library of Congress Cataloging-in-Publication Data

West from Fort Bridger : the pioneering of the Immigrant Trails
    across Utah, 1846–1850 / original diaries and journals edited and
    with introductions by J. Roderic Korns and Dale L. Morgan ;
    revised and updated by Will Bagley and Harold Schindler.
       p.   cm.
    Includes index.
    ISBN 0-87421-178-6
    ISBN 0-87421-189-1
    1. Pioneers—Utah—Diaries. 2. Overland journeys to the Pacific—
History—Sources. 3. Utah—Description and travel—Sources. 4.
Utah—History—Sources. I. Korns, J. Roderic, 1890–1949.
II. Morgan, Dale Lowell, 1914–1971. III. Bagley, Will, 1950–.
IV. Schindler, Harold, 1929–.
    F821.W47   1994
    979.2'02—dc20   94–16876
                                                        CIP

CONTENTS

ILLUSTRATIONS

MAPS

INTRODUCTION TO THE NEW EDITION

In THE AUTUMN of 1941, Dale Lowell Morgan opened what was to become an eight-year correspondence with Salt Lake City businessman J. Roderic Korns. It was a fascinating and altogether astonishing exchange of ideas between three men—the third being Salt Desert historian Charles Kelly—who were obsessed with the history of the American West. This letter to Korns explained Morgan's purpose:

> One thing after another that has occupied my attention sooner or later turns out to be something you have already looked into. We seem to have minds that work alike, only yours works much sooner. Half a dozen times, now, I have mentioned something to Charlie Kelly that has attracted my interest, and he tells me, "Rod Korns looked into that"; "Korns did some research on that"; "Korns probably knows—he checked the facts." And then at times, in taking books from the library, I have noted shrewd marginal comments which could not be made by the man on the street, and although I may be wide of the mark here, I wouldn't be surprised to have you tell me that Mr. Korns knows something about this.

That was how it all started. Over the best part of the 1940s, the letters continued, addressed "Dear Rod and Charlie," or "Dear Rod and Dale," or "Dear Dale and Charlie." The flow of information was, in any terms, awesome, covering every aspect of their mutual interest: the Great Basin, the opening of the West, overland travel and wagon roads, Indians, fur traders and trappers, and the gold rush, to say nothing of Mormon history, the Great Salt Lake, and the Great Salt Desert.

The overland pioneers who challenged the rivers, mountains, deserts, and tribes to conquer the new lands in the West fascinated Korns, and by 1943 it was obvious to Morgan that Korns was a great resource going to waste. Their single-spaced letters—often filling six, eight, even ten pages written over many days—were crowded with facts, theories, arguments, and new discoveries sufficient to fill a bookshelf. Morgan, who preached and practiced the doctrine of shared information, pressed Korns to write a book.

In April, 1943, after discussing Edwin Bryant's adventures in Utah, Morgan suggested, "I propose that as soon as you can, you write out your findings and conclusions in a monograph to be entitled 'The 1846 Emigrant Trails Through the Wasatch Mountains' (or 'From Fort Bridger to Great Salt Lake Valley') . . . the sooner the better." Morgan wrote, "you owe it to yourself and the cause of history to publish your findings. . . . It would be desirable to make [a] close study of all the Bryant, Donner, Harlan-Young, etc., documents you can lay your hands on, plus the Mormon journals and your own field research. . . . [I] would be glad to offer any help I could."

So was born the volume you hold in your hands, *West from Fort Bridger*.

As a text and guide to the pioneering of immigrant trails across Utah from 1846–1850, it is unmatched and invaluable. By the same measure it likely is the most obscure, overlooked, uncelebrated, and poorly promoted book in recent memory. Perhaps *the* classic study of western trails, the book is truly history with its boots on. Since its publication in an edition of 986 copies as volume XIX of the *Utah Historical Quarterly*, it has acquired a small but devoted following, and it remains the most complete and compelling recounting of the dramatic history of Lansford W. Hastings' "cutoff" to California.

Awarded the American Association for State and Local History's Award of Merit, the volume certainly met A. R. Mortensen's hopes that it would be a "most important contribution to western Americana." It stands—as Charlie Kelly commented—as "one of the most important contributions to Utah history ever assembled."

In the course of forty years, the book itself has become a historical document. Built upon the field research of Roderic Korns, who could "remember the narrow, one track road winding up Parley's canyon and continually curving to follow the base of the mtns, and always north of the stream," *West from Fort Bridger* provides precise descriptions of trails, such as the Golden Pass road, which is now buried beneath the fill and concrete of a modern interstate highway built through a canyon originally impassable for wagons. Physical evidences of even more obscure trails have often fallen victim to time (not to mention the ravages of man), and Rod Korns' book preserves observations that simply could not be duplicated today.

The truth of the book's authorship reveals the character and integrity of Dale L. Morgan. *West from Fort Bridger* was very much a collaboration between Charles Kelly, Dale Morgan, and Roderic Korns—as Kelly wrote, "the three of us worked this out together"— but Morgan actually committed it to paper.

By 1950, Morgan, at 36 the youngest of the three, was coming into his own as a preeminent scholar of the American West. He had written *The Humboldt: Highroad of the West* and *The Great Salt Lake*, and had edited a number of other important books, including *Utah: A Guide to the State*. He had already begun to establish a shining reputation that would grow brighter with every passing year until his untimely death in 1971.

To describe Dale L. Morgan as a prodigious researcher and writer is an understatement. Stricken as a youngster with meningitis, which robbed him of his hearing, he was fated to live in a silent world, alone with his thoughts and ambitions. His concentration was total; his ability to reason through the most difficult and complex array of data was immense. Having secured a wartime job in Washington, D.C., Morgan spent his free time in the Library of Congress and the National Archives, where he discovered and transcribed the manuscript journals Capt. Howard Stansbury kept during his 1849–1850 topographical expedition to Utah.

As a measure of Morgan's astonishing work ethic, it is enough to say that during his stay in Washington, he read and transcribed every article pertaining to Utah, the Mormons, and the West in the Library of Congress' huge file of newspapers. The thousands of pages of typescript became an integral part of his personal research library and permitted him to write on virtually every aspect of western history with authority far and above that of any other scholar.

In their often-heated correspondence, Morgan, Kelly, and Korns worked through the significance of this information in light of the known sources. After hundreds of pages of letters and many road trips, Korns died in July, 1949, without actually beginning the book that would "give Rod's work such immortality as print affords."

At Korns' deathbed, Morgan promised to see their research published. In a February, 1951, letter to Kelly, Morgan explained the proposal he made to the Utah State Historical Society:

> At that time, most of the members of the Editorial Board did not know Rod from Adam, and those who did, like [Leland] Creer, never got on well with him. They more or less had to go on my assurance that there was or someday would be a manuscript, because I then had nothing to show

them except the texts of the Clyman, Bryant, Lienhard, and Reed journals themselves. . . . I was glad to make any kind of deal that would give Rod his chance to go down in history as he so much wanted to. Since then I have written his book almost wholly from his point of view, including even its occasional references to myself. I don't want or expect that this book shall make me a reputation. I have had and will have other books to attend to that, whereas this is Rod's one chance. Although perhaps 50 percent of the basic material that has gone into the book has come from my own researches, all this would have been at Rod's disposal had he lived, and I am glad to place it at his disposal now that he is dead. In his time he contributed much to our own books; and it is significant in that some of the basic material in this, e.g., the treatment of Parley P. Pratt's Golden Pass Road, Rod wrote out originally for my use when I should come to publish Stansbury's journals. He never dreamed that it would thus serve for a book of his own, and I take a good deal of satisfaction that things should have worked out like that to reward his generous motives.

Immediately after Korns' death, Morgan began giving shape to the manuscript material they had collected during the previous decade. The process involved an extraordinary and productive search for original historical sources. "Isn't it amazing what journals have turned up in the last couple of years?" Morgan wrote. "I am getting almost beyond surprise."

By July, 1950, Morgan had outlined the present structure of the book to Charles Kelly. That September, however, Morgan tracked down the complete manuscript of Heinrich Lienhard's narrative, which included almost twice as much material as the published version. Morgan, with no formal instruction in German, deciphered the text's antique script and by December had created a brilliant "transliteration"—to use his own term. The translation so impressed the dean of the graduate school at the American University that he offered to certify Morgan as an expert German-English translator. Morgan noted, "How wonderfully funny this is, no one but myself will ever know, because no one else was in the apartment here to watch me through that interminable job."

In the spring of 1951, after almost two years' work on the manuscript, Morgan noted that his "textual contribution to the book was done," and reported to widow Sara Korns on April 20, 1951, "Rod's book is indeed finished." His peace was once more disturbed by "incredible news" from San Jose historian Clyde Arbuckle that a journal of the Harlan-Young company had surfaced in Salinas, California. Morgan appreciated that "the pressure of time is now so fearful" that he could not include the complete James Mathers diary, but he was able to extract enough information from the diary's owner to include its most significant information in *West from Fort Bridger*. In 1963, he published the complete journal in *Overland in 1846*.

Morgan was explicit about who should be credited as editor of the book: "First, with respect to my own part in this volume. My position is this: This is the one and only book Rod Korns will ever have, and his whole professional immortality is bound up with it. . . . I desire nothing said that will diminish in any way what Rod rightfully has coming to him; I want this to be thought of as his book, not mine."

In presenting this updated and expanded edition, the current editors have carefully weighed Morgan's desires against the demands of history and have concluded to acknowledge Morgan's role as editor on the title page. Still, we have preserved the book's original viewpoint and voice, keeping the occasional use of the first-person singular, so that readers should note that the occasional "I" remains Roderic Korns. Rod Korns' spirit informs the book. "While the work is 90% yours," Kelly wrote Morgan, "we both appreciate Rod's contribution in hammering away at the subject until every possible clue had been run down." The present editors recognize *West from Fort Bridger* will always be "Rod's book."

Morgan maintained a long-standing affection for the work, noting in his own masterpiece, *Overland in 1846*, "the posthumously published *West from Fort Bridger*, [was] edited by myself and express[es] my own views." It is our hope that the new edition will make the book easily available to a wider audience, and will in some measure win it the recognition that is long overdue.

UPDATE STRATEGY

In 1966, Morgan began discussions about editing a new edition of *West from Fort Bridger*. To this end, he left a clear description of his revision strategy and marked up a copy of the book with detailed corrections. Morgan died before completing the revision, but the corrected copy came into the possession of publisher Fred Rosenstock and ultimately was purchased by George Ivory, who made it available for our revision. This information provided a concise outline of Morgan's intentions.

Neither of the present editors would take on the task of editing Dale Morgan without the utmost humility and respect. With Morgan's notes before us, however, and with mutual moral support, we believe we have created a new edition that closely matches the work Morgan would have produced had he been granted the time.

Four decades of road construction and the creation of the interstate highway system have made many of the references in the first edition obsolete. We updated these descriptions to reflect modern highway routes and names. We have kept most of the original map references, except where Morgan noted the lack of adequate maps, and these comments have been updated to reflect the revolution in cartography that has created a new generation of topographic maps. The following 1:100,000-scale maps can be used to trace the Hastings Cutoff west from Fort Bridger: *Evanston, Ogden, Salt Lake City, Promontory Point, Tooele, Newfoundland Mountains, Bonneville Salt Flats, Wendover, Wells, Ruby Lake,* and *Elko.* The Utah quadrangles *Ogden, Tremonton,* and *Grouse Creek* and Idaho's *Oakley* quadrangle depict the country through which the Salt Lake Cutoff passes. These maps are available from the Bureau of Land Management and the U.S. Geological Survey, and the township and coordinate references Morgan used in the original edition apply to the new maps.

Richard Howe has updated and corrected the original maps of Herbert Fehmel, providing an overlay that shows the route of modern interstate highways on the "West from Fort Bridger: Pioneer Trails across Utah, 1846–1850" map.

Most chapters preserve their original form, including the first edition's stylistic conventions, with only minor corrections made where they were specifically indicated by Morgan. Some changes were based on comments in Morgan's letters to A. R. Mortensen and Charles Kelly. The Virginia Reed letter has been corrected against Morgan's later transcription in *Overland in 1846.* Occasional new material has been added to further enlighten the record, but the strikingly small number of these corrections is a tribute to Morgan's scholarship and attention to detail.

In his proposal for a new edition, Morgan wrote, "I go on hoping there will be some development on the Edward Kern diary of 1845 held [in private possession] in Pennsylvania; but so far nothing. Maybe there will be a turn for the better in the next year; devotedly let us hope so." The "turn for the better" did not occur for 26 years, but in 1993 Harold Schindler located Kern's long-lost "Journal of a Trip to California 1845–46–47," which describes his service with John C. Frémont and clarifies several points that perplexed Korns, Morgan, and Kelly due to the silence of other records. The Kern manuscript has a curious history. It was among two crates of Richard and Edward Kern papers stored in the crawl space of a hotel in Dingman's Ferry, Pennsylvania, and forgotten until 1958, when they were discovered during a cleanup. *Life* magazine published a portion of the journal in 1959, together with some sketches. Scholars, however, were not permitted to see or quote from the papers, as the owners feared this would lessen their value. It was not until 1990 that Yale University's Beinecke Library acquired portions of the collection. There the journal now resides as MS 111 (uncatalogued Western Americana). Unfortunately, the journal is not as helpful as was hoped; it was composed at least a year after the events it describes, and Kern did not write a detailed description of the trek across the Salt Desert. In several instances, however, his remarks untangle points of confusion, and the entries from October 21 to November 4, 1845, are here published for the first time.

Two documents that Morgan also longed to see were the Lansford W. Hastings waybill and map described in Thomas Bullock's 1847 Mormon Pioneer company journal. In the late 1940s, in response to a request from Morgan, church historians looked for, but did not find, these items in their disorganized collection. The documents were eventually located and catalogued, and a new chapter in this edition includes two Hastings waybills and Thomas Bullock's copy of Hastings' map. In addition, several references to the elusive T. H. Jefferson have been located in old newspaper files to supplement the thin biography of this remarkable cartographer.

The most radical editorial surgery is confined to "The Salt Lake Cutoff." Morgan and Korns pioneered research on this subject and were forced to work with a few ambiguous sources. In the original edition, Morgan noted, "Henry Bigler, Israel Evans, Azariah Smith, and Addison Pratt kept journals of this eastbound march, while James S. Brown . . . has left some reminiscences of it." Unfortunately, "save for the journal of Addison Pratt . . . the present whereabouts of none of the original journals kept by the pioneering Mormons of 1848 is now known." Thus, Morgan was forced to rely on a version of Bigler's journal from the *Utah Historical Quarterly*, extracts from Addison Pratt's diary in the Journal History of the LDS church, and Andrew Jenson's loose paraphrase of Azariah Smith's diary, which made it "impossible to tell how much of the narrative owes to Smith, and how much is Jenson's personal interpretation." The recent publication of several 1848 journals (noted below) has made it possible to make changes Morgan outlined in 1967. In the spirit of completing Morgan's work, the Salt Lake Cutoff chapter has been reconstructed to include excerpts from all six of the known journals—those of Henry Bigler, Ephraim Green, Jonathan Holmes, Addison Pratt, Samuel Rogers, and Azariah Smith—resolving several problems of identification and dating raised in the original footnotes. The chapter now also includes both Bigler's daybook and the *Utah Historical Quarterly* version of the journal.

One other pertinent collection came to light when Harold Schindler located the papers of Charles E. Davis at the Sutter's Fort Historical Park Archives in Sacramento. The collection consists of journal notes, scrapbooks, and more than a thousand photographic negatives. Davis inspired Charles Kelly's early interest in the Hastings Cutoff, as noted in *Salt Desert Trails*: "Through his activities I first heard of the existence of the Salt Desert Trail, and determined to follow it from Salt Lake City." Davis was an amateur explorer who had traveled the Amazon, northern Alaska, Siberia, and the great deserts of America. With the support of curator H. C. Peterson of the Sutter's Fort Museum, Davis spent the autumn of 1927 retracing the Donner-Reed trail from Sutter's Fort east to Fort Bridger. Davis made his home on Mullett Island, Salton Sea, California, and was evidently a man of comfortable means and some influence, which allowed him to pursue such an extravagant avocation.

He began his automobile trek from the west slope of the Sierra with Emile Coté, as his driver and assistant. On September 23, 1927, Davis led a party of ranchers, including 73-year-old Eugene Munsee and Pete McKellar of Pilot Peak, across the Salt Desert on a search for relics, especially James Frazier Reed's "Pioneer palace car." The party found the ruins of two wagons six miles east of Silver Island, one showing "some blacksmithing iron parts. . . . I judged this wagon to be James Reed's as it was a large wagon." Davis described corroded hubs, broken felloes, and wagon box remains scattered along a line for some nine or ten miles, and the men collected a number of these artifacts and shipped them to Sutter's Fort Museum.

Davis met with residents and old-timers along the way, including 76-year-old Joseph Yates, a Utahn who had lived in Lake Point, Tooele County, since its founding. Fifty yards off the route of the Victory Highway as it passed through Lake Point, Yates "pointed out a spot where the two emigrants were buried and these same graves were known to have been made between the years of 1845 and '47." Yates and Davis were convinced they had found the location of the graves of Luke Halloran and John Hargrave, the first overland emigrants to be buried in Utah. They marked the spot with a cross and "built up mounds of rocks."

It is not clear if Dale Morgan or Roderic Korns knew of Davis' expedition, but Charles Kelly certainly did, and spent much time investigating his conclusions. Nevertheless, it seems unlikely that Morgan would have been swayed from his conviction that Halloran and Hargrave lie buried near the site of Grantsville.

SUPPLEMENTARY BIBLIOGRAPHY AND ACKNOWLEDGMENTS

A few of Dale L. Morgan's later works that shed light on material in *West from Fort Bridger* include *Jedediah Smith and the Opening of the West* (Indianapolis, 1953); "Miles Goodyear and the Founding of Ogden," *Utah Historical Quarterly*, XXI (July and October, 1953); *The Overland Diary of James Pritchard, from Kentucky to California in 1849* (Denver, 1959); *Overland in 1846: Diaries and Letters of the California-Oregon Trail* (2 vols., Georgetown, Calif., 1963); *The West of William H. Ashley* (Denver, 1964); *In Pursuit of the Golden Dream: Reminiscences of San Francisco and the Northern and Southern Mines, 1849–1857 by Howard C. Gardiner* (Stoughton, Mass., 1970); with James R. Scobie, *Three Years in California: William Perkins' Journal of Life at Sonora, 1849–1852* (Berkeley, 1964); and, with Eleanor Towles Harris, *The Rocky Mountain Journals of William Marshall Anderson: The West in 1834* (San Marino, Calif., 1967). Richard L. Saunders, *Eloquence from a Silent World: A Descriptive Bibliography of the Published Writings of Dale L. Morgan* (Salt Lake City, 1990) provides a comprehensive picture of Morgan's lifework.

Two Charles Kelly articles require special notice: "Gold Seekers on the Hastings Cutoff," and "The Journal of Robert Chalmers," both in *Utah Historical Quarterly*, XX (January, 1952). Kelly and Morgan originally planned to include "Gold Seekers" in volume XIX, with Kelly even offering to rewrite it and credit it to Korns, but printing deadlines and the length of *West from Fort Bridger* required publishing Kelly's works in the next volume.

Editions of two important primary accounts of the opening of the Salt Lake Cutoff, David L. Bigler's *The Gold Discovery Journal of Azariah Smith* and S. George Ellsworth's *The Journals of Addison Pratt*, were published in 1990. Further research led to the location of the journals of Ephraim Green, Jonathan Holmes, and Samuel H. Rogers in 1991, and of an additional Henry Bigler narrative written under his Hawaiian pen name. Reminiscent accounts by Joseph W. Bates, Thomas Dunn, Zadok Judd, Samuel Miles, Robert Pixton, and Francis Hammond all shed some light on the opening of the cutoff. Will Bagley, ed., *A Road from El Dorado: The 1848 Trail Journal of Ephraim Green* (Salt Lake City, 1991) presents the complete Green journal and outlines the current knowledge of original documents from the "Thompson Company." At long last available, these sources, plus first-hand accounts of Mormon dissenters who left Salt Lake for Fort Hall in March, 1848, solve many of the problems that bedeviled Morgan and Korns.

Many of the manuscripts and books referenced in the text have since been published or issued in new editions. A small sample includes Charles Camp's masterful reworking of his 1928 edition of James Clyman's diaries, which was republished with extensive new material provided by Dale Morgan, as *James Clyman, Frontiersman* (Portland, Oregon, 1960); George P. Hammond, ed., *The Larkin Papers: Personal, Business, and Official Correspondence of Thomas Oliver Larkin, Merchant and United States Consul in California* (10 vols., Berkeley, 1951–68) made this invaluable correspondence accessible to scholars; Robert V. Hine and Savoie Lottinville, eds., *Soldier in the West: Letters of Theodore Talbot during His Services in California, Mexico, and Oregon, 1845–53* (Norman, 1972) describes the 1845 exploration of the route that became the Hastings Cutoff. Mary Lee Spence and Donald Jackson, eds., *The Expeditions of John Charles Frémont* (3 vols., Chicago, 1970–1984) includes a portfolio containing Charles Preuss' maps; Doyce B. Nunis, Jr., ed., *The Bidwell-Bartleson Party, 1841 California Emigrant Adventure: The Documents and Memoirs of the Overland Pioneers* (Santa Cruz, Calif., 1991) is a definitive work, and we have adopted Dr. Nunis' name for this significant party; Scott G. Kenny, ed., *Wilford Woodruff's Journal* (10 vols., Midvale, Utah, 1983) contains information Morgan and Korns sought unsuccessfully in the LDS historian's office; and finally, the journals of the Stansbury expedition quoted in "The Golden Pass Road" have been published in full by Brigham D. Madsen, ed., *Exploring the Great Salt Lake: The Stansbury Expedition of 1849–50* (Salt Lake City, 1989).

We recognize the assistance of Dr. George Miles, Yale Library curator, who made the Edward Kern journal available to us. Mary Lou Lentz, interpretive specialist at Sutter's Fort State Historical

Park, provided valuable information from the Charles E. Davis collection. William W. Slaughter of the Historical Department, Archives Division, The Church of Jesus Christ of Latter-day Saints (cited hereafter as LDS Archives), helped us locate and copy documents and portraits in the church's possession. Susan Whetstone of the Utah State Historical Society helped us track down much of the first edition's artwork in the Society's collections. Marta Lienhard Vincent graciously provided us with photographs of her great-great-grandfather, Heinrich Lienhard.

Finally, we must acknowledge the inspiration, insights, and encouragement of David L. Bigler, Peter H. DeLafosse, Robert K. Hoshide, Kristin Johnson, Michael N. Landon, Brigham D. Madsen, W. L. Rusho, Jack Shapiro, Rush Spedden, Roy D. Tea, Jack B. Tykal, and our skilled and dedicated editor, John Alley, for their part in making this dream a reality.

HAROLD SCHINDLER
WILL BAGLEY
Salt Lake City
May, 1994

PREFACE

FROM THE VERY beginning the Utah State Historical Society, like most if not all other state societies of similar purpose, has had as its main reason for existence the collection, preservation, interpretation, and dissemination of the history of its own immediate state and region. However, the Society always has felt that this history could not be told in a vacuum; it has always exhibited an interest in the broader aspects of history as against losing itself in purely local antiquities.

Since early numbers of the *Quarterly*, the Society has published articles and volumes which are of significance to the history of Western America, if not to the entire country itself. In recent years the publishing of the full-scale studies of the Powell Colorado River Explorations, as well as the several studies concerned with the pre-settlement explorations in the Rocky Mountain region (as exemplified by the latest volume on the Escalante Expedition, under the authorship of Dr. Herbert E. Bolton)—all bear testimony to the relatively widespread interest of the State Historical Society.

While the focal point of the present volume is necessarily confined for the most part to Utah, because of ruggedness of terrain, number of travelers, distance, and other factors, this sector—a vital part of what came to be the great overland highroad to the Pacific—is of extreme importance to the entire story of overland travel and consequently brings more than local significance to the book.

Through the medium of the basic documents, diaries, and journals, this work for the first time identifies all the routes of 1846 across Utah; it prints for the first time in English or direct from the manuscript the most significant part of the Lienhard diary, which will eventually come to be regarded as one of the classic diaries of overland travel; it presents a wealth of new information about the Donner party on the Hastings Cutoff—of such character that every book about the Donner party ever written from 1848–1950 now requires to be rewritten; and it explores and identifies in detail the trails across Utah used by the Forty-Niners. The publishing of the documents alone would be a valuable contribution to scholarship, but by careful annotation, extensive notes, and introductions to the journals themselves, the author has given background and cohesion to his subject that is both interesting and informative. Perhaps it would not be too optimistic to predict that this volume by Mr. Korns will be a most important contribution to Western Americana.

Besides the individuals and institutions to whom the author is directly indebted for aid, the Utah State Historical Society is grateful to a host of people, for the most part unnamed, for cheerful and gratuitous help rendered in diverse ways. The entire office staff of the Society has given service beyond the call of duty to the task of seeing the volume through the printers. To the Deseret News Press for advice, professional and otherwise, and to Mr. Herbert Fehmel for his cartographic work sincere thanks is due.

A. R. MORTENSEN
Editor

One of my first duties as executive director of the Utah State Historical Society and editor of the *Utah Historical Quarterly* was to see to the completion and publication of Volume XIX, *West from Fort Bridger: The Pioneering of Immigrant Trails across Utah, 1846–1850*. It gives me great personal satisfaction, therefore, that this classic volume, revised and updated, will once again be available to scholars, researchers, and all those interested in the history of the American West. Republication of this important work testifies to the enduring legacy of the late Dale L. Morgan to western historiography and stands as a testament to Morgan's friendship for J. Roderic Korns. Utah State University Press and editors Will Bagley and Harold Schindler are to be congratulated.

A. R. MORTENSEN
Escondido, California
May, 1994

—*Sara Merrill Korns photo, Utah State Historical Society*

J. RODERIC KORNS

—*Harold Schindler photo*

DALE LOWELL MORGAN

IN MEMORIAM
J. RODERIC KORNS
July 24, 1890–July 2, 1949

IN PUBLISHING his definitive account of the pioneering of the immigrant trails across Utah, *West from Fort Bridger*, the Utah State Historical Society pays final tribute to one of its most able members, J. Roderic Korns. The months that have intervened between the time of his death and this publication of his most brilliant and most characteristic work have not in any way served to reconcile those who knew him to his passing, and it is deeply satisfying to feel that nothing, not death itself, has sufficed to subdue the turbulent energy, critical discernment, and skeptical temper he brought to his study of the West's engrossing history.

J. Roderic Korns was born at Tekamah, Burt County, Nebraska, on July 24, 1890, the son of William Henry and Roberta (Stalcup) Korns. His forebears had lived in this country since 1752, when Carl Korn immigrated to Pennsylvania from Wurtemberg, Germany. The Korns family history will not be developed at length here, having been the subject of a recent inquiry by Charles Byron Korns, *The Genealogy of Michael Korns, Sr. of Somerset County Pennsylvania* (Berlin, Pa., 1949)—a work published just at the time of Rod's own death to which characteristically he had contributed much information. However, in 1855 Rod's grandfather, Solomon Korns, succumbed to the irresistible pull of the West, and Rod's father, William Henry Korns, was born at Raritan, Illinois. The powerful attraction of the West seized upon William in turn, and he grew up to publish a series of newspapers always farther west, first the *Unionville Democrat* at Rockwell City, Iowa, and subsequently the *Burt County Herald* at Tekamah, Nebraska.

The only son born to his parents, Rod was their second child, his elder sister, Rowena (now Mrs. Charles A. Maly of Salt Lake City), having been born at Tekamah, March 18, 1889. Rod's name originally was Rodric Korns, but in the course of time he became acquainted with a Scot who pronounced his name with a broad burring of the "r"s; Rod found this pronunciation congenial to his ear, and altered the spelling of his name from "Rodric" to "Roderic." A family nickname in his childhood had been "Jimmy the Kid," and when, as he grew older, a distinguishing initial became desirable, he arbitrarily prefixed a "J" to his name.

He was, however, still "Rodric" at the time he made his first appearance in print. In the spring of 1895 his father had moved still farther west, to Casper, Wyoming, where he published the *Wyoming Derrick* and led the local Democrats in what is still regarded as the most bitterly fought political campaign ever waged in Natrona County. After Rod's death, his wife found in one of his old books a clipping which dates from this period, cut from the *Derrick* of August 13, 1896:

THE YOUNGEST TYPE SETTER.

The youngest compositor who now sets type in Wyoming is Master Rodric Korns son of W. H. Korns editor and publisher of the Casper (Wyoming) *Derrick*. The youngster is said to take to the "stick and rule" with great aptness, doing the type setting act in a manner truly wonderful for one of his age. He is too young to write legibly and puts his letters to his grandparents in type perfect in all particulars—and has them printed. Master Korns is not only the youngest compositor in Wyoming but *The Auxiliary* believes him to be the youngest in the west. If there are others of more tender age this publication would like to make the fact known.—*Printers Auxiliary.*

I set up the piece above. I am 6 years [old] how [old] is Master Korns?

Yours Truly,
FRANK L THOMAS
Lewiston, Mo.

I was six years old on the twenty-fourth of July, last past. I set type when I was five years and eight months old. Rodric Korns.

A second clipping is dated a week later:

I like Mr. Barrie. He pays me to clerk in his store when he goes to dinner. He is a nice man and makes my burro some harness. I want every body to buy harness from Mr. Barrie.

RODRIC KORNS.

Shortly after the outbreak of the Spanish-American War, the Korns family returned east as far as Chadron, Dawes County, Nebraska, where the elder Korns published another Democratic paper, the *Chadron Chronicle*. In 1901 they moved again, this time to Salt Lake City, where they settled permanently. William H. Korns bought a half-interest in the *Mining Weekly*, a weekly magazine devoted to the interests of that industry, but four years later he left the publishing business to found the Korns Warehouse Company. This flourishing concern he operated until his death on March 29, 1922, and it has since been carried on by his son and grandson. At the time of the change in Salt Lake City's government from the aldermanic to the commission form, in 1911, W. H. Korns was elected one of the first commissioners, being assigned to the water department. Rod's first vote was cast to help elect his father, and the energetic part taken by W. H. Korns in the Mountain Dell Reservoir project in Parleys Canyon, ever since a key source of supply in Salt Lake City's water system, gave Rod a lasting interest in terrain and stream courses—an interest which illuminates all the historical researches of his later years.

Apart from his early celebrity as a printer, Rod first achieved distinction as an athlete. Active of body and gifted with a notable competitive will, he won acclaim as Utah's first amateur heavyweight boxing champion, and as a football player was no less prominent. Playing for the old Salt Lake High School, he was all-state center in 1907, and captain of the team in 1908, when it won the state championship. In 1909 he entered the University of Utah as an engineering student, and—freshmen being then eligible for conference competition—became center on the varsity football team. In later life Rod had some amusing reminiscences of that year, particularly of his frustrations in playing against Colorado Mines' muscular all-conference center.

The excessive effort required to hold down a job and get an education on the side forced him after a year to give up his college studies. As time went on, he assumed an increasingly heavy share of the responsibility for running the warehouse, and he managed it from 1912 to 1922, when at his father's death he became owner as well.

Early in life Rod became active in Masonry, on October 10, 1916, being made a Master Mason in Argenta Lodge No. 3, Salt Lake City. From this lodge demitted, he and his father were instrumental in organizing Progress Lodge No. 22, F. & A. M., which he served as treasurer during the three-year term, 1920–22. A Royal Arch Mason, he was exalted in Salt Lake Chapter No. 5 on April 18, 1917, and served that Chapter as High Priest during 1922. He affiliated with Utah Chapter No. 1 when the two Chapters were consolidated in 1932, being a life member at the time of his death. Rod was also a Knight Templar, having been knighted in Utah Commandery No. 1 on May 23, 1918. He became a member of El Kalah Temple, A. A. O. N. M. S., on November 5, 1919, and was an active member of the Shrine Patrol for 25 years.

In contrast to his father, Rod was a Republican in political affiliation. During both world wars he was active in all phases of civilian work, serving as a district air-raid warden and a Red Cross and bond drive worker.

On January 30, 1917, he married Sara Beck Merrill in Salt Lake City. Born July 15, 1898, she was herself a descendant of two prominent pioneer families. Two children were born to them, James Roderic (January 20, 1918–June 12, 1933) and William Lester (November 18, 1921–). Rod became interested in golf the year after his second son was born, and the boy grew up virtually with a golf club in his hand. To his father's unbounded delight, "Billy" began winning state championships at the age of 16, and today he is familiar to Utah sports fans as one of the state's outstanding amateur golfers. During World War II Bill was commissioned a second lieutenant of Infantry. A graduate of the University of Utah, he married Jane Elizabeth Bracken on December 24, 1943, and they have two children, William Robert and Susan Leslie. His grandson was one of the great pleasures of Rod's last years, and it was instructive to hear him remark upon the grave consideration a child receives today as compared with the arbitrary discipline under which he himself grew up.

The furiously active life he lived caught up with Rod in 1944, when high blood pressure precipitated a heart attack. The valves to his heart were damaged beyond repair, and the last five years of his life were a constant rear-guard action fought against the ravages of high blood pressure. He had serious sieges in the hospital in the spring of 1948 and again in the spring of 1949 before the illness which brought an end to his life on July 2, 1949. He was buried with Masonic ceremonies in Mount Olivet Cemetery.

In all that has been said of him, there is little to hint at the existence of that J. Roderic Korns whose memory the Utah State Historical Society now honors. To all who knew his spirit of restless inquiry and his combative temperament, the accident that channeled his energies into the sphere of history will be found wonderfully characteristic. As he explained it to me once, during the time Boulder Dam was under construction, he and his wife visited the site. A guide pointed out a nearby mesa and related impressively that in early days a group of Mormons had taken refuge there from the Indians, but in vain; all had been massacred. Rod decided that he didn't believe a word of the story, and on returning home, went around to inquire of his old friends, Alvin F. Smith and A. William Lund, at the LDS Historian's Office, who quickly assured him that he was entirely justified in his skepticism. Rod's interest in old stream channels through Salt Lake Valley soon brought him back to the Historian's Office to consult some early maps, and in the course of these visits he became involved in an argument concerning some details of the route by which the Mormon pioneers entered the valley. That argument launched him upon the exhaustive studies which led finally to the authoritative work dealing with the trails of 1846–1850 that is now published.

Lacking any formal academic training in history, Rod turned this lack into one of his greatest assets. He wasted no piety on pronouncements by "authority" and attached no special sanctity to any assertion just because it had been printed in a book. With an instinctive feeling for fundamentals he went directly to the sources to form his opinions. Fresh and original in his vision, he had nevertheless a deep respect for facts.

Rod had also, and this was of great importance for the present volume, a feeling for terrain that is rare in this generation—rare perhaps in any generation, for the mountain men who possessed it a century ago were one of the wonders of the age to the army officers who hired them as guides. Rod might have been up a certain canyon once only, and that 13 years before, but he could give you a general picture of that canyon and even map it for you, showing how the road was situated with reference to the creek, where a branch came in, where a white ranchhouse or a red barn would be found; and this information would stand up under investigation. To this special gift of memory he united a notable power of observation. He could see and immediately appreciate the significance of old rope burns on a tree, evidence that wagons in times long gone had been let down a steep slope; the rectangular outlines of a slightly sunken grave stood out for him like a mountain range; and a rusty discoloration on a rock outcropping readily explained itself to him, evidence that an iron wagon tire once had scraped upon that stone. Rod also adopted as a working hypothesis the refreshing idea that any diarist was entitled to credence until proved wrong, and in all my acquaintanceship I have met with no historian more steadily insistent upon conclusions that would embrace *all* the stated facts in the study of any source document.

Rod was a person of notable candor. He felt, himself, that this virtue was something of a vice, because dogmatic ignorance—especially pretentious ignorance—always impacted upon him like a personal affront; he regretted that he seemed to possess so little of tact. This very forthrightness, however, was a part of the special tang his personality held for his friends, and they recognized, as he perhaps did not, that he was also a person of rare sensitivity of feeling. In the course of his wide-ranging researches, he became interested in the Mississippi Saints, who wintered with the mountain men in 1846–47 at Pueblo, Colorado. He went down to St. George and talked with Manomas (Gibson) Andrus, "Aunt Nome," as everyone called her, who as a child of four had been a member of the Mississippi Company. At the time of the interview, the 95-year-old pioneer had been blind for some years, but her memory was still clear, and she took much pleasure in talking to one so genuinely interested. The substance of the interview Rod published in a long article in the *Salt Lake Tribune*, March 10, 1938, Aunt Nome's 96th birthday. Later Aunt Nome had an opportunity to come up to Salt Lake City, and she accepted it for the purpose of coming to visit Rod and talking with him again. He was out of town at the time and did not learn until later how keenly disappointed Aunt Nome had been to miss him. No other opportunity offered to visit with her before her death on May 31, 1940. Rod told me this story on two different occasions, and the deep tenderness he felt for Aunt Nome, and the painful sense he had of having failed her, shone through all that he said. The vigorous intellectual curiosity, the deep response to the lure of history, the true feeling for scholarship, and even the joy of combat which brought Rod bounding into a historical fray, shillelagh whirling about his head, were not more characteristic of him than this gentleness and delicacy of feeling.

Had Rod lived a little longer, we might have had several books from him, for his enthusiasms ran wide as well as deep. He was much interested in the contribution made by the obscure French *voyageurs* to the exploration of the Trans-Mississippi West, and over a period of years gathered many notes on the subject. This interest extended to the mountain men of a later period, and no one was better informed about them. Rod would especially have liked to complete another work in progress, a study of the pioneering of the wagon roads across the Green River Valley after 1824 to which he devoted much time and thought, and which would have been a work as illuminating as that now published.

But if Rod had to be limited to one book, we can be glad it was this one, for it is in every way appropriate that his researches should have come full circle to their place of beginning, the trails to and through the Great Salt Lake country. During nearly two decades while this book has been in the making, Rod's researches have reached out to influence many of the new books which have impinged upon his special field of authority, as is shown by acknowledgments in works published by Charles Kelly, Bernard DeVoto, Charles L. Camp, and myself. Refracted through other minds, however, his ideas by no means have always been properly represented, so that a book of his own, prior to his death, had become a necessity.

The manuscript was not yet completed when he died, and I have assumed the responsibility of preparing it for publication. Thus in a sense it is a collaboration between myself and Rod, since it has fallen to me to find expression for many of the ideas which over a period of ten years were threshed out between us in conversation and correspondence. If it were possible for Rod to give the manuscript a final editing, he would no doubt effect many small improvements, and the language would acquire the kind of force and pungency which he alone could give to the work of J. Roderic Korns. I think, however, that Rod would find this volume a faithful presentation of his ideas and that he would feel that I have served him well in this last service I have the power to do him.

He would also want to join with me in thanking his wife, Sara Merrill Korns, for all that she has done to bring this project to fruition. She has been altogether energetic and persistent in making the local inquiries and obtaining the special documents that have given final authority to many of the notes. Other acknowledgments Rod himself has made, scattered throughout his text, but I would like to express my personal thanks to the President and Board of the Utah State Historical Society, who took this means of honoring the memory of one of the Society's most respected members, and to Mr. Charles Kelly, Mr. Carroll D. Hall, Mr. Walter E. Dansie, Mrs. E. J. Magnuson, Mrs. Marguerite Sinclair Reusser, Mrs. Elizabeth M. Lauchnor, Miss Barbara Kell, Dr. Charles L. Camp, Mr. Joseph Micheli, Mr. T. Gerald Bleak, Mr. Leslie E. Bliss, Dr. George P. Hammond, Mrs. Helen Harding Bretnor, Mrs. Juanita Brooks, Mr.

Darel McConkey, Dr. Ernst Correll, Mrs. Marguerite Eyer Wilbur, Mr. Glen Dawson, Mr. Charles Eberstadt, Dr. Frederick W. Hodge, Mr. Clyde Arbuckle, Miss Agnes McDowell, Miss Haydée Noya, and Miss Dorothy W. Bridgwater. All in diverse ways have helped to make this work possible.

DALE L. MORGAN
Washington, D. C.
January, 1951

INTRODUCTION

FOR ALL ITS RICH and varied history, the West has few episodes more thoroughly fascinating than the pioneering of immigrant trails across the Great Salt Lake region during the years 1846–1850. The absorbing story of the Donner party and the Cutoff which became for them a road to death, the settling of Mormons in the Great Salt Lake Valley, and the surge of goldseekers to California—these great themes stand up monumentally in any account of the West and are embraced by a single five-year span of trail history.

The trails worked out during this time at the cost of such laborious trial and painful error occasionally serve as the arterial routes of our own time. Often, they wander off to one side or the other of our relentlessly engineered modern highways, for grass, wood, and water are no longer, as they once were, controlling factors in the location of a road, and motorists are content to take the long way around rather than traverse a steep divide which wagons routinely challenged. Following old trails can become an infinitely diverting pastime, for now they afford one the luxury of pursuit on a superhighway, and next moment they veer adventurously into the wildest of terrain, occasionally into country where automobiles were never meant to travel.

Notwithstanding the ravages of erosion and other forces inexorably changing the face of the earth, land has a stubborn character. In no better way, perhaps, than by following an old trail can the physical and spiritual kinship with generations of men now laid away to rest be felt. The dry sage uplands west of Fort Bridger are now as they have ever been; the Copperas Spring west of the Muddy still stains the earth blood-red; the far view from the pass over Big Mountain enchants the heart now as a hundred years ago; the white hell of the Salt Desert yet burns the eye; and the canyon of the Humboldt's South Fork remains what it was for James Frazier Reed in 1846, "a perfect snake trail." Those who travel the West sometimes find its vast dry expanse of plain and mountain monotonous and depressing, but not those who are familiar with its trails. Hardly a square mile lacks its personal eloquence, or ghosts of the past to take on flesh and blood and walk beside us.

Although the present study is centered upon the pioneering of the Hastings Cutoff in 1846, the story we have to tell begins in the timeless past when the trails that were to be marked out by wagons first came into existence. It is one of the conventions of American

[1]

history that all the great trails were trodden out successively by the buffalo, the Indians, the white frontiersmen, and finally by Conestoga wagons and railroads. This convention, like most others, has only a limited applicability to the West, and particularly to that part—western Wyoming, northern Utah, southern Idaho, and eastern Nevada— which now concerns us. Here the character of terrain has been the first and often the final consideration in the making of any trail. Game, Indian, and white man, all moved as the conformation of the country permitted. Where water ran, ordinarily, there would a trail go also, through mountains or around them. A gap in a mountain range, whether or not low enough to allow passage of a stream, would exert an equal compulsion. The stern facts of geography—including in the more arid localities the absence or presence of a succession of springs—loom forcefully through any study of the West's historic trails.

Much of the mountain-desert country was never very hospitable to the buffalo or deer, and its traveled ways owe little to these animals. There is no doubt, however, that within the possibilities of the terrain the contribution of the Indians to the making of the trails we shall describe was enormous. Since this special obligation to Indians cannot be continually acknowledged in the notes to the journals, let us insist upon it now. No wagon, it is safe to assume, was ever taken anywhere in the Great Salt Lake country save upon paths already beaten out by the red men. The journals of James Clyman and Edwin Bryant bespeak this indebtedness to the Indians, both for the trails themselves and for aid and advice received. If I seem to labor this point, it is because our near-sighted view of the exploration and settlement of the West tends to picture it as having been a virgin wilderness with never a trace or track of humankind when the whites first penetrated it.

The mountain men who spread through the Rockies in the 1820s and made of the West a kingdom which even today retains a regal splendor for the imagination, fell heir to trails already age-old. They renamed the mountains, passes, and streams to their taste, often in memory of one another, and absorbed from the Indians the wisdom which was to be tapped in turn by the immigrants of the 1830s and 1840s. The mountain men were not, in a sense, actual trail-makers; their accomplishment consisted in learning to distinguish from among the multiplicity of Indian trails the one that would best serve a given need. From a larger point of view, however, the mountain men brought much more than this local sagacity to their eventual calling as immigrant guides, for they acquired what Bernard DeVoto has happily called the "continental mind." Their rovings took them from the country of the Blackfeet to that of the Apaches, from the domain of the Pawnees to that of the Nez Percés, and they brought a breadth of viewpoint to the trails that went far beyond the circumscribed outlook of the Indian. The mountain men bridged two eras, and it is appropriate that the journal of one of their number, James Clyman, should launch us upon our narrative of the Hastings Cutoff.

The first tracks left by wheeled vehicles west of the Missouri River must have been made very early, certainly by 1820. When, in the fall of 1824, William H. Ashley set out up the Loup and the Platte to join his trappers in the mountains, he took a wagon with him.[1] It was abandoned along the way, no one knows where. The first wheeled vehicle actually to cross the Continental Divide must have been the four-pounder cannon Ashley sent to the mountains nearly three years later. It was this cannon which boomed out the welcome to Jedediah Smith at Bear Lake on his return from California on July 3, 1827. The sources provide no real evidence as to where the cannon reached the valley of the Bear, possibly south of Cokeville, Wyoming, by a route approximating what became the Greenwood Cutoff, but it is reasonably clear that the piece of artillery was then hauled down the Bear to the Bear Lake Outlet and up the west shore of Bear Lake to the rendezvous on the site of Laketown.[2]

In 1830 William L. Sublette, Jedediah Smith's partner, took ten wagons and two Dearborn buggies from the Missouri River to the Wind River Mountains, and two years later Captain B. L. E. Bonneville brought 20 wagons across South Pass to Horse Creek.[3] Slowly, as bulky buffalo hides replaced beaver pelts as the standard product of the fur trade, carts and wagons came into use on the plains and in the mountains. In 1836 Marcus Whitman, enroute to Oregon,

---

[1] Harrison Clifford Dale, *The Ashley-Smith Explorations and the Discovery of a Central Route to the Pacific, 1822–1829* (Glendale, Calif., 1941), 116. Ashley wrote General Henry Atkinson in December, 1825, "I left Fort Atkinson on the 3rd November, 1824. On the afternoon of the fifth, I overtook my party of mountaineers (twenty-five in number), who had in charge fifty pack horses, a wagon and teams, etc." This is the last mention of the wagon.
[2] *Ibid.*, 167; Maurice S. Sullivan, ed., *The Travels of Jedediah Smith* (Santa Ana, Calif., 1934), 26.
[3] Jedediah S. Smith, David E. Jackson, and William L. Sublette to Secretary of War John Eaton, St. Louis, October 29, 1830, *Senate Document* No. 39, 21 Congress, 2 session (Serial 203), 21–23; Washington Irving, *The Rocky Mountains; or, Scenes, Incidents, and Adventures in the Far West; digested from the journal of Capt. B. L. E. Bonneville* (2 vols., Philadelphia, 1837), I, 30.

brought a wagon over the Bear River Divide by the route of the Greenwood Cutoff, and from the Bear River Valley took it on to Fort Hall. Stripping down the wagon to make a two-wheeled cart of it, the valiant doctor got this symbol of civilization as far as Fort Boise before giving up the endeavor.[4] Four years later Robert Newell, Joe Meek, and other mountain men succeeded in taking wagons the rest of the way to the Columbia,[5] so that by 1840 a wagon road of sorts had been made virtually the whole width of the continent.

The first wagons known to have entered the Great Salt Lake country were brought in during the summer of 1841 by the venturesome Bidwell-Bartleson company.[6] From Soda Springs they left the developing Oregon Trail with their nine wagons to descend the Bear River to the Great Salt Lake. They followed the right bank of the Bear down through Cache Valley and eventually struck the Malad. After much difficulty, they succeeded in getting their wagons across, and then followed the Malad and the Bear to Bear River Bay. From the vicinity of present Corinne they turned west across the Promontory Mountains, around the north shore of Great Salt Lake, but at a point east of Kelton veered northwest to reach the springs at the southeastern base of the Raft River Mountains. Uncertain of the country, they sent scouts west in unavailing search for a practicable route to the head of the Humboldt and then turned southwest and south, along the rim of the Salt Desert and down the chain of springs which breaks out at the eastern base of the Pilot Range. One of their wagons was abandoned on this stretch of the trail, apparently at Owl Springs, but the other eight were taken around the shoulder of Pilot Peak and on across Silver Zone Pass into Gosiute Valley, there to be abandoned and subsequently found by the immigrants of 1846. Crossing the Pequop Mountains into Independence Valley and proceeding on through Clover Valley to Ruby Valley, the Bidwell-Bartle-

---

[4] Clifford Merrill Drury, *Marcus Whitman, M. D., Pioneer and Martyr* (Caldwell, Idaho, 1937), 139–50. The itinerary appears from William H. Gray's letter of September 9, 1836, printed in A. B. and D. P. Hulbert, eds., *Marcus Whitman, Crusader, Part One* (Denver, 1936), 216–29.

[5] Harvey E. Tobie, *No Man Like Joe* (Portland, 1949), 83–88.

[6] I thus qualify the achievement of the Bidwell-Bartleson party because no one knows what became of Bonneville's wagons or others brought to the Rockies by fur traders and Oregon missionaries prior to 1841. J. Cecil Alter, in *Utah Historical Quarterly*, IX (January, April, 1941), 92n., presents shreds of evidence to indicate that in 1833 some of Bonneville's wagons may have been brought as far south as the Cub River in Cache Valley.

son company at last reached the object of their hopes and fears, the Humboldt, by way of Secret Pass.[7] West of Pilot Peak, their route anticipated in a number of places the Hastings Cutoff, and some reference is made hereafter to their experiences.

Two years after the Bidwell-Bartleson party's abortive effort to work out a road to California through the Great Salt Lake country, the government explorer, Lt. John Charles Frémont, contributed another chapter to the history of wheeled travel in this area.[8] Like the Bidwell-Bartleson party, though at first on the opposite side of the river, he started down the Bear from Soda Springs, carrying with him a howitzer mounted on a wheeled carriage. Sheering away from the Bear at Standing Rock Pass, Frémont made his way up Weston Creek and down Deep Creek to the valley of the Malad, which stream and the Bear he followed nearly to the lake. Just above the mouth of the Bear he crossed to its left bank and proceeded south around Bear River Bay to the Weber River. From a base camp west of present Ogden, he visited Frémont Island in Great Salt Lake but was too short of provisions to extend his explorations farther and turned back to Fort Hall. Frémont's return route, up the Malad and Little Malad, over to the Bannock River, and down it to the Snake, was subsequently adopted when intercourse between Great Salt Lake City and Fort Hall began in 1847–48. Stansbury described the road in detail in the autumn of 1849, and it served for many years as a highroad for travel between the Mormon communities around the Salt Lake and points in eastern Idaho and southwestern Montana.

More significant for the history of the great immigrant trails so soon to be marked out across Utah were the experiences of one of the companies which helped to swell to its great proportions the Oregon immigration of 1843. Not all who took the trail that year had Oregon as their objective. Joseph C. Chiles, a member of the Bidwell-Bartleson party, no sooner had returned to the States in 1842 than he set about organizing a new company for California. This party set out from the Missouri frontier in the spring of 1843, its identity not submerged even by the year's tidal wave of Oregon travel. East of Fort Bridger, Chiles fell in with the great mountain man, Joseph Reddeford Walker, who will constantly reappear in this trail history, and

<hr/>

[7] John Bidwell, *A Journey to California* (San Francisco, 1937), 15–19.

[8] John Charles Frémont, *Report of the Exploring Expedition to the Rocky Mountains in the Year 1842, and to Oregon and North California in the Years 1843–'44* (Washington, 1845), 139–62.

Walker agreed to guide Chiles' wagons on to California by the Humboldt route. Relieved of a wearing responsibility, Chiles undertook to investigate yet another possible route to California. With a small pack party, he kept to the Oregon Trail as far as Fort Boise, and then made his arduous way into the upper Sacramento Valley via the headwaters of the Malheur and Pit rivers.[9]

The immigrants given into Walker's keeping had not, while in the buffalo country, been able to lay in a sufficient supply of meat to see them through to California. Walker had traveled the Humboldt country in 1833–34 in taking a detachment of Bonneville's party to and from California, and he had no illusions about its resources. It was advisable to attempt to lay in a supply of deer and elk meat before launching into such barren climes. Accordingly, when he was ready to move from Fort Bridger, instead of following the now deeply beaten track north to the Little Muddy and up it to its headwaters, the trace beginning to be thought of as the Oregon Trail, Walker struck out from the fort southwest toward what one of his party called "the Utah Mountains, at the head of Bear River." This meatmaking expedition in the Uintas was not an unqualified success, and after ten days Walker resignedly set out with his charges down the Bear to regain the Oregon road where it came down Bridgers Creek. The notes appended to the journals make it evident how much the later travelers owed to Walker's road from Fort Bridger to the Bear, for with small variation, the Hastings-Donner-Mormon trail as far as the Bear River Valley was that over which Walker took the Chiles wagons in August, 1843.[10]

---

[9] The experiences of this division of the Chiles party are recorded in the diary of Pierson B. Reading, published in the *Quarterly of the Society of California Pioneers*, VII (September, 1930), 148–98. Regrettably, no diary is known for Walker's detachment beyond the point it finally left the Oregon Trail on lower Raft River to strike over to the head of the Humboldt.

[10] The "Journal of John Boardman," published in *Utah Historical Quarterly*, II (October, 1929), 99–121, describes the experience of a member of the Chiles-Walker party who subsequently changed his mind and went to Oregon. Overton Johnson and William H. Winter, whose *Route across the Rocky Mountains* (Lafayette, Ind., 1846; reprinted at Princeton, 1932) is quoted above, were two Oregon immigrants who accompanied Walker to the Bear, being as much in need of provender as the Californians. P. B. Reading did not make this side tour; he joined Chiles at Fort Hall. Much the best account of the Walker route is by Theodore H. Talbot, in charge of Frémont's baggage train, who followed it about two weeks later. See the Edwin Bryant journal, note 8. Talbot says eight wagons were with Walker along the Bear River.

Before Walker with his eight wagons passes from our view, let us remark the interesting flirtation he conducted that summer with the boundaries of the present state of Utah. The meanderings of the Bear along the Utah-Wyoming line brought him at several points within the present confines of the state; and later, beyond Fort Hall, when Walker took his wagons up the Raft River, through City of Rocks, and on to Goose Creek, from that time the standard California Trail, he also crossed the extreme northwestern tip of Utah.

The Western trails, in the mid-1840s, were still very much in a state of flux. All along their length, determined efforts were being made to shorten the wearisome distances. A disastrous effort at a cutoff in Oregon in 1845 did not dampen the enthusiasm for improvement, and 1846, in particular, was noteworthy for the blazing of new routes. The celebrated Applegate Cutoff to Oregon, which took off from the California Trail below the great bend of the Humboldt River, was worked out by Jesse Applegate at the same time Lansford W. Hastings was addressing himself to the country west of Fort Bridger.

The Hastings Cutoff, the dominant theme of these studies, came into being because of the obvious irrationality of traveling northwest from Fort Bridger to Fort Hall and then, beyond Fort Hall, turning southwest again to reach the head of the Humboldt. Why not cut straight across that bend and save several hundred miles' travel? This was the gospel which Lansford W. Hastings preached so eloquently and which won converts enough to enable him to mark out a new wagon road through the Great Salt Lake country. However, the willingness of these immigrants to take a chance on Hastings' new route beyond all doubt was heightened by the reports that the popular hero, Frémont, had looked out the greater part of it. Consequently we must take a close look at Frémont's famous Third Expedition.

It would add very much to our understanding of the history of the Hastings Cutoff had John Charles Frémont kept clear of politics long enough, while his journals still survived and his memory was unimpaired, to provide us with a detailed account of his expedition of 1845. Unfortunately, by the time he came to publish his *Memoirs*, in 1887, his journals had gone up in smoke, and he remembered practically nothing of his experiences. The account he published is mainly an elaboration of the sketchy data he had incorporated into his *Geographical Memoir* of 1848,[11] and to give his narrative life and color he

---

[11] John Charles Frémont, *Geographical Memoir upon Upper California, in*

was reduced to borrowing incidents from John Bigelow's early biography of himself and DeWitt C. Peters' biography of Kit Carson.[12]

Edward M. Kern's journal was long lost, and until recently all that we had of it was an extract describing the experience of Theodore Talbot's contingent after Frémont divided his party at Mound Springs.[13] Fortunately, Kern's journal has finally become available, and it now supplements the scanty data in Frémont's *Geographical Memoir*, the map Charles Preuss drew to accompany it, and a few miscellaneous sources to create a reasonably clear view of Frémont's experiences in the most creditable piece of exploration he ever accomplished. With a large, well-equipped party, he left Bent's Fort on the Arkansas on August 16, 1845. Crossing the Rockies in central Colorado, he entered present Utah by way of the White River, following it to its mouth in the Green. He then ascended the Duchesne to the vicinity of Wolf Creek Pass, crossed the Great Basin Divide to the Provo River, and followed this stream down to Utah Valley, which he reached about October 9. Moving north along the Jordan River, he encamped on the site of Salt Lake City on October 14. Here his party remained for six days while he took observations for latitude and longitude and visited Antelope Island. Frémont's account of this visit to the island—which, as the Preuss map shows, was reached by following the east bank of the Jordan to its mouth, and then splashing across the shallow bar which connects the island

---

Illustration of His Map of Oregon and California (Washington, 1848, 67 pp.). The first edition was printed for the use of the Senate, and its feature of greatest present-day interest, the itinerary of the expedition, appears on pp. 56–58. An edition in 40 pp. was printed in 1849 for the use of the House.

[12] Compare, for example, the incident at Sagundai's Spring, *Memoirs of My Life* (Chicago, 1887), 436–37, which Frémont borrowed almost verbatim either from John Bigelow, *Memoir of the Life and Public Service of John Charles Frémont* (New York, 1856), 126–27, or from one of the editions (1873 or after) of DeWitt C. Peters' *Kit Carson's Life and Adventures*, 247–48. If from Frémont's *Memoirs* what he clearly borrowed from these two biographies and his *Geographical Memoir* be subtracted, practically nothing remains. Worse yet, he did not use these sources with entire accuracy. Altogether, his reminiscences of the expedition of 1845 are a pathetic comment on the state of his memory in the 1880s.

[13] If Talbot himself kept a journal while on this expedition, it has not come with his other papers into the keeping of the Library of Congress. A manuscript narrative of the Third Expedition by Thomas S. Martin, in the Bancroft Library, contributes nothing of interest or value concerning his experiences between the Rockies and the Sierra. Various sources supply useful sidelights on the expedition as far west as Bent's Fort, and after its arrival in California, but the record between is remarkably barren.

with the mainland—is the only real contribution *Memoirs* makes:

> There is at the southern end of the lake a large peninsu-
> lar island, which the Indians informed me could at this low
> stage of the water be reached on horseback. Accordingly on
> the 18th I took with me Carson and a few men and rode from
> our encampment near the southeastern shore across the
> shallows to the island—almost peninsular at this low state of
> the waters—on the way the water nowhere reaching above the
> saddle-girths. The floor of the lake was a sheet of salt re-
> sembling softening ice, into which the horses' feet sunk to the
> fetlocks. On the island we found grass and water and several
> bands of antelope. Some of these were killed, and, in mem-
> ory of the grateful supply of food they furnished, I gave their
> name to the island. . . . Returning to the shore we found at
> the camp an old Utah Indian. Seeing what game we had
> brought in he promptly informed us that the antelope which
> we had been killing were his—that *all* the antelope on that
> island belonged to him—that they were all he had to live
> upon, and that we must pay him for the meat which we had
> brought away. He was very serious with us and gravely re-
> proached me for the wrong which we had done him. Pleased
> with his readiness, I had a bale unpacked and gave him a
> present—some red cloth, a knife, and tobacco, with which he
> declared himself abundantly satisfied for this trespass on his
> game preserve. With each article laid down, his nods and
> gutturals expressed the satisfaction he felt at the success of
> his imaginary claim. . . .[14]

Apparently Frémont broke up camp on what he called "Station

---

[14] *Memoirs of My Life*, 431. Compare Kit Carson's account, found alterna-
tively in Blanche C. Grant, ed., *Kit Carson's Own Story of His Life* (Taos, 1926),
66; and Milo M. Quaife, ed., *Kit Carson's Autobiography* (Chicago, 1935), 89:
"There was in our front a large island, the largest of the lake. We were informed
by Indians that on it there was abundance of fresh water and plenty of antelope.
Frémont took a few men, I being one, and went to the Island to explore it. We
found good grass, water, timber and plenty of game. We remained there some
two days killing meat and exploring. It was about fifteen miles long and in
breadth about five miles. . . . In going to the Island we rode over salt from the
thickness of a wafer to twelve inches. We reached it horseback. . . ."
The Indian Frémont mentions was quite possibly Wanship's son, old only
in Frémont's recollection. See Osborne Russell's *Journal of a Trapper* (Boise,
1921), 122.

Creek," present City Creek, on the morning of October 21, for his itinerary places him that day at "Spring point, (extremity of a promontory at south end of Salt Lake, opposite Antelope island)." This was the locality of Garfield, at the north end of the Oquirrh Mountains. On the 23rd he was in "Spring Valley, opening on southern shore of the Great Salt lake"—the springs at present Grantsville in Tooele Valley—and by the 25th had moved on to a "Valley, near southwestern shore of Salt lake." He had thus moved along the route of the future Hastings Cutoff as far as Skull Valley. He had also reached the jumping-off place for his crossing of the Salt Desert.

Kit Carson recalls, in his dictation of 1856:

> [We] kept around the south side of the Lake to the last water. Fremont started [Lucien] Maxwell, [Auguste] Archambeau, [Basil] Lajeunesse and myself to cross the desert. It had never before been crossed by white man. I was often here. Old trappers would speak of the impossibility of crossing, that water could not be found, grass for the animals, there was none.
>
> Fremont was bound to cross. Nothing was impossible for him to perform if required in his exertions.
>
> Before we started it was arranged that at a certain time of [the] next day he should ascend the mountain near his camp, have with him his telescope, so that we could be seen by him, and if we found grass or water, we should make a smoke, which would be the sign to him to advance. We travelled on about sixty miles no water or grass, not a particle of vegetation could be found, (ground as level as a barn floor), before we struck the mountains on the west side of the Lake. Water and grass was there in abundance. The fire was made. Fremont saw it and moved on with his party. Archambeau started back and met him when about half way across the desert. He camped on the desert one night and next evening at dark, he got across, having lost only a few animals.[15]

A second version of the desert crossing, which must have been based upon information had from Frémont himself, was printed by John Bigelow in his campaign biography of 1856. By reason of its early date, the additional details it provides are of special interest:

[15] *Own Story*, 66–67; *Autobiography*, 89–91.

Their previous visit to the lake had given it a somewhat familiar aspect, and on leaving it they felt as if about to commence their journey anew. Its eastern shore was frequented by large bands of Indians, but here they had dwindled down to a single family, which was gleaning from some hidden source enough to support life, and drinking the salt water of a little stream near by, no fresh water being at hand.[16] This offered scanty encouragement as to what they might expect on the desert beyond.

At its threshold and immediately before them was a naked plain of smooth clay surface, mostly devoid of vegetation—the hazy weather of the summer hung over it, and in the distance rose scattered, low, black and dry-looking mountains. At what appeared to be fifty miles or more, a higher peak held out some promise of wood and water, and towards this it was resolved to direct their course.

Four men, with a pack animal loaded with water for two days, and accompanied by a naked Indian—who volunteered for a reward to be their guide to a spot where he said there was grass and fine springs—were sent forward to explore in advance for a foothold, and verify the existence of water before the whole party should be launched into the desert. Their way led toward the high peak of the mountain, on which they were to make a smoke signal in the event of finding water. About sunset of the second day, no signal having been seen, Fremont became uneasy at the absence of his men, and set out with the whole party upon their trail, travelling rapidly all the night. Towards morning one of the scouts, Archambault, was met returning.

The Indian had been found to know less than themselves, and had been sent back, but the men had pushed on to the mountains, where they found a running stream, with

---

[16] Frémont made use of this detail from Bigelow in writing his *Memoirs*, 432, saying, "On the 23d I encamped at a spring in a valley opening on the southern shore of the lake. On the way, near the shore, we came to a small run flowing into the lake, where an Indian was down on his hands and knees, drinking. Going there also to drink, we were surprised to find it salt. The water was clear, and its coolness indicated that it came from not far below the surface." Frémont picked up his date from the *Geographical Memoir*, which would place this episode near Grantsville. It fits the character of Skull Valley much better, and more probably happened there.

wood and sufficient grass. The whole party now lay down to rest, and the next day, after a hard march reached the stream. The distance across the plain was nearly seventy miles, and they called the mountain which had guided them Pilot Peak. This was their first day's march and their first camp in the desert.[17]

To these accounts must be added that of Frémont himself. He adopted the tales of his *Geographical Memoir*, added the Bigelow account and the Carson narrative as presented in DeWitt Peters' biography, stirred vigorously, and came up with the following:

Some days here [in Skull Valley] were occupied in deciding upon the direction to be taken for the onward journey. The route I wished to take lay over a flat plain covered with sage-brush. The country looked dry and of my own men none knew anything of it; neither Walker nor Carson. The Indians declared to us that no one had ever been known to cross the plain, which was upon the line of our intended travel, and at the farther edge of the desert, apparently fifty to sixty miles away, was a peak-shaped mountain. This looked to me to be fertile, and it seemed safe to make an attempt to reach it. By some persuasion and the offer of a tempting reward, I had induced one of the local Indians to go as guide on the way to the mountain; willing to profit by any side knowledge of the ground, or water-hole that the rains might have left, and about which the Indians always know in their hunts through the sage after small game.

I arranged that Carson, Archambeau, and Maxwell should set out at night, taking with them a man having charge of a pack-mule with water and provisions, and make for the mountain. I to follow with the party the next day and make one camp out into the desert. They to make a signal by smoke in case water should be found.

The next afternoon when the sun was yet two hours high, with the animals rested and well watered, I started out on the plain. As we advanced this was found destitute of any vegeta-

---

[17] Bigelow, *op. cit.*, 124–25. It is possible that Bigelow drew his information from the Frémont diaries, still in existence in 1856, but even if received verbally, his version must be accounted more authoritative than what Frémont could remember 30 years later.

tion except sage-bushes, and absolutely bare and smooth as if
water had been standing upon it. The animals being fresh I
stretched far out into the plain. Travelling along in the night,
after a few hours' march, my Indian lost his courage and
grew so much alarmed that his knees really gave way under
him and he wobbled about like a drunken man. He was not a
true Utah, but rather of the Pi-utes, a Digger of the upper
class, and he was becoming so demoralized at being taken so
far from his *gîte*. Seeing that he could be of no possible use I
gave him his promised reward and let him go. He was so
happy in his release that he bounded off like a hare through
the sagebrush, fearful that I might still keep him.

Sometime before morning I made camp in the sagebrush, lighting fires to signal Carson's party. Before daybreak
Archambeau rode in; the jingling of his spurs a welcome
sound indicating as it did that he brought good tidings. They
had found at the peak water and grass, and wood abundant.
The gearing up was quickly done and in the afternoon we
reached the foot of the mountain, where a cheerful little
stream broke out and lost itself in the valley. The animals
were quickly turned loose, there being no risk of their straying from the grass and water. To the friendly mountain I
gave the name of Pilot Peak. . . . Some time afterward, when
our crossing of the desert became known, an emigrant caravan was taken by this route, which then became known as
The Hastings Cut-off.[18]

Edward Kern's journal adds some intriguing information and
provides the earliest eyewitness account of the first known crossing of
the route that became the Hastings Cutoff:

On the 21st [October] after a travel of 15 miles we
camped at the base of a rocky ridge [Oquirrh Mountains].
Crossing the Valley in South Westerly course Vegetation is
becoming more sparse and the grass is of a salty nature, gives
but poor food to our animals—Numerous salt springs.
[October 22] Over a prairie and march [marsh] close to
the borders of the lake camping at some springs. Making 15
miles.[19] sage in abundance

---

[18] *Memoirs of My Life,* 432–33.
[19] After crossing the Salt Lake Valley on the 21st, Frémont's party camped

23rd Today we have had close to our left a ridge of burnt
rock [Stansbury Mountains] almost devoid of vegetation. A
narrow strip of salty and bunch grass mixed seems close to its
foot—The country is fast assuming a most desolate appearance. 19 miles [Timpie Point].

[October 24] Continuing along this ridge for 6 miles
nearly in a South of West course [into Skull Valley], we
crossed a plain of dry soil. Sage is now becoming the prevailing growth. Camped at some springs [Burnt Springs] at the
foot of a barren rocky ridge [Stansbury Mountains]   15 m.

Traveling today (25th) over a broken country at the foot of
the ridge we camped at a small spring stream [Redlum
Spring]. Bill Williams leaves us at this camp to return to the
settlements on the Arkansas. [October 27?] Kit Carson, Archambeau and Dick Owens,[20] were sent to see what prospect
of water ahead, this being as far as the eye could reach
Nothing but a large barren plain.

On the 28th after a couple of hours travel through the
mountain [Cedar Mountains] we entered on one of the most
disolate looking places I have seen—with but a small
prospect of water ahead and less of grass, we commenced our
journey over what has since been called by the emigrants the
"Long Drive".[21] We were the first white men without doubt
who had ever attempted it. At five o'clock we camped, tired
and worn out, among some low sand hills—without water and
but little wood—25 miles—Striking Camp at 5 o'clock next
morning [October 29] we passed at 10 [o'clock] a small isolated range [Floating Island], previous to reaching this point
the road had become muddy—at 11 o'clock we nooned
among some bunch grass at the foot of a low range of [hills];
no water.[22] We kept among these hills until 4 [o'clock] when
we again entered the plain—the mud on this afternoon's road
is very heavy—water salty. at 6-20 [o'clock] we reached some
springs of good water, grass, and timber plenty [Pilot

---

at the site of Grantsville on the 22nd.

[20] Carson recalled the party comprised Basil Lajeunesse, Lucien Maxwell,
Auguste Archambault, and himself. See page 10.

[21] This revealing sentence shows that this is a reminiscent journal, not a
daily diary, composed after 1846.

[22] Like the emigrants of 1846, Fremont's company had vain hopes of finding
water on Silver Island.

Springs]—Extremely fatigued with their two days travel many
of our animals rested.

[October] 30—3 miles to a spring creek in the mountain
[Pilot Peak]. Piñon abundant. The day cold and disagreeable.

Friday Oct 31—Along the ridge over broken and sterile
country for 12 miles when we struck a level plain [Tecoma
Valley] and an old wagon trail. This was the sign of an old
party who had attempted to cross the Desert. To save themselves [two words illegible] many men were obliged to throw
away their effects and return.[23] After crossing this plain we
struck another ridge [Toano Range] and camped near its
summit at some holes of water [with] Pine timber [and]
bunch grass   24 miles

November 1st 7 mi   Camped on the slope of a mountain
of the same ridge as yesterday. There was no water save in
some holes and that only to be procured by digging. Our
mules had had none the night previous and it was amusing to
see them fight one another. It was with difficulty they could
be kept out of the holes, until a supply could be procured for
them and dealt out in buckets as the holes were very slow in
filling up

2nd [November]   Raising camp at 7:45 [o'clock] we
crossed the summit of the ridge and descending continued
among the hills till 10:20 [o'clock] when we came onto another plain covered as usual with wild sage—Camping at a
spring and marsh[24]   grass and water tolerable. 14 miles

[November 3]   Left our camp this morning at 7:35
[o'clock]   continued for 3 miles on the plains   8:30 [o'clock]
West we raised another range of mountains in which we
travelled until 9:50 [o'clock] when we commenced crossing a
similar plain to those already passed   camping at some
springs of good water at 11:55 [o'clock] making 13 miles of
travel.[25]

[23] These were the tracks of the Bidwell-Bartleson party. Kern's account is
the first to show that Frémont saw evidence of the company's passing. See the
Bryant journal, note 67.

[24] After traversing the Toano Range via a canyon Dale L. Morgan dubbed
"Frémont's Pass," the explorers crossed Gosiute Valley to Flowery Lake.

[25] The party crossed the Pequop Mountains via Jasper Pass to reach Mound
Springs in Independence Valley. Kern made no entry for November 4, which
was undoubtedly spent resting.

November 5 1845—Today we parted company, the Captain passing to the Southward with a small party to examine the great basin. Supposed to be an immense desert, lying between the Sierra Navada and the Rocky Mountains.[26]

These four accounts have numerous points of agreement and several discrepancies.[27] Frémont says he set out across the desert in the late afternoon and continued "travelling along in the night," while Kern recalled making camp at five o'clock in the evening. While this may be another indication of a failing memory, it suggests Frémont sent his men across the desert in detachments, traveling himself with the rear guard. Carson says nothing about an Indian going with his advance party, but this is plausible, much more so than one going with Frémont. Carson declares that Frémont saw the smoke signal; Frémont and Kern are silent on the point; Bigelow says nothing was seen of it. Considering normal visibility conditions, Bigelow very likely has the straight of it; only from the crest of the Cedar Mountains could Frémont have had any prospect of seeing a smoke signal from Pilot Peak. Bigelow says Frémont finally set out into the desert without any assurance of water, out of concern for his

---

[26] Edward M. Kern, "Journal of a Trip to California 1845–46–47," Beinecke Library, Yale University. Used by permission. For this date's entry in the edited version of Kern's journal published in J. H. Simpson's *Report*, see the James Clyman journal, note 2, which continues Kern's account to November 8 when the Talbot party reached the Humboldt River.

[27] Captain Howard Stansbury's original journals, published in Brigham D. Madsen, ed., *Exploring the Great Salt Lake: The Stansbury Expedition of 1849–50* (Salt Lake City, 1989), 186, contain a little information related to these events. Guided by Archambault, Stansbury came east across the Salt Desert on the Hastings Road on November 5, 1849, and wrote:

> Crossed the mountains through the pass following the wagon road. It is about 5 miles north of where Fremont crossed. . . . After crossing continued down the east slope of the mountain for about two miles when we came to a spring with some green grass growing in the water. . . . This was one of Fremont's camping grounds before crossing the mountain which he did through a pass at this place. From this spring our course lay about East across a broad valley of 10 miles wide. . . . Reaching the eastern mountain foot came to a Spring where had been another Camping ground of Fremont here was some good green grass.

The first campsite Stansbury describes was Redlum Spring, on the west side of Skull Valley; the second was Burnt Spring, on the east side of the valley. With respect to Frémont's crossing of the Cedar Mountains, see the Clyman journal, note 19. Frémont's camp at Redlum Spring is also mentioned by Edwin Bryant; see his entry for August 3.

men; although Bigelow was writing a presidential campaign biography, in which little touches of the kind would be well received, it is entirely consistent with Frémont's character that he should have done so. Frémont's night march into the desert could have taken him to Kern's camp "among some low sand hills" at a point beyond Grayback Mountain. Since the site provided "but little wood" and Kern made no mention of Frémont's sagebrush beacon fire, the signal fire tales seem unlikely. Neither Bigelow nor Frémont mentions any difficulty in getting across the salt, but Carson remembered that a few animals were lost, and four years later Archambault told Stansbury that the desert passage cost Frémont ten mules and several horses.[28] The memory must have influenced Joe Walker a year later when he expressed his low opinion of the new route to Edwin Bryant and others.

It seems probable that Carson's scouting party began its crossing on October 27, 1845. Kern left Redlum Spring on the morning of October 28, reaching the springs at Pilot Peak finally at nightfall on October 29.[29] The *Geographical Memoir* shows observations made at "Pilot peak creek" on October 30.

Frémont was doubtless mistaken in supposing that even the Indians had never directly crossed this desert, but his party must be accorded the credit for making the first white traverse of it; Jedediah Smith in 1827 had rimmed the desert to the south, while the Bidwell-Bartleson party of 1841 had skirted it to the north.

Frémont left Pilot Peak on October 31, and on November 1 the *Geographical Memoir* places him at a "Spring at head of ravine." The Preuss map locates this camp high in the Toano Mountains, nearly due west of present Wendover, and some 20 miles south of the pass that had been used by the Bidwell-Bartleson party and was to be used by all the immigrant wagons of 1846, as it is by I-80 today. From their mountain camp Frémont's party turned directly west,

---

[28] Stansbury noted this information in his journal on October 30, 1849, and subsequently incorporated it into his published report. See Madsen, ed., *Exploring the Great Salt Lake*, 182.

[29] Perhaps, however, Carson set out on the 26th. For its bearing on these dates, note the information Alpheus H. Favour developed from Frémont's accounts in the records of the General Accounting Office, which indicated Old Bill Williams, who was hired on August 28, separated from Frémont on October 27, 1845. Obviously Williams did not like the Salt Desert, and was paid off the eve of Frémont's attempted crossing. Alpheus H. Favour, *Old Bill Williams, Mountain Man* (Chapel Hill, N. C., 1936), 138–39.

and in two days they were at "Whitton spring."

It is difficult to believe that Frémont could have missed the springs at Flowery Lake after descending the west slope of the Toanos; especially because Clyman, coming east on the Frémont trail seven months later, made these springs one of his campsites. However, it should be pointed out that the Preuss map shows Frémont to have crossed a dry valley after coming down out of the Toanos and to have found water only across another divide, which indicates that "Whitton spring" actually was Mound Springs in Independence Valley. To support such a view, neither the Preuss map nor Kern's diary locates a spring between "Whitton spring" and the water at the base of the East Humboldt Mountains.[30]

Apart from mere historical curiosity, the actual location of the spring is important because it was here that Frémont divided his party. Taking ten men, he himself turned south around Spruce Mountain to reach Ruby Valley between Franklin and Ruby lakes. He then went directly up over the Ruby Mountains by Harrison Pass, and on reaching Huntington Valley, turned south and west again to go on to the appointed place of rendezvous at Walker Lake through Diamond, Antelope, Monitor, Big Smoky, and Soda Springs valleys.

Although Frémont was chiefly impressed with his own travels, history has found more significant the movements of the other portion of his party, entrusted to Lieutenant Theodore H. Talbot and guided by Joe Walker. Their route to the Humboldt became the route next year of James Clyman and Edwin Bryant, and save for the evidences left by Talbot's passing, which Lansford Hastings carefully watched for next spring and which became the point of departure from the established trail, the history of the Hastings Cutoff might have been different beyond all recognition.

We have now set the stage for the dramatic trail-making endeavors of 1846. These are studied at close range through the texts of the source documents, which have preserved the story in remarkable detail. Each of these documents is suitably introduced and annotated to bring out the wealth of information it contains, so extended comment would be inappropriate here. It is nevertheless desirable to point out the wonderful fullness with which these journals develop a notably complex story. We have James Clyman's diary to follow Lansford Hastings eastward along the Frémont route as far as Great

---

[30] Another deficiency of the Preuss map: It does not show the springs in Clover Valley either, though they are mentioned by Kern.

Salt Lake, and to give us some insight into the view of the terrain between that point and Fort Bridger which confirmed Hastings in his opinion that wagons could be taken directly west from the fort. The Clyman journal is followed by Edwin Bryant's narrative, which picks up the story at Fort Bridger and relates the adventures of a mounted party that went in advance of the wagons Hastings engaged to guide over his new cutoff. The experiences of this party affected the movements of the wagons in a decisive manner by inducing them to try the Weber Canyon route to the valley of the Great Salt Lake. One lack persists in our documentation of this engrossing story; we have no journal of the Harlan-Young party's pioneering of the route down Echo Canyon or later circuit of the Ruby Mountains.[31] But by rare good fortune a new narrative of the greatest importance, kept by a Swiss immigrant, Heinrich Lienhard, who traveled a few days behind the Harlan-Young company and just ahead of the Donner party, has been made available for publication here; that part of it relating to the famous Cutoff is now printed for the first time in its entirety, in English, and it alters radically many of our ideas about Hastings and his Cutoff. The Lienhard journal is the more valuable because it indicates that he traveled much of the time with T. H. Jefferson, whose *Map of the Emigrant Road from Independence Mo. to St. Francisco, California,* depicting the route of the Hastings Cutoff, is one of the central documents for any study of the western trails. As though in this abundance we had not enough to be grateful for, an actual journal by James Frazier Reed has appeared, in the light of which the experiences of the Donner party on the Hastings Cutoff can be authoritatively treated for the first time. All the books about

---

[31] While this volume was in press in 1951, a hitherto unknown journal by James Mathers came to light in the possession of Miss Frances E. Campbell, Salinas, California. Mathers reached Fort Bridger on July 21, and two days later, in company with two others, Carolan Mathers and Otis Ashley, set out on the new Hastings road, overtaking the rear wagons of the Harlan party at Bear River on July 25. Mathers reached the Weber River on July 29 but did not emerge finally from the canyons of the Weber until August 5. Arriving at the Jordan River on August 7, he went on south around the lake and with the rest of the Harlan company set out on the Salt Desert crossing on August 16. When some of the wagons had to be left in the desert, he stayed with them, and is doubtless the unnamed man Heinrich Lienhard talked to on the night of the 18th (see p. 158). Traveling in close proximity to Jefferson and Lienhard, he ultimately reached the main California Trail again on September 8. The Mathers diary has since been published in Morgan, *Overland in 1846,* I, 219–236, making "a notable addition to the history of the Hastings Cutoff."

the Hastings Cutoff and the Donner party must be rewritten under the impact of these new-found records.

These impressive documents have served me as a vehicle for presenting my personal researches, which have extended over a period of nearly 20 years, on the pioneering of the immigrant roads into and across Utah, including the routes and the companies who marked them out. The special studies of the Golden Pass Road and of the Salt Lake Cutoff north of Great Salt Lake, roads designed to obviate the difficulties of the Hastings route, should be received as necessary supplements. These studies could be extended further to include an account of the pioneering of the Southern Road to California, down through the heart of Utah and across the Vegas and Mojave deserts, but such an account, embracing necessarily all the themes of the Spanish Trail, would be a book in itself. Perhaps the value of the present publication would be heightened by including, too, a study of the Hudspeth Cutoff from Soda Springs to the Raft River below City of Rocks—a route that Benoni Morgan Hudspeth worked out in the summer of 1849. No wholly accurate account of the itinerary of the Hudspeth Cutoff has yet been published. But it has not seemed advisable to take it up here—for geographical reasons (it lay wholly within the confines of what is now Idaho) and for the practical reason that I can bring the authority of field research to only a part of its length.

The conclusions voiced in the notes to the documents in this volume are based for the most part on direct field research. In particular, all that is said of the Hastings Cutoff and its variant routes between the Bear River Divide and Skull Valley; of the Golden Pass Road; and of the Salt Lake Cutoff is based on prolonged personal study of the terrain. Identification of the trails between Fort Bridger and the Bear River rests on field trips made in company with Charles Kelly in 1937 and with Dale L. Morgan in 1948. For the Salt Desert I lean heavily on Mr. Kelly's first-hand investigations, of which I have had the benefit both from personal intercourse and from his book, *Salt Desert Trails*. The Nevada stretches of the Hastings Cutoff are least satisfactorily treated in my notes, since the state of my health in late years has prevented my going over this part of the trail in its entirety, and I have seen it only at tangential points. What I say about the westernmost reaches of the Hastings Cutoff is mainly based upon map study backed up by second-hand information and quite possibly is subject to the adjustment that field research always exacts.

My special acknowledgments with respect to the documents are made in my introductions to each of them. But I have some personal obligations perhaps more appropriately expressed here. I have to thank scores of people who have helped me through the years, most of whose names I do not even know. Farmers, ranchers, miners, forest rangers, housewives—all manner of people who have given me five minutes or an hour at their door, in their barns, in their fields, or beside the road have helped to invest these studies with the measure of authority they possess. On the more personal plane, I am especially indebted to Charles Kelly, companion on so many trips which for both of us are cherished memories; he has shared with me his library and all his resources of information and has been the anvil against which I have hammered out many of my ideas. I have the same kind of obligation to Dale L. Morgan, with whom I did much of the final field work; he has placed at my disposal the fruits of his researches in libraries the length and breadth of the land and has given me very great aid in the preparation of my manuscript. My wife, Sara Merrill Korns, with all else she has given me, has been boon companion on yet other field trips, sharing with me in adventures and misadventures neither of us would want to forget. Nor could I fail to mention two friends since high school days, A. William Lund and the late Alvin F. Smith. As assistant church historian and church librarian, respectively, they have made me welcome at the LDS Church Historian's Office over a long period of time, given me access to many of the records in their custody, argued amiably with me on many subjects, and not minded my occasional derision of their views. To these friends and all others who have helped, I extend my thanks.

Because such a work as this is not written without the help of organized scholarship, I wish to acknowledge also a special obligation to the Salt Lake City Free Public Library, the Utah State Historical Society, the California Historical Society, the California State Library, the Missouri Historical Society, the Bancroft Library, the Henry E. Huntington Library, the Yale University Library, the New York Public Library, the Sutter's Fort Historical Museum, the Southwest Museum, the Kentucky Historical Society, the National Archives, and last but very far from least, the Library of Congress. Perhaps these institutions will receive this now finally published work as an adequate return for their varied and generous aid.

—*Charles Kelly photo, Utah State Historical Society*

LANSFORD WARREN HASTINGS

—*Utah State Historical Society*

JAMES CLYMAN

—*Utah State Historical Society*

JAMES M. HUDSPETH

THE JOURNAL OF JAMES CLYMAN

May 21–June 7, 1846

INTRODUCTION

DECEMBER, 1845, was for Sutter's Fort a month of historic arrivals. The last month of the year was not one which ordinarily brought visitors down out of the mountains. Of late years there had been an annual wave of arrivals overland from Oregon in July or August, and another, direct from the States, in October. But the two bronzed men who rode down from the upper valleys in December, 1845, were not travelers of quite this kind.

First to reach the fort was John Charles Frémont, Brevet Captain in the Topographical Corps of the United States Army; his arrival the *New Helvetia Diary* faithfully chronicled on December 10. Frémont on this occasion certainly cut a better figure than when he had come in over the Sierra 21 months before with the half-starved, half-naked party of explorers he had brought down from the Columbia. There had been no trail then but the one he found for himself, and the finding had been infinitely painful and laborious. This time Frémont came in jauntily. The large, excellently equipped exploring expedition he had brought west through the Rockies to the Great Salt Lake had, after splitting at Mound Springs, gone two ways to Walker Lake and rendezvoused there with no difficulty whatever. Splitting his party a second time, with Joe Walker instructed to guide the greater number in to the San Joaquin Valley by the southern pass which bore his name, Frémont had turned north with a small detachment of his company. His purpose was to look into this new route across the mountains which immigrants of the last two years had discovered for themselves—a route said to go up the Truckee River to a practicable if difficult pass and down the far slope to Sutter's post on the American River.

The reports had turned out to be true, the immigrants more successful than he in finding a route for travel across the Sierra. Frémont only had to follow the tracks of their wagons in to the settlements. He did not begrudge them their achievement, for he had the ebullient conviction that he himself had discovered an entire new route across the continent, a route which would vastly shorten the road to California. While outfitting himself at Sutter's preparatory to going south in search of his party, he set the fort to buzzing with talk of his discoveries. Time pressed, however, and on December 13 the *New Helvetia Diary* conscientiously recorded, "Started Capt. Frémont to meet Capt. Walker to the South."

Shortly the *Diary* had to be reopened for an entry equally interesting. On Christmas Day Sutter's clerk took up his pen to record the news: "Arr^d Capt. Hastings from the U.S."[1] The notation was spare enough. But now, indeed, there would be a stirring and fluttering in California.

The reappearance of Frémont upon the California scene was a surprise, that of Hastings astonishing only in that he had come so late, with the Sierra passes still open only by a vagary of the weather. For months California had been buzzing with rumors of this enterprising young man's fantastic activities. A fledgling Ohio lawyer who had gone overland to Oregon with the immigration of 1842, Hastings had come down the coast to California next year and fallen in love with this brown, sunburnt land. If he had returned to the States by way of Mexico, it was only for the purpose of publishing an *Emigrants' Guide, to Oregon and California* which glowingly represented to intending immigrants the country about the Bay of San Francisco.[2] Never had he permitted California to doubt that he would be back. So early as August 12, 1845, John Marsh at San Jose was writing Thomas O. Larkin, the American consul at Monterey, "I have lately received information from Mr Hastings who passed through this country some two years ago. It is highly probable,— almost certain that he is now on his way to this place with a numerous company of immigrants—it is said two thousand, principally *families* from Ohio & Kentucky, & that they are mostly of good character & some property."[3]

The expectantly awaited immigration of 1845, when it rolled down out of the Sierra in October, hardly measured up to such

---

[1] The quotations are from John A. Sutter, *New Helvetia Diary* (San Francisco, 1939), 16–19.

[2] First published at Cincinnati, Ohio, in 1845; reprinted in photofacsimile with an introduction by Charles Carey, Princeton, 1932.

[3] Marsh to Larkin, Pueblo of St. Joseph, August 12, 1845, George P. Hammond, ed., *The Larkin Papers: Personal, Business, and Official Correspondence of Thomas Oliver Larkin, Merchant and United States Consul in California* (10 vols., Berkeley, 1951–68), III, 310. Note that future citations of the Larkin Papers simply reference the date of the item.

advertising, numbering no more than a few hundreds, and when Hastings in person reached New Helvetia so remarkably late in the season, it was at the head of a party of only ten men. He came in, nonetheless, sanguine that his book would stir up a vast immigration in 1846, and it was soon known far and wide that his purpose was to return east on the trail next spring and divert that immigration to California.

What Hastings himself stood to gain by this furious activity is not, at this distance, quite clear. John Bidwell has said that Hastings' hope was to build up a sufficient American population in California to wrest that province from Mexico, envisioning himself as the president of a new republic on the model of Texas.[4] There is some contemporary evidence for this, brought to Oregon in the spring of 1846,[5] but it seems likely that Hastings had many irons heating in the fire, all of them dependent for their usefulness on the building up of a large American population in California. Whatever his motives, Hastings was completely dedicated to the cause. A letter of March 3, 1846, illustrates the expansive character of his ideas. "The emigration of this year to this country and Oregon," he assured Larkin at Monterey, "will not consist of less than *twenty thousand* human souls, a large majority of whom, are destined to this country. Our friend [Thomas J.] Farnham, and many other highly respectable and intelligent gentlemen, will accompany the emigration of this year, among them are also, many wealthy gentlemen and capitalists, who design to make large investments in California, in both agricultural and commercial pursuits." Thousands more, he added, might be expected by sea. "Thus, Sir, you c[a]n not but observe, that a new era in the affairs of California, is about to arise; these now wild and desolate plains must soon abound with all the busy and int[e]resting scenes of highly civilized life. And what a change, what a scene, to behold such a vast amount of dorment intelligence, inert energy, and dead and buried enterprise, as the Mexicans and Californians here possess, bursting forth in a day, as it were, into brilliant intelligence, commendable activity, and unbounded enterprise!"[6]

To a new and improved route to California Hastings had already given thought. Not having himself traveled directly overland to the Bay of San Francisco, he had necessarily been somewhat vague in

---

[4] John Bidwell, *Echoes of the Past* (Chico, Calif., n.d.), 49, 50.
[5] *Oregon Spectator* (Oregon City), June 25, 1846.
[6] Hastings to Larkin, New Helvetia, March 3, 1846, Larkin Papers.

his book about how to get there. "Those who go to California," he had
written, "travel from Fort Hall, west southwest about fifteen days, to
the northern pass, in the California mountains; thence, three days, to
the Sacramento; and thence, seven days down the Sacramento, to the
bay of St. Francisco." But immediately he had ventured to suggest
the possibility of something better: "The most direct route for the
California emigrants, would be to leave the Oregon route, about two
hundred miles east from Fort Hall; thence bearing west southwest, to
the Salt lake; and thence continuing down to the bay of St. Francisco,
by the route just described."[7]

As printed, this suggestion for a cutoff was no more than the expression of a pious hope. It was gratifying if hardly amazing for
Hastings to learn on his arrival at Sutter's that Frémont during the
autumn had found just such a route. Frémont was still in the south
searching for his party and did not get back to Sutter's until January
15, but without waiting for the details, Hastings cheerfully appropriated the new route to himself and began to spread the glad tidings
abroad. In a letter of January 12, Jacob P. Leese wrote to Larkin
from Sonoma, "Capt. Hastings has Jest arived at Sutters, from the
U. S. by land with 10 men he says he has found a road through the
Stony Mountains 400 miles shorter than has ever been travell'd. A
Larg Emigration will be through this Summer."[8]

When Frémont finally returned, Hastings had four days to question him about the new route before the explorer left for Yerba
Buena, the embryo San Francisco. What Hastings was told then must
have been similar to what Frémont wrote his wife on January 24:

> You know, that on every extant map, manuscript or
> printed, the whole of the Great Basin is represented as a
> sandy plain, barren, without water, and without grass. . . .
> with a volunteer party of fifteen men, I crossed it between the
> parallels of 38° and 39°. Instead of a plain, I found it,
> throughout its whole extent, traversed by parallel ranges of
> lofty mountains, their summits white with snow (October);
> while below, the valleys had none. Instead of a barren coun-
> try, the mountains were covered with grasses of the best
> quality, wooded with several varieties of trees, and containing

[7] *Emigrants' Guide, to Oregon and California*, 135, 137–38.
[8] Leese to Larkin, January 12, 1846, Larkin Papers. It is perfectly clear that
Hastings kept to the known trail in coming West in 1845, so that the character of
such talk as this is also clear.

more deer and mountain sheep than we had seen in any
previous part of our voyage. . . . By the route I have explored
I can ride in thirty-five days from the *Fontaine qui Bouit*
River to Captain Sutter's; and, for wagons, the road is decidedly better [than the established immigrant trail].[9]

Much of this was nonsense, but it was the kind of language
Hastings himself used with so much flamboyance, and he was the
last person to find fault with it. As it turned out, Hastings would see
very little of Frémont's own route; the Hastings Cutoff owed much
more to the explorations of Talbot's detachment, hardly so much as
intimated in Frémont's letter to his wife. It was not until weeks later,
when Frémont's reunited party passed by Sutter's Fort enroute to the
Klamath country, that Hastings had an opportunity to question those
who had looked out the route which chiefly interested him. But one
of his temperament needed nothing more than the bare assurance
that a trail through the deserts to the Great Salt Lake had actually
been found.

Through the winter Hastings remained at New Helvetia, laying
out for Sutter a new townsite along the Sacramento calculated to
appeal to the year's immigration.[10] With the onset of the early California spring, however, he began to prepare for his journey. Sutter
wrote Larkin on March 2, "Some of the Emigrants which arrived the
last fall are preparing for Oregon, and likewise a party for the U.
States, Capt. Hastings is going one Way or the other." Although Sutter had no doubt that, as Hastings predicted, fall would bring "a
powerful Emigration" and although himself as sanguine a man as
California ever saw, he was admittedly skeptical in the face of a
soaring optimism which could envision an influx of from 10,000 to
20,000 immigrants; "if 2 or 3000 would come," he remarked sagely,
"it would be a great many."[11]

On April 11 Hastings and his man, James M. Hudspeth, a Mis-
sourian, left Sutter's for Johnson's Ranch in Bear Valley, the place of
rendezvous for those intending to return to the States.[12] By that date
Hastings' plans had so far matured that Sutter could be informed of
them in detail. This is shown by a letter the master of New Helvetia
wrote William A. Leidesdorff on June 28, a full ten weeks after Hast-

---

[9] John Charles Frémont, *Memoirs of My Life*, 452.
[10] *New Helvetia Diary*, 26.
[11] Sutter to Larkin, New Helvetia, March 2, 1846, Larkin Papers.
[12] *New Helvetia Diary*, 35.

ings' departure: "The Emigrants from the U. States will be here this time in the Month of August, because Capt. Hastings is gone so far as fort Pritcher to bring them a new route Discovered by Capt. fremont which is about 3 or 400 Miles shorter as the old route over fort Hall."[13]

It was at the place of rendezvous in the Bear Valley that Hastings and Hudspeth came into the life of James Clyman, to whom, as the diarist of their eastward journey, we are indebted for so much that we now know about the complex history of the Hastings Cutoff.

The Virginia-born Clyman had the distinction of having been an Ashley man, a comrade of Jedediah Smith, William L. Sublette, Thomas Fitzpatrick, and the rest of that great company of adventurers who opened up the West. Clyman had been with Jedediah Smith in the rediscovery of South Pass in 1824; during the next two years he had taken beaver on all the waters of the Green and the Bear; and in the spring of 1826 he had been one of the party of trappers who, in a bullboat, made the first circumnavigation of Great Salt Lake. He had left the mountains in 1827 to take up land in Illinois and Wisconsin, but in the spring of 1844, to "see the country and try to find a better climate," for he had been troubled by a cough, he had made a horseback journey down into Arkansas and back up into Missouri. At Independence, on impulse, he had joined the year's immigration to Oregon. In the spring of 1845 he had ridden south from the Columbia to California, and now he was embarking upon the long journey home. About noon of April 16, 1846, he reached Hastings' camp, being welcomed, as he says, "in a warm and Polite manner."

We could have asked no better diarist for this journey. With his unrivaled experience as a frontiersman, his eminent good judgment, and his attentive regard to the country through which they passed, Clyman was clearly the effective head of the group with which he traveled; it is not merely because he chanced to become its historian that his detachment of the eastbound travelers has become identified as the Clyman-Hastings party.

The company which broke up its encampment at Johnson's Ranch on April 23 to ride up into the Sierra consisted, by Clyman's accounting, of "19 men and boys 3 women and 2 children and about

---

[13] Sutter to Leidesdorff, New Helvetia, June 28, 1846, Leidesdorff Papers, Huntington Library. Hastings had no means of communication with Sutter after leaving Johnson's Ranch, therefore Sutter had this information from him before Hastings set out.

150 mules and Horses." This was too large a party to travel together with the grass yet so short, and on May 16, after reaching the valley of the Humboldt, it split in two. The Clyman-Hastings party, which went on ahead, was made up, as Clyman says, of "8 men and 37 animals." The eight men evidently included one boy, and there was also a woman in the group, as is shown by a later entry in the diary.[14] The names of those who made up the party are not definitely known, but a reasonable probability is that the group primarily included (aside from Clyman, Hastings, Hudspeth, and Hastings' Indian vaquero) the Sumner family who were returning east from Oregon. Clyman had journeyed with the Sumners down from the Columbia in 1845 and had noted on April 20 their presence in the party going back to the States: "Mr Sumner has been in Oregon from thence to California and still being dissatisfied is now returning to the states again after haveing [spent] nearly five years in Traveling from place to place as Likewise a small fortune." The family apparently consisted of Owen Sumner, Sr., Owen Sumner, Jr., the latter's wife, and a second son or grandson who very likely was the boy Clyman mentions. If the presence of the Sumners be granted, only one member of the party remains unidentified. It has sometimes been suggested that the old mountain man, Caleb Greenwood, was the man, but it is much more likely that he and his 2 sons traveled with the rear detachment which went by way of Fort Hall.

On May 20 the Clyman-Hastings party reached the site of Elko, Nevada, encamping a few miles above the hot springs. That night Clyman made note in his journal of having observed during the day "what I supposed to be the E Branch [South Fork] of Marys River comeing in through a deep Kenyon from a range of snow capd mountains [Ruby Mountains] to the E of us." Thus the little party had reached the western limits of the country thereafter to be indelibly associated with Hastings' name. The excerpt from the Clyman journals that now follows is reprinted by permission of the Huntington Library, San Marino, Calif., which owns the originals, the California Historical Society, which first printed the Clyman journals in its *Quarterly* and later as *James Clyman, American Frontiersman, 1792–1881*, and Dr. Charles L. Camp, whose original editing of the journals contributed so largely to the classic status they have achieved.

---

[14] Compare Clyman's journal entries for May 18 and June 8, as published in Charles L. Camp, ed., *James Clyman, American Frontiersman, 1792–1881* (San Francisco, 1928), 216, 224.

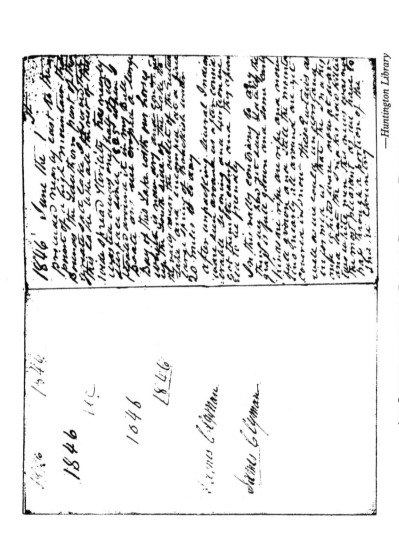

AN OPENING IN THE JAMES CLYMAN DIARY

Describing the Great Salt Lake and Valley, June 1, 1846.

THE CLYMAN JOURNAL

May 21 [1846] On the way again as usual N. E. course 1 1/2 hours
ride brought us to whare the stream came through a Kenyon [Osino
Canyon] for a short distance but the trail led over a sandy ridge to the
N and after passing another of the same discription we came to a
handsome little Brook h[e]ading to the N. W. [North Fork of the
Humboldt]   On each side of this brook the earth was covered white
with a salin incrustation and when broke By the tramping of our
mules it nearly strangled them and us causing them to caugh and us
to sneeze   at 14 miles we encamped[1] this being the point whare Mr
Freemant intersected the wagon Trail last fall on his way to california[2] and Mr Hastings our pilot was anxious to try this route but my

---

[1] The night's camp was a mile or two southwest of present Halleck, Nevada.
The country traveled over during the next two days is shown with a wealth of
detail on the *Halleck* quadrangle of the U. S. Geological Survey.

[2] Not Frémont, but the detachment of his party under Lt. T. H. Talbot,
guided by Joe Walker, from which he had separated at "Whitten's Spring"
(Mound Springs) on November 5, 1845. Talbot's group headed west and northwest to reach the Humboldt, descend it to its Sink, and then follow along the
base of the Sierra to Walker Lake while the party under Frémont's command
took a more southerly course to Walker Lake. Of more immediate interest to us
is Talbot's party, whose trail Hastings was so eager to follow. For purposes of
comparison with the other journals of this route, the relevant extract from the
journal of Edward M. Kern, Talbot's topographer, is reprinted from J. H.
Simpson's *Report of Explorations Across the Great Basin of the Territory of Utah
for a Direct Wagon-Route from Camp Floyd to Genoa, in Carson Valley, in 1859*
(Washington, 1876), Appendix Q, 477, 478:

    November 5, 1845.—Whitten's Spring. To-day we parted compa-
ny, the captain passing to the southward with a small party, to examine
that portion of the Great Basin supposed to be a desert lying between
the Sierra Nevada and the Rocky Mountains. The main body of the
camp, under the guidance of Mr. Joseph Walker, are to move toward
the head of Mary's or Ogden's River [the Humboldt], and down that
stream to its sink or lake. From thence to Walker's Lake, where we are
again to meet. I am to accompany the latter party in charge of the topography, &c. Crossing the [Spruce] mountains near our camp, we arrived about 1 o'clock p.m. at several springs of excellent water. These
springs spread into a large marsh, furnishing an abundant supply of
good grass for the animals [south of Snow Water Lake, in Clover Val-
ley]. On the 6th, owing to a severe snow-storm, we were obliged to remain in camp. Having no timber but a few green cedars, fires were not
very abundant.

    On the 7th we commenced our ascent by a steep and rocky road

beleef is that it [is] verry little nearer and not so good a road as that
by fort Hall   our encampment is in a large fine looking vally but too
cold and dry for any kind of grain   the mountains which are no
greate elivation above the plain are covered nearly half way down in
snow

22   after long consultation and many arguments for and against
the two different routs one leading Northward by fort Hall and the
other by the Salt Lake we all finally tooke Fremonts Trail by the way
of Salt Lake Late in thee day   the Stream brances again in this vally
the Larger comeing From the S the smaller from the N. up this
Northern branch the Wagon Trail leads by the way of Fort Hall[3]

Crosing the N. Branch we struck S. E. for a low gap in a range of
snow cape[d] mountains[4]   soon crossed the vally and commenced as-

---

[across the East Humboldt Mountains]. The snow was falling lightly
when we started, but before we reached the summit, we were nearly
blinded by the storm. A short descent brought us into a pleasant valley
[north end of Ruby Valley], well watered by several small streams, and
timbered with aspen and cottonwood. This is, really, a beautiful spot,
surrounded by high mountains, those on the west [Ruby Mountains]
covered with snow. Crossing a low range of hills [Secret Pass], we entered another valley [Secret Valley], that takes its waters from the
snowy mountains on either side. The stream [Secret or Cottonwood
Creek], after winding among the grass-covered hills, emerges into a
plain, through which we could see Ogden's River flowing. Walker has
given this creek the name of Walnut Creek, from one of his trappers
[evidently on his California expedition of 1833–34] having brought into
his camp a twig of that tree found near its head; a tree scarcely known
so far west as this. Camped on Walnut Creek, having made 14 1/2 miles.

November 8.—At about 6 miles from our camp of last night, we
struck Ogden's [Humboldt] River. It is about 25 feet wide here and
about 2 feet deep, with a tolerable current. Crossing without difficulty,
we struck the emigrant wagon-trail. Continuing down it for a few miles,
we encamped a little below where the river receives a tributary of considerable size, coming from the northwest [North Fork of Humboldt].
Made to-day about 14 miles.

[3] The large branch is Lamoille Creek, which enters the Humboldt from the
south a mile below the point where Secret Creek reaches the river. Above the
mouth of Secret Creek, the East Fork of the Humboldt branches several times,
Mary's River, Tabor Creek, and Bishops Creek all heading in the mountains to
the north and northeast. The original wagon trail to Fort Hall followed up Bishops Creek, the gorge of which is still locally called Emigration Canyon.

[4] Variously known as Humboldt Pass and Secret Pass, this inviting gap
between the East Humboldt and Ruby ranges is clearly apparent to a traveler ascending the Humboldt. Clyman's route to Ruby Valley is followed today by
Nevada State Route 229.

sending the mountain out of which issues a small Brook [Secret Creek]   followed up this brook to neare its source and encamped nearly on the summit of the mountain[5] and within perhaps less than one mile of the snow   the air was Quite cool and a few drops of rain fell. On this elevated ridge the grass we found to be nearly full grown while that in the vally was Quite short   Here I observed large beds of rock resembling marble   12 mile

23   Late in the evening last heard rumbling thunder   after dark a few drops of rain fell   The night was cool and froze a little in fact every night has produced some Ice since we left the plains of California   Early this morning the snow fell so as to whiten earth at our camp and laid on the mountains all day   another shower fell during the forenoon   Continued withe some difficulty to follow Freemonts trail up the brook [Secret Creek] to a handsome little valy [Secret Valley] and over a ridge [Secret Pass proper] to a nother larger vally [north end of Ruby Valley]   several small streams fall into this vally and run off to the S & S W and no doubt fall into marys river and the last water seen passing into that stream[6]

Crossed the vally S. E. and assended a steep narrow mountain[7] some remnants of snow drifts were laying on the summit of this mountain   desended the mountain on the South side to a large spring of warm water flowing into a large vally [Clover Valley] and spreading into a large swale covered in marsh grass[8]   here we encamped at the distance of 12 miles   the day was cloudy and several light showers of snow fell on the mountains

24   S. E. across the vally of the warm spring and over a ridge of hills[9] covered with shrubby Junts of cedars and into another vally of

---

[5] This was a mistaken estimate of their elevation; the night's encampment was near the mouth of Mineral Springs Creek, some 5 miles short of the summit of the pass.

[6] The southward-flowing streams combine to form the Franklin River, which once spread out as a marsh called Franklin Lake some 30 miles to the south. But this suggestion of a water-level route to the Humboldt helps to explain Hastings' action in later taking the wagons south around the Rubies.

[7] The southern extension of the East Humboldt Mountains, which were crossed at about the northern line of T. 33 N., R. 61 E.

[8] Warm Spring. Compare the Kern, Bryant, and Reed journals, and the Jefferson map, which calls it "Mill Spring."

[9] The northern extension of Spruce Mountain. Clyman's course would better have been described E. by S. E. The *Ruby Lake, Wendover, Newfoundland Mountains, Bonneville Salt Flats,* and *Tooele* U.S.G.S. 30 by 60 minute topographical maps depict the country for the next nine days of the journey.

considerable length but not more than 6 or 8 miles wide [Independence Valley]   disance to day 14 miles   stoped at a lot of small springs on several low mounds but so thirsty is the earth that the water does not run more than 20 or 30 feet before it all disappears[10]   to the S. W. of this vally the hills rise in considerable peaks covered in snow[11]   at this time animal life seem all most Extinct in this region and the few natives that try to make a precarious subsistanc here are put to all that ingenuety can invent   roots herbs insects and reptiles are sought for in all directions   in some parts moles mice and gophers seem to be Quite plenty and in order to precure those that live entirely under the surface of the earth when a suitable place can be found a Brook is damned up a ditch dug and the habitation of the mole inundated when the poor animal has to take to the surface and is caught by his enemy

25   again under way E. of S [i.e., S. of E.?] across another dry clay plain covered in shrubs of a verry dwarfish character and over as dry a range of low mountains clothed in dwarfish cedars and pines[12] Came to a hole of water or rather a cluster of small springs[13] which like the last night disappeared in the parched earth immediately here we stoped and watered and nooned   on again nearly east to a rather rough looking rang of mountains [Toano Range]   asended and found several snow drifts about the summit   here we lost Fremonts trail and desended a southern ravine to all appearanc dry as a fresh burnt brick Kiln   unpacked and prepared ourselves for a night without water   I assended one of the dry Cliffs and to my astonishment saw a well of good cool water[14]   from the top of this rang we could have a fair view of one of those great Salt plains [the Salt Desert itself] you may give some Idea of its [extent] when I assure you that we stood near the snow drifts and surveyed this plain stretching in all directions beyond the reach of vision

---

[10] Mound Springs, which Kern called "Whitten's Spring." It was here that Frémont and Talbot separated to take their diverse ways to Walker Lake.

[11] Spruce Mountain rises imposingly to an elevation of 11,051 feet.

[12] The Pequop Mountains, which were crossed by Jasper Pass. The Western Pacific Railroad has tunneled through the same pass.

[13] So-called Flowery Lake, 10 miles south of Shafter, Nevada, in arid Gosiute Valley.

[14] The *Map of Oregon and Upper California* prepared by Charles Preuss to accompany Frémont's *Geographical Memoir upon Upper California*, shows a spring high in the Toanos as Frémont's first camp after leaving Pilot Peak. It is apparent from the experience of Clyman and Bryant that water could be found in springs or pot holes in this locality, but always at the cost of some searching.

26 Spent the whole day in searching for the Trail which I succeeded in finding late in the afternoon[15]

27 Left our camp near the top of the mountain an took a N. E. cours to a high ruged looking bute standing prominent and alone with the tops whitned in snow[16] along the East side of this bute which stands in the salt plains to near the Eastern point 22 miles and encamped on a fine spring Brook that comes tumbling from the mountain in all its purity [Pilot Peak Creek] This bute affrd's numerous springs and brooks that loose themselves immediately in the salt plain below but the grass is plenty generally and the main bulk of the county produces nothing but a small curly thorn bush [greasewood] winding on the earth To the S. s. E. and East you have a boundless salt plain without vegitation except here and there a cliff of bare rocks standing like monumental pillars to commemorate the distinction of this portion of the Earth

28 Left our camp at the Snowy or more properly the spring Bute for this Bute affords several fine Brooks and took the Trail East and soon entered on the greate salt plain the first plain is 6 or 7 miles wide and covered in many places three inchs deep in pure white salt[17] passed an Island of rocks[18] in this great plain and entered the

---

[15] From this day's entry and the next it is evident that the Clyman-Hastings party remained at their camp in the Toanos, east of Flowery Lake, until they were able to locate the Frémont trail to take them on to Pilot Peak. This in itself disposes of any idea that Frémont had used Silver Zone Pass, nearly 20 miles to the north, but there is still other evidence. The Preuss map shows that Frémont took a southwest rather than a west course from Pilot Peak to the Toanos; and Captain Howard Stansbury, on reaching the Hastings Road at Pilot Peak from the north, made note in his journal on November 2, 1849, "The road runs around the foot of the Ridge [Pilot Range], passes to the north of another high one [Toano Range] (crossed by Frémont) & then goes on to the head of Marys River." Stansbury's information came from his guide, Auguste Archambault, who had been with Frémont in 1845; the quotation is from his original diary, in the National Archives, as Stansbury did not incorporate the remark about Frémont in his published *Report*.

[16] Pilot Peak, just west of the Utah-Nevada line and 20 miles north of Wendover, was so named by Frémont for its service to his party in the crossing of the Salt Desert in 1845. Its snow-crowned heights are visible from far off. Note that Clyman's camp in the Toanos was nearly west of modern Wendover, so that his route of May 27 and that of I-80 make an "X" in Tecoma Valley.

[17] The flat plain lying between Pilot Peak and Silver Island.

[18] Silver Island, which Stansbury described on November 2, 1849, as composed of "altered black limestone seamed with veins of gypsum all altered by fire." It derives its name not from its color, which is a sullen reddish-brown, but from some hopeful mining operations carried on in the 1870s.

greate plain over which we went in a bold trot untill dusk when we Bowoiked for the night without grass or water and not much was said in fact all filt incouraged as we had been enformed that if we could follow Mr Fremonts trail we would not have more than 20 miles without fresh water   In fact this is the [most] desolate country perhaps on the whole globe there not being one spear of vegitation and of course no kind of animal can subsist and it is not yet assertaind to what extent this imminse salt and sand plain can be south of whare we [are]   our travel to day was 40 miles

    29   As soon as light began to shew in the East we ware again under way crossed one more plain and then assended a rough low mountain[19]   still no water and our hopes ware again disapointed Commenced our desent down a ravine made 14 miles and at length found a small spring of Brackish water which did not run more than four rods before it all disappeared in the thirsty earth[20]   but mean and poor as the water was we and our animals Quenched our burning thirst and unpacked for the day after our rapid travel of about 20 hours and 30 hours without water

    30   At an Eearly hour we ware on our saddles and bore south 4 miles to another small spring of the same kind of water[21]   stoped and

---

[19] The Cedar Mountains, bounding Skull Valley on the west. It has been supposed that the Clyman-Hastings party crossed the mountains by Hastings Pass, where the wagons went later in the summer, but assuming that they were still following the Frémont trail, we must suppose that they, like Frémont, crossed the Cedar Mountains farther south. For this detail we are again indebted to Stansbury, whose original journal says on November 5, 1849, "Crossed the [Cedar] mountains through the pass following the wagon road. It is about 5 miles north of where Frémont crossed." However, the Preuss map would indicate that Frémont, like the later wagon road, went north some miles from Redlum Spring before crossing the Cedars.

[20] Presumably Redlum Spring, northernmost of the scanty springs which break out along the east slope of the Cedar Mountains. Five miles west, on the far slope, is a similar watering place, Lone Rock Spring, which the overland travelers did not see owing to the fact that the trail across the Cedars angled northwest and southeast.

[21] According to information provided by Mr. Walter E. Dansie of the Deseret Livestock Company, the first spring south of Redlum now existing is Henrys Spring, which however is only a mile and a quarter distant. The next water, Eight-Mile, or Sulphur, Spring, is another 5 miles south and a mile east of Henrys Spring. Clyman's 4 miles does not fit either spring, but his water most probably was Sulphur Spring. The alternative name of this spring refers to its distance from Iosepa, which lies across Skull Valley 8 miles east and 1 1/2 miles south.

drank and continued changing our course to S E passed a small salt plain and several large salt springs changed again to E. or N. of E. a rugged mountain [Stansbury Mountains] to oure right and a salt marsh to our left[22] this mountain is The highist we have seen in these plains allthough 20 peaks are visable at all tines 20 miles to day

M. 30 long before day was visibele a small Bird of the mocking bird kind was heard to cheer us with his many noted Song an this is the only singing Bird that I have heard for the last 10 days in fact this desolation afords subsistance to nothing but Lizards, and scorpions which move like Lightning ove the parched Earthe in all directions as we pass along the spring we camp at to night is large and deep sending off a volume of Brackish water to moisten the white parched earth[23] nearly all the rocks seen for .7 days pas^d. is Black intersperced with white streaks or clouds and I judge them to be a mixture of Black Bassalt and Quarts. Our spring has greate Quantities of fish in it some of considerable size

31 N. E. along the mountains to the N. point whare is an extensive spring of salt water[24] after turning the point of the mountain

---

[22] This great semicircle in Skull Valley was forced upon the party by the then-marshy character of the north end of the valley, which was so pronounced that it was even possible to conceive it as a southern extension of Great Salt Lake. Stansbury, when journeying eastward on the same trail on November 6, 1849, commented: "On account of numerous springs which come out of the Eastern mountain & render the whole valley immediately before us miry & impassable for animals we were forced very much Out of our course to the Southward, to make a circuit around this soft portion of the valley, making at least a semicircle if not more, before regaining the course from which we started at the [Redlum] Spring." It is evident that there have been marked changes in the water supply of this end of the valley since 1846, for I-80, in cutting directly across northern Skull Valley to the depression at the north end of the Cedar Mountains which is called Low Pass, today has parched terrain on either hand.

[23] From the courses, the distance traveled, and the brackish character of the water, it would appear that the night's encampment was at Burnt Spring, 9 1/2 miles north of present Iosepa. On reaching the east side of Skull Valley, Clyman came into the trail of his old associate, Jedediah Smith, who in returning from his first journey to California traveled north through the valley in June 1827. Smith had come in northeasterly out of the desert to the water at Orr's Ranch on June 25, 1827, and had encamped the following night, probably at Big or Horseshoe Spring, 3 1/2 miles south of Burnt Spring. See Maurice Sullivan, ed., *The Travels of Jedediah Smith*, 22, 23, and compare the U. S. Bureau of Land Management's township maps of Skull Valley.

[24] From Burnt Spring it is 5 1/2 miles to the Big Salt Spring at Timpie Junction, with no good water between. Jedediah Smith's journal entry, describ-

we changed again to the S. E. along betwen the mountain and the greate Salt Lake   Travel to day 20 miles and we passed some 15 or 20 large springs mostly warm and more or less salt some of them verry salt   camped at some holes of fresh water[25]   in sight are several snowy mountains in fact snow may be seen in all most all directions and two peaks one to the S. W. and the other to the S. E. seem to be highg enough to contain snow all the season.[26]   we have had two nights only since we left the Settelments of California without frost and to day is cold enough to ride with a heavy coat on and not feel uncomfortabl

1846 June the 1st. proceeded nearly east to the point of a high mountain [Oquirrh Mountains] that Bounds the Southern part of the greate salt lake   I observed that this lake like all the rest of this wide spread Sterility has nearly wasted away one half of its surface since 1825 [1826] when I floated around it in my Bull Boate and we crossed a large Bay of this Lake with our horses which is now dry and continued up the South side of the Lake to the vally near the outlet [Jordan River] of the Eutaw Lake and encamped at a fine large spring of Brackish water 20 miles to [*sic*] today[27]

after unpacking several Indians ware seen around us   after considerable signing and exertion we got them to camp and they apeared

---

ing the same ground in 1827, is interesting to read in comparison: "June 27th North 10 miles along a valley in which were many salt springs. Coming to the point of the ridge which formed the eastern boundary of the valley I saw an expanse of water Extending far to the North and East. The Salt Lake, a joyful sight, was spread before us." The route of Clyman and Smith along the east side of Skull Valley was closely followed by the old Lincoln Highway, near the county road that enters I-80 at Rowley Junction just west of the Big Salt Spring.

[25] At present Grantsville, which the immigrants were to know variously as Twenty Wells and Hastings Wells. Jedediah Smith's parallel entry, after rounding the Stansbury Mountains, reads: "After coming in view of the lake I traveled East [more nearly southeast], keeping nearly paralel with the shore of the lake. At about 25 Miles from my last encampment I found a spring of fresh water and encamped. The water during the day had been generally Salt." Frémont went over the same ground, westbound in 1845.

[26] Clyman probably has reference to Deseret Peak, in the Stansbury Mountains, and to Lowe Peak in the Oquirrh Mountains, which bound Tooele Valley on the east.

[27] During the day, the party rounded the southern shore of Great Salt Lake to camp for the night near present Magna, close to the site of Garfield, a once-prosperous company town now abandoned. Frémont gave the name Spring Point to this area at the north end of the Oquirrh Mountains in 1845. Clyman's encampment was at any of half a dozen springs that here break out.

to be friendly

In this vally contrary to any thing we had yet seen Lately the grass is full grown and some early Kinds are ripe are ripe [sic] and now full grown and still the mountains nearly all around are yet covered in snow

These Ewtaws as well as we could understand informed us that the snakes and whites ware now at war and that the snakes had killed two white men this news was not the most pleasant as we have to pass through a portion of the snake country

2 acording to promis our Eutaw guide came this morning and conducted us to the ford on thee Eutaw river[28] which we found Quite

---

[28] Where Clyman forded the Jordan River has a significant bearing upon the routes through Salt Lake Valley adopted by the westbound parties later in the summer, and must here be considered in detail. The earliest crossing of the Jordan of which we have any record is that of Jedediah Smith in 1827. Bound for Cache Valley, Smith headed northeasterly from the northern point of the Oquirrhs, roughly paralleling the shore of the lake, to cross the Jordan River somewhere near the north end of Salt Lake Valley, the exact spot difficult to establish because he speaks of crossing an extensive swamp, "thick covered with flags and Bulrushes," bordering the river on the *west* as well as the east bank. The existence of such a swamp west of the river is not shown by any of the early surveys. It may be that a series of wet years in the 1820s and earlier, giving rise to such a swamp, was followed by a dryer era; note Clyman's remark of June 1 about the shrinkage of Great Salt Lake between 1826 and 1846.

The next recorded crossing was that of Frémont, westbound in 1845. After breaking up his camp on City Creek, on or very near the present Temple Square, Frémont had gone (as the Preuss map makes clear) straight west to cross the Jordan by the fine ford at the foot of present North Temple Street where Highway 186 now bridges the river. In early days Mill Creek flowed in a westerly direction from its canyon until it reached 9th East Street, whence it angled northwest a couple of miles and in the vicinity of 21st South and 3rd West streets turned nearly north, paralleling the Jordan River. Picking up enroute the waters of a large spring run, Parleys, Emigration, Red Butte, Dry Canyon, and the South Fork of City Creek, it finally flowed into the Jordan a few yards south of North Temple Street, in so doing creating the gravelly bar in the Jordan which made the North Temple ford so superior a crossing. South of this point, for nearly 4 miles, any crossing of the Jordan was attended by great difficulties, because the meandering Mill Creek, east of the river, constituted a nearly impassable morass.

In view of the familiarity his journal displays with the Wasatch Mountains east of Salt Lake Valley, there can be little question that Clyman knew in general how the party would have to travel in going on across the mountains to Fort Bridger. Although his memory of the canyons opening upon Salt Lake Valley must have faded a little in 20 years, it is clear that he knew they would have to ascend a central canyon, and this consideration significantly affected his choice of route to reach and cross the Jordan.

full and wetting several packs on our low mules but we all got safely over and out to the rising ground whare we found a fine spring brook and unpacked to dry our wet baggage[29]

This [Jordan River] is about 40 yards wide running in a deep channel of clay banks and through a wide vally in some place well set in an excelent kind of grass But I should think that it would not be moist Enough for grain   the mountains that surround this vally are pictureesque and many places beautifull being high and near the base smoothe and well set in a short nutericious grass Especially those to the West

Afternoon took our course E into the Eutaw [Wasatch] mountains and near night we found we had mistaken the Trail and taken one

---

On rounding the Oquirrhs he would have seen the mighty panorama of the Wasatch open up before him. He could see the red sandstone cliffs which soon were to give name to Red Butte Canyon, and immediately to the south the apparently wide-open canyon, Emigration, down which the Reed-Donner party was to cut its way later in the summer. But these canyons lay too far north; had he wanted to take his party up either, the Frémont crossing of the Jordan would have been entirely satisfactory. His true course east was through Parleys Canyon, but from where he surveyed the mountain wall, its mouth was entirely hidden. The next canyon south of Parleys, Mill Creek, was much the most inviting, a deep gash in the skyline. It was toward the mouth of Mill Creek Canyon, accord- ingly, that he now directed the course of the party, the Indian a welcome guide to the nearest practicable ford of the Jordan. The route adopted east across Salt Lake Valley was, generally speaking, that of State Route 201, swinging in a shal- low arc to the south to keep clear of the alkali lakes, mud flats, and tule beds which occupy depressions in the valley floor. State Route 201 crosses the Jordan at 21st South, but it is probable, in the light of the information Edwin Bryant's journal affords, that Clyman's party crossed the river a little more to the south, near present 27th South Street.

[29] If we may assume that Clyman's language means exactly what it says, that the party made their noon halt on a "fine spring brook" rather than upon one of the creeks flowing out of the canyons, this halt was upon the run which rises in the northeast corner of Fairmont Park, about a quarter of a mile south of the intersection in Sugar House of 21st South and 11th East streets, and flows southwesterly to Mill Creek, its waters augmented along the way by smaller springs so as to become a stream of respectable size. The fact that this "spring brook" lies directly in the path of the route Clyman's party was pursuing toward the mouth of Mill Creek Canyon, and that no such brook would have been en- countered had they crossed at the North Temple ford is further evidence for the theory of the route here set forth. The "rising ground" Clyman alludes to is a terrace of old Lake Bonneville above 7th East Street. For details of the terrain between the Jordan and the base of the mountains, see the U. S. Geological Sur- vey's advance sheet, *Salt Lake City*, and compare the 1856 Land Office plat for T. 1 S., R. 1 E.

that bore too much to the South[30]   camped in a cove of the mountain making 25 miles[31]   the ravines and some of the side hills have groves of oak and sugar maple on them all of a short shrubby discription and many of the hill sides are well clothed in a good bunch grass and would if not too cold bear some cultivation

3   N. E. up the Brook [Parleys Canyon] into a high ruged mountain [Big Mountain] not verry rocky but awfull brushy   with some dificulty we reached the summit and commenced our dissent which was not so steep nor Quite so brushy[32]   the Brush on this ridge

---

[30] Close under the mountains, Clyman corrected the impression under which he had labored during the day, that Mill Creek was the canyon to ascend. Above 27th East, in the vicinity of 30th South Street, Parleys suddenly opens up to sight, and this canyon at its mouth has several characteristics by which it differs from Mill Creek, an outcropping of golden-colored rock on its north wall, and the deep gully its creek has cut where it emerges from the mountains, which is in striking contrast to the shallow bed in which Mill Creek winds down off the bench. How close Clyman got to the mouth of Mill Creek before realizing his mistake it is impossible to know, but it is improbable that he actually entered that canyon.

[31] For some years I inclined to the opinion that this night's camp was on Mill Creek, since there is a pronounced recess or cove in the Wasatch Mountain wall where Mill Creek issues from its canyon. However, the implication of Clyman's language is that he rectified as well as discovered his mistake in the route; and moreover it seems necessary to suppose that he camped this night on "the" brook he ascended next morning. By dictionary definition a "cove of the mountains" could be either an opening in a canyon or a recess in the face of a mountain wall; evidently Clyman intended the former. As there was no suitable place at the mouth of Parleys Canyon where a party might picket 37 horses overnight, Clyman and his companions must have ascended the canyon some distance. Above Suicide Rock there are four small "coves" within less than 3 miles, but the largest and most attractive opening, nearly half a mile in length, begins 3 1/4 miles above the canyon mouth. The night's camp probably was in this largest of the coves. The day's travel, 25 miles, accords well with this hypothesis.

[32] The party rode perhaps 2 miles up Parleys Canyon, the route of I-80, to where the canyon forked at the present Mountain Dell Reservoir. Following up the north fork, Mountain Dell Canyon, they ascended it 5 miles and then turned abruptly to their right to climb 2 miles up to the Big Mountain summit. The Little Dell Dam now floods part of this trail, but the Pioneer Memorial Highway approximates this second stage of the day's journey by switchbacks along the canyon sides that lift the graded highway by easy stages to the summit.

The pass over Big Mountain has been known unofficially as Pratt's Pass, in honor of Orson Pratt, who led the Mormon vanguard over it in 1847. It would be an appropriate honor to the first man who described this summit to rename it Clyman Pass.

For details of terrain on this day's journey and the first few miles of the next, see the U. S. Geological Survey's *Fort Douglas* quadrangle.

consists of aspen, oak cherry and white Firr the later of which is
Quite like trees   this ridge or mountain devides the waters of Eutaw
from those [of] Weebers rivers and desended the South branch of
Weebers river[33] untill it entered a rough Looking Kenyon[34] when we
bore away to the East up a small Brook [Dixie Creek] and encamped
at the head springs makeing to day about 18 miles[35]   on the top of
the mountain we passed several snow drifts that had not yet thawed
and the whole range to the S. W. and N. is more or less covered in
snow and many peaks heavily clothed and the air cold and
disagreeable   some few light Showers of rain fell during the day and
one shower of snow fell in the afternoon   service berry in bloom as
Likewis choke cherries   no game seen through this region and it is
difficult to determin what the few natives that inhabit this region
subsist on   23 miles

    4th   North 4 miles down a ravin[36] to Weabers [Weber] River   we

----

[33] East Canyon Creek, which until the Mormon entrance into Utah was
called by the trappers "Bossman's" or "Bauchmin's" Fork. Stansbury concluded
that by this they had intended "Beauchemin's Fork," and so rendered the name
on his map. Beauchemin probably was the name of a trapper. Account books of
the American Fur Company's Western Department at the Missouri Historical
Society list several employees named "Beauchemin," any of whom might be the
East Canyon Creek namesake. The most likely candidate is Jean Baptiste Beauchemin, who had a long history with the Company in various capacities beginning in 1823 as a boatman. In 1830 he was at Fort Union, then disappeared until
1843 when he turned up with the Western Outfit. Hudson's Bay Company correspondence refers to Beauchemin Creek as early as 1845.
    Logically, the route by which Clyman descended into East Canyon was by
way of Little Emigration Canyon, which heads directly upon the eastern side of
the Big Mountain pass, and from the fact that the Donner party, later in the
summer, and the Mormons, a year later, brought their wagons up to the divide
by way of this canyon, it seems mandatory to believe that Clyman got down into
East Canyon by this route.
    [34] The East Canyon dam was built in these narrows and its reservoir was
expanded in 1966. Compare Bryant's journal for July 24, 1846.
    [35] Clyman here gives the day's travel as 18 miles, but at the end of the day's
entry he gives the distance as 23 miles. It must be supposed that 23 miles ending
at the head springs of Dixie Hollow was the complete day's travel, for plainly 18
miles would not have sufficed for the journey as described. To examine their
itinerary in reverse: From the springs in Dixie Hollow it was 3 miles down to
East Canyon. Thence 7 miles up East Canyon and 4 miles up Little Emigration
Canyon makes the distance to the pass over Big Mountain 14 miles. From this
point to the camp in Parleys is another 9 miles, or a total day's journey of 23
miles.
    [36] Main Canyon, as it is locally called; Little East Canyon, as the maps have
it. It opens out upon the Weber at present Henefer.

struck this stream a short distance above the Junction of the N. and S. Branches and immideately above whare it enters the second Kenyon above its mouth[37] followed up the vally some 3 miles and crossed over[38] found the stream about 50 yards wide muddy from the thawing of snow in the mountains south it has a rapid current over a hard gravelly bottom and it has a considerable Sized intervale through which it pases thickly covored in shrubby cotton wood and willows after crossing we took a deep cut ravin coming direct from the N. E. [Echo Canyon] the Bluffs of this ravin are formed of red rock made of smoothe water washe^d pebbles and the North side in particular are verry high and perpendicular and in many places hanging over the narow vally is completely Strewn over with the boulder which have fallen from time to time from the cliffs above passed to day several clumps of oak and sugar maple the cliffs however have scattering clumps of cedar on them To day saw one Lonesome looking poor grisly Bear

This [Weber River] like the Eutaw river heads in the Eutaw mountains[39] and running North some distance Turns to the West and breaks through two ranges of mountains falls into the salt Lake 30 or 40 miles south of the mouth of Bear rivir and has a shallow barr at its mouth stuck over in drift wood.[40]

26 [miles].[41]

5th N. E. Up the Brook on which we encamped in a few miles

---

[37] Clyman's perfect acquaintance with the Weber River is not the least interesting feature of his journal. By the North Branch he means present Lost Creek; by the South Branch he has reference to East Canyon Creek. The "second Kenyon" of the Weber has Devils Slide as a distinguishing feature of its south wall.

[38] In contrast to the wagon route later in the summer, which crossed from the north to the south bank approximately where old US 30S bridged the Weber at Henefer, Clyman's party crossed the river immediately below the mouth of Echo Canyon, some 3 miles higher up.

[39] By "Eutaw mountains" the trappers ordinarily intended the Uintas, but in his entry for June 2 Clyman used this term in reference to the Wasatch. He may have regarded the two ranges as a single T-shaped mountain mass. He also uses the term, "Eutaw river," which he previously has employed in reference to the Jordan, in obvious allusion to the Provo. Perhaps Clyman considered the Provo and the Jordan a continuous river notwithstanding the one flows into and the other out of Utah Lake.

[40] For the second time in the diary, here is a memory Clyman seemingly owes to his circumnavigation of the lake 20 years before.

[41] The night's encampment was in Echo Canyon in the vicinity of Castle Rock.

it parted into several smaller Brooks and we continued up the most central[42]

notwithstanding the frosty morning several summer songsters ware warbling their loves or chirping amongst the small willows which skirted the little Brook as we passed along   in a few hours ride we arived at the summit of the ridge that devides the waters of We-abers River from those of Bear River   this ridge is high and several drifts of winters snow was still Lying a fiw miles to the Souths of our rout notwithstanding this summit ridge is smoothe and handsomely clothed in young grass

Continued down the East side of the ridge and crossed over a small muddy stream [Yellow Creek] running N. into Bear River struck Bear River a rapid stream 40 yards wide and running over a smoothe rocky Bed[43]   we found this stream fordabel and greate thickets of willows and catton wood growing in the bends   Continued our course up a small Brook[44] a few miles and camp[d]. several times to day we had a sight of the Eutaw [Uinta] mountains completely covered in snow as the weather has been Quite to cool to have much effect upon the peaks of this rang of mountains

30 Miles

6   proceeded N. E. through a Barren range of wild sage hill and plains and deep wash[d]. gutters with little alteration Except now and then a grove of shrubby cedars untill late in the afternoon when we struck the wagon trail leading from Bridgers Trading house to Bear River[45]   Turned on our course from N. E. to S. E. and took the road

---

[42] As does present I-80, enroute to Evanston. The Union Pacific takes a northerly fork, while still another branches off to the south in the direction of Chalk Creek. The divide here consists of gently rolling hills which can be crossed at virtually any point.

[43] The site of Evanston, Wyoming. For all practical purposes, Clyman's route from the mouth of Echo to this point has been that of I-80.

[44] Sulphur Spring Creek, not to be confused with the better-known Sulphur Creek which flows into the Bear some 6 miles farther south. The night's encampment was in this barren canyon a few miles northeast of Evanston. The terrain for the travels of Clyman and the other travelers of 1846 west of Fort Bridger is best depicted on the map, "Areal Geology of a Portion of South-western Wyoming," prepared to illustrate A. C. Veatch, *Geography and Geology of a Portion of Southwestern Wyoming with Special Reference to Coal and Oil*, U. S. Geological Survey Professional Paper No. 56 (Washington, 1907).

[45] This was the branch of the Oregon Trail which from Fort Bridger headed northwest to strike the Little Muddy 10 miles east of Cumberland Gap. It followed that stream to its head, crossed the Bear River Divide, and descended Bridgers Creek to reach the Bear River Valley about 7 miles south of present

Toward Bridger   near sun set we came to a small Stream of muddy water[46] and Encamped

7   Packed up before sun rise and Took the road and at 10 A. M. arived at the old deserted Trading house   Judge of our chagrin and disapointment on finding this spot so long and so anxiously saught for standing solitary and alone without the appearance of a human being having visited it for at least a month and what the caus conjectur was rife but could [not] be certain except that Bridger and his whole company had taken the road N. W. Toward the Lower part of Bear River havin had no grass whare we encamped last nig and finding plenty here about we unsadled and concluded to remain here today and consult what was next to be done

In our weak and deffenceless state it was not easy to fix on any safe plan of procedure   some proposed to return to Bear River and risk the hostility of the snake Indians others proposed to take the trail Travel slowly and risk the Sioux[s]. which ware supposed to be on our rout to Fort Larrimie so that the day was taken up in discusing what would be the most safe way of disposing ourselves a sufficant time to await the company from oregon to the states which was generally supposed would be Quite large this season   the day was warm and the creek [Blacks Fork] rose rapidly from the thawing of the snow on the Eutaw mountains and this is the season of high water in this region   nothing can be mor desolate and discouraging than a deserted fort whare you expect relief in a dangerous Indian country and every imaginary Idea was started as to what had been the caus of Bridgers leaving his establishment   But nothing satisfactory could possibly be started and we ware still as far in the dark as ever

Sage, Wyoming. Clyman's party probably struck the wagon road not far south of where it reached the Little Muddy. He found it familiar, having traveled it en-route to Oregon in 1844.

[46] The Big Muddy, or as it is sometimes called, Muddy Creek, at present Carter, Wyoming.

THE JOURNAL OF EDWIN BRYANT

July 17–August 8, 1846

INTRODUCTION

To FOLLOW in detail the movements of Lansford W. Hastings during the three weeks after his arrival at Fort Bridger with Clyman is not possible on the basis of the documents that have so far come to light. At the time he left California in April, it had been his intention, as we have seen, to await the oncoming immigration in the vicinity of Fort Bridger. The absence of Bridger from his fort, however, made it highly inadvisable to linger there.

In these circumstances, Clyman tells us, "Mr Hastings his man and Indian servant wished to go some 50 or 60 miles N. stop and await the arrival of the company from oregon" (that is, go directly north up the Green River Valley to where the Greenwood [Sublette] Cutoff crossed it and there wait for parties eastbound along the trail), while on the other hand "4 men of us one woman and one boy ware detirmined to go back to Bear River there being two trails from green river to bear rever it was uncertain which the oregon company might take if allready not passed." It was agreed to part. But they did not separate then and there, for Clyman adds, "so wa all started togather once more and after comeing to the separating place we all continued on for the day...."[1]

The "separating place," one may suppose, was the point 2 miles below Fort Bridger where the trail northwest to the Bear left Blacks Fork. Clyman does not again mention Hastings, and it is impossible to say which of three things Hastings may have done: (1) On reaching the "separating place," continued north and west with the others to the Bear River Valley, as Clyman's reiteration "we all" might indicate (though in this case Clyman's words "separating place" are meaningless); (2) accompanied the others as far north as the Cumberland Gap, and then veered northeast to intersect the Greenwood Cutoff on Hams Fork; (3) turned down Blacks Fork in the direction of South Pass.

---

[1] Camp, ed., *James Clyman, American Frontiersman, 1792–1881*, 224, being Clyman's journal entry for June 8, 1846.

Not for three weeks can we definitely locate Hastings. During that time Clyman's little party met, in the Bear River Valley, the rear division of the company from California from whom they had separated in May, and with numbers thus augmented, set out east again, crossing South Pass June 18, meeting the first companies of the immigration June 23, opposite the Red Buttes, and arriving at Fort Laramie June 27.

It is in the laconic journal of W. E. Taylor, traveling with John Craig and Larkin Stanley, who got the first wagons into California this year, that we meet again with the redoubtable Hastings. Taylor writes in his journal on July 1, "23 miles [from the previous night's encampment at South Pass] brought us to Little Sandy. Extremely sterile country; in sight of eternal snow on the Bear River mountains." And next day, "Broke a waggon, a man sick. Dist. 10 miles. Camped on Big Sandy. Mr. L. [W.] Hastings visited our camp."[2]

This placing of Hastings on the Big Sandy on the afternoon of July 2—at a point, it will be noted, west of the intersection of the Fort Bridger and Greenwood roads—is important in that it helps us to evaluate a reminiscent account published by John R. McBride over 30 years later. McBride with his parents was bound for Oregon, and he relates that they met Hastings, Hudspeth, and the Indian vaquero on the morning of July 3, 1846, "about twenty miles east of the summit of the South Pass." There is some error here, of date if not of place, in view of Hastings' definitely established location the day before. But McBride tells of Hastings' efforts to induce the company to go to California rather than to Oregon—efforts which if not quite successful, were sufficiently persuasive that the McBride family took the trail past Fort Bridger in preference to the Greenwood Cutoff. We are chiefly indebted to McBride for descriptions of Hastings and Hudspeth as he remembered them from this wilderness encounter. Hastings he recalled as "a tall, fine-looking man, with light brown hair and beard, dressed in a suit of elegant pattern made of buckskin,

---

[2] W. E. Taylor, manuscript journal, April 20–September 13, 1846, in the Sutter's Fort Historical Museum, Sacramento, Calif., quoted by courtesy of the curator, Mr. Carroll D. Hall. The company with which Taylor was traveling was at this time, as it had been from the time it left the frontier, in advance of all others on the trail; hence it was the first to hear Hastings' story. This company arrived at Fort Bridger on July 9, but Taylor wrote in his journal only: "16 miles. Brought us to Bridger. Shoshones in abundance. Mr. Joseph Walker et al from California." Taylor remained at the fort over the 10th, but again all he committed to his diary was: "Lay by. Indians visited us in great numbers."

handsomely embroidered and trimmed at the collar and openings, with plucked beaver fur . . . an ideal representative of the mountaineer." Less favorably impressed with Hudspeth, McBride thought him "about as repulsive in manner as Hastings was attractive. He was a coarse, profane creature, who seemed to feel that loud swearing was the best title to public favor."[3]

Wherever he may have been during the three weeks in which he is off the record, on July 2 Hastings was plainly moving east along the trail, stopping to sing the praises of his new cutoff to each company he encountered. He reached his farthest east about July 7, evidently at the point east of South Pass where the wagon road left the Sweetwater. A lone traveler from Oregon, Wales B. Bonney, unexpectedly appeared from the West, and Hastings seized upon the providential circumstance to send a letter to the oncoming immigration while he himself turned back to Fort Bridger.

No copy of Hastings' letter to the immigration has survived, but its contents are sufficiently summarized in the narratives of Edwin Bryant and J. Quinn Thornton. Bryant's little party met the lone wayfarer, Bonney, on the morning of July 10, on the Sweetwater 30 miles above Devils Gate. After marveling over the foolhardiness of the man in making such a journey alone, Bryant goes on to say, "Mr. Bonney brought with him an open letter from L. W. Hastings, Esq., of California, dated on the head-waters of the Sweetwater, and addressed to the California emigrants on the road. The main contents of the letter I will not recite. It hinted, however, at probable opposition from the Californian government to the ingress to that country of American emigrants; and invited those bound for California to concentrate their numbers and strength, and to take a new route which had been explored by Mr. H., from Fort Bridger via the south end of the Salt Lake, by which the distance would be materially shortened."[4] Writing in retrospect, Thornton adds that Hastings had "proceeded as far as the eastern side of the Rocky Mountains, and encamped at a place where the Sweetwater breaks through a cañon, at the point where the emigrants leave that river to enter the South Pass. . . . After meeting some of the advanced companies, and sending forward a messenger with a letter to those in the rear, informing

---

[3] John R. McBride, "Pioneer Days in the Mountains," *Tullidge's Quarterly Magazine*, III (July, 1884), 311–20. This account was published originally in the *Salt Lake Tribune* in 1879.

[4] Edwin Bryant, *What I Saw in California* (New York, 1848), 127.

them that he had explored a new and much better road into California than the old one, he returned to Fort Bridger, where he stated that he would remain until the California and Oregon emigrants should come up, when he would give a more particular description of his 'cut-off.'"[5]

Bryant himself reached Fort Bridger July 16, arriving, he says, "at the encampment of Mr. Hastings about eleven o'clock at night." Hastings had been back at the fort only a few hours, but his dream was on the verge of being realized, for encamped with him was a company numbering 40 wagons willing to try his cutoff. The better to exhibit the state of mind of those who were to pioneer the new trail for wagons, two letters by immigrants written immediately before and after Hastings' departure are here reprinted.

The first was written by Dr. T. Pope Long, not hitherto identified in the year's California immigration, to his brother back in Clay County, Missouri:

> Fort Bridger, July 19, 1846.
>
> Dear Brother:—We arrived here on Thursday [July 16], and are now waiting for a sufficient number of waggons, in order to take a nearer route crossing the country on the south end of the great salt lake. This route will cut off at least 250 miles, and is the one through which Capt. Frémont passed last season. It is proposed by Mr. Hastings, (who has been with us for some time;) he came through on horseback, and reports the route perfectly practicable for wagons. The fort at which we are stationed, is surrounded by high mountains covered as deeply in snow as if it were the middle of winter. We have got this far extremely well. Our oxen are in good order, and travel almost as well as they did when we started. About forty wagons are now with us waiting to take the cutoff. I have met with several old mountain friends, who have treated us very kindly. * * * The different companies that

---

[5] J. Quinn Thornton, *Oregon and California in 1848* (New York, 1849), II, 95-6. See also Vol. I, p. 142. Carrying this letter, Bonney met the Donner party at Independence Rock on July 12. See Virginia Reed's letter of that date, published in the Southwest Museum's *The Masterkey*, XVIII (May, 1944), 82. Bonney subsequently made his way to Pueblo and thence on to the States by the Santa Fe Trail. See the *Autobiography of Pioneer John Brown* (Salt Lake City, 1941), 70. Bonney's arrival at Independence on September 30 was noted by the Independence *Western Expositor* of October 3, reprinted in the St. Louis *Weekly American*, October 9, 1846.

started in the spring have had no difficulties with the Indians, except the occasional loss of a few horses. But difficulties are occurring almost every day *amongst themselves*. They are continually dividing, and sub-dividing. Experience has taught us that small companies, of about fifteen wagons are the best, to travel with. * * * We have received news that war is raging between the U. States and Mexico. It has occasioned much speculation in our little camp, and some disbelieving the report. It has alarmed some, and will turn them towards Oregon. I apprehend no danger myself, and we are generally anxious to get to our destination. * * * We will arrive in California, I think, about the middle of September—a long and tedious trip to some, but others do not mind it. I have enjoyed myself finely; and as the country through which we have to pass is healthy, I apprehend no sickness. We have used but little more than one-half of our provisions, and have performed two-thirds of the journey to California.[6]

The second of these letters, by an unnamed correspondent, was printed in summary in the St. Louis *Missouri Republican*:

A letter from a young man of this city, one of the party that left for California last spring, was received by his friends yesterday, and kindly placed in our hands, from which we have extracted the following particulars. The letter is dated on the 23d of July, at Fort Bridger, which is near the head of Black's Fork of Green river, not far from Bear river mountains, and was brought in by Capt. [Joseph R.] Walker, who was returning from California [from service] with lieut. Fremont. At Fort Laramie, col. [William H.] Russell and many others of the emigrants, sold off their wagons, and with a pack containing a few articles, pursued their journey on horseback. The grass on the route from Fort Laramie was deficient, and the animals fared badly—For one hundred miles west of the States, the country is represented as being miserably poor and barren; though fifty to one hundred miles further, the valleys of the Platte and other streams, afforded very good grazing. The soil, however, is sandy and full of

---

[6] *St. Louis Daily Union*, November 28, 1846, reprinted from the *Liberty* [Mo.] *Tribune*. The asterisks which indicate elisions are doubtless those of the *Tribune*.

salt. The parties were in the South Pass of the Rocky Mountains on the 13th of July, and had then seen no Indians after leaving Fort Laramie, and considered themselves beyond their dangerous vicinity, and only a few of the emigrants kept a night guard. From Fort Laramie, they had pleasant weather, with cool nights and warm days—though very dusty roads, till they reached Fort Bridger, and during the whole route they had not seen more than a dozen buffalo.

Col. Russell and his party, by hard travelling, reached Fort Bridger two or three days before the others, but his horses had their backs badly worn, and he remained there four days to recruit. At that place they were met by Mr. Hastings, from California, who came out to conduct them in by the new route, by the foot of Salt Lake, discovered by capt. Fremont, which is said to be two hundred miles nearer than the old one, by Fort Hall. The distance to California was said to be six hundred and fifty miles, through a fine farming country, with plenty of grass for the cattle.

Companies of from one to a dozen wagons, says the writer, are continually arriving, and several have already started on, with Hastings at their head, who would conduct them to near where the road joins the old route, and there leave them, and push on with his party. Russell had also started, guided by a man who came through with Hastings. He is said to be very sick of the journey, and anxious to complete it. Instead of entering California as the commander of a half military caravan, he had been forsaken by his most cherished companions, and even his understrappers have treated him with indignity. [Andrew J.] Grayson had quarrelled with all his companions, and every one who could raise a horse had left him. [Lilburn W.] Boggs and many others had determined to go to Oregon, and were expected to arrive at Fort Bridger in a day or two. [George L.] Curry had also been persuaded to go to Oregon, and from thence he would go to California and the Sandwich Islands. He was still in bad health.

The Oregon route may be considerably shortened by avoiding Fort Bridger [via the Greenwood Cutoff], and passing a stretch of forty five miles without water—but most companies go that way. The emigrants were heartily tired of their journey, and nine tenths of them wished themselves back in the States. The whole company had been broken up into squads by dissatisfaction and bickerings, and it was pretty much every man for himself. The accounts they have received of Oregon and the Californias, by the parties they met returning to the States, had greatly disheartened them, and they had horrible anticipations of the future, in the country which they believed to be, when they set out, as beautiful as the Elysian fields.

The climate at Fort Bridger is described as delightfully pleasant; the days were clear and warm, refreshed by pleasant breezes, and the nights were cool, with light dews and occasional frost. Fort Bridger is said to be a miserable pen, occupied at times by Messrs. [James] Bridger and [Louis] Vasques, and resorted to by a number of loafing trappers to exchange furs and moccasins with the emigrants for flour, bacon and whiskey. The latter sells at two dollars a pint.[7]

The background having been lightly sketched in, we may take up the journal of Edwin Bryant, one of the most informative and readable records left by the overland travelers of this or any other year. Born in Massachusetts in 1805, Bryant moved to Kentucky with his parents in 1816. Although he studied medicine, he did not practice, becoming instead one of the editors of the Louisville *Courier-Journal*. Impelled, it is said, by failing health, in the spring of 1846 he set out for California with two Louisville friends, Richard T. Jacob and Robert Ewing. It seems to have been understood from the start that a book would result, for when he passed through St. Louis in late April, the *Missouri Republican* commented, "Mr. Bryant will, it is supposed, collect the material for a book which shall give a faithful account of the country which he visits. He is fully competent to the task."[8]

Bryant left the frontier early in May as one of the large company led by William H. Russell. The Colonel enjoyed his place in the sun only a few weeks, the temper of the Oregon and California immigrants being such that no leader could make his authority stick for very long. On grounds of ill-health, Russell eventually resigned his office. He and a number of friends, Bryant among them, sold their wagons and went on by muleback, arriving at Fort Bridger on the

---

[7] *Missouri Republican*, October 26, 1846, transcript furnished by Miss Barbara Kell, Librarian, Missouri Historical Society, St. Louis, Mo.

[8] Quoted in the *Jefferson* [Mo.] *Inquirer*, May 6, 1846. See also the St. Louis *Missouri Reporter*, April 25, 1846.

evening of July 16.

The entries from Bryant's journal as here reprinted, covering the period July 17–August 8, 1846, comprise pp. 142–93 of his *What I Saw in California*. This book was written immediately after his return to the States in August, 1847, and was published in New York late in 1848, just in time to reap the benefit of the excitement over the gold discoveries. It went through seven American and two English editions in two years, and was published in French, German, and Dutch translations. The book is also sometimes met with under the title, *Rocky Mountain Adventure*, which reprint publishers gave it in the eighties. It appears that the reprint editions were made from the plates of the original, since the pagination is the same and even the typographical errors are repeated, although three paragraphs are eliminated at the end and a table of thermometrical observations omitted, shortening the reprints by three pages. Twentieth-century editions, under the original title, include those of the Fine Arts Press, Santa Ana, Calif., 1936, edited by Marguerite Eyer Wilbur; a photo-reprint by Ross & Haines, Inc., Minneapolis, Minn., 1967; and the University of Nebraska Press, Lincoln, Neb., 1985, edited by Thomas C. Clark.

Bryant returned to California in 1849, guiding a large company of gold-hunters, and for a few years he was active in real estate promotion. In 1853 he returned to Kentucky, where he lived until his death in 1869.[9] His book is his chief memorial, as engrossing now as when written, and his account of his experiences on the Hastings Cutoff will remain one of the great source narratives for the history of Utah and the West.

---

[9] See Georgia Willis Read and Ruth Gaines, eds., *Gold Rush: The Journals, Drawings, and Other Papers of J. Goldsborough Bruff* (New York, 1944), I, 628–30.

—Harold Schindler photo

DEVILS SLIDE

—Harold Schindler photo

THE ELEPHANT'S STATUE

July 17 [1846].—We determined to encamp here [at Fort Bridger] two or three days, for the purpose of recruiting our animals, which being heavily packed, manifest strong signs of fatigue. We pitched our tent, for the first time since we left Fort Laramie, near the camp of Messrs. Hastings and Hudspeth. These gentlemen left the settlements of California the last of April, and travelling over the snows of the Sierra, and swimming the swollen water-courses on either side, reached this vicinity some two [six] weeks since, having explored a new route, via the south end of the great Salt Lake, by which they suppose the distance to California is shortened from one hundred and fifty to two hundred miles. My impressions are unfavorable to the route, especially for wagons and families; but a number of the emigrant parties now encamped here have determined to adopt it, with Messrs. Hastings and Hudspeth as their guides; and are now waiting for some of the rear parties to come up and join them.

"Fort Bridger," as it is called, is a small trading-post, established and now occupied by Messrs. Bridger and Vasquez. The buildings are two or three miserable log-cabins, rudely constructed, and bearing but a faint resemblance to habitable houses. Its position is in a handsome and fertile bottom of the small stream [Blacks Fork] on which we are encamped, about two miles south of the point where the old wagon trail, via Fort Hall, makes an angle, and takes a northwesterly course [to the Little Muddy]. The bottom produces the finest qualities of grass, and in great abundance. The water of the stream is cold and pure, and abounds in spotted mountain trout, and a variety of other small fish. Clumps of cotton-wood trees are scattered through the valley, and along the banks of the stream. Fort Bridger is distant from the Pacific Spring, by our estimate, 133 miles.[1]

About five hundred Snake Indians were encamped near the trading post this morning, but on hearing the news respecting the movements of the Sioux, which we communicated to them, most of them left immediately, for the purpose, I suppose, of organizing elsewhere a war-party to resist the threatened invasion. There are a number of traders here from the neighborhood of Taos, and the

---

[1] As measured by the Mormon odometer next year, the actual distance was 115 miles.

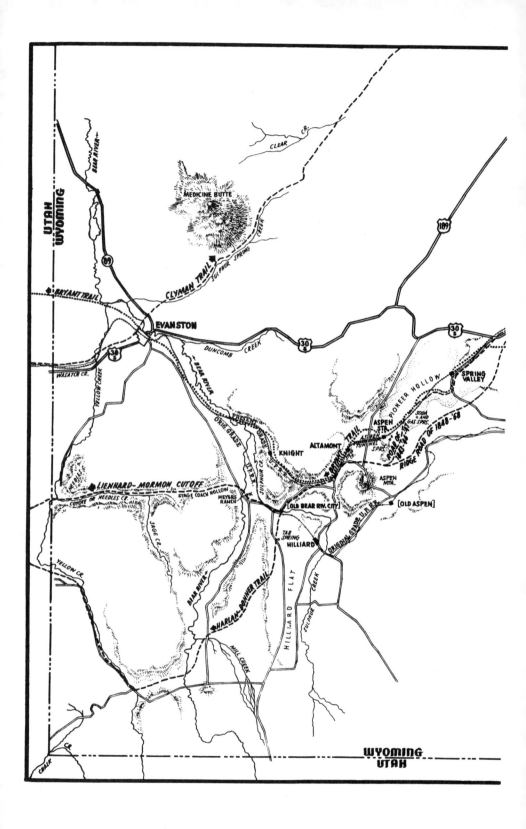

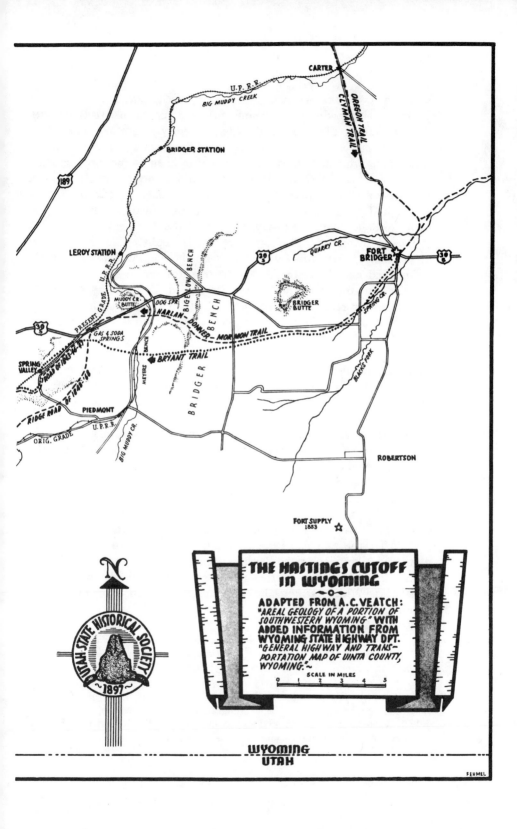

head-waters of the Arkansas, who have brought with them dressed buckskins, buckskin shirts, pantaloons, and moccasins, to trade with the emigrants. The emigrant trade is a very important one to the mountain merchants and trappers. The countenances and bearing of these men, who have made the wilderness their home, are generally expressive of a cool, cautious, but determined intrepidity. In a trade, they have no consciences, taking all the "advantages;" but in a matter of hospitality or generosity they are open-handed—ready, many of them, to divide with the needy what they possess.

I was introduced to-day to Captain [Joseph Reddeford] Walker, of Jackson county, Missouri, who is much celebrated for his explorations and knowledge of the North American continent, between the frontier settlements of the United States and the Pacific. Captain W. is now on his return from the settlements of California, having been out with Captain Frémont in the capacity of guide or pilot. He is driving some four or five hundred Californian horses, which he intends to dispose of in the United States. They appear to be high spirited animals, of medium size, handsome features, and in good condition. It is possible that the trade in horses, and even cattle, between California and the United States may, at no distant day, become of considerable importance. Captain W. communicated to me some facts in reference to recent occurrences in California, of considerable interest. He spoke discouragingly of the new route via the south end of the Salt Lake.[2]

Several emigrant parties have arrived here during the day, and others have left, taking the old route, via Fort Hall. Another cloud, rising from behind the mountains [Uinta Mountains] to the south, discharged sufficient rain to moisten the ground, about three o'clock, P.M. After the rain had ceased falling, the clouds broke away, some of them sinking below and others rising above the summits of the mountains, which were glittering in the rays of the sun with snowy whiteness. While raining the valley, it had been snowing on the mountains. During the shower the thermometer fell, in fifteen minutes, from 82° to 44°.

---

[2] Walker, as we have seen, had been with Frémont in the first exploration of the new route. His presence at Fort Bridger enroute back to the States was remarked by many of the overland immigrants, beginning with W. E. Taylor on July 9. Walker was still there, no doubt to let his horses recruit, as late as July 24, when Heinrich Lienhard mentions his presence at the fort.

July 18.—We determined, this morning, to take the new route, via the south end of the great Salt Lake. Mr. Hudspeth—who with a small party, on Monday [July 20], will start in advance of the emigrant companies which intend travelling by this route, for the purpose of making some further explorations[3]—has volunteered to guide us as far as the Salt Plain, a day's journey west of the Lake. Although such was my own determination, I wrote several letters to my friends among the emigrant parties in the rear, advising them *not* to take this route, but to keep on the old trail, via Fort Hall. Our situation was different from theirs. We were mounted on mules, had no families, and could afford to hazard experiments, and make explorations. They could not.[4] During the day I visited several of the emigrant *corrals*. Many of the trappers and hunters now collected here were lounging about, making small trades for sugar, coffee, flour, and whiskey. I heard of an instance of a pint of miserable whiskey being sold for a pair of buckskin pantaloons, valued at ten dollars. I saw two dollars in money paid for half a pint.

Several [Shoshoni] Indians visited our camp, in parties of three or four at a time. An old man and two boys sat down near the door of our tent, this morning, and there remained without speaking, but watchful of every movement, for three or four hours. When dinner was over, we gave them some bread and meat, and they departed without uttering a word. Messrs. [George L.] Curry and [R. H.] Holder left us to-day, having determined to go to Oregon instead of California. Circles of white-tented wagons may now be seen in every direction, and the smoke from the camp-fires is curling upwards,

---

[3] In view of the fact that Hastings' wagons set out from Fort Bridger the same day as the Bryant-Russell pack party which Hudspeth accompanied, it is very doubtful that Hudspeth had any idea of influencing the route of the wagons this year, not east of Great Salt Lake, at any rate, though as it turned out he played a decisive part in the decision to take the wagons down through the canyons of the Weber.

It seems likely that Hudspeth's prime object was to investigate the possibilities of what Clyman on June 4 had referred to as the North Branch of the Weber—present Lost Creek, known to the trappers as Pumbar's Fork (after Louis Pombert, a member of Jedediah Smith's first expedition to California). It was the conviction of the mountain men that a feasible route from the Bear River into the valley of the Great Salt Lake could be found using this canyon; three years later Jim Bridger guided Stansbury on a reconnaissance of this area, and Hudspeth no doubt was seeking to establish whether a route superior to that through Echo Canyon could be found for the immigration of succeeding years.

[4] See the introduction to the Reed journal, note 10.

morning, noon, and evening. An immense number of oxen and horses are scattered over the entire valley, grazing upon the green grass. Parties of Indians, hunters, and emigrants are galloping to and fro, and the scene is one of almost holiday liveliness. It is difficult to realize that we are in a wilderness, a thousand miles from civilization. I noticed the lupin, and a brilliant scarlet flower, in bloom.

July 19.—Bill Smith,[5] a noted mountain character, in a shooting-match burst his gun, and he was supposed for some time to be dead. He recovered, however, and the first words he uttered upon returning to consciousness were, that "no d—d gun could kill him." The adventures, hazards, and escapes of this man, with his eccentricities of character, as they were related to me, would make an amusing volume. I angled in the stream, and caught an abundance of mountain trout and other small fish. Another shower of rain fell this afternoon, during which the temperature was that of a raw November day.

July 20.—We resumed our march, taking, in accordance with our previous determination, the new route already referred to. Our party consisted of nine persons. Mr. Hudspeth and three young men from the emigrant parties, will accompany us as far as the Salt Plain.[6]

---

[5] More probably this was the celebrated Old Bill Williams, as stated by Jacob Wright Harlan, *California '46 to '88* (San Francisco, 1888), 42. The gun which burst, Harlan says, Old Bill had bought for $20 from one of his fellow immigrants; and following the accident, "after Bridger had restored him with some whiskey, he cried out that since he had hunted and trapped in the mountains he had been wounded a hundred times, and had been struck by lightning twice, and that nothing, not even a —— mean rifle, could kill him." The probability of Old Bill's being here at this time is heightened by the fact that he had separated from Frémont's party the previous October 27 in Skull Valley. See pps. 14 and 17.

[6] The nine men comprising the Bryant-Russell party were William H. Russell, Edwin Bryant, Richard T. Jacob, William H. Nuttall, Hiram O. Miller, James McClary, John C. Buchanan, A. V. Brookie, and W. B. Brown. The three young men with Hudspeth were J. C. Ferguson, John Minter, and James Kirkwood. With the exception of Brookie, these identifications are established by H. H. Bancroft's "Pioneer Register and Index," appended to the several volumes of his *History of California* (7 vols., San Francisco, 1884–1890), with supplementary information from the Fort Sutter Papers, XIV, 50, in the Huntington Library. As to Brookie, John R. McBride, *op. cit.*, 320, gives his name as "Major A. V. Brookie," and speaks of him as having lived in Salt Lake City between 1870 and 1876. In 1857, Brookie came from California to try to sell Brigham Young land in Henry L. Kinney's Mosquito Republic speculation in Nicaragua. Failing that, Brookie was sworn in as a U.S. deputy marshal for Utah in 1858. See the *New York Times*, July 24, 1858, and *Kirk Anderson's Valley Tan*, November 26, 1858.

We ascended from the valley in which Fort Bridger is situated, on the left of a high and rather remarkable *butte* which over looks the fertile bottom from the west.[7] There is no trail,[8] and we are guided in

[7] Note that Bryant left Fort Bridger on the left of, which is to say south of, Bridger Butte, which was also the case with the wagons under Hastings that set out the same day. The modern highway, I-80, goes north of the butte.

[8] On the contrary, as we have remarked, a wagon trail as far as the Bear had been made three years before by the Chiles party, which Joe Walker had engaged to guide to California. In view of the fact that Walker was at the fort at the same time as Bryant, it is curious that Bryant appears to be ignorant of the history of the Chiles party. The "Journal of John Boardman," *Utah Historical Quarterly*, II (October, 1929), 107–109, describes their experiences west of Fort Bridger, but does not detail their route except to note on August 17 that the first day's travel (which would have been to the Big Muddy) was over a bad road, and the second day's travel, to the Bear River, on August 18, was over a good road, "Not as much sage."

To remedy to some extent the deficiencies of the Boardman diary, we have Theodore Talbot's journal as, in company with Thomas Fitzpatrick, he passed on west with the rear detachment of Frémont's Second Expedition. Talbot writes under date of August 31, 1843:

Followed the trail of Walker & Childs party. . . . In the evg. we camped on the head of [Big] Muddy creek. We had a magnificent view from the high ridge [Bridger Bench] between Black and Muddy creeks of the valley of Blacks Fork and the whole Youta range of mountains.

Fri. 1st. Went a mile to the north down Muddy creek, then in a southwest direction across the divide which lies between Muddy creek and Bear River, which latter we struck not far from its source at the junction of its forks [Bear River and Mill Creek] in a beautiful valley lying under the Anahuac Mountains. The lofty balsam firs and the thick groves of Athenian poplar, the rapid current and the wayward rocky channel, give Bear River more character than any stream we have yet seen. We found it very unpleasant travelling today, as we had an incessant and very intense cold wind blowing in our faces. About ten o'clock A. M. when we were on the highest point of the divide, we had a considerable hail and snow storm.

Charles H. Carey, ed., *The Journals of Theodore Talbot 1843 and 1849–52* (Portland, 1931), 43.

Since in the travel here described Talbot was following the trail of the Walker-Chiles wagons, his description is helpful in determining their route, which inquiry certainly should have disclosed to Hastings and Hudspeth. From the fact that after striking the Muddy Talbot had to go down its valley one mile before he could continue west, it seems likely that Walker's trail reached the Muddy about 3 miles south of Dog Springs, where old US 30S crossed the stream one-half mile south of I-80, and went down a mile to round a ridge and go up into Spring Valley where the Union Pacific Railroad line now runs. Except that he reached the Muddy a mile higher up, Walker's trail of 1843 was that by which Hastings reached the Bear in 1846, and which the Mormons largely fol-

our course and route by the direction in which the Salt Lake is known to lie. The face of the upland country [Bridger Bench], after leaving Fort Bridger, although broken, presents a more cheerful aspect than the scenery we have been passing through for several days. The wild sage continues to be the principal growth, but we have marched over two or three smooth plains covered with good grass. The sides of the hills and mountains have also in many places presented a bright green herbage, and clumps of the aspen poplar frequently ornament the hollows near the bases of the hills.

We crossed a large and fresh Indian trail, made probably by the Snakes. Many of their lodge-poles were scattered along it, and occasionally a skin, showing that they were travelling in great haste. As usual for several days past, a cloud rose in the southwest about three o'clock, P.M., and discharged sufficient rain to wet us. The atmosphere during the shower had a wintry feel. On the high mountains in sight of us to the left [Uinta Mountains], we could see, after the clouds broke away, that it had been snowing.

We reached a small creek or branch called "Little Muddy" by the hunters, where we encamped between four and five o'clock.[9] Our camp is in a handsome little valley a mile or more in length and half a mile in breadth, richly carpeted with green grass of an excellent quality. An occasional cotton-wood tree, clumps of small willows, and a variety of other shrubbery along the margin of the stream, assist in composing an agreeable landscape. The stream is very small, and in places its channel is dry. The wild geranium, with bright pink and purplish flowers, and a shrub covered with brilliant yellow blossoms, enliven the scenery around. The temperature is that of March or April and winter clothing is necessary to comfort. Many of the small early spring flowers are now in bloom, among which I noticed the

---

lowed in 1847. The only other possibility is that Walker's wagons reached the Big Muddy at a point some 4 miles higher up and descended it to the vicinity of present Piedmont, then crossing over to Sulphur Creek and the Bear by the original line of the Union Pacific, abandoned in 1901 and now employed for the county road between Piedmont and Hilliard.

[9] Korns and Morgan placed Bryant's "Little Muddy" camp on the Big Muddy, but historian Rush Spedden has noted that a third watercourse, Little Creek, located about a mile northeast of Piedmont, matches Bryant's description perfectly, and positioned the Bryant-Russell party to climb a ridge and drop into Soda Hollow. The Little Creek location also checks with Bryant's mileages. In following Bryant's trail this day and the next, the most helpful map is the Veatch map, for which see the Clyman journal, note 44.

strawberry. Large numbers of antelopes were seen. Distance 15 miles.

July 21.—Our buffalo-robes and the grass of the valley were white with frost. Ice of the thickness of window-glass, congealed in our buckets. Notwithstanding this coldness of the temperature, we experience no inconvenience from it, and the morning air is delightfully pleasant and invigorating. Ascending the hills on the western side of our camp, and passing over a narrow ridge,[10] we entered another grassy valley, which we followed up in a southwest course, between ranges of low sloping hills, three or four miles.[11] Leaving the valley near its upper end, or where the ranges of hills close together,[12] we ascended a gradual slope to the summit of an elevated ridge, the descent on the western side of which is abrupt and precipitous, and is covered with gnarled and stunted cedars, twisted by the winds into many fantastic shapes.[13] Descending with some difficulty this steep mountain-side, we found ourselves in a narrow hollow [Pioneer Hollow], enclosed on either side by high elevations, the bottom of which is covered with rank grass, and gay with the bloom of the wild geranium and a shrub richly ornamented with a bright yellow blossom. The hills or mountains enclosing this hollow, are com-

---

[10] The tongue of land between the Muddy and Spring Valley.

[11] Spring Valley, which the Union Pacific today ascends toward the Aspen Tunnel by which it crosses the Bear River Divide; the terrain is described geologically by W. T. Lee in U.S. Geological Survey Bulletin 612, *The Overland Route, Part B* (Washington, 1916), 77–81. From where he arrived in the valley to the point a mile or so beyond where old US 30S left the railroad, that old highway followed Bryant's route; I-80 now runs well to the north of the emigrant trails. Bryant is here describing the trail over which Hastings would bring his wagons the following day, and over which the Mormons in their turn would come next year.

[12] The Union Pacific had the resources to cut a passage through this constriction of the valley, but the immigrants of 1846, and the Mormons in 1847, had to climb up over the obstructing ridge and descend its rough western slope into the upper valley of Antelope Creek, sometimes called Pioneer Hollow. By some mischance Bryant failed to note the "copperas" spring at the base of this ridge which figures so prominently in the other journals.

[13] The wagons of 1846 and 1847 faithfully followed Bryant down into Pioneer Hollow and then climbed out of the hollow to the south. This turned out to be unnecessary; in returning east in August, 1847, the Mormons found that it was possible to stay up on the first ridge and follow it around to where the wagons had climbed up to the divide, and in consequence the toilsome road Bryant describes was abandoned for wagons after 1847. Stansbury rode over the original trail in 1849 and agreed that the distance it saved was not worth the extra trouble it occasioned.

posed of red and yellow argillaceous earth. In the ravines there are a few aspen poplars of small size, and higher up some dwarfish cedars bowed by winds and snows.

Following up this hollow a short distance, we came to an impassable barrier of red sandstone, rising in perpendicular and impending masses, and running entirely across it.[14] Ascending with great difficulty the steep and high elevation on our right hand, we passed over an elevated plain of gradual ascent, covered with wild sage, of so rank and dense a growth that we found it difficult to force our way through it. This ridge overlooks another deeper and broader valley,[15] which we entered and followed in a southwest course two or three miles, when the ranges of hills close nearly together, and the gorge makes a short curve or angle, taking a general northwest direction.[16] We continued down the gorge until we reached Bear river, between one and two o'clock, P.M.

Bear river, where we struck and forded it, is about fifty yards in breadth, with a rapid current of limpid water foaming over a bed so unequal and rocky, that it was difficult, if not dangerous to the limbs of our mules, when fording it. The margin of the stream is thinly timbered with cottonwood and small willows. The fertile bottom, as we proceeded down it, varying in width from a mile and a half to one-eighth of a mile, is well covered with grasses of an excellent quality; and I noticed in addition to the wild geranium, and several other flowers in bloom, the wild flax, sometimes covering a half acre or more with its modest blue blossom. Travelling down the stream on the western side, in a course nearly north, six miles, we encamped on its margin about 3 o'clock, P.M.[17]

---

[14] The culminating ridge between the Green and Bear rivers, through which the 5,900-foot Aspen Tunnel was driven in 1901. When Hastings approached this point with wagons he had to veer to the south to get the wagons up to the divide; consequently Bryant's trail diverges from the later wagon roads at the fork in Pioneer Hollow. See the Lienhard journal, note 4.

[15] The broad upper valley of Stowe Creek in which Altamont is located, at the west portal of the Aspen Tunnel. On descending into this valley Bryant again for a short distance anticipated the route of Hastings' wagons.

[16] Stowe Creek Canyon. Following down it, Bryant reached and crossed the Bear about 4 miles southeast of present Evanston. The Union Pacific now descends this canyon, but it was too much for wagons in 1846, and Hastings turned left across a low divide to the valley of Sulphur Creek.

[17] The night's encampment was on the west bank of the Bear some 2 miles northwest of present Evanston. In proceeding down the river after fording it, Hudspeth crossed his eastbound trail of June 5 and could not have failed to orient

The country through which we have passed to-day, has, on the whole, presented a more fertilized aspect than any we have seen for several hundred miles. Many of the hillsides, and some of the table-land on the high plains, produce grass and other green vegetables. Groves of small aspen poplars, clumps of hawthorn, and willows surrounding the springs, are a great relief to the eye, when surveying the general brownness and sterility of the landscape. I observed strawberry-vines among the grass in the hollows, and in the bottom of Bear river; but there was no fruit upon them. We have passed the skeletons of several buffaloes. These animals abounded in this region some thirty years ago; but there are now none west of the Rocky Mountains.

Brown shot three antelopes near our camp this afternoon. A young one, which was fat and tender, was slaughtered and brought to camp; the others were so lean as not to be considered eatable. The sage-hens, or the grouse of the sage-plains, with their broods of young chickens, have been frequently flushed, and several shot. The young chickens are very delicate; the old fowl is usually, at this season, lean and tough.

McClary has been quite sick with a fever which has prevailed among the emigrants, and frequently terminated fatally. This afternoon he was scarcely able to sit upon his mule, from weakness and giddiness. Distance 25 miles.

July 22.—Cold, with a strong wind from the snowy mountains to the southwest, rendering the atmosphere raw and uncomfortable. We rose shivering from our bivouacs, and our mules picketed around were shaking with the cold. McClary was so much relieved from his sickness, that he considered himself able to travel, and we resumed our march at seven o'clock. Crossing the river bottom on the western side, we left it, ascending and descending over some low sloping hills, and entering another narrow, grassy valley, through which runs a small stream in a general course from the southwest.[18] We travelled

---

himself; Medicine Butte is an unmistakable landmark. It was therefore not accidental that he did not turn immediately west to the head of Echo Canyon; he was seeking to reconnoiter the country farther north.

[18] Naming this valley up which Bryant traveled has been one of the most troublesome questions that has attended identification of his route. On November 24, 1990, David L. Bigler, Rush Spedden, Kent Malan, and Harold Schindler, through the kind cooperation of Rochelle Whitlock, manager of the Deseret Livestock Company, were allowed access to company property across which the Bryant-Russell party journeyed after leaving Bear River on July 22, 1846. Using

up this gradually ascending valley about twelve miles, to a point w[h]ere the stream *forks*. Near this place there are several springs of very cold water.[19] Following up the right-hand fork some miles farther, in a northwest course, we left it by climbing the range of hills on the right hand, passing along an elevated ridge, from which we descended into a deep mountain gorge [Trail Canyon], at about one o'clock, P.M.

The mountains on either side of the *cañada* or gorge are precipitous, and tower upwards several thousand feet above the level upon which we are travelling. At 3 o'clock[20] we crossed a small stream [Rochelle Creek] flowing into the *cañada* from the northeast. Continuing down, the space between the ranges of mountains becomes narrower, and choked up with brush, prostrate trees, and immense masses of rock (conglomerate) which have fallen from the summits of the mountains, affording us no room to pass. We were compelled to leave the bottom of the gorge, and with great caution, to find a path along the precipitous side of the mountains, so steep in many places that our mules were in constant danger of sliding over the precipices, and being thus destroyed.

The snows have recently disappeared. Their fertilizing irrigation has produced a verdant carpet of grass in the bottoms of the small

---

Bryant's journal as a guide, this group determined that the '46 mule party entered Utah through Thomas Canyon, striking present Crane Creek near its northernmost point. They followed that creek (Bryant's "right-hand fork") some 10 miles west to the "elevated ridge" and into Trail Creek Canyon, descended that canyon to its junction with Lost Creek, and proceeded southwest along Lost Creek to Croyden.

[19] The forks of Crane Creek above the present Crane Reservoir. Bryant's language is inexact in saying that he had ascended the creek itself 12 miles to its forks; this was, rather, the distance from the Bear River. In general, his route can be followed on the *Cache National Forest* map, which is based on the township maps. Roads today run up both of the forks Bryant mentions. He followed the right-hand fork only for another mile before climbing up on the dividing ridge. Staying up on the divide for the distance of a mile and a half while following it in a southwesterly direction, he then, as he remarks, descended into the deep gorge of Trail Canyon.

[20] The two hours between the time Bryant reports beginning the descent of Trail Canyon and crossing the "small stream" scarcely 2 miles distant can be accounted for by the party stopping to "noon" and rest their animals. The nameless small stream (which Morgan and Korns identified as Francis Creek, and is here christened Rochelle Creek) is obviously not Francis Creek, which flows from the southeast, and Bryant is correct in describing the stream as flowing from the northeast.

hollows, bespangled with a variety of blooming plants and shrubs. The geranium, wild flax in bloom, and a purple phlox, have been the most conspicuous. In some places the blight of recent frosts is visible. I noticed several fir-trees in one place, while descending through the gorge, from 20 to 100 feet in height. Some of them were standing upon inaccessible projections from the mountain-side. The mountains on either side of us, during our march this afternoon, have raised their rocky and barren summits to a great height, presenting in places perpendicular walls and impending projections of red sandstone and conglomerate rock. Immense masses of many thousand tons' weight have fallen from the sides, and rolled from the summits into the trough of the gorge, where they lie imbedded deep in the earth, or shattered by the concussion of the fall. In other places, the soft red sandstone has been worn by the action of the atmosphere into many remarkable and sometimes fantastic shapes. Some of these are spiral and columnar, others present the grotesque forms of nondescript animals and birds. A very conspicuous object of this kind, of colossal magnitude, exhibited the profile of a rhinoceros or elephant. We named it the "Elephant's Statue."[21]

---

[21] This landmark is in Trail Canyon just above its junction with Francis Canyon. In May, 1948, Dale L. Morgan and I attempted to drive up these two canyons but in each case we were quickly frustrated by ranchers' locked steel gates. Subsequent local inquiry, and information from Mr. Walter E. Dansie of the Deseret Livestock Company, is relied upon to establish that the landmark we photographed was in fact the "Elephant's Statue."

Note that Trail Canyon is the "Red Chimney Fork" of Stansbury's journal of 1849, the pass at its head offering easy access to and from Saleratus Valley. The canyon is somewhat better described by Stansbury than by Bryant:

Aug. 23. . . . After traveling down [Lost Creek] we came to a branch coming in from the East which Bridger declared headed near the ridge from which we had descended yesterday   I accordingly determined to follow it up, & did so & found it was as he had said. We encamped on the head of the ravine heading in the ridge which we should have followed yesterday. The ascent is very moderate & even, & with the exception of some three or four miles of side lying ground which will require to be worked, some large boulders, & detritus of the high conglomerate cliffs removed, & considerable brush & small trees cut out of the way. By keeping up the last valley traced from Bear River [Saleratus Valley], following the [dividing] ridge spoken of & descending this valley which we have called "Red Chimney fork," from the remarkable resemblance of one of the projections of the Cliffs to this object, I think a good road can be obtained to its mouth or junction with Pumbars [Lost] Creek. The timber is small oak or Black jack, quaking Asp Cherry Service Berry & box Elder of considerable size.

The dislocated skeletons of buffaloes which perished here many years ago, have been frequently seen. Large flocks of antelope have been in sight during the day's march. We have seen as many as five hundred. A red fox, and an animal of a brown color, which I never saw described, approached within a short distance this afternoon.

Just before sunset we reached a small opening between the mountain ranges,[22] covered with a dense growth of willows, wild currants, and wild rose-bushes. The mountainsides presented clumps of hawthorn, and a few diminutive and scattering cedars. Here we encamped in the small openings among the willows and other shrubbery, where we found grass and water sufficient for our animals. Distance 35 miles.

July 23.—Ice froze in our buckets and basins one-fourth of an inch in thickness. On the surface of the small shallow brook which runs through the valley, the congelation was of the thickness of window-glass. At home, in the low and humid regions of the Mississippi valley, at this stage of the thermometer we should suffer from sleeping in the open air. But here the atmosphere is so elastic, dry, and bracing, that we experience no inconvenience.

Continuing our march down the narrow defile in a southwest course, generally along the side of the mountains, (the bottom being choked up with willows, vines, briers, and rosebushes,) we crossed the channels at their mouths, of two small streams emptying into the branch upon which we are travelling.[23] These streams flow through narrow mountain defiles which, as far as we could discern, were tim-

---

Aug 24. Returned on our trail as far as the mouth of Red Chimney Fork a distance of 6 or 8 miles, where it runs into Pumbars Creek. About a mile above the mouth a larger Ravine [Francis Canyon] puts in on the left, but the ascent to the ridge seems to be not so good as the Chimney fork. Entering the valley of Pumbars creek the road will have to keep in the bottom for about a mile crossing & recrossing several times as the banks on each side are entirely too steep & high for any thing but a bridle path. . . .

This quotation, as with others from the journals of the Stansbury Survey, is from transcripts of the originals in the National Archives placed at my disposal by Mr. Morgan.

[22] Apparently this opening was a short distance above the junction of Trail and Lost creeks.

[23] The first of these would seem to have been Lost Creek proper, the second the rivulet out of Hell Canyon. Stansbury turned west up the latter ravine, eventually descending into Ogden's Hole. He then went on to Ogden by way of North Ogden Canyon.

bered with cedars and poplars. One of these gorges [Hell Canyon] presents a most savage and gloomy aspect. It is so narrow and deep that the rays of the sun never penetrate to its bottom. Mr. Hudspeth thinks this is what is called by the hunters, "Ogden's Hole." It derives this name from the circumstance that a trapper by the name of Ogden concealed himself here from a body of pursuing and hostile Indians, and perhaps perished.[24] I am not sufficiently acquainted with the facts to relate them with accuracy. The romantic interest of the story is doubtless much enhanced by a view of the wild and forbidding spot where its incidents and catastrophe occurred.

The ranges of mountains, as we proceeded down the gorge, became more and more elevated, but less precipitous.[25] I noticed, at a height of six or eight hundred feet above the level of the stream, numberless small white fossil shells, from half an inch to an inch in diameter. In places bare of vegetation, the ground was white with these crustaceous remains. About eleven o'clock, we passed through a grove of small poplars, at the upper end of a triangular valley.[26] The stream down which we have been travelling, here runs through a perpendicular *cañon* of great elevation,[27] and empties into the main Weber river, which flows into the Great Salt Lake, running in a nearly west course. Ascertaining by examination that we could not pass this *cañon*, without following a considerable distance the rocky channel of the stream, we crossed some low hills, or a gap in the mountains at the northeast [southeast] corner of the valley. While marching over these hills, we were overtaken by five or six Indians mounted on horses. The Indians rode up and saluted us with much apparent friendship and cordiality. They were a small party encamped in the valley that we had just left, whose animals and lodges

---

[24] Hudspeth had evidently been taken in by some spell-binding mountain man. Ogden's Hole was the trappers' name for Ogden Valley, east of Ogden, where Huntsville now stands. For other examples of the desperate folklore attaching to the name, see William Kelly, *An Excursion to California over the Prairie, Rocky Mountains, and Great Sierra Nevada* (London, 1851), I, 240–41, and Mrs. B. G. Ferris, *The Mormons at Home* (New York, 1856), 220, 221. The valley took its name actually from Peter Skene Ogden, the great brigade leader of the Hudson's Bay Company, who trapped the valley in the spring of 1825.

[25] This is characteristic of the canyon all the way from the junction of Lost Creek and Trail Creek.

[26] The valley in which Croyden now stands, immediately north of Devils Slide in Weber Canyon.

[27] The locality of the present cement plant at Croyden. Over the course of a century, Lost Creek has lost some of its formidable character here.

we had seen at a distance in the brush skirting the stream. After riding two miles, we entered a fertile valley several miles in length and breadth, covered with luxuriant grass, through which flows Weber river;[28] but tracing the channel down to where it enters the mountains, we found a *cañon* more difficult to pass than the one we had just left.[29] Observing at a distance a party of Indians, whose encampment was some two miles up the valley, coming towards us, we determined to halt for an hour or two, and gather from them such information as we could in reference to the route to the Salt Lake.

The first Indians that came up were two men and a small boy. One of the men called himself a Utah, the other a Shoshonee or Snake. The Utah appeared to be overjoyed to see us. He was not satisfied with shaking hands, but he must embrace us, which, although not an agreeable ceremony, was submitted to by several of our party. This ceremony being over, he laughed merrily, and danced about as if in an ecstasy of delight in consequence of our appearance. He examined with great curiosity all of our baggage; tried on, over his naked shoulders, several of our blankets, in which costume he seemed to regard himself with great satisfaction. He was, for an Indian, very comical in his deportment and very merry. The

[28] The open valley of the Weber extends from the mouth of Echo Canyon some 6 miles west to where the canyon begins west of Henefer. The trail Bryant followed from Croyden Valley over to the Weber is today approximated by a county road. This road, after crossing the gentle divide, goes to Henefer to join old Highway 30S at the crossing of the Weber. Bryant reached the river about 2 miles below the town. Hudspeth was again in full view of his eastbound trail, having come down Main Canyon, back of Henefer, on June 4.

[29] The area immediately above Devils Slide, since blasted open for the Union Pacific and the modern highway. Lt. E. G. Beckwith, reconnoitering routes for Pacific railroads, inspected this area on April 7, 1854. The river, he noted in his journal, had cut through

a red conglomerate sandstone mountain six or eight hundred feet high, which is rapidly disintegrating, the talus at some points being entirely swept away by the river, and at all others it stands at too steep an angle towards the water to be easily climbed over.

The Indian trail, however, passes through this canon at low water, a part of the way in the stream. It is five hundred yards long. We rode to its upper end [by way of Croyden Valley] and clambered in to examine it. The trail by which we passed ascends Dry Creek [Lost Creek] half a mile, and then passes without difficulty to its head, by a low pass in the ridge through which the canon itself is cut."

"Report of Explorations for the Pacific Railroad, on the Line of the Forty-First Parallel of North Latitude," *House Executive Document* No. 129, 33 Congress, 1 session, Serial 737.

number of Indians about our camp soon accumulated to fifteen or twenty, all of whom were Utahs, except the one Snake mentioned, who had married a Utah squaw.[30] A hasty dinner was prepared, and we distributed very sparingly among them (for our stock of provisions is becoming low) something from each dish, with which display of hospitality they appeared to be gratified. Most of these Indians were armed with bows and arrows. There were among them a miserable rifle and musket, which they had evidently procured from Mexican trappers or traders, as, when I inquired of the owner of one of them its name, he pronounced the word *carabina*. Those who had these guns were desirous that we should wait until they could ride some distance and bring dressed deer or elkskins, which they wished to trade for powder and balls. They were all miserably clothed, some wearing a filthy, ragged blanket, others a shirt and gaiters made of skins, and others simply a breech-cloth of skins. Their countenances, however, were sprightly and intelligent, and several of them were powerfully formed.

The result of our inquiries in reference to the route was not satisfactory. The merry old fellow we first met, advised us by signs to go southwest a distance until we struck water, and then go northwest.[31] Another advised us to return to the small valley, and from thence to pass through the mountains parallel with Weber river. We determined on the latter route, it appearing to be the shortest.

Saddling up, we retraced our trail into the small valley [Croyden Valley], where we were overtaken by the Indians, desirous of trading skins for powder and balls. Several trades were made, generally at the rate of twelve charges of powder, and as many ounce-bullets, for a large elk or deer skin well dressed. We ascended from the valley through a winding and difficult ravine,[32] to the summit of the range of mountains on the west, from which we could see nothing but mountain after mountain, one rising behind another, in the course we designed taking. A halt was called, and Mr. Hudspeth and my-

---

[30] This was Little Soldier's mixed band of Utes and Northern Shoshoni.

[31] That is, they were advised to follow in reverse Hudspeth's eastbound trail of June as far as East Canyon, then descend that canyon to where it opened out upon the Weber at present Morgan.

[32] Up the steep slopes of this draw a dugway had recently been built when I drove up Lost Creek in May, 1948. If it has a name, local inquiry did not disclose it; and as Bryant's name is nowhere else on the map of Utah, it might fittingly be placed here. The new road reportedly winds down to the Weber a few miles below.

self, leaving our party, entered a ravine and followed it down steep declivities, (our mules frequently sliding ten or fifteen feet over bare and precipitous rocks,) with a view of ascertaining the practicability of passing along the bank of the river. Forcing our way, after our descent, through the thick brush and brambles, and over dead and fallen timber, we finally reached the stream and crossed it. The result of our observations was that the route was impracticable, without the aid of axes to clear away the brush and dead and fallen timber, unless we took the rocky bed of the river for a road, wading water generally three feet deep, and in places, probably of swimming depth to our animals. We returned after considerable difficulty to our party, and countermarching, encamped just as the sun was setting, in the small valley so often referred to.[33]

There are two Indian lodges near our camp. We visited them, and made exchanges of small articles with the women for parched and pulverized sunflower and grass seeds. Its taste was much like that of parched corn, and agreeable. All the men, women, and children, some eight or ten in number, visited us during the preparation and discussion of our supper, watching with much curiosity and interest the culinary operations and other movements. They were good-natured and sociable, so far as there can be sociability between persons making known their thoughts by vague signs. Our supper to-night, with the exception of bread and coffee, consisted of a stew made of antelope flesh, which, as it happened, was very highly seasoned with pepper. I distributed several plates of this stew among the Indians. They tasted of it, and immediately made most ludicrous grimaces, blowing out and drawing in their breath, as if they had been burnt. They handed back the plates without eating their contents. To satisfy them that we were playing no tricks upon them, which they seemed to suspect, I ate from the same dishes; but they could not be prevailed upon to eat the stew. Coffee, bread, and a small lump of sugar to each was distributed among them, with which they seemed much pleased. The sugar delighted them beyond measure, and they evidently had never seen or tasted of it before. During the visit of these Indians, I noticed the females hunting for the vermin in the heads and on the bodies of their children; finding which, they ate the animals with an apparent relish. I had often heard of this disgusting practice, but this is the first instance of it I have seen. They retired to their lodges about nine o'clock, and so much

---

[33] For the third time the party is back in Croyden Valley.

confidence did we feel in their friendship, that no watch was set for the night. Distance from our last camp, seven miles.

July 24.—Crossing for the third time the low gap at the southeastern corner of the small valley, we entered the large, level, and fertile bottom, on the edge of which we had halted yesterday [Weber Valley]. Fording the river, we took a south course over this bottom, which is about three miles in breadth, covered with tall grass, the bloom upon which shows that, when ripe, it must be heavily seeded and nutritious. From the valley we ascended gradually five or six miles to the summit of a ridge of hills,[34] from which, descending about the same distance in a southwest course, we struck another branch of Weber's river, flowing in a northwest course [East Canyon Creek]. Following the stream about a mile, much to our disappointment we found another impassable *cañon*. This *cañon* resembles a gate, about six or eight feet in width, the arch and superstructure of which have fallen in immense masses, rendering a passage by the channel of the stream impossible.[35] The mountains on either side raise their perpendicular walls of red sandstone to a great elevation.

Looking up the side of the mountain on our right, we saw a small Indian trail winding under and over the projecting and impending cliffs. This evidence that the Indians had passed this way, satisfied us that we could do the same; although to the eye, when standing in the valley and looking upwards, it seemed impossible. We commenced the ascent, mules and men following each other along the narrow and dangerous path in single file. After much labor we reached the summit of the ascent. This first difficulty being over, we travelled about two miles along the side of the mountain, in a path so narrow that a slight jostle would have cast us over a precipice to the bottom of a gulf a thousand feet in depth. Continuing down the stream five miles, our progress being obstructed by many difficulties, we at length, much to our gratification, reached an opening between the mountains, displaying an extensive valley [Morgan Valley] covered with grass, and the meanderings of the stream upon which we were travelling by the line of dark green shrubbery and herbage

---

[34] Up Main Canyon to the summit, locally called the Hogsback. On the far side they descended Dixie Creek to the floor of East Canyon. Since Hudspeth had ridden over this section on June 3–4, it is curious that some comment upon the circumstance was not made by Bryant.

[35] The "rough Looking Kenyon" of which Clyman had taken note on June 3. The narrows Bryant describes have been closed up by the East Canyon dam. Compare the *Fort Douglas* quadrangle.

upon its banks. We reached the junction of this stream with Weber river between four and five o'clock, and encamped for the day [2 miles below Morgan].

A number of Utah Indians accompanied us several miles this morning. Among them was the pleasant and comical old fellow, who amused us so much yesterday. They all appeared to be much gratified by our visit, and were very pressing in their invitations to us to stop and trade with them. Near the last *cañon* there was a solitary lodge, from which the inhabitants, with the exception of an old man and woman, fled as soon as they saw us, driving before them their horses. The old man and woman, being unable to run, hid themselves under the bank of the stream. I noticed in one of the ravines to-day, the scrub-oak, or what is commonly called *black-jack*, also a few small maple-trees. The trunks of none of these are more than two inches in diameter. Distance 24 miles.

July 25.—We determined to remain encamped to-day, to rest and recruit our mules, the grass and water being good. The valley in which our camp is situated is about fifteen miles in length, and varies from one to three miles in breadth. The mountains on both sides rise in benches one above another, to an elevation of several thousand feet above the level of the valley. The summits of this range, on the west, exhibit snow. It is scarcely possible to imagine a landscape blending more variety, beauty, and sublimity, than is here presented. The quiet, secluded valley, with its luxuriant grass waving in the breeze; the gentle streamlet winding through it, skirted with clumps of willows and the wild rose in bloom; the wild currant, laden with ripe fruit; the aspen poplar, with its silvery, tremulous foliage; the low, slopping hills, rising at first by gentle ascents, and becoming gradually more and more elevated and rugged, until their barren and snowy summits seem almost to cleave the sky, compose a combination of scenery not often witnessed.

I noticed this morning, about ten o'clock, a column of smoke rising from the mountains to the west. The fire which produced it continued to increase with an almost frightful rapidity, and the wind, blowing from that quarter, has driven the smoke into the valley, darkening the sun, and imparting to everything around a lurid and dismal coloring.

Jacob, Buchanan, and Brown started early this morning, with the intention of ascending one of the snowy mountain peaks. They returned about four o'clock, P.M., overcome with the fatigue of their walk, and without having accomplished their design, being prevented by distance, and the tangled brush in the hollows and ravine. Mr. Hudspeth rode down the valley to explore Weber's river to the Salt Lake. He returned in the afternoon, having passed through the next *cañon*.[36] I noticed several magpies, and other small birds, in the valley during the day.

July 26.—The fires in the mountains were burning with great fury all night, threatening, although probably at a distance of twenty miles, to reach us before we decamped. Burnt leaves and ashes, driven by the winds, whirled through the atmosphere, and fell around us in the valley. Mr. Hudspeth and two of the men with him left us here, to explore the *cañon* above, and ascertain the practicability of wagons passing through it. Resuming our march, we proceeded down the valley about ten miles, passing through, at its lower end, a grove of poplars, in which a fire had been burning, and some of the fallen trees were yet blazing. Entering between the walls of the mountains forming the *cañon*, after laborious exertions for several hours, we passed through it without any serious accident. The *cañon* is four or five miles through, and we were compelled, as heretofore, to climb along the side of the precipitous mountains, frequently passing under, and sometimes scaling, immense overhanging masses and projections of rock. To be thus safely enlarged from this natural prison-house, locked at every point, was an agreeable, if not an important event in the history of our journey.

At four o'clock, P.M., we encamped on the bank of the Weber river, just below the *cañon*.[37] The stream, at this point, is about thirty feet in breadth, with a limpid and rapid current, and a rocky channel. The grass along its margin is dry and dead, but well seeded, and consequently nutritious to our animals. A few small poplars, generally from two to three inches in diameter at the trunk, skirt the stream.

---

[36] The "second canyon" of the Weber—the mountain walls close in again below Morgan Valley. Devils Gate was this canyon's most famous feature, and still is, though blasting has opened up a passage for railroad and highway. Hudspeth evidently saw nothing in his reconnaissance to make him think wagons could not get through; use of the water-level route down the Weber for the Hastings Cutoff consequently depended upon the possibility of forcing a way through the upper canyon. Devils Gate was called "the Devils Chair" in 1878. See Edward W. Tullidge, *Tullidge's Histories* (Salt Lake City, 1889), II, 121.

[37] The night's encampment was in the lovely little valley at the mouth of the canyon where Uintah now stands. Here is the junction of I-84 with US 89, which as straightened in the early 1950s follows the path of Bryant and the Hastings wagons south to Farmington Junction and I-15.

I ascended the range of hills [the Sand Ridge] bordering the valley of the river to the south, from which I had a most extensive and interesting view of the Great Salt Lake. My position was about ten miles distant from the lake, but my elevation was such that I could discern its surface from the north to the south, a distance which I estimated at sixty or eighty miles. The shore next to me, as far as I could see it, was white. Numerous mountainous islands, dark and apparently barren, sometimes in ranges of fifteen or twenty miles, sometimes in solitary peaks, rise to a considerable elevation above its surface; but the waters surrounding these insulations could be traced between them as far as the eye could reach. The evening was calm, and not a ripple disturbed the tranquil bosom of the lake. As the sun was sinking behind the far distant elevations to the west, the glassy surface of this vast inland ocean was illuminated by its red rays, and for a few minutes it appeared like a sea of molten fire. The plain or valley of the lake, to the right, is some eight or ten miles in width, and fertile. The Weber river winds through it, emptying into the lake some ten miles to the north of our camp. A few trees fringe its margin. I could smell a strong and offensive fetor wafted from the shore of the lake.

Returning to camp, Miller, who had employed his leisure in angling, exhibited a piscatory spectacle worthy the admiration of the most epicurean ichthyophagist. He had taken with his hook about a dozen salmon-trout, from eight to eighteen inches in length; and the longest weighing four or five pounds. A delicacy such as this, and so abundant, we determined to enjoy, and from the results of Miller's sport we feasted this evening upon a viand which epicures would give much to obtain; but they nor my "Tonglythian" friends, Higgins and Frazer,[38] would scarcely undergo the fatigues and privations to which we had been subjected for its acquisition. Distance 16 miles.

July 27.—By an arrangement with Mr. Hudspeth, we remained encamped, awaiting his return from his exploring trip through the upper cañon of Weber river. Fishing apparatus was in great demand this morning; and most of the party, as soon as breakfast was over, were enjoying the Waltonian sport, in angling for the delicious salmon-trout with which the stream abounds. Our bait is the large insect resembling the cricket, heretofore described, myriads of which are creeping and hopping among the grass, and other vegetation of the valley. Every angler was more or less successful, according to his

[38] Evidently personal friends of Bryant.

luck or skill. A quantity of fish, weighing each from two to five pounds, was taken,—more than sufficient for our wants, although our appetites at this time are not easily satisfied. The fires noticed day before yesterday, and yesterday, have continued to burn; and this afternoon they seemed to have found fresh fuel. The wind changing to the southeast, and blowing a gale, just before sunset, dense clouds of smoke and ashes were driven down upon us.

July 28.—Some of the party went into the hills to gather service-berries. (I do not know that this orthography is correct. It is in accordance with the orthoepy.) The service-berry is produced by a shrub, generally from four to six feet in height. It is of a dark color, larger than the whortleberry, and not very unlike it in flavor. This fruit is abundant here.

July 29.—Mr. Hudspeth and two young men came into camp early this morning, having bivouacked last night a short distance from us, on the opposite side of the river. They had forced their way through the upper cañon, and proceeded six miles further up Weber river,[39] where they met a train of about forty emigrant wagons under the guidance of Mr. Hastings, which left Fort Bridger the same day that we did.[40] The difficulties to be encountered by these emigrants by the new route will commence at that point; and they will, I fear, be serious. Mr. Hudspeth thinks that the passage through the cañon is practicable, by making a road in the bed of the stream at short distances, and cutting out the timber and brush in other places.

Resuming our march, we took a south course over the low hills bordering the valley in which we have been encamped; thence along

---

[39] To the mouth of Echo Canyon.

[40] Hastings therefore left Fort Bridger with the wagons on July 20; and up to the time of his departure none had been added to the 40 wagons mentioned in Dr. Long's letter of July 19. It may be assumed that Hudspeth met these wagons at the mouth of Echo on the evening of July 26 or the morning of July 27. This chronology is significant for two reasons: (1) It had taken the wagons only seven days to cut their way through the upland country from Fort Bridger to the mouth of Echo; consequently they had relatively little trouble on the first section of the new route. (2) Heinrich Lienhard's journal shows that Hastings spent the night of July 27 with a rear company at Bear River; consequently he was almost 40 miles away when Hudspeth met the immigrants who were breaking trail, and could have had no part in their decision to descend the Weber through its canyons. It is evident from Lienhard's further entry of August 3 that Hastings at no time had contemplated taking the wagons down the Weber, that his intention had been that all should take the route across the mountains he himself had followed in coming east.

the base of a range of elevated mountains [Wasatch Mountains] which slope down to the marshy plain of the lake. This plain varies in width from fifteen to two miles, becoming narrower as we approach what is called the "Utah Outlet" [Jordan River], the channel through which the Utah Lake empties its waters into the Salt Lake.

The Great Salt Lake has never been accurately surveyed. It is situated between 40 and 42 degrees of north latitude, and between 35 and 36 degrees of longitude west from Washington. Its length is variously stated by the hunters and trappers who have travelled along its shores, at from one hundred and fifty to one hundred and eighty miles. But in this estimate, the numerous large bays and other irregularities are included. Its extreme length in a straight line is probably one hundred [75] miles, and its extreme breadth between forty and sixty miles. At this season the shore, as we pass along it, is white with a crust of the muriate and carbonate of soda combined. The muriate of soda predominates, but the alkali combined with it is sufficient to render the salt bitter and unfit for use in its natural state. When the wind blows from the lake, the stench arising from the stagnant water next to the shore is highly offensive to the smell. The surface of the lake does not present that rippling and sparkling appearance when the sudden breeze passes over it, so frequently seen on fresh-water lakes, and on the ocean. The waters undoubtedly are thoroughly saturated with saline matter, and hence, from their weight, when they move at all, it is with a lazy and sluggish undulatory motion. It is stated that no fish exist in the lake. I have already mentioned that there are numerous mountainous islands in the lake. There are also several large bays indenting its shores. The plain or valley along which we have travelled to-day is in some places argillaceous, in others sandy and gravelly. Where there is a soil, it is covered with a growth of luxuriant vegetation,—grass, a species of cane, rushes, and a variety of small shrubs and flowering plants. A few scrub-oaks and stunted cedars can be seen on the mountain-sides, and along the ravines. There are many small streams of pure cold water flowing from the mountains.

The heat of the sun during our march this afternoon was excessive. My bridle reins were frequently so hot that it was painful to hold them in my hands. The road has been difficult, and our progress slow. We encamped about three o'clock for the day, on a small spring branch.[41] The sunset scene this evening was splendid. The surface of the lake appeared like a sheet of fire, varying in tint from crimson to a pale scarlet. This flame-like ocean was bordered as far as we could see to the north and south of us, with a field of salt, presenting all the appearances of freshly fallen snow.

When I took out the thermometer this evening, much to my regret I discovered that the bulb was broken.[42] I hung the frame and glass tube on a willow for the observation of the Indians. It will be some time before they will venture to touch it. They stand in great awe of the mysterious instruments which science has invented, and never handle them except with due caution. Distance 18 miles.

July 30.—At sunrise, clear and calm, with an agreeable temperature. The morning scene was beautifully grand. Our camp being in the shadow of the mountains, the face of the sun was invisible to us, long after his golden rays had tipped, one after another, the summits of the far-distant islands in the lake. By degrees the vast expanse of waters became illuminated, reflecting the bright beams of the god of day with dazzling effulgence.

Our route to-day continued south, near the base of the range of mountains on our left.[43] We frequently crossed deep ravines and piles of granite debris, with which the slope of the mountains in places is covered. Travelling about ten miles we reached the southern extremity of one of the bays of the Salt Lake [Farmington Bay]. Beyond this there is a basin of water some three or four miles in circumference, surrounded by a smooth sandy beach.[44] An immense number of ducks were walking and flying over this beach and playing in the basin. Approaching the shore of the pond, a solitary Indian rose from the weeds or grass near the water, and discovering us, he started immediately and ran with considerable speed towards a point of the mountains on our left. Several of us pursued and overtook him. He appeared much alarmed at first, but after shaking hands with us,

---

[41] At present Farmington, doubtless on Farmington Creek, although properly speaking it is not a "spring" branch.

[42] Accordingly, the thermometrical observations Bryant appended to *What I Saw in California* terminate here.

[43] The route of old Alternate US 91, close under the mountains through Farmington, Centerville, and Bountiful.

[44] Hot Springs Lake, now dried up. A half mile across, it extended about a mile and a half north and the same distance south of the site of Becks Hot Spring, its eastern shore being just a few yards west of U.S. 89; see the 1856 township plat for T. 1 N., R. 1 W.

and discovering that we had no hostile intentions, he soon forgot his fright. He carried in his hand a miserably lean duck, which he had just killed with an arrow. A quiver slung across his bare and tawny shoulders, was well supplied with this weapon. He was naked, with the exception of a small covering around his loins, and his skin was as dark as a dark mulatto. Learning from him that he was a Utah, we endeavored to make him comprehend that we wished to trade with his tribe for elk-meat. He shook his head, and appearing desirous of leaving us, we dismissed him. He was soon out of sight, hurrying away with long and rapid strides.

Proceeding about two miles and turning the point of the mountain, we came to seven warm springs, so strongly impregnated with sulphur as to have left a deposite of this mineral in some places several feet in depth. These springs gush out near the foot of a high precipice, composed of conglomerate rock and a bluish sandstone. The precipice seems to have been uplifted by some subterraneous convulsion. The temperature of the water in the basins was about 90°. The water of most of them was bitter and nauseous.[45]

From these springs we crossed a level plain, on which we encamped at 11 o'clock, A.M., near a small stream of cold water [City Creek] flowing from the mountains, which is skirted with a few poplars and small willows. The grass immediately around our camp is fresh and green, but a short distance from us it is brown, dry, and crisp.

After dinner we were visited by three Indians, one of whom was the man with the duck we saw this morning. The eldest of the three signified that he wished a friendly smoke and a "talk." A pipe was produced and filled with tobacco. Lighting it, I drew two or three puffs and handed it to the old man, and it passed from him to his comrades until the tobacco was consumed. They appeared to enjoy the fumes of the smoke highly. We informed them of our wish to trade for meat. They signified that they had none. Three females of middle age, miserably clad and ugly, soon made their appearance, bringing baskets containing a substance, which, upon examination, we ascertained to be service-berries, crushed to a *jam* and mixed with pulverized grasshoppers. This composition being dried in the sun until it becomes hard, is what may be called the "fruit-cake" of these

---

[45] This site, located at the northern edge of Salt Lake City, was long famous as Warm Springs. Once municipally operated as Wasatch Springs Plunge, in 1994 the building houses the Children's Museum of Utah.

poor children of the desert. No doubt these women regarded it as one of the most acceptable offerings they could make to us. We purchased all they brought with them, paying them in darning-needles and other small articles, with which they were much pleased. The prejudice against the grasshopper "fruit-cake" was strong at first, but it soon wore off, and none of the delicacy was thrown away or lost.

Two of our party mounted their mules and rode to the Indian encampment[46] to ascertain if there were not more Indians, and some from whom meat could be obtained. As soon as the men and women in our camp saw them riding in the direction of their lodges, they hastened away with great speed and in much alarm. Returning from the Indian encampment, Jacob and Brookey reported that there were no more Indians, and that no meat could be obtained. They saw a large quantity of grasshoppers, or crickets, (the insect I have before described,) which were being prepared for pulverization.

The Indians of this region, in order to capture this insect with greater facility, dig a pit in the ground. They then make what hunters, for brevity of expression, call a *surround*;—that is, they form a circle at a distance around this pit, and drive the grass-hoppers or crickets into it, when they are easily secured and taken. After being killed, they are baked before the fire or dried in the sun, and then pulverized between smooth stones. Prejudice aside, I have tasted what are called delicacies, less agreeable to the palate. Although the Utahs are a powerful and warlike tribe, these Indians appeared to be wretchedly destitute.

A fire was raging on the mountain-side all night, and spread down into the valley, consuming the brown vegetation. The water of the small stream was made bitter with the ashes. Our campground, we conjecture, is the same that was occupied by Captain Frémont last year.[47] Distance 15 miles.

July 31.—Morning clear, with a delightful temperature, and a light breeze blowing from the west. Our route to-day runs in a west course across the valley of the "Utah Outlet" [Jordan River], about

---

[46] This was undoubtedly Wanship's band, which the trapper Osborne Russell found in Salt Lake Valley in the winter of 1840–41, and which remained until several years after the coming of the Mormons.

[47] Frémont had encamped here the previous October; see p. 8. The campground of Bryant and Frémont was on, or within a few yards of, present Temple Square; originally City Creek branched in the neighborhood of North Temple and State streets, one fork running south into Mill Creek, the other north of west to the Jordan.

ten miles south from the bay or arm of the Salt Lake upon which we have been travelling. The waters of the Utah Lake are emptied into the Salt Lake through this channel. The Utah Lake is a body of fresh water between sixty and eighty miles in circumference, situated about twenty miles south of the Salt Lake. The shape of the extensive plain of this lake was made apparent to us by the mountains surrounding it. The plain of the lake is said to be fertile, but of the extent of its fertility I have no certain knowledge. The eastern side of the valley of the "Outlet" is well watered by small streams running from the mountains, and the grass and other herbage on the upland are abundant, but there is no timber visible from our position.*

Descending from the upland slope on which we encamped yesterday, we crossed a marsh about two miles in width, covered with grass so dense and matted that our animals could scarcely make their way through it.[48] This grass is generally from five to eight feet in height. A species of rush called *tule* is produced on the marsh. It grows to the height of eight and ten feet. The ground is very soft and tremulous, and is covered for the most part with water to the depth of two or three inches. But our mules were prevented from sinking into it by the forest of herbage which they prostrated under their feet as they advanced. From the marsh we ascended a few feet upon hard, dry ground, producing a coarse grass with an ear resembling our small grains, wheat or barley, and some few flowers, with bunches of wild sage. The colors of the flowers were generally yellow and scarlet.

We reached the Utah Outlet after travelling four miles, and forded it without difficulty.[49] The channel is about twenty yards in

---

* In 1847 the Mormons made a settlement between the Utah and the Salt Lake [note by Bryant].

[48] This was the difficult marsh created by Mill Creek, flowing in its original channel north into the Jordan. See the Clyman journal, note 28.

[49] The fact that it required 4 miles' travel to reach the Jordan ford is strong evidence for the hypothesis set forth in the notes to the Clyman journal, that Clyman's crossing was in the vicinity of present 27th South Street. Note that this crossing was the only one with which Hudspeth was acquainted. Had he known of the North Temple crossing, Hudspeth undoubtedly would have led the company to it and they would have reached it in a little more than a mile. Although Bryant opens his account of the day's events by saying that their route "ran in a west course across the valley," this was simply a statement of their objective. They had to go 4 miles south before they could turn west toward the point of the Oquirrh Mountains. Clyman's estimate of the breadth of the channel was double that of Bryant, reflecting the circumstance that he crossed it at the time of the spring runoff.

breadth, and the water in the deepest places about three feet. The bed of the channel is composed of compact bluish clay. The plain or valley, from the western bank of the "Outlet" to the base of the range of hills to the west [Oquirrh Mountains], is level and smooth, and in places white with a saline deposite or efflorescence. There is but little vegetation upon it, and this is chiefly the wild sage, indicative of aridity, and poverty of soil. From this plain we struck the shore of another bay of the Salt Lake, bordered by a range of mountains running parallel with it.[50] The shore, next to the white crust of salt, is covered with a debris precipitated from the rocky summits of the mountains.

Our route for several hours described nearly a semicircle, when there was a break in the range of mountains, and we entered upon another plain [Tooele Valley]. About three o'clock, P.M., we passed several remarkable rocks rising in tower-like shapes from the plain, to the height of sixty or eighty feet.[51] Beyond these we crossed two small streams bitter with saline and alkaline impregnation. The plain presents a sterile appearance, but little vegetation appearing upon it, and that stunted and withered. At seven o'clock, P.M., we reached a spring branch descending from a mountain ravine, and fringed with small willows, the water of which is comparatively fresh and cool.[52] Here we encamped after a march without halting, of twelve hours. There is a variety of vegetation along the stream—grass, weeds, some few flowers, briers, and rose-bushes.

Soon after we encamped, three Utah Indians visited us. They were mounted on horses, rather lean, and sore-backed from hard usage. The men appeared to be of a better class and more intelligent than those we had before met with. They were young and manifested much sprightliness, and an inquisitive curiosity, which they took no pains to conceal. We invited them to sup with us, and they partook of our simple viands with a high relish. A renewal of our overtures to trade for meat met with no better success than before. They had no meat to dispose of. They were dressed in buckskin shirts, gaiters, and moccasins; and armed with bows and arrows. Two of these men, the most intelligent, concluded to encamp with us for the night. The

[50] He is again referring to the Oquirrhs.

[51] Adobe Rock. Compare the Jefferson map. State Route 138 passes within a stone's throw of this prominent formation half a mile before turning southwest toward Grantsville at Mills Junction.

[52] North Willow Creek, at Grantsville. The night's camp was on the creek a little south of present State Route 138.

principal of these, a young man of about twenty-five, with an amiable but sprightly expression of countenance, was so earnest and eager in his inquiries respecting every thing appertaining to us, and into our language, that I sat conversing with him until a late hour of the night. From him I learned the names of many things in the Utah dialect. I give some of these below. The orthography is in strict accordance with the sound.[53]

ENGLISH.	UTAH.	ENGLISH.	UTAH.
Tobacco	Pah.	Water	Poh.
Fire	Coutouch.	Eye	Pooh.
Grass	Shawnip.	Ear	Nank.
Hair	Pamp.	Nose	Tamoucher.
Sun	Tarp.	Hand	Moh.
Powder-horn	Naup.	Flint	Tuck.
Spur	Tannegan.	Wood	Schnip.
Mule	Moodah.	Blanket	Tochewanup.
Bullet	Navak.	Pipe	Toh.
Knife	Weitch.	Teeth	Tamp.
Horse	Punk.	Bear	Padewap.
Finger	Mushevan.	Rifle	Wokeat.
Foot	Mamp.	Powder	Noketouch.
Bear's Claw	Musheta.	Pantaloons	Wannacouch.
	Middenah.	Saddle.	

These are some of the words of the Utah language which I wrote down, from his pronunciations, by the light of our campfire. Furnishing him and his companion some skins, we requested them to retire for the night, which they seemed to do with reluctance. Distance 40 miles.

August 1.—Morning clear, with a delightfully soft breeze from the south. I purchased, this morning, of one of the Utahs, a dressed grisly bear-skin, for which I gave him twenty charges of powder and twenty bullets. Several other small trades were made with them by our party. Having determined to cross a range of mountains, instead of following to avoid it, the shore of another cove or bay of the Salt Lake,—by doing which we should lose in distance twenty-five or thirty miles,—we laid our course nearly west, towards the lowest gap we could discover in the range.[54]

---

[53] This is the earliest printed Ute vocabulary by any traveler, and after William Ashley's of May 27, 1825, the oldest known. See Dale L. Morgan, ed., *The West of William H. Ashley* (Denver, 1964), 115, 281.

[54] North Willow Canyon, the deep cleft in the Stansbury Mountains immediately southwest of present Grantsville. The route was adopted in preference

After we had proceeded two or three miles up the sloping plain, towards the base of the mountains, Colonel Russell recollected that he had left his rifle at the camp—a "nine-shooter." Accompanied by Miller, he returned back to recover it. I was very well satisfied that the Indians would have discovered it, and considering it a valuable prize, would not wait for the return of the loser. According to their code of morals, it is not dishonest to take what is left in camp, and they never fail to do it. I halted for an hour, and long after our party had disappeared in a gorge of the mountains, for the return of Colonel Russell and Miller. I could see, from my elevated position, the dust raised by the horses of the retreating Indians on the plain, at a distance of six or eight miles from the camp. Becoming impatient, I commenced a countermarch, and while moving on, I saw, at a distance of a mile and a half, a solitary horseman, urging his animal with great speed towards me. There being but one instead of two, I felt considerable anxiety, not knowing but some disaster might have occurred. I moved faster towards the horseman, and, at the distance of a quarter of a mile, discovered that it was Colonel Russell. Riding towards him, I inquired what had become of Miller? He did not know. He had lost him in hunting through the willows and ravines. My anxiety was much increased at this report, and I started to return to the camp, when Miller, proceeding at a slow gait, appeared on one of the distant elevations. The result of the search for the "nine-shooting" rifle was fruitless. The Indians had carried it away with them. The only consolation I could offer to Colonel Russell for his loss was, that a more useless burden was never carried on the shoulders of man or mule. It was a weight upon the beast, and an incumbrance to the rider, and of no practical utility on this journey. This consolation, however, was not very soothing.

(I will state here, that this rifle was recovered by Mr. Hudspeth, brought into California, and returned to Colonel Russell. The Indian who took it from our camp, after he had returned to the village of his tribe, was much elated by his prize. But in discharging it, the ball, instead of making its passage through the barrel, took another direction, and wounded him in the leg. An instrument so mysterious and eccentric it was considered dangerous to retain, and the chief ordered its restoration to the emigrant parties following us. It was rec-

---

to the circuitous course north around the Stansbury Range into Skull Valley. To this day, as a route to Skull Valley, it remains only a pack trail.

ognized by Mr. Hudspeth, and returned to its owner, as above stated.)[55]

Following the trail of our party, we entered the narrow mountain-gorge, or valley, where I saw them disappear. Proceeding up this valley, we passed several temporary wigwams, erected by the Indians along the side of the small stream which flows through it from the summit of the mountain. These wigwams were all deserted; but fires were burning in front of them, dogs were barking, and willow-baskets, some of which contained service-berries, were standing about. A few poplar and pine trees, service-bushes, willows, and a variety of small shrubbery, with an occasional sunflower, ornament this narrow and romantic gorge. As we ascended, the sides of the mountain presented ledges of variegated marble, and a debris of the same was strewn in our path. We overtook our party when they were about halfway up the steep ascent to the crest of the range. Mules and men were strung out a mile, toiling and climbing up the almost insurmountable acclivity.

The inhabitants of the wigwams, who had fled and concealed themselves until we had passed, now commenced whooping far below us, and we could see several of them following our trail. After much difficulty in urging our animals forward, and great fatigue to ourselves and them, we reached the summit of the ridge. Here we halted to take breath. Several of the Indians, whose whoops we had heard, came up to us. They were naked, and the most emaciated and wretched human objects I had ever seen. We shook hands, however, and greeted them kindly. The descent on the western side of the mountain, although steep, is not difficult, there being but few obstructions. Four miles from the summit brought us to a gentle slope, and to a faint stream which flows from the hills and sinks in the sands just below.[56] Here we encamped for the day. Near us, on the slope, there is a grove of small cedars, the deep verdure of which is some relief to the brown and dead aspect of vegetable nature surrounding us. Distance 15 miles.

August 2.—Morning clear, with a soft breeze from the south. We were visited early by three miserable Digger Indians, calling them-

---

[55] Compare this story with the one related by Heinrich Lienhard under date of August 20, 1846.

[56] Kanaka Creek, at present Iosepa. Having crossed the Stansbury Mountains instead of circling them, the Bryant-Russell party had come farther south in Skull Valley than had Frémont the previous autumn or Clyman in the spring, and thus they stumbled upon the welcome supply of fresh water at Iosepa.

selves Soshonees. They were naked, with the exception of a few filthy, ragged skins, fastened around their loins. They brought with them a mixture composed of parched sunflower seed and grasshoppers, which they wished to exchange with us for some articles we possessed. We declined trading with them. One of them signified, that he knew where there was water over the next ridge of mountains.[57] Water at the western base of the next range would diminish the long march without this necessary element, over the great Salt Plain, some ten or twelve miles. For a compensation in shirts and pantaloons, he consented to accompany and guide us to the water; but when we started, he declined his engagement.

Descending into the plain or valley [Skull Valley] before us, we took a northwest course across it, striking Capt. Frémont trail of last year after we had commenced the ascent of the slope on the western side.[58] The breadth of this valley at this point from the base of one range of mountains to the other, is about twenty miles. Large portions of it are covered with a saline efflorescence of a snowy whiteness. The only vegetation is the wild sage; and this is parched and shrivelled by the extreme drought. Not a solitary flower or green plant has exhibited itself. In our march we crossed and passed several deep ravines and chasms [washes], plowed by the waters from the mountains during the melting of the snows, or hollowed out by the action of the winds. Not a living object, animal, reptile, or insect, has been seen during our day's march.

We encamped at two o'clock, P.M. There are a few dwarf cedars in our vicinity, and scattered bunches of dead grass. In a ravine near us the sand is moist; and by making an excavation, we obtained a scant supply of water, impregnated with salt and sulphur.[59] A dense smoky vapor fills the valley and conceals the summits of the distant mountains. The sun shining through this, dispenses a lurid light,

---

[57] This was possibly Lone Rock Spring, on the west slope of the Cedar Mountains (see the Clyman journal, note 20).

[58] The trails came together below Redlum Spring, to which Bryant came by a northwest, and Frémont by a west, course from the east side of Skull Valley.

[59] Redlum Spring produces little water late in the summer, and that may be the explanation of Bryant's remark about the scant supply. It is also to be remarked, however, on the basis of the experience of those who traveled the Hastings Cutoff in 1850, that water could be had in many places here by digging for it. This may explain some of the variant information about the character and location of the sulfur-tainted water to which, in reading through the journals of the overland immigrants, we have given the generic name of Redlum Spring.

coloring the brown and barren desert with a more dismal and gloomy hue. As soon as our afternoon meal had been prepared and discussed, we commenced preparations for the march over the Salt Desert to-morrow, which employment occupied us until a late hour of the night. Distance 20 miles.

August 3.—I rose from my bivouac this morning at half-past one o'clock. The moon appearing like a ball of fire, and shining with a dim and baleful light, seemed struggling downwards through the thick bank of smoky vapor that overhung and curtained the high ridge of mountains [Cedar Mountains] to the west of us. This ridge, stretching far to the north and the south as the eye can reach, forms the western wall (if I may so call it) of the desert valley we had crossed yesterday, and is composed of rugged barren peaks of dark basaltic rock, sometimes exhibiting misshapen outlines; at others, towering upwards, and displaying a variety of architectural forms, representing domes, spires, and turreted fortifications.

Our encampment was on the slope of the mountain; and the valley lay spread out at our feet, illuminated sufficiently by the red glare of the moon, and the more pallid effulgence of the stars, to display imperfectly its broken and frightful barrenness, and its solemn desolation. No life, except in the little oasis occupied by our camp, and dampened by the sluggish spring, by excavating which with our hands we had obtained impure water sufficient to quench our own and our animals' thirst, existed as far as the eye could penetrate over mountain and plain. There was no voice of animal, no hum of insect, disturbing the tomb-like solemnity. All was silence and death. The atmosphere, chill and frosty, seemed to sympathize with this sepulchral stillness. No wailing or whispering sounds sighed through the chasms of the mountains, or over the gulfy and waterless ravines of the valley. No rustling zephyr swept over the scant dead grass, or disturbed the crumbling leaves of the gnarled and stunted cedars, which seemed to draw a precarious existence from the small patch of damp earth surrounding us. Like the other elements sustaining animal and vegetable life, the winds seemed stagnant and paralyzed by the universal dearth around. I contemplated this scene of dismal and oppressive solitude until the moon sunk behind the mountain, and object after object became shrouded in its shadow.

Rousing Mr. Jacob, who slept soundly, and after him the other members of our small party, (nine in number,) we commenced our preparations for the long and much-dreaded march over the great Salt Desert. Mr. Hudspeth, the gentleman who had kindly con-

ducted us thus far from Fort Bridger as our pilot, was to leave us at
this point, for the purpose of exploring a route for the emigrant wagons farther south.[60] He was accompanied by three gentlemen,
Messrs. Ferguson, Kirkwood, and Minter. Consequently, from this
time forward we are without a guide, or any reliable index to our
destination, except our course westward,[61] until we strike Mary's river
and the emigrant trail to California, which runs parallel with it, some
two hundred miles distant. The march across the Salt Plain, without
water or grass, was variously estimated by those with whom I
conversed at Fort Bridger, at from sixty to eighty miles. Captain
Walker, an old and experienced mountaineer, who had crossed it at
this point as the guide of Captain Frémont and his party, estimated
the distance at seventy-five miles, and we found the estimate to be
nearly correct.

We gathered the dead limbs of the cedars which had been cut
down by Captain Frémont's party when encamped here last autumn,
and ignited them, they gave us a good light during the preparation
and discussion of our frugal breakfast, which consisted to-day of
bread and coffee, bacon being interdicted in consequence of its in-
citement to thirst—a sensation which at this time we desired to avoid,
as we felt uncertain how long it might be before we should be able to
gratify the unpleasant cravings it produces.

Each individual of the party busied himself around the blazing
fires in making his various little but important arrangements, until
the first gray of the dawn manifested itself above the vapory bank
overhanging the eastern ridge of mountains, when the word to saddle
up being given, the mules were brought to the campfires, and every
arm and muscle of the party was actively employed in the business of
saddling and packing "with care!"—with unusual care, as a short

---

[60] In the whole of Bryant's journal, this is the only explanation of the
"explorations" Hudspeth may have had in mind at the time of the departure
from Fort Bridger. Nothing is known of Hudspeth's activities in behalf of the
year's immigration after parting this day from Bryant. Whether he actually tried
to find a route that would skirt the Salt Desert to the south (as Beckwith did in
1854 and Simpson in 1858–59) we have no means of knowing. It is probably to
Hudspeth, however, that the immigrants owed the route across the Cedar Mountains by Hastings Pass, 5 miles north of where Frémont, and presumably
Clyman and Bryant, crossed.

[61] They were not quite so helpless as Bryant's language might indicate, for
they had verbal information as to the character of the country ahead not only
from Hudspeth and Hastings but from Joe Walker. See Bryant's entry for
August 6.

detention during the day's march to readjust the packs might result
in an encampment upon the desert for the coming night, and all its
consequent dangers, the death or loss by straying in search of water
and grass of our mules, (next to death to us,) not taking into the account our own suffering from thirst, which for the next eighteen or
twenty hours we had made up our minds to endure with philosophi-
cal fortitude and resignation. A small powder-keg, holding about
three or four pints of coffee, which had been emptied of its original
contents for the purpose, and filled with that beverage made from the
brackish spring near our camp, was the only vessel we possessed in
which we could transport water, and its contents composed our entire
liquid refreshment for the march. Instructions were given to Miller,
who had charge of this important and precious burden, to husband it
with miserly care, and to make an equitable division whenever it
should be called into use.

Everything being ready, Mr. Hudspeth, who accompanied us to
the summit of the mountain, led the way. We passed upwards
through the *cañada* or mountain-gorge, at the mouth of which we had
encamped, and by a comparatively easy and smooth ascent reached
the summit of the mountain after travelling about six miles. Most of
us were shivering with cold, until the sun shone broadly upon us after emerging, by a steep acclivity, from the gorge through which we
had passed to the top of the ridge [summit of Cedar Mountains].
Here we should have had a view of the mountain [Pilot Peak] at the
foot of which our day's journey was to terminate, but for the dense
smoke which hung over and filled the plain, shutting from the vision
all distant objects.

Bidding farewell to Mr. Hudspeth and the gentleman with him,
(Mr. Ferguson,) we commenced the descent of the mountain. We
had scarcely parted from Mr. H. when, standing on one of the peaks,
he stretched out his long arms, and with a voice and gesture as loud
and impressive as he could make them, he called to us and exclaimed—"Now, boys, put spurs to your mules and ride like h——!"
The hint was timely given and well meant, but scarcely necessary, as
we all had a pretty just appreciation of the trials and hardships before
us.

The descent from the mountain on the western side was more
difficult than the ascent; but two or three miles, by a winding and
precipitous path through some straggling, stunted, and tempest
bowed cedars, brought us to the foot and into the valley, where, after
some search, we found a blind trail which we supposed to be that of

Captain Frémont, made last year.[62] Our course for the day was nearly due west; and following this trail where it was visible, and did not deviate from our course, and putting our mules into a brisk gait, we crossed a valley some eight or ten miles in width sparsely covered with wild sage (artemisia) and grease-wood. These shrubs display themselves and maintain a dying existence, a brownish verdure, on the most arid and sterile plains and mountains of the desert, where no other vegetation shows itself. After crossing the valley, we rose a ridge of low volcanic hills, thickly strewn with sharp fragments of basaltes and a vitreous gravel resembling junk-bottle glass [Grayback Mountain]. We passed over this ridge through a narrow gap, the walls of which are perpendicular, and composed of the same dark scorious material as the debris strewn around. From the western terminus of this ominous-looking passage we had a view of the vast desert-plain before us, which, as far as the eye could penetrate, was of a snowy whiteness, and resembled a scene of wintry frosts and icy desolation. Not a shrub or object of any kind rose above the surface for the eye to rest upon. The hiatus in the animal and vegetable kingdoms was perfect. It was a scene which excited mingled emotions of admiration and apprehension.

Passing a little further on, we stood on the brow of a steep precipice, the descent from the ridge of hills, immediately below and beyond which a narrow valley or depression in the surface of the plain, about five miles in width, displayed so perfectly the wavy and frothy appearance of highly agitated water, that Colonel Russell and myself, who were riding together some distance in advance, both simultaneously exclaimed—"We must have taken a wrong course, and struck another arm or bay of the Great Salt Lake." With deep concern, we were looking around, surveying the face of the country to ascertain what remedy there might be for this formidable obstruction to our progress, when the remainder of our party came up. The difficulty was presented to them; but soon, upon a more calm and scrutinizing inspection, we discovered that what represented so perfectly the "rushing waters" was moveless, and made no sound. The illusion soon became manifest to all of us, and a hearty laugh at those who were the first to be deceived was the consequence; denying to them the merit of being good pilots or pioneers, etc.

---

[62] The fact that Bryant comments on this trail at the west foot of the Cedar Mountains may indicate some variance from the Frémont trail in surmounting the range.

Descending the precipitous elevation upon which we stood, we entered upon the hard smooth plain we had just been surveying with so much doubt and interest, composed of bluish clay, incrusted, in wavy lines, with a white saline substance, the first representing the body of the water, and the last the crests and froth of the mimic waves and surges. Beyond this we crossed what appeared to have been the beds of several small lakes, the waters of which have evaporated, thickly incrusted with salt, and separated from each other by small mound-shaped elevations of a white, sandy, or ashy earth, so imponderous that it has been driven by the action of the winds into these heaps, which are constantly changing their positions and their shapes. Our mules waded through these ashy undulations, sometimes sinking to their knees, at others to their bellies, creating a dust that rose above and hung over us like a dense fog.

From this point on our right and left, diagonally in our front, at an apparent distance of thirty or forty miles, high isolated mountains rise abruptly from the surface of the plain [the Silver Island Range]. Those on our left were as white as the snow-like face of the desert, and may be of the same composition, but I am inclined to the belief that they are composed of white clay, or clay and sand intermingled.

The mirage, a beautiful phenomenon I have frequently mentioned as exhibiting itself upon our journey, here displayed its wonderful illusions, in a perfection and with a magnificence surpassing any presentation of the kind I had previously seen. Lakes, dotted with islands and bordered by groves of gently waving timber, whose tranquil and limpid waves reflected their sloping banks and the shady islets in their bosoms, lay spread out before us, inviting us, by their illusory temptations, to stray from our path and enjoy their cooling shades and refreshing waters. These fading away as we advanced, beautiful villas, adorned with edifices, decorated with all the ornaments of suburban architecture, and surrounded by gardens, shaded walks, parks, and stately avenues, would succeed them, renewing the alluring invitation to repose, by enticing the vision with more than Calypsan enjoyments or Elysian pleasures. These melting from our view as those before, in another place a vast city, with countless columned edifices of marble whiteness, and studded with domes, spires, and turreted towers, would rise upon the horizon of the plain, astonishing us with its stupendous grandeur and sublime magnificence. But it is in vain to attempt a description of these singular and extraordinary phenomena. Neither prose or poetry, nor the pencil of the artist, can adequately portray their beauties. The whole distant view around, at this point, seemed like the creations of a sublime and gorgeous dream, or the effect of enchantment. I observed that where these appearances were presented in their most varied forms, and with the most vivid distinctness, the surface of the plain was broken, either by chasms hollowed out from the action of the winds, or by undulations formed of the drifting sands.

About eleven o'clock we struck a vast white plain, uniformly level, and utterly destitute of vegetation or any sign that shrub or plant had ever existed above its snow-like surface. Pausing a few moments to rest our mules, and moisten our mouths and throats from the scant supply of beverage in our powder-keg, we entered upon this appalling field of sullen and hoary desolation. It was a scene so entirely new to us, so frightfully forbidding and unearthly in its aspects, that all of us, I believe, though impressed with its sublimity, felt a slight shudder of apprehension. Our mules seemed to sympathize with us in the pervading sentiment, and moved forward with reluctance, several of them stubbornly setting their faces for a countermarch.

For fifteen miles the surface of this plain is so compact, that the feet of our animals, as we hurried them along over it, left but little if any impression for the guidance of the future traveller. It is covered with a hard crust of saline and alkaline substances combined, from one-fourth to one-half of an inch in thickness, beneath which is a stratum of damp whitish sand and clay intermingled. Small fragments of white shelly rock, of an inch and a half in thickness, which appear as if they once composed a crust, but had been broken by the action of the atmosphere or the pressure of water rising from beneath, are strewn over the entire plain and imbedded in the salt and sand.

As we moved onward, a member of our party in the rear called our attention to a gigantic moving object on our left, at an apparent distance of six or eight miles. It is very difficult to determine distances accurately on these plains. Your estimate is based upon the probable dimensions of the object, and unless you know what the object is, and its probable size, you are liable to great deception. The atmosphere seems frequently to act as a magnifier; so much so, that I have often seen a raven perched upon a low shrub or an undulation of the plain, answering to the outlines of a man on horseback. But this object was so enormously large, considering its apparent distance, and its movement forward, parallel with ours, so distinct, that it greatly excited our wonder and curiosity. Many and various were the conjectures (serious and facetious) of the party, as to what it might be, or portend. Some thought it might be Mr. Hudspeth, who had concluded to follow us; others that it was some cyclopean nondescript animal, lost upon the desert; others that it was the ghost of a mammoth or Megatherium wandering on "this rendezvous of death;" others that it was the d——l mounted on an Ibis, &c. It was the general conclusion, however, that no animal composed of flesh and blood, or even a healthy ghost, could here inhabit. A partner of equal size soon joined it, and for an hour or more they moved along as before, parallel to us, when they disappeared, apparently behind the horizon.

As we proceeded, the plain gradually became softer, and our mules sometimes sunk to their knees in the stiff composition of salt, sand, and clay. The travelling at length became so difficult and fatiguing to our animals that several of the party dismounted, (myself among the number,) and we consequently slackened our hitherto brisk pace into a walk. About two o'clock, P.M., we discovered through the smoky vapor the dim outlines of the mountain [Pilot Range] in front of us, at the foot of which was to terminate our day's march, if we were so fortunate as to reach it. But still we were a long and weary distance from it, and from the "grass and water" which we expected there to find. A cloud rose from the south soon afterwards, accompanied by several distant peals of thunder, and a furious wind, rushing across the plain and filling the whole atmosphere around us with the fine particles of salt, and drifting it in heaps like the newly fallen snow. Our eyes became nearly blinded and our throats choked with the saline matter, and the very air we breathed tasted of salt.

During the subsidence of this tempest, there appeared upon the plain one of the most extraordinary phenomena, I dare to assert, ever witnessed. As I have before stated, I had dismounted from my mule, and turning it in with the *caballada*, was walking several rods in front of the party, in order to lead in a direct course to the point of our destination. Diagonally in front, to the right, our course being west, there appeared the figures of a number of men and horses, some fifteen or twenty. Some of these figures were mounted and others dismounted, and appeared to be marching on foot. Their faces and the heads of the horses were turned towards us, and at first they appeared as if they were rushing down upon us. Their apparent distance, judging from the horizon, was from three to five miles. But their size was not correspondent, for they seemed nearly as large as our own bodies, and consequently were of gigantic stature. At the first view I supposed them to be a small party of Indians (probably the Utahs) marching from the opposite side of the plain. But this seemed to me scarcely probable, as no hunting or war party would be likely to take this route. I called to some of our party nearest to me to hasten forward, as there were men in front, coming towards us. Very soon the fifteen or twenty figures were multiplied into three or four hundred, and appeared to be marching forward with the greatest action and speed. I then conjectured that they might be Capt. Frémont and his party with others, from California, returning to the United States by this route, although they seemed to be too numerous even for this. I spoke to Brown, who was nearest to me, and asked him if he noticed the figures of men and horses in front? He answered that he did, and that he had observed the same appearance several times previously, but that they had disappeared, and he believed them to be optical illusions similar to the mirage. It was then, for the first time, so perfect was the deception, that I conjectured the probable fact that these figures were the reflection of our own images by the atmosphere, filled as it was with fine particles of crystallized matter, or by the distant horizon, covered by the same substance. This induced a more minute observation of the phenomenon, in order to detect the deception, if such it were. I noticed a single figure, apparently in front in advance of all the others, and was struck with its likeness to myself. Its motions, too, I thought, were the same as mine. To test the hypothesis above suggested, I wheeled suddenly around, at the same time stretching my arms out to their full length, and turning my face sidewise to notice the movements of this figure. It went through precisely the same motions. I then marched deliberately and with long strides several paces; the figure did the same. To test it more thoroughly, I repeated the experiment, and with the same result. The fact then was clear. But it was more fully verified still, for the whole array of this numerous shadowy host in the course of an hour melted entirely away, and was no more seen. The phenomenon, however, explained and gave the history of the gigantic spectres which appeared and disappeared so mysteriously at an earlier hour of the day. The figures were our own shadows, produced and reproduced by the mirror-like composition impregnating the atmosphere and covering the plain. I cannot here more particularly explain or refer to the subject. But this phantom population springing out of the ground as it were, and arraying itself before us as we traversed this dreary and heaven-condemned waste, although we were entirely convinced of the cause of the apparition, excited those superstitious emotions so natural to all mankind.

About five o'clock, P.M., we reached and passed, leaving it to our left, a small *butte* rising solitary from the plain [Floating Island]. Around this the ground is uneven, and a few scattering shrubs, leafless and without verdure, raised themselves above the white sand and saline matter, which seemed recently to have drifted so as nearly to conceal them. Eight miles brought us to the northern end of a short range of mountains [Silver Island], turning the point of which and bending our course to the left, we gradually came upon higher ground, composed of compact volcanic gravel. I was here considerably in the rear, having made a detour toward the base of the *butte* and thence towards the centre of the short range of mountains, to discover, if such existed, a spring of water. I saw no such joyful presentation nor any of the usual indications,[63] and when I reached and turned the point, the whole party were several miles ahead of me, and out of sight. Congratulating myself that I stood once more on terra firma, I urged my tired mule forward with all the life and activity that spur and whip could inspire her with, passing down the range of mountains on my left some four or five miles, and then rising some rocky hills connecting this with a long and high range of mountains on my right. The distance across these hills is about seven or eight miles. When I had reached the most elevated point of this ridge the sun was setting, and I saw my fellow-travellers still far in advance of me, entering again upon a plain or valley of salt, some ten or twelve miles in breadth. On the opposite side of this valley rose abruptly and to a high elevation another mountain [Pilot Peak], at the foot of which we expected to find the spring of fresh water that was to quench our thirst, and revive and sustain the drooping energies of our faithful beasts.

About midway upwards, in a *cañada* of this mountain, I noticed the smoke of a fire, which apparently had just been kindled, as doubtless it had been, by Indians, who were then there, and had discovered our party on the white plain below; it being the custom of these Indians to make signals by fire and smoke, whenever they notice strange objects. Proceeding onward, I overtook an old and favorite pack-mule, which we familiarly called "Old Jenny." She carried our meat and flour—all that we possessed in fact as a sustenance of life. Her pack had turned, and her burden, instead of being on her back was suspended under her belly. With that sagacity and discre-

---

[63] There are two seeps in the Silver Island Range, but so cursory a search would hardly find them.

tion so characteristic of the Mexican pack-mule, being behind and following the party in advance, she had stopped short in the road until some one should come to rearrange her cargo and place it on deck instead of under the keel. I dismounted and went through, by myself, the rather tedious and laborious process of unpacking and repacking. This done, "Old Jenny" set forward upon a fast gallop to overtake her companions ahead, and my own mule, as if not to be outdone in the race, followed in the same gait. "Old Jenny," however, maintained the honors of the race, keeping considerably ahead. Both of them, by that instinct or faculty which mules undoubtedly possess, had scented the water on the other side of the valley, and their pangs of extreme thirst urged them forward at this extraordinary speed, after the long and laborious march they had made, to obtain it.

As I advanced over the plain—which was covered with a thicker crust of salt than that previously described, breaking under the feet of the animals like a crust of frozen snow—the spreading of the fires in the *cañada* of the mountain appeared with great distinctness. The line of lights was regular like camp-fires, and I was more than half inclined to hope that we should meet and be welcomed by an encampment of civilized men—either hunters, or a party from the Pacific bound homewards. The moon shone out about nine o'clock, displaying and illuminating the unnatural, unearthly dreariness of the scenery.

"Old Jenny" for some time had so far beat me in the race as to be out of my sight, and I out of the sound of her footsteps. I was entirely alone, and enjoying, as well as a man could with a crust of salt in his nostrils and over his lips, and a husky mouth and throat, the singularity of my situation, when I observed, about a quarter of a mile in advance of me, a dark, stationary object standing in the midst of the hoary scenery. I supposed it to be "Old Jenny" in trouble once more about her pack. But coming up to a speaking distance, I was challenged in a loud voice with the usual guard-salutation, "Who comes there?" Having no countersign, I gave the common response in such cases, "A friend." This appeared to be satisfactory, for I heard no report of pistol or rifle, and no arrow took its soundless flight through my body. I rode up to the object and discovered it to be Buchanan sitting upon his mule, which had become so much exhausted that it occasionally refused to go along, notwithstanding his industrious application of the usual incentives to progress. He said that he had supposed himself to be the "last man," before "Old

Jenny" passed, who had given him a surprise, and he was quite
thunderstruck when an animal, mounted by a man, came charging
upon him in his half-crippled condition. After a good laugh and
some little delay and difficulty, we got his mule under way again, and
rode slowly along together.

We left, to us, in our tired condition, the seemingly interminable
plain of salt, and entered upon the sagey slope of the mountain about
10 o'clock. Hallooing as loudly as we could raise our voices, we obtained, by a response, the direction of our party who had preceded
us, and after some difficulty in making our way through the sage,
grass, and willows, (the last a certain indication of water in the
desert,) we came to where they had discovered a faint stream of water, and made their camp. Men and mules on their first arrival, as we
learned, had madly rushed into the stream and drank together of its
muddy waters,—made muddy by their own disturbance of its shallow
channel and sluggish current.[64]

Delay of gratification frequently gives a temporary relief to the
cravings of hunger. The same remark is applicable to thirst. Some
hours previously I had felt the pangs of thirst with an acuteness almost amounting to an agony. Now, when I had reached the spot
where I could gratify my desires in this respect, they were greatly
diminished. My first care was to unsaddle my mule and lead it to the
stream, and my next to take a survey of the position of our encampment. I then procured a cup of muddy water, and drank it with a
good relish. The fires before noticed were still blazing brightly above
us on the side of the mountain, but those who had lighted them, had
given no other signal of their proximity. The moon shone brilliantly,
and Jacob, Buchanan, McClary, and myself, concluded we would
trace the small stream of water until we could find the fountain
spring. After considerable search among the reeds, willows, and luxuriant grass, we discovered a spring. Buchanan was so eager to obtain
a draught of cold, pure water, that in dipping his cup for this purpose, the yielding weeds under him gave way, and he sank into the
basin, from which he was drawn out after a good "*ducking*," by one of
those present. The next morning this basin was sounded to the depth
of thirty-five feet, and no bottom found. We named this spring

---

[64] The now-dry Pilot Peak Creek on the present TL Bar Ranch (once the
Pete McKellar Ranch and originally the Cummings Ranch) at the eastern base of
Pilot Peak. Although Pilot Peak itself is in Nevada, the springs that break out be-
low it all are on the Utah side of the boundary line between the two states.

"Buchanan's well."[65] We lighted no fires to-night, and prepared no evening meal. Worn down by the hard day's travel, after relieving our thirst we spread our blankets upon the ground, and laying our bodies upon them, slept soundly in the bright moonshine. Several of our party had been on the road upwards of seventeen hours, without water or refreshment of any kind, except a small draught of cold coffee from our powder-keg, made of the salt sulphur-water at our last encampment, and had travelled the distance of seventy-five miles. The Salt Plain has never at this place, so far as I could understand, been crossed but twice previously by civilized men, and in these instances two days were occupied in performing the journey.[66] Distance 75 miles.

August 4.—We did not rise from our grassy couches this morning until the sun shone broadly and bright upon us, above the distant mountain ridges to the east. The scene around, with the exception of the small but highly fertile oasis encircling our encampment, is a mixture of brown and hoary barrenness, aridity, and desolation, of which no adequate conception can be conveyed by language. The fires in the *cañada* of the mountain were still smoking, but no blaze was discernible. Last night they appeared as if not more than half a mile or a mile distant but considerably to our surprise this morning, by a daylight observation, we saw that the *cañada*, from whence the smoke was curling upwards in graceful wreaths, was some four or five miles from us.

Our first care was to look after and collect together the animals, which, upon our arrival last night, we had let loose to refresh themselves in the manner most agreeable to them. We found them busily employed in cropping the tall seeded grass of the oasis. The anxieties respecting the health, strength, and safety of our animals, constitute one of the most considerable drawbacks upon the pleasures of our trip,—pleasures, as the reader may suppose, derived almost exclusively from the sublime and singular novelties presented to the vision. The significance of the word is in no other respect applicable to this stage of our journey. To fathom the motives of an all-wise Providence, in creating so vast a field of desolation; to determine in our minds whether the little oases we meet with are the beginnings of a system or process of fertilization which is to ramify and extend, and to render this hitherto abandoned and uninhabitable waste a garden

[65] Now called Pilot or Donner Spring.
[66] Bryant is referring to the Frémont and the Clyman parties.

of flowers, teeming with its millions of life; or whether they are evidences of the last expiring struggles of nature to sustain animal and vegetable existence, which will leave this expansive region impenetrable to the curiosity of man, furnish a study for the thoughts, fruitful of interest and provocative of investigation.

For the purpose of resting and recruiting our over-labored mules, we had predetermined to remain encamped to-day. We cleared away with our hands and willow sticks the thickly-matted grass and weeds around "Buchanan's well," making a handsome basin, some five or six feet in diameter. The water is very cold and pure, and tasted to us more delicious than any of the invented beverages of the epicure to him. While engaged in this work, Brown brought forward a remarkable blade of grass which he had pulled up a short distance from us, to which he called my attention, and desired its measurement. It was measured and found to be thirty-five feet in length. The diameter of the stalk was about half of an inch, and the distance between the joints about eighteen inches. It was heavily seeded at the top. With this prodigiously tall vegetable production, we endeavored to sound the depth of the spring; but after thrusting it down to its full length we could discover no bottom.

In the afternoon we saw two antelopes above us. Col. Russell and Miller saddled their mules and rode further up the slope of the mountain, for the purpose of hunting and to make other discoveries. During their absence a very dark cloud rose from the west, accompanied by distant thunder and a strong wind. The indications, judging as we would of the signs on the Atlantic side of the continent, were that we should have a heavy shower of rain; but our experience in this dry region had been such, that we felt but little dread of all the waters in the clouds. A few sprinkling drops of rain fell; just enough to leave a scarcely perceptible moisture upon the grass. Col. R. and M. returning, reported that they had killed no game. They found a small running stream of water from the *cañada* where the fires were burning, which sank in the sands and debris of the mountain before it reached the valley; and they also saw three Indian huts, constructed of cedars and grass, but unoccupied. The occupants of these huts, doubtless, after making their signal-fires upon discovering us, had all fled. Their probable motive for inhabiting temporarily this dismal region, was to trap for the few animals which roam in the neighborhood of the spring, and are compelled to approach it for water and grass.

During the course of our journey, nothing has contributed so largely to the depression of the spirits of our small party as inaction. I found to-day that the absence of our usual active employments, added to the desolate aspect of the scenery surrounding us, had produced much despondency in the minds of several of our company; and I felt a strong desire myself to be moving forward, to throw off those formidable mental incubi, ennui and melancholy.

August 5.—A most delightful, clear morning, with a light, soft breeze from the south fanning the parched and arid desert, playing over the waving grass, and sporting with the silvery leaves of the willows of the oasis.

Our mules, notwithstanding the day's rest we had allowed them after the long and laborious ride over the Salt Plain, evinced much stiffness and exhaustion. We took a southwest course along the slope of the range of mountains under which we had encamped. This slope is covered with a debris of gravel and sharp fragments of dark volcanic rock, and is furrowed from the base of the mountains down to the verge of the plain with deep and almost impassable ravines. The hoary and utterly desolate plain of salt on our left expands in breadth, and stretches, interminably to the eye, away to the southeast and the southwest. The brisk breeze having cleared the atmosphere of the smoke, our view is much more extensive than it was yesterday.

After travelling about ten miles we struck a wagon-trail, which evidently had been made several years [before?].[67] From the indentations of the wheels, where the earth was soft, five or six wagons had passed here. The appearance of this trail in this desolate region was at first inexplicable; but I soon recollected that some five or six years ago an emigrating expedition to California was fitted out by Colonel Bartlettson, Mr. J. Chiles, and others, of Missouri, who, under the guidance of Captain Walker, attempted to enter California by passing

---

[67] The trail made by the eight wagons of the Bidwell-Bartleson party of 1841, the first immigrant train to California. See p. 4. Skirting the Salt Desert at its northwestern extremity, they had turned south along the east base of the Pilot Range to reach on September 14, 1841, the locality where Bryant's party came upon their trace. See Bidwell's *A Journey to California*, 19, and compare Lienhard's journal for August 24–25. Edward Kern recorded seeing the tracks on October 31, 1845. It would appear that the Bidwell-Bartleson party crossed the shoulder of Pilot Peak higher up than Frémont or Clyman, taking a west course toward Silver Zone Pass while Frémont traveled southwest to cross the Toano Range farther to the south. Clyman coming east on the same trail in 1846 apparently saw no evidence of their passing.

round the southern terminus of the Sierra Nevada; and that they were finally compelled to abandon their wagons and every thing they had, and did not reach their destination until they had suffered incredible hardships and privations.[68] This, it appeared to me, was evidently their trail; and old as it was, and scarcely perceivable, it was nevertheless some gratification to us that civilized human beings had passed here before, and left their mark upon the barren earth behind them. My conjectures, above stated, have been subsequently confirmed by a conversation with Mr. Chiles.

Following this old trail some two or three miles, we left it on the right, and crossed some low and totally barren hills, which appear to have been thrown up by the action of volcanic fires at no very remote period of geological history. They are composed of a white, imponderous earth, resembling ashes, intermingled with fragments of scoria, resembling the cinders from an iron-foundry, or a blacksmith's furnace. A vitreous gravel, or glass, was also thickly strewn over the surface, and glittered brightly in the sunbeams.

From these hills, changing our course more to the west, we descended into a spacious and level valley, about fifteen miles in width, and stretching north and south as far as the vision could penetrate [Tecoma Valley]. A continuous range of high mountains [Toano Range] bounds this valley on the west, and a broken and irregular range on the east. The only vegetation consists of patches of wild sage, and a shrub ornamented with a yellow flower, resembling the Scotch broom of our gardens. A considerable portion of the plain is covered with salt, or composed of a white, barren clay, so compact that our horses' hoofs scarcely left an impression upon it. Crossing this valley, we entered the range of mountains on the west of it by a narrow gorge, and following its windings, we reached the foot of the steep dividing ridge about six o'clock, P.M. Here we had expected to find water,[69] but the ravine was entirely dry, and the grass bordering it was brown and dead. An elevated *butte* of red sandstone towered upwards on our right, like the dome of some Cyclopean cathedral. On our left was a high but more sloping mountain; and in front, the steep and apparently impassable crest of the Sierra.

---

[68] Bryant here confuses the Bidwell-Bartleson party of 1841—of which, as he remarks, Joseph Chiles was a member—with the Chiles-Walker party of 1843. This second company did not traverse any part of the future Hastings Cutoff west of the Bear River.

[69] See the Clyman journal, note 14.

After a fruitless search for water at the bottom of the gorge, among the rocks and crevices of the ravine, I accidentally discovered, near the top of the mountain on our left, a few straggling and stunted cedars, and immediately beneath them a small patch of green shrubs, which I conjectured were willows, a most welcome indication of water, after a ride of eleven hours without rest or refreshment of any kind. Dismounting from my mule, and accompanied by McClary, I ascended the mountain as far up as the little green oasis, in the centre of which, much to our joy, we found a small spring. No water flowed from its basin, although the ground immediately around was damp, and the grass green and luxuriant. Our party was soon apprized of the discovery, and following us up the mountain, we made our camp near the spring, which the mules soon completely exhausted of its scant supply of water, without obtaining sufficient to quench their thirst.

Ascending to the summit of the mountain, just as the sun was setting, I had a more extended view of the great Salt Plain than at any time previously. Far to the southeast apparently from one hundred to one hundred and fifty miles, a solitary mountain of immense height rises from the white surface of the desert, and lifts its hoary summit so as almost to pierce the blue ceiling of the skies, reflecting back from its frozen pinnacle, and making frigid to the eye the warm and mellow rays of the evening sun [Wheeler Peak?]. No words can describe the awfulness and grandeur of this sublime desolation. The only living object I saw to-day, and the only sign of animal existence separate from our party, was a small lizard.

About three o'clock, P.M., while we were on the march, a violent storm of wind, with some rain, raged in the valley [Tecoma Valley] to the south of us, raising a dense cloud of dust, which swept furiously up the eastern side of the valley in drifting masses that would have suffocated us, had we been travelling within its range. Fortunately, we were beyond the more disagreeable effects of the storm, although where we were the wind blew so violently as almost to dismount us from our horses.

We grazed our mules on the dry grass along the ravine below us, until nine o'clock, when they were brought up and picketed around the camp, as usual. The basin of the spring was enlarged so as to hold water enough, when filled, to satisfy the wants of our mules in the morning. These matters all being attended to, we bivouacked on the side of the mountain. Distance 30 miles.[70]

August 6.—The knowledge that our mules had fared badly, and were in a position, on the steep side of the mountain, where they could neither obtain good rest nor food, kept me more wakeful than usual. The heaviest calamity that could befall us, at this time, would be the loss, by exhaustion or otherwise, of our animals. Our condition in such an event would be deplorable. I rose at two o'clock, and having first filled all our buckets and vessels with water from the spring, let the mules loose to satisfy their thirst. One of them I found tangled in its rope, thrown down, and strangled nearly to suffocation.

The night was perfectly serene. Not a cloud, or the slightest film of vapor, appeared on the face of the deep blue canopy of the heavens. The moon and the countless starry host of the firmament exhibited their lustrous splendor in a perfection of brilliancy unknown to the night-watchers in the humid regions of the Atlantic; illuminating the numberless mountain peaks rising, one behind the other, to the east, and the illimitable desert of salt that spread its wintry drapery before me, far beyond the reach of the vision, like the vast winding-sheet of a dead world! The night was cold, and kindling a fire of the small, dead willows around the spring, I watched until the rich red hues of the morning displayed themselves above the eastern horizon, tinging slightly at first, and then deepening in color, the plain of salt, until it appeared like a measureless ocean of vermilion, with here and there a dark speck, the shadow of some solitary *buttes*, representing islands, rising from its glowing bosom. The sublime splendors of these scenes cannot be conveyed to the reader by language.

As soon as it was light, I saddled my mule, and ascended to the crest of the ridge to observe the features of the country, and determine our route for the day. I returned just as our morning meal was prepared, and at seven o'clock we were all in our saddles and on the march. We passed around the side of the mountain on which we had encamped, and rose gradually to the summit of the range. Here we were delayed for some time in finding a way to descend [west slope of Toano Range]. There are several gorges or ravines leading down, but they appeared to be choked up with rocks and brush so as to render them nearly impassable.

------

[70] Clyman's estimated mileage for the equivalent section of his trail was 22 miles. Bryant traveled in less of a direct line and started farther north, which may account for the difference.

In searching to find a passage presenting the fewest difficulties, I discovered, at the entrance of one of these gorges, a remarkable picketing or fence, constructed of the dwarf cedars of the mountain, interlocked and bound together in some places by willow withes. It was about half a mile in length, extending along the ridge, and I supposed it at the time to have been constructed for defensive purposes, by some of the Indian tribes of this region, against the invasion of their enemies. At the foot of the mountain there was another picketing of much greater extent, being some four or five miles in length, made of the wild sage; and I have since learned from trappers that these are erected by the Indian for the purpose of intercepting the hares, and other small game of these regions, and assisting their capture.

We descended the mountain through a very narrow gorge, the rocky walls of which, in many places, are perpendicular, leaving us barely room to pass. Emerging from this winding but not difficult passage, (compared with our former experience,) another spacious and level valley or plain spread itself before us [Gosiute Valley]. The breadth of this valley is about twenty miles, and its length, judging from the apparent distance of the mountains which exhibit their summits at either end, is about one hundred and fifty miles. The plain appears to be an almost perfect level, and is walled in by ranges of mountains on both sides, running nearly north and south. Wild sage, grease-wood, and a few shrubs of a smaller size, for the most part leafless, and apparently dead or dying, are the only vegetation of this valley. The earth is composed of the same white and light composition, heretofore described as resembling ashes, imbedded in and mixed with which is a scorious gravel. In some places it is so soft that the feet of our animals sink several inches; in others it is baked, and presents a smooth and sometimes a polished surface, so hard that the hoofs of our mules leave but a faint impression upon it. The snowy whiteness of the ground, reflecting back the bright and almost scorching rays of the sun, is extremely painful to the eyes, producing in some instances temporary blindness.

About two o'clock, P.M., after travelling three-fourths the distance across the valley, we struck an oasis of about fifty acres of green grass, reeds, and other herbage, surrounding a number of springs, some of cool fresh water, others of warm sulphur water. These waters rise here, and immediately sink in the sands [Flowery Lake]. Our information at Fort Bridger led us to expect a spring and grass at this point, and in order to make sure of it, we extended the flanks of our small party some three or four miles from the right to the left. The grass immediately around the springs, although not of the best quality, is very luxuriant, and on the whole, it being a favorable place for grazing our mules,—no apprehensions being entertained of their straying, or of Indian depredations,—we determined to encamp for the day.

In the course of our march to-day, we saw three hares, and near the spring, Miller saw an antelope. McClary and Brookey each killed a duck in one of the basins of the spring soon after our arrival, and later in the afternoon Brown killed a hawk. The signs of animals around the springs are numerous, and the wolves [coyotes] were howling near our camp until a late hour of the night. Distance 18 miles.

August 7.—A disagreeable altercation took place between two members of our party about a very trivial matter in dispute, but threatening fatal consequences. Under the excitement of angry emotions, rifles were levelled and the click of the locks, preparatory to discharging the death-dealing contents of the barrels, was heard. I rushed between the parties and ordered them to hold up their pieces, and cease their causeless hostility towards each other. I told them that the life of every individual of the party was, under the circumstances in which we were placed, the property of the whole party, and that he who raised a gun to take away a life, was, perhaps inconsiderately, worse than a common enemy or a traitor to all of us, and must be so considered in all future controversies of this nature, and be denied all further intercourse with us. It was truly a startling spectacle, to witness two men, in this remote desert, surrounded by innumerable dangers, to guard against which they were mutually dependent, so excited by their passions as to seek each other's destruction. The ebullition of insane anger was soon allayed, and we commenced our day's march about the usual hour of the morning.[71]

Our course was due west, and after travelling some four or five miles, we commenced the ascent of the range of mountains in our front [Pequop Mountains]. We ascended and descended this range through winding *cañadas* such as I have previously described [Jasper Pass]. Another spacious valley or plain opened to our view from the western side of this sierra, nearly as large in dimensions as that which we entered upon and partly crossed yesterday, and varying but little from it in its general characteristics [Independence Valley]. Crossing

---

[71] See the Reed journal, note 45.

this valley, the sun pouring its scorching rays down upon us with such fervor as nearly to parch our bridle reins into a crisp, we found on the slope of the western side, near the foot of the mountain, another small oasis, of an acre or two of green vegetation, near the centre of which were one or two small springs or wells of cool fresh water. The waters of these springs [Mound Springs] rise to the surface and sink immediately, moistening only the small patch of fertile ground which I have described.

Refreshing ourselves and our animals with the most grateful beverage of this fountain of the desert, we pursued our wearisome journey over the next sierra [north slope of Spruce Mountain], through a narrow gap, which brought us into another broad valley of an oval shape [Clover Valley], walled in on all sides, apparently, by an elliptical circle of elevated mountains. The hue of the wild sage and grease-wood of this valley, is a shade greener than in the other valleys we have crossed since we entered the Desert Basin. The composition of the earth is nearly the same. A fine white sand, impalpable almost as ashes, mingled with which is a scorious gravel, in some places soft and yielding to the hoofs of our mules, in others baked and compact almost to the hardness of brick, are the leading characteristics of the *soil*, if soil it can be called.

Fifteen miles brought us to the slope of the mountain on the western side of this valley, where we found a bold spring gushing forth a volume of water sufficient to turn the most powerful mill-wheel, but like all the other springs of this desert which we have seen, after running a short distance, the water sinks and disappears in the thirsting sands.[72] Around this spring there are a few small willows and a luxuriant growth of grass, with some handsome yellow flowers. Here we encamped at six o'clock, after a march of eleven hours, without rest to ourselves or our animals, which begin to manifest much fatigue and exhaustion.

The signs of game around our encampment are numerous, but nothing in the shape of bird or beast shows itself. In the course of our day's journey we started three hares, which are all of animal life that has been seen.

Nothing can exceed the grandeur and sublimity of these magnificent valleys, walled in by the tall and spiral mountains when

---

[72] The Warm Spring at which Clyman had encamped on May 23. The immigrants who followed Bryant on the trail were so much impressed with its flow that they named it Mill Spring. See the Jefferson map.

lighted as they now are, by the brilliant and powerful rays of the moon, and the sparkling radiance of the starry host, suspended as it were, like chandeliers from the deep, soft, blue canopy of the heavens. Their desolation is mellowed, and there is a purity, a holiness about them, which leads the imagination to picture them as vast salons of nature, fashioned by the hand of the Almighty for the residence of uncontaminating and unsinful essences, and not for the doomed children of passion, want, sorrow, and care! Should the economy of Providence, in the course of centuries, fertilize and adapt them to the residence of man, the fabled glories of Elysium would scarcely exceed their attractions. Distance 35 miles.

August 8.—The morning was clear and cool. A slight dew was perceptible on the grass and on our blankets. Our course to-day was nearly the same as yesterday. We passed over the range of mountains [East Humboldt Mountains] under which we had encamped, by ascending one of its most elevated peaks. When we reached the summit of this peak, after repeatedly stopping on the side of the mountain to breathe our mules, they seemed nearly exhausted and scarcely able to proceed on the journey. The descent on the western side was so steep and difficult, that our animals and ourselves (dismounted of course) slid or jumped down rather than walked. At the foot, we entered a small valley, with comparatively strong signs of fertility [north end of Ruby Valley]. A faint stream of water [Franklin River] runs through it, from north to south, the margin of which is fringed with green grass; and a few stunted cotton-wood trees and other shrubbery relieve the everlasting monotony of sage. The sight of these trees and of a stream of running fresh water, was more agreeable to us than can be conceived by those who have never been deprived of such scenic objects.

Crossing this stream and the bottom opposite, we passed through a low gap of a range of hills,[73] on the western side of which we struck

---

[73] Secret Pass, used by the Bidwell-Bartleson party in 1841 (their wagons having been abandoned in Gosiute Valley, at the first springs west of Pilot Peak), by Talbot's detachment of Frémont's party, and by Clyman. The route was rejected for wagons by Hastings when he came along a few weeks after Bryant, and Lt. Beckwith's journal indicates why. Pursuing his exploration for a Pacific railroad route, Beckwith reconnoitered Secret Pass on May 22, 1854. After crossing a branch of the Franklin River, Beckwith says, his party

> passed over spurs of hills descending from the pass, and in 2.05 miles came upon a small rill descending from the lowest point in its summit, which was but 0.84 mile distant, 1.15 miles below which we encamped

another small stream of water [Secret Creek], which flows through a fertile, grassy valley [Secret Valley], in a northwestern course. After descending this valley some five or six miles, the stream *cañons* between high and precipitous hills, along the sides and over the tops of which we were compelled to select our way to the best advantage, until we emerged into the spacious valley of Mary's [Humboldt] river, the sight of which gladdened our eyes about three o'clock, P.M.

At this point the valley is some twenty or thirty miles in breadth, and the lines of willows indicating the existence of streams of running water are so numerous and diverse, that we found it difficult to determine which was the main river and its exact course. After wandering about for some time, in compliance with the various opinions of the party, I determined to pursue a course due west, until we struck the river; and at sunset we encamped in the valley of the stream down which we had descended, in a bottom covered with most luxuriant and nutritious grass. Our mules fared most sumptuously both for food and water.

---

in a side ravine, finding it impracticable to descend with our wagons, on account of the miry character of the soil and of a rocky ravine, commencing 1.33 miles below camp, to the valley of Humboldt river, which lies directly west of this pass. Numerous small creeks descending from various parts of the pass unite, forming a stream five feet in depth, at present, above the head of the ravine, through which it descends with a rapid current to the valley below. Its banks in the ravine are lined with willows and a small growth of cotton-wood, and large fallen rocks obstruct its easy passage, did not the soft soil forbid it. The narrow part of the ravine is three miles in length, and its rocky sides very abrupt; and some parts, particularly near its head, rise vertically to the height of 40 and 60 feet. On the north side, immediately above these rocky walls, the mountain spurs are rolling, or intersected by ravines, and rise rapidly to a much greater height than they attain directly above the summit of the pass. They are easily ridden over, however, in any direction near the stream. On the south side these hills are more abrupt, both towards the stream and the east, and are more rocky and broken, the narrow ravines partaking slightly of the character of cañones. Below this the ravine opens and is easily accessible on horseback, although the mountains are still high above it for three miles, whence they subside gradually into the Humboldt valley on the south side of the stream; but on the north side, are terminated quite abruptly by a remarkable round bald butte, standing directly in front of the pass in looking eastward from the Humboldt river. From the summit of this butte the country to the west is seen to great advantage. The Humboldt valley is broad and open for 30 miles between its main branches which are seen descending from the north and south of this position. . . .

After dark, fires lighted by Indians were visible on the mountains through which we had passed, and in several places in the valley a few miles distant. Our watch, with which we had dispensed in crossing the desert, was set to-night, and it was fortunate for us that we were thus cautious, as an attempt was made by the Indians to steal our mules, which was frustrated by the man on duty at the time.

The mountains on either side of the valley of Mary's river at this point, tower upwards to a great elevation, and are composed of dark basalt. I noticed near the summits of some of the peaks, small patches of snow. Distance 23 miles.[74]

---

[74] The night's camp was about 7 miles above the mouth of Secret Creek, and the same distance southeast of Halleck, Nevada, where they would come into the established trail down Bishops Creek. Here, with however much regret, we take our leave of Bryant. With many interesting adventures, he and his companions made their way down the Humboldt and across the Sierra, on August 31 arriving at Sutter's as the first immigrants to reach California overland this year.

—*Charles Kelly photo, Utah State Historical Society*

WAGON RUINS AND OX BONES ON THE SALT DESERT

Artifacts on the Hastings Cutoff trace the route of the emigrant wagons across the salt.

—Charles Kelly photo, Utah State Historical Society

PILOT PEAK

Guiding point for all emigrants who crossed the Salt Desert.

THE JOURNAL OF HEINRICH LIENHARD

July 26–September 8, 1846

INTRODUCTION

Having followed the Bryant-Russell party the whole length of the Hastings Cutoff and seen them through to the relative security of the Humboldt Valley, we must return to Fort Bridger and take up the fortunes of the immigrants to whom Edwin Bryant said his farewells on the morning of July 20, 1846. The Harlan-Young company, with their wagons, are distinguished in having made the Hastings Cutoff a traveled road, and it was their example, when all is said, that induced the Donner party to enter so blithely upon the new route.

According to the story his nephew tells, George Harlan had probably known Hastings in Michigan in 1844, presumably having met him after Hastings' return from his visit to the Pacific. When, a year later, a copy of the *Emigrants' Guide* came into Harlan's hands, he concluded to sell his farm and migrate to California. The Harlans set out for the frontier in October, 1845, their party consisting at first of 14 persons—Harlan himself, his wife, his mother-in-law, then 90 years of age and blind, his two married daughters and their husbands, Ira and John Van Gordan, two younger children, two nephews, G. W. and Jacob W. Harlan, two nieces, Sarah and Malinda Harlan, and "some others." They were joined along the way by a Mr. Clark, and by spring had reached Westport, near Independence, prepared to begin the long journey.[1]

In Missouri the Harlan company was further enlarged to include Peter L. Wimmer and his family. Wimmer had married Harlan's daughter, Polly, and although he remarried after her death, taking the widow Elizabeth Jane (Cloud) Bays as his wife, he remained on cordial terms with his father-in-law. The addition of the Wimmers and their five children to the Harlan party is the more interesting in that they are said to have been Mormon converts, and thus were

---

[1] Jacob Wright Harlan, *California '46 to '88*, 20–28. The Mr. Clark mentioned may be William Squire Clark, or is perhaps the same Clark in whose presence J. Quinn Thornton interviewed the survivors of the Donner party at San Francisco in the fall of 1847.

among the small number of Saints privileged to inspect Salt Lake
Valley before Brigham Young arrived there with his Pioneers.[2]

When, in May, 1846, the intending California immigrants organized for the long journey, electing William H. Russell to be their
captain, George Harlan withdrew with his wagons, expressing the
conviction, as Edwin Bryant says, "that companies of moderate size
would travel with much more convenience and celerity than large
companies, and that his party added to those on the ground . . .
would render the train too unwieldy for convenience and progress.
This view was afterwards found to be entirely correct."[3]

The Harlan train organized separately, electing Judge Josiah
Morin of Jackson County, Missouri, as their captain when George
Harlan declined the command.[4] No daily diary recounting the ex-
periences of this company east of Fort Bridger has yet been found,
though Heinrich Lienhard and Jacob Wright Harlan later wrote
reminiscent accounts of some of their experiences along the way.
Their progress as far west as Fort Laramie may be followed, after a
fashion, through occasional allusions in the narratives of Edwin
Bryant and J. Quinn Thornton, and in the unpublished journal of
George McKinstry, Jr., all three of whom were traveling with the
Russell company. On May 12, 1846, McKinstry mentions that Harlan's 40 wagons had embarked upon the journey, slightly in advance
of the Russell company, and on June 23, having left the Russell wag-
ons to ride ahead to Fort Laramie, he remarks that he nooned "at
Harlens & Youngs camp east of the [Scotts] bluff."[5]

Aside from its date and place, McKinstry's notation of June 23 is
interesting for its association of the names Harlan and Young, indicating that the two families found one another congenial traveling
companions long before the question of a cutoff arose. The Ten-
nessee-born Samuel C. Young had moved to Western Missouri in

---

[2] See H. H. Bancroft, *History of California*, V, 778; VI, 29–31; W. W. Allen
and R. B. Avery, *The California Gold Book* (San Francisco, 1893), *passim*; and
The Pony Express, January, 1948. Mrs. Wimmer was cooking for the Mormon
Battalion veterans at Coloma at the time of the discovery of gold in 1848.

[3] Edwin Bryant, *What I Saw in California*, 31.

[4] Jacob Wright Harlan, *op. cit.*, 33.

[5] George McKinstry, Jr., Manuscript Diary, May 12–June 30, 1846, in the
Bancroft Library. If McKinstry kept a diary for the rest of the journey, it has
been lost. Because he traveled the Hastings Cutoff with one or another of the
companies which ventured upon it under Hastings' personal guidance, his finely
detailed journal would be a superlative source of information.

1831, and he started for California originally as a member of the Russell train. When that unwieldy company began to break up, the segment which has become known as Young's party apparently came to consist, besides himself, his wife, and his children, of "Arthur Caldwell, Mrs. Margaret Caldwell, John McCutchen, Mr. Buchalass, Joseph Gordon, Jacob Gordon, Duncan Dickenson, W. Hooper and wife"—all of these were men with families and from the same place—and four young men, "Jacob Ross, Simpson, McMonagill [William McDonald?] and one other."[6] It does not follow that all of these took the Hastings Cutoff; some may have separated from the others at the Little Sandy or Fort Bridger to go the Fort Hall route; but it is probable that the majority contributed their share to the digging down and chopping out of the new road.

The Harlan-Young company very likely reached Fort Bridger July 16, the same day as Edwin Bryant, for Jacob Harlan says they halted three days at the fort.[7] As with all other companies on the trail this year, the Harlan train had grown and diminished by turns as the dissatisfied broke away and others took their place. The original commander, Judge Morin, seemingly ended by going to Oregon,[8]

[6] "Biographical Obituary. Samuel C. Young—a Pioneer of 1846," *San Jose Pioneer*, November 9, 1878. One of the minor mysteries in the history of the Hastings Cutoff has been that until the entry in the McKinstry diary was found, no allusions to the Young party had appeared in the records of the year's immigration. A probable explanation is that references in various diaries and narratives to the Gordon family encompass the Youngs as well. Bryant mentions the Gordons in his journal on May 8: "we overtook ten emigrant wagons, with a numerous drove of cows and other stock. Most of these wagons are the property of Mr. Gordon, of Missouri, who, with his entire family, consisting of several sons and daughters, is removing to California." Sixteen days later he noted the fact when 13 wagons, "about half of which belonged to Mr. Gordon, of Jackson county, Mo.," separated from the Russell party. I am informed by Mr. Clyde Arbuckle, San Jose historian, that Joseph and Matilda (Henderson) Gordon migrated to California with a family of six sons and two daughters.

[7] Jacob Wright Harlan, *op. cit.*, 41. The letter of Dr. Long, printed in the introduction to the Bryant journal, fully supports this conclusion, for it speaks of Hastings as having been with the company for some time, and almost in the same breath mentions having reached Fort Bridger on July 16. Clearly, Hastings reached the fort in company with the Harlan-Young party.

[8] The homeward-bound James Clyman wrote in his diary on June 27, 1846:
    we met numerous squad of emigrants untill we reached fort Larrimie whare we met Ex govornor [Lilburn W.] Boggs and party from Jackson county Mi[ss]ourie Bound for California and we camped with them   several of us continued the conversation untill a late hour. And here I again obtained a cup of excellent coffee at Judge Morins camp

and if the train had any acknowledged captain other than Hastings himself when the wagons began to roll west of Fort Bridger, his name has not been preserved. It is established, however, that when the company left the fort, it numbered 40 wagons.[9] The biographical sketch of Samuel C. Young says that "four companies formed at [Fort Bridger], of about ten families to a company, to travel the Hastings' Cut-off,"[10] and it may be supposed that they averaged a wagon to a family. The Harlans constituted one of these four companies, the Youngs and Gordons apparently another, but the other two have not been even tentatively identified.

A journal of the company which left Fort Bridger on July 20 may yet be discovered, but for the present their experiences must be followed through the diaries of those who traveled a little behind them on the trail—in the present instance, through the journal of Heinrich Lienhard. A record of the highest importance, the Lienhard narrative has been remarkably neglected, attributable in some part to its having been written in German. A book version was published in Zurich in 1898, significant even in this drastically abridged form, but the book itself largely escaped notice, being printed in German. Now, for the first time, as they read the portion of his narrative here published, scholars can begin to appreciate Heinrich Lienhard's notable contribution to the history of the western trails.

---

the first I had tasted since in the early part of last winter and I fear that during our long conversation I changed the purposes of Governor and the Judge for next morning they both told me they inte[n]ded to go to Oregon

Next day Clyman moved along the trail as far as Fort Bernard, 8 miles east of Fort Laramie, and on the 29th recorded further:

29 Parted with some of my old acquaintances who ware on their way (to) some for Oregon and some for california   the Ex govornor Boggs and Judge Morin changed their notion to go to Oregon in place of california. . . .

Camp, ed., *James Clyman, American Frontiersman, 1792–1881*, 229–30.

Ex-governor Boggs did eventually go to California, though by the Fort Hall route. But Morin seems actually to have gone to Oregon. In addition to its other interest, Clyman's mention of Morin is important as the last definite date for the Harlan-Young party before Edwin Bryant found them at Fort Bridger—assuming, of course, that Morin himself had not already gone his own way, which is more than merely possible.

[9] See Dr. Long's letter, heretofore cited, and compare Bryant's entry for July 29, 1846.

[10] *San Jose Pioneer*, November 9, 1878.

This ingratiating young man was born January 19, 1822, at Uss-
buhl, Canton Glaurus, Switzerland. He sailed for America from
LeHavre, France, in September, 1843. After living for a time at
Highland, Illinois, near St. Louis, he sought unsuccessfully to take
up a land claim in Wisconsin. He worked at Galena and St. Louis,
and then seized an opportunity to set out for California in the spring
of 1846. It is that overland journey which makes the young Lienhard
so interesting and has brought him into these pages. On reaching
New Helvetia Lienhard became one of Sutter's most trusted men,
and in 1849 he was sent back to Switzerland to bring his employer's
family to America. Having accomplished that mission, he returned a
second time to Switzerland to marry Elsbeth Blumer. In 1854, however, he sold his home in a Zurich suburb and with his wife and
their two small children immigrated to Wisconsin. Two years later he
settled, by a peculiarly interesting historical coincidence, at Nauvoo,
Illinois, buying Heber C. Kimball's old home and 200 acres of
grazing and timber lands. There he lived until his death on December 19, 1903. Besides the two children born in Switzerland, seven
others were born in America.

About 1868, it is said, Lienhard began writing his memoirs,
completed some six years later as an enormous manuscript of 238 folios. One of his old Zurich friends, while on a visit to America, read
the manuscript, and was so impressed that he arranged to publish an
abridgment of it as a feature of the worldwide celebration of California's Golden Jubilee. The book appeared under the title *Californien
unmittelbar vor und nach der Entdeckung des Goldes* [California Immediately Before and After the Discovery of Gold] (Zurich: Fasi & Beer,
1898), and it was well enough received to require another edition two
years later.

Notwithstanding the publication of his reminiscences, Lienhard
remained an almost unknown figure. His book was translated as a
master's thesis by Reuben L. Spaeth at the University of California in
1914, but this thesis did not engage the attention of scholars. In 1939
students of German at C. K. McClatchy Senior High School in
Sacramento, California, translated the tenth chapter of Lienhard's
book, and under the title, *I Knew Sutter,* this was published in a small
edition at Sacramento in 1939. The following year the Swiss-Ameri-
can Historical Society published at Madison, Wisconsin, a compila-
tion entitled, *The Swiss in the United States,* which included a section
devoted to Lienhard, but with respect to his overland journey this

work contented itself with translating the chapter headings to Lienhard's book.

The Swiss pioneer began to emerge into the warm sun of scholarly enthusiasm with the publication of Marguerite Eyer Wilbur's *A Pioneer at Sutter's Fort, 1846–1850; the Adventures of Heinrich Lienhard* (Los Angeles: The Calafia Society, 1941). Not content to translate the book of 1898, Mrs. Wilbur succeeded in locating Lienhard's original manuscript in the possession of his children. Her translation was made directly from the manuscript and does full justice to Lienhard's life from the time he arrived at Sutter's Fort in October, 1846.

Considerations of space made it impossible for Mrs. Wilbur to include in her book Lienhard's account of his overland journey, which is certainly not outmatched in interest or importance by his reminiscences of life at Sutter's Fort. When Mr. Dale L. Morgan made inquiry of her about Lienhard's experiences on the overland trail, Mrs. Wilbur generously presented him with a copy of the Zurich book, and that marked the beginning of the complicated undertaking which is the present publication. Mr. Morgan lent the book to me, and with some effort, not having the same facility in German as my remote ancestors, I translated Chapters V, VI, and a portion of Chapter VII, the part of it dealing with Lienhard's experiences on the Hastings Cutoff. Mr. Morgan also lent the book to the LDS Church Historian's Office, for whom Mr. Frank I. Kooyman translated Lienhard's entire narrative, down to the point of beginning of Mrs. Wilbur's book. Mr. Kooyman's translation was compared with my own, and in anticipation of publication the finished text was read critically by Dr. Ernst Correll, professor of economic history at American University, Washington, D. C.

Mrs. Wilbur had provided information which meanwhile enabled Mr. Morgan to locate the original manuscript itself, in the hands of Lienhard's granddaughter, Mrs. E. J. Magnuson, of Minneapolis, Minn. The inquiries Mr. Morgan set on foot served to reawaken interest in the manuscript, and it was acquired by the Bancroft Library. Generously that library made available for study a photostatic copy of that part of the manuscript which relates to the Hastings Cutoff. It became at once apparent that the book of 1898 was a cruel abridgment of the original manuscript, reducing its proportions by fully one half, leaving out the entries for whole days, and omitting significant information even from the entries printed. Consequently it was necessary to start all over again. The Bancroft Library gave permission for the publication of so much of Lienhard's original manuscript as was concerned with the Hastings Cutoff, and a translation of these folios, by Mr. Morgan, again read critically by Dr. Correll, is the text now finally published. Specifically, the part of the manuscript here published extends from Folio 67, page 1, line 38, to Folio 73, page 4, line 33, comprising Lienhard's entries for July 26–September 7, 1846, with a part of that for September 8. Perhaps it should be added that as Lienhard has his own often highly original spellings of the names of his fellow travelers, where these names first occur they are printed as Lienhard wrote them and then corrected in brackets, but thereafter the names are properly spelled as a function of the translation. Lienhard had picked up a certain amount of English before setting out on the overland journey, so that occasional English words and phrases appear in his narrative, especially when he is quoting his fellow travelers or taking account of their point of view; to distinguish these English phrases in the translation, all are italicized.

The surpassing importance of the Lienhard narrative is that although it partakes somewhat of the character of reminiscences, it has the authority of a daily diary. As Lienhard explains in his narrative, he kept a diary from the first day of his journey, a part of which later was lost, in consequence of which his account as far as Fort Laramie is largely reminiscent. But from a point 7 miles west of Fort Laramie, and on as far as Donner Pass, covering the period June 26–October 5, 1846, Lienhard's travels are described on the basis of the original journal still in his possession in the 1870s. The narrative has some obvious, and therefore in no way troublesome, later additions, and doubtless has more of literary continuity than the diary itself possessed, but it is a faithful daily record, and introduces into the history of the Hastings Cutoff what has been a pressing want, a reliable chronology for the companies in advance of the Donner party. Nor is this all; it gives us a totally new insight into the ideas Hastings brought to his cutoff, shows him at work improving it, reveals how different the Donner story might have been, and as if this were not enough, explains and illuminates much that has been inexplicable in the remarkable map of T. H. Jefferson; study of the Lienhard journal develops the surprising fact that he traveled in company with Jefferson much of the way west from Fort Bridger.

The few reminiscent accounts that tell the story of the Harlan-Young party's crossing of the Salt Desert make clear the immense value of Lienhard's work. Let us quote the three source narratives upon which our knowledge of their experiences, up to the present, has depended. The first is from the obituary of Samuel C. Young:

Hastings had made them believe that the desert was but forty miles across. When they arrived there they made every preparation that the country and their circumstances would allow; they filled all their vessels full of water, procured all the grass they could take with them, to feed and sustain their stock; and when they had finished their preparations, they began their perilous journey in the evening and traveled all night, stopping now and then to rest and give the stock a little hay. Morning came at last; and such a sight! The sun arose in full splendor, reflecting his rays on this vast salt plain, as white as snow, and as far as the eye could reach not a thing to be seen, not a spear of grass or a drop of water, and the end could not be detected by the eye. The stock was showing signs of great fatigue; a little hay and some water revived them, and a cup of coffee and a cold snack had as good effect on the emigrants. It was a blessing that they were ignorant of what was in store for them. They were led to believe that they would reach water and grass by noon; full of hope they again started their jaded and trusted teams. They traveled until noon; the stock showing great distress, they stopped to feed them some grass and give them a little water, which comprised nearly all they had lain in. The emigrants by this time had become very much discouraged. The eye could not detect the end of the plain. But no time was to be lost, so they started again, in the midst of the glare of the sun at noon-day, upon this still vast, white, salt plain. Every mile traveled that evening produced its effect; oxen gave out and lay down, some to rise no more; others, from extreme thirst, became crazy and nothing could be done with them and finally they would become exhausted and drop down dead. From the middle of the evening, one disaster after disaster happened nearly every step of the way. Wagons were abandoned; such of the oxen as could travel were taken out and driven along, others would give up and lie down, even after the yoke was taken off, and neither persuasion nor the whip could make them budge. These misfortunes continued and increased during that evening, until it seemed as if all were lost. But night came at last; that at least shut off the reflection of the

sun. In the midst of all but despair they stopped to give the
last pound of grass to the surviving stock, and a few favorites
got a little water, and such as had wagons left went to them
and got out and ate and divided with others their frugal meal.
At last they started on their long night-tramp, hoping to get to
water and grass before morning. On they traveled, every mile
so full of disaster that the recital would fill pages; but they
struggled on through that long, dark, and lonely night, still
praying for water and grass, but morning was again ushered
in with the sun's reflection upon the white, salt plains, with
no signs of the end. The loss of stock through the night could
now be realized. A halt was ordered, a little rest was taken,
with a morsel to break the fast, and the order was given to
make the last effort to get through. From this until noon more
stock was lost than during the last twenty-four hours. At noon
they reached water and grass in a most worn-out and de-
spondent condition. Some of the teams were left; some as far
back as thirty miles. Water and grass were hauled back and
some of the stock saved and some of the wagons were brought
in; others were abandoned and it took many days to collect
everything together and get ready to start again. Here was
eighty-two miles of desert these emigrants had passed over,
instead of forty. Volumes could be written, on the suffering of
man and beast that occurred during this eighty-two mile
march across the desolate wastes. At last they reached St.
Mary's River with the loss of most of their stock, worn out and
greatly discouraged—to find that the Fort Hall emigrants had
passed on, three weeks ahead of them, posting notices of that
fact.[11]

Next let us place in the record Jacob Harlan's account, beginning at the point of emergence from Weber Canyon:

We ... continued on round the south end of the lake,
crossing the river Jordan, a small stream, which runs out of
Utah lake into Salt Lake. We passed many beautiful springs,
but on trial the water was found to be saltish, and we were
distressed by want of good water till we reached a range of
mountains, where we laid in a supply of fresh water for the
ninety-mile desert. We started on our passage over this desert

---

[11] *Ibid.*

in the early morning, trailed all day and all night, and all next day and next night, and on the morning of the third day our guide told us that water was still twenty-five miles distant. Our teams were so exhausted that they could not haul the wagons. We had to unyoke them and drive them to the water, and then back again to fetch the wagons. William Fowler here lost his seven yoke of oxen. The man who was in charge of them went to sleep, and the cattle turned back and re-crossed the desert—or perhaps died there. Thus he was left with his two wagons, and no teams to haul them. It was a hard case, as he had a large family with him. He had mar-ried my sister, Malinda, after we left Fort Bridger. Then he had his mother, a half brother, and three sisters, one of whom was a Mrs. Hargrave (wife of John Hargrave, who died and was buried here), and her four small children. Also he had with him two brothers named Musgrave, one of whom was his stepfather. The rest of our company helped him with teams, and he managed to keep with us.

After having passed the desert, we found it necessary to rest our animals for three days, they were so exhausted and spirit-broken.[12]

Finally, W. W. Allen and R. B. Avery tell us:

The route of the band was on the south side of Salt Lake and skirting the mountain so as to be sure of water. When the edge of the real desert was reached which was readily recog-nized . . . preparations were made for crossing the desolate wastes. Provided with an ample supply of water, and thor-oughly rested, the train started across, and was two days and nights almost uninterruptedly moving on before safety for the stock from thirst and starvation was reached.[13]

It would be gratifying if Lienhard's narrative could be studied with reference to the diary from which it was elaborated. However, Lienhard's granddaughter, Mrs. E. J. Magnuson, who has lent every assistance and encouragement to the present work, has been unable to trace it in any branch of her family, and herself knows nothing of the diary other than as Lienhard mentions it in his manuscript. The

---

[12] Harlan, *op. cit.*, 42–44.
[13] Allen and Avery, *op. cit.*, 65.

narrative itself is so picturesque and so enlightening that we will not complain of this one lack.

Having said so much of the document, let us provide some preface for the story it has to tell. Lienhard's attention had been fixed upon California, it seems, almost from the time he reached America. In the early spring of 1846 he happened to fall in with two of his fellow emigrants from Switzerland, Heinrich Thomen and Jacob Ripstein. They were in the midst of preparations to leave for California, and persuaded Lienhard to go with them. Two others joined subsequently, George Zins, a German from Lorraine, and Valentine Diel, another German from Darmstadt. The former, Lienhard says, was small but stout, somewhat of a joker but very touchy and even hottempered, though remorseful when he went too far. Diel had been in America several years and lately had run a cigar store in St. Louis. A few years older than Lienhard, he was physically strong but suffered from an ailment which made him unfit for physical exertion, and—at least in Lienhard's view—was not quite honest and straightforward. The five became known in the immigration as the "five German boys," a term Lienhard emphasizes by employing it in English in his German text.[14]

The five young men, Lienhard, Thomen, Ripstein, Zins, and Diel, had only one wagon among them, three span of young oxen, and two young cows. Through most of the journey, until far down the Humboldt, they traveled in close proximity to three other wagons. Two of these belonged to a Swiss, Samuel Kyburz, later Sutter's majordomo. Kyburz had an American wife and two children, and one of his wagons was driven for him by "his old but still vigorous and joyous father-in-law," John Barber. The third wagon was the property of Barber's sons, John and Samuel. This little company of four wagons underwent together all the vicissitudes consequent upon taking the Hastings Cutoff.

---

[14] Bancroft's "Pioneer Register and Index" supplies a few details as to the later lives of Lienhard's four companions. Thomen was subsequently a resident of Sacramento and San Francisco. Ripstein became a farmer in Yuba County. Zins built one of the first brick houses in Sacramento, and was for some years a manufacturer of bricks; he spent his last days on a ranch near Oakland, where he died in 1885. Diel was a grocer in San Francisco in the fifties and later a rancher near Mayfield, Calif., where he died about 1882. It is of some interest to note, as recorded by the *New Helvetia Diary*, that on June 20, 1847, Zins married Mrs. Wolfinger, one of the survivors of the Donner party.

Lienhard's group started from the frontier in the Harlan company, but on the Little Blue joined a company under G. D. Dickenson, an example soon followed by Kyburz, the Barbers, and Jacob D. Hoppe. The latter, whose name is rendered by Lienhard "Hapi" or "Hapy," was a Marylander who was to be prominent in California affairs until his death in a steamboat explosion in 1853. Lienhard says that Hoppe had killed a slave and thus had found it advisable to move across the Missouri line into the Indian Territory until the immigration of 1846 began to roll. He had a beautiful wife and three children, and on setting out, his entourage included a maidservant named Lucinda (who, as we shall see, achieved a certain notoriety along the way) and also a young man Lienhard calls Mike, who drove one of Hoppe's two wagons. Mike had left Hoppe's service before the arrival at Fort Bridger, and who took his place as driver is not known. This company of six wagons after a time separated from the Dickenson company as casually as it had united with it. Reinforced at Fort Bridger by several other wagons—with one of which our mysterious cartographer, T. H. Jefferson, apparently traveled—this little group became known to the rest of the immigration as "Hoppe's Company," although as Lienhard points out, Hoppe was not actually their captain. Lienhard and his fellow travelers reached the immigrant encampment on Blacks Fork, 2 miles below Fort Bridger, on July 23. Here for two days they rested their worn oxen, while they traded with the mountain men, giving alcohol, sugar, lead, and powder for skins and moccasins. The "five German boys" also seized the opportunity to trade their two dry cows to a red-headed mountain man, Miles Goodyear, for two more oxen.[15] Finally, on July 26, 1846, six days behind the Harlans, they set out on the new Hastings road. During those six days they had been preceded by several other companies, ranging in size from one to a dozen wagons. Lienhard lists the total, including the 40 wagons of the Harlans, as 52, but the Mathers diary gives the number who had reached Bear River by the night of July 25—two days before Lienhard reached that point—as 57 in all. There may or may not have been yet other wagons traveling one day behind Mathers and one day ahead of Lienhard, but it is quite clear that "Hoppe's company" was the last on the trail ahead of the Donner party, and their experiences are the more important for that reason.

Lienhard's story may now be given over to the diarist himself. Not, however, until I have expressed my gratitude and that of Mr.

---

[15] See the introduction to the Reed journal, note 13.

Morgan to Mr. Glen Dawson, Mrs. Marguerite Eyer Wilbur, Mrs. E. J. Magnuson, Mrs. Irene D. Paden, Mrs. Helen Harding Bretnor, Dr. Ernst Correll, Mr. Charles Kelly, Mr. Darel McConkey, Mr. A. William Lund, Mr. Frank I. Kooyman, and above all the Bancroft Library and its director, Dr. George P. Hammond, for their help in making it possible to publish the most significant part of the Lien- hard overland narrative in this, its most meaningful setting.

LIENHARD AS A YOUNG MAN

LIENHARD IN LATER YEARS

THE LIENHARD JOURNAL

Beyond Fort Britcher [Bridger] there are two roads, the old one past the so-called Soda Springs and Fort Hall, and a new one called Captain Hastings' Cutoff which is said to be much shorter and passes by the Great Salt Lake.[1] Many companies ahead of us already had chosen Hastings' Cutoff as their route, and we, too, thought it preferable.

On July 26 we finally broke camp again and entered upon the new road past the Fort, leaving the Fort Hall road to our right. After following the road through a rapid ascent we came to a dry valley, and having passed the rising ground found it again to descend a little. On the right, by the side of the road, scarcely 6 miles from the Fort, we came upon an ice-cold spring flowing out of the ground near a thicket.[2] We passed yet another spring into the right near the road, but camped by a brook, approximately 6 miles from the first spring and about 12 miles from the Fort. The stream [the Big Muddy] contained only a little water, but on the other hand we found enough grass for the draft animals here.[3]

---

[1] The point of divergence, as Bryant's journal and the Mormon diaries of 1847 make clear, was on Blacks Fork 2 miles below the Fort. Five of these diaries kept by members of the Mormon Pioneer party are hereafter quoted in clarifying the journals of Lienhard and Reed:

Clayton: *William Clayton's Journal* (Salt Lake City, 1921).

Lyman: Unpublished journal of Amasa Lyman, kept for him by Albert Carrington; typed transcription in the Utah State Historical Society's WPA collection.

Pratt: Journal of Orson Pratt, published in *L. D. S. Millennial Star*, XI–XII (1849–50); reprinted separately as *Exodus of Modern Israel* (Salt Lake City, [194–]).

Smith: Unpublished journal of George A. Smith, kept for him by Albert Carrington, and nearly identical with the Lyman journal; original in the LDS Archives.

Snow: Journal of Erastus Snow, published in *Improvement Era*, XIV–XV (1911–12); and again in part in *Utah Humanities Review*, II (April, July, 1948).

[2] See the Jefferson map and the spring it depicts (though to the left of the road) in "Cottonwood Valley." Jefferson also locates Sugar Loaf Hill, hereafter described in the Mormon journals. It will become evident as Lienhard's narrative progresses that he and Jefferson set out from Fort Bridger together and continued in company until the afternoon of August 5.

[3] The Mormon diaries give a somewhat more detailed picture of the country traveled over than do Lienhard or Reed, and are correspondingly helpful in establishing the exact routes traveled in 1846. The Mormon Pioneer party of

On the 27th, our road led through many hollows between rocky
hills, whereby we passed several springs of water, of which a few had
an unpleasant taste of mineral salts. Around one of these springs the
surface of the ground had taken on a rust color, from which it would
appear that the water contained iron. In these narrow, deep little
valleys through which the road wound, grass springs up everywhere
that water exists, but the grass was coarse in spots, like rushes. In the
evening, near sunset, after having traveled about 18 miles, we
reached the Bear River, where we camped.[4] In the afternoon Captain

---

course had the Hastings road to guide them west across the mountains; as Erastus Snow commented, "Fortunately for us a party of emigrants bound for the
coast of California passed this way last Fall, though their trail is now in many
places scarcely discernable."

The Mormons left their camping-place a half-mile south of Fort Bridger on
the morning of July 9, 1847, setting out "westward over pretty rough roads"
(Clayton). The road "continued gradually to ascend, and in 6 1/4 miles came to a
small brook [Cottonwood Creek], formed by a spring and melting snow, which
lay in places upon its banks" (Pratt). After resting their teams here, the Saints
moved on and in about three-quarters of a mile crossed the spring brook "near a
high square table mound [Sugar Loaf Butte], with thick beds of indurated green
clay, plenty of Quaking Asps & a few snow banks" (Lyman). Pulling up a long,
stony hill for about half a mile, they came out upon "an elevated sage plain
[Bigelow Bench]," a "comparatively level table land" across which they continued for 2 or 3 miles before descending "150 or 200 feet down a very steep hill"
(Pratt), this descent of the western slope of Bigelow Bench "the steepest and
most difficult we have ever met with, being long and almost perpendicular"
(Clayton). Having reached the base of the hill, the wagons wound their way
"down a hollow to a creek called *Muddy Fork* which here runs North and winds
round the hills to the North of Fort Bridger" (Snow). At the end of a 13-mile
journey, the Saints crossed the Muddy to encamp on its left bank. The better to
identify the place of crossing, Albert Carrington writes in the Lyman journal that
red mineral clay there cropped out in the bluffs, adding an evident description of
the stratification in these bluffs: "Grind & Sythe Stone r[ed] c[lay] 20 ft. 1 g[ray]
s[andstone] 15 r[ed] c[lay] 1 d[ark] s[andstone] 12 r[ed] c[lay] 20 g[reen] c[lay] 25
to 30 close on the right of the road as you cross Muddy going W."

From the above details, as also from the fact that on resuming the journey
next day the Mormon wagons did not have to pull over the ridge between the
Muddy and lower Antelope Creek which Edwin Bryant describes, it would seem
that the wagon road reached the Muddy perhaps a mile south of where old US
30S bridged it at Dog Springs, now one-half mile south of I-80. Hastings' road of
1846 thus ran southwest from Fort Bridger to where it climbed up on Bigelow
Bench, nearly west over the high table land, leaving Bridger Butte to the right,
and then a little north of west to the encampment on the west bank of the
Muddy. The wagons of 1843 apparently went down the steep western slope of
Bigelow Bench a mile or so south of where those of 1846 reached the Muddy.

[4] Lienhard's 18-mile figure for the day's travel was a revision of his first es-

timate, which was 17 miles, the same as Jefferson's. The quality of the detail in the Jefferson map for this day's journey is remarkable, especially when seen in the perspective the Mormon journals afford. The Mormon diaries for July 10, 1847, indicate that the first $3\,1/2$ miles west from the Muddy were very easy going; Orson Pratt alone takes note of any grade, observing that the road "commenced gradually to ascend." At the $3\,1/2$-mile mark, the Saints passed what William Clayton describes as "a small copperas spring at the foot of a mountain a little to the left of the road. The water is very clear but tastes very strong of copperas and alum and has a somewhat singular effect on the mouth. It runs a little distance over the red sand which abounds in this region and where it is saturated with water almost looks like blood at a little distance." Orson Pratt adds that the Saints called this spring "Red Mineral Spring," from the extreme redness of the soil out of which it issued. This spring, and the nearby Soda Spring, are located in the S. E. quarter of Sec. 18, T. 15 N., R. 117 W.

Beyond this point, the road the Mormon Pioneers were following crossed what Pratt calls "a ridge between two branches of Muddy Fork"—that is, the ridge between Soda Hollow and Pioneer Hollow (or Antelope Creek), one arm of which extended around to constrict the passage between Pioneer Hollow and Spring Valley. Clayton most clearly describes the road from this point on:

> After passing this spring the road winds around the foot of the mountains gradually ascending [Antelope Creek] for some distance till finally arriving on the summit of a high ridge. Here Elder Pratt took a barometrical observation and found the height to be 7,315 feet above the level of the sea. On arriving at the west side of the ridge two and a half miles from the last mentioned spring we found a very steep, rough place to descend and found it necessary to halt and fix the road. About half way down there is a place over huge rocks, leaving barely enough room for a wagon to get down, but by labor it was soon made passable. A little farther, the brethren had to dig a place considerably to make a pass between the mountains. . . . At twenty miles from Fort Bridger passed another spring and a little farther after arriving on the bottom land, the road turns nearly south through a beautiful low bottom filled with grass, at 1:45 we halted for noon, having traveled nine miles.

The Lyman journal fills in the picture by saying that after descending the ridge into Pioneer Hollow, the Saints "soon passed a similar tasting spring" and at the noon halt there were "2 good springs of pure water & a red & gunpowder spring opposite, across the bottom." These springs are in the S. W. quarter of Sec. 4, T. 15 N., R. 118 W.

The afternoon journey of July 10, 1847, which presumably had been Hastings' of July 21, 1846, as it was Lienhard's six days later, is best described by Clayton:

> . . . we proceeded again and after traveling three and a half miles began to ascend the dividing ridge between the Colorado waters and the great basin. This mountain [Aspen Divide] is very high and the ascent steep, rendering it necessary to make a crooked road to gain the summit. The height is 7,700 feet according to Elder Pratt's observations. The surface at the top is narrow. Here three bears were seen to run over a still higher mountain [Aspen Mountain] on the left. The descent was

Hastings met us; he turned back again with us and remained overnight in our camp. The weather continued as it had for several days, quite even. The morning was cool; during the day it was sunny but rather windy.[5]

---

very steep, having to lock wagons for half a mile. We then descend and travel on the bottom a few miles between high rugged mountains till the road seems suddenly to be shut up by a high mountain ahead. The road here turns suddenly to the left and goes east about 200 yards then winds again southwest. After ascending and descending another high ridge, we crossed a small creek about ten feet wide and at 7:45 formed our encampment on the southwest banks, having traveled this afternoon nine miles and during the day eighteen over the most mountainous course we have yet seen.

To interpret: Above the place of noon encampment, Pioneer Hollow forks. One fork [Choppy Draw?] heads south of west, and up this valley Bryant's party had gone in anticipation of the present line of the Union Pacific. Another fork heads west of south, and up this valley the wagon road of 1846–47 made its way. After reaching the Great Basin divide, in the S. E. quarter of Sec. 18, T. 14 N., R. 118 W., it descended a steep grade for half a mile west to arrive in the upper valley of Stowe Creek, not far south of present Altamont, at the west portal of the Aspen tunnel. There was not in 1847 much water in Stowe Creek, for Pratt says, "no running water, but some standing in pools"; some overland journals of later years indicate that this water had an alkaline character. From the vicinity of Altamont the road, as Pratt tells us, wound southwesterly for several miles, when the way ahead was blocked by the canyon of Stowe Creek. To avoid this "gorge," a term Edwin Bryant and Albert Carrington employed in preference to Clayton's "high mountain," the road turned sharply to the left and zigzagged southwesterly over the divide between Stowe Creek and Sulphur Creek, descending a draw to reach the latter stream at the site of old Bear River City, in the S. W. quarter of Sec. 28, T. 14 N., R. 119 W. The Mormon encampment of July 10, 1847, was on the south bank of Sulphur Creek, 1 3/4 miles east of the Bear River, but Lienhard's party went on to the east bank of the Bear before encamping. See the Jefferson map.

To the place of the Mormon encampment, the road of 1846–47 probably followed without material variation the route over which Walker had brought the Chiles wagons in 1843; see the Bryant journal, note 8.

[5] By the 27th, as we have noted in the Bryant journal, note 39, the advance wagons of the Harlan-Young company had reached the Weber River, nearly 40 miles farther west, although it appears from the important new diary of James Mathers that as late as the 25th some of the Harlan company were as far back on the trail as Bear River. (Mathers indicates that to that time 57 wagons had taken the Hastings Cutoff, of which 30 had gone on ahead.) Hastings' preoccupation with the back trail was obviously motivated by his desire to shorten the road between the crossing of Sulphur Creek and the head of Echo Canyon. The more roundabout road to the south followed by the Harlan-Young wagons and later by the Donner wagons is described in the Reed journal, notes 3 and 5, and is tentatively depicted on the Jefferson map. It seems likely that Lienhard's company

On the 28th when I went out in the morning to drive our cattle to
the wagons, I scared up in the thicket along the river bank a short-
legged animal which at first I took to be a young gray bear. I had
with me no other weapon than my usual walking-stick, but even so I
would not suffer the animal to escape. I immediately engaged it and
administered to it as it ran a few vigorous blows with the stick, whereupon it suddenly wheeled about to offer resistance, and showed me at
close range a mouth full of splendid, sharp teeth, with which it did its
best to seize me by the legs. So furious became the onslaught that for
a short time I thought it would succeed in seizing me. I struck as
rapidly as possible at the head of the animal, which must have observed a small hole in the ground; it sought to back into this and in
fact succeeded in doing so, but the hole was so shallow that the head
remained outside. This gave me a better opportunity; after two or
three heavy blows over the eye. all at once it lay dead and I had
knocked out an eye. The animal proved to be a fine fat badger rather
than a young bear; it had flesh much resembling that of a bear,
which by all was heartily relished.

We now had always on our left the Uinta Mountains;[6] in that direction conifer forests appeared to exist. In the valley of this river, the
water of which was clear and good, there were a few trees resembling
red fir, but cottonwood trees and willow thickets were the most
characteristic feature of the Bear River Valley here where we crossed
it. The Bear River is not entirely insignificant; it must deliver the
greatest amount of water to the Great Salt Lake; however, in flowing
to the lake it makes a great bend and during its course several
considerable affluents empty into it. To the right and in front of us
there was no real mountain but only rocky hills, which here and
there were sparsely overgrown with miserable cedars. Yesterday we
went through a growth of giant sagebrush which often reached a
height of more than 4 feet and grew so close together that one could
scarcely go between them.

Today the sagebrush fields made room over the hills for a scanty
growth of some kind of grass. After we had gone about 7 miles, we
camped near the channel of a nearly dry brook, where however we

---

encountered Hastings near the crossing of Sulphur Creek, a stream Jefferson calls
"Hare Creek" (rendered by his engraver "Hane Creek").

[6] In the original manuscript Lienhard wrote "Uta," then crossed it out and
wrote "Uinta." It is probable that his diary of 1846 used the word, "Uta," for the
present name, as applied to these mountains, did not come into general use until
about eight years later.

found a spring of excellent water, together with sufficient grass for our cattle. The 52 wagons traveling ahead of us here had taken two different routes, and Hastings had shown us still another which he considered the better way, and which we thought to put to the test. Hastings left us in the evening to overtake a company in advance of us.[7]

---

[7] Thus economically, in three sentences, Lienhard describes the first wagon travel over what became the fixed road from the Bear River to Yellow Creek. For a proper understanding of the route, let us again turn to the Mormon journals.

The fork in the road east of the Bear, at the crossing of Sulphur Creek, is most clearly described in the Lyman journal: "there are two roads here, one to the right keeps down the creek further, the other bears more south." Orson Pratt adds that "a few wagon tracks [were to be seen] bearing off to the South, while a few others bore down the small creek on which we were encamped." It so happened that the Mormons encountered at Bear River, on the evening of July 10, a little party which had just come from California by way of the Hastings Cutoff. Among their number was the mountain man, Miles Goodyear, who the previous autumn had settled at the site of Ogden (see the introduction to the Reed journal, note 13). July 11 being a Sunday, the Saints remained encamped that day, and Porter Rockwell, J. C. Little, and some others went out with Goodyear to inspect the right-hand or northern road—or as Clayton puts it, "to view the route he [Goodyear] wishes us to take." Clayton's entry here is a curiosity: "They represent it as being bad enough, but we are satisfied it leads too far out of our course to be tempted to try it. . . . After dark, a meeting was called to decide which of the two roads we shall take from here. It was voted to take the right hand or northern road, but the private feelings of all the twelve were that the other would be better. But such matters are left to the choice of the camp so that none may have room to murmer at the twelve hereafter."

History has vindicated the judgment of the camp as against the prejudices of the Twelve, in that the road thus chosen became the established trail. So far from leading "out of our course," it was a shorter and more direct route. No doubt Clayton's remark of July 10, when Goodyear first visited the Mormon encampment, explains the attitude of the Twelve: "Mr. Miles Goodyear came into camp. . . . He says it is yet seventy-five miles to his place, although we are now within two miles of Bear River. His report of the [Great Salt Lake] valley is more favorable than some we have heard but we have an idea he is anxious to have us make a road to his place through selfish motives."

To consider the roads from this fork in the trail to where they reunited, compare the details from the Mormon diaries with the Veatch map heretofore cited and with the *Sulphur Creek Reservoir* and *Millis, Wyoming* quadrangles.

The Mormon journey resumed on July 12, taking, as Orson Pratt writes:

the right hand fork of the road down the [Sulphur] creek, which is represented as being the nearest, and 1 3/4 miles brought us to Bear River ford. The river here is about 60 feet wide, 2 1/2 feet deep; a very rapid current, and the bottom completely covered with round boulders, some of which were about as large as a human head. . . . The road again forks at this place. We took the right hand, which bore a few degrees south of west. For about 2 miles our road gradually ascended, and

On the 29th we remained at the same camping place while some

---

crossing a ridge we commenced descending, following down for several miles a ravine [Coyote or Needles Creek] in which there was little water. Plenty of grass, of an excellent quality, is found in almost every direction. The country is very broken, with high hills and vallies, with no timber excepting scrubby cedar upon their sides. . . . The road is exceedingly difficult to find, excepting in places where the grass has not completely obscured it. We halted for noon a little east of a pudding stone formation. This ledge [The Needles] is on the right of the road, which passes along at its base. The rocks are from 100 to 200 feet in height, and rise up in a perpendicular and shelving form, being broken or worked out into many curious forms by the rains. Some quite large boulders were cemented in this rock. . . . We continued down the ravine but a short distance, where it empties its waters into a small tributary of Bear River [Yellow Creek, almost on the Utah-Wyoming line], which we crossed and again began to ascend for some distance, when we crossed another ridge and descended rather abruptly at first but afterwards more gradually into another ravine, at the head of which was a good spring of cold water. We continued descending this ravine until towards evening, when we encamped at the foot of a ledge of rocks on the right [a quarter of a mile east of Cache Cave].

Again to recapitulate: Following the route of the present county road west from Piedmont, the Hastings-Mormon road continued down Sulphur Creek to where the stream bent to the north, and then left it to climb over a small ridge to the Bear. The river was forded a few hundred yards north of the present bridge at the Meyers Ranch, in the N. E. quarter of Sec. 30, T. 14 N., R. 119 W., some 7 miles southeast of Evanston. On the west bank of the river the Mormons came to yet another fork in the trail (further discussed in note 10). Choosing the right-hand fork, the trail of Lienhard's own party, the Mormons proceeded down the river about a half mile, and then pulled up what subsequently became known as Stagecoach Hollow, at the head of which they descended directly west into the canyon of Coyote Creek, which they followed down to Yellow Creek at The Needles. This stage of the journey, up over the divide between the Bear River and Yellow Creek, Jefferson calls "Hastings Pass," by way of thanking Hastings for his services in guiding the Lienhard-Jefferson party over it.

The Mormon detachment with which Pratt was traveling did not halt at Yellow Creek, but continued on west, up over the divide to the tiny branch of Echo Creek which rises near Cache Cave. Lienhard himself camped at a spring in Yellow Creek Valley, called by Jefferson "Basin Spring." This spring has not been conclusively identified, but Mr. A. J. Barker, whose ranch lies in Yellow Creek Valley under The Needles, told me in August, 1948, of a spring located from 1 1/2 to 2 miles southwest of his ranchhouse, which conceivably was the spring which interests us.

To this point the Veatch map is the most illuminating single map for studying the Hastings-Mormon trail. From Yellow Creek west, see the *Wasatch National Forest* map, which is based on the township surveys of the 1870s, and the *Evanston, Ogden,* and *Salt Lake City* quadrangles.

gave needed repairs to their wagons, others mended their footgear or clothing, and yet others washed. The last two nights the still water was covered with a thin crust of ice; the days however were bright and warm. Yesterday morning we had intended to proceed on our journey, and taking his rifle and hunting knife Ripstein set off to look out the way—or rather, went ahead in the direction our road would lead us in the hope of shooting an antelope. It was only after he had gone that we found that repairs to our wagon were absolutely necessary before we could pursue our onward journey. We feared that this had occasioned Ripstein some inconvenience, for of course he supposed that he would meet us on the way, not that we would remain at yesterday's camp. Evening came, but Ripstein had not returned; where he could be, nobody knew.

After breaking camp on the 30th, our way led up a long, moderately steep slope, thence rapidly down through a hollow between the hills, passing a spring about 3 miles from the last campsite, and soon afterwards reaching the dry channel of a brook, which we followed until we had gone about 14 miles from our previous camp, where again we found water and grass, our two prime necessities.[8] Ripstein

---

[8] Again compare the Jefferson map. This day's travel brought the company from Yellow Creek to upper Echo Canyon, the night encampment probably being about 2 miles above Castle Rock. Neither Lienhard nor the Mormon diarists of 1847 mention the place of junction with the original road which had gone around to the south, but it is obvious from the Jefferson map that the two roads united up on the divide west of Yellow Creek, and above the spring Lienhard mentions.

Following Lienhard's route in the Mormon records is a little difficult, for the movements of the Saints were complicated by Brigham Young's falling ill of "mountain fever" on the morning of July 12, 1847. Part of the Pioneer party was sent ahead under Orson Pratt, another part went on only as far as Cache Cave, while a rear detachment stayed behind with Young near The Needles. As a result of this illness, Young himself required from July 12 to July 16 to cover the ground Jefferson and Lienhard traversed in a single day. Having made this clear, let us see what Clayton says of the route from the point where Young was left behind, the noon halt of July 12, 1847, Clayton being with the intermediate section of the Pioneer party:

After traveling one and a half miles we crossed the creek [Coyote Creek] at the foot of a high mountain [The Needles] and a little farther crossed back again [not so: this second crossing was of Yellow Creek itself]. A mile farther, began to ascend a long steep hill, narrow on the summit and steep descent. We then wound around between high hills till arriving again on a narrow rich bottom. At the foot of the hill we crossed last, there is a spring of very good cold water, and in fact, there are many good springs all along the road. At six o'clock we formed our enstill had not returned and we were seriously concerned about him.

Most of the day, July 31, we followed this watercourse and its windings. To our right rose spike-rocks (conglomerate) of a reddish color, several of them from 3 to 4 hundred feet high; to our left were various knolls and hills, at times quite rocky, then again overgrown with scanty grass and small underbrush. The narrow gorge led us entirely to the south [southwest] and became ever more constricted, so that we were very often compelled to cross the bed of the stream, and finally had to cut the road through a dense willow thicket. Here we found an abundance of red, black, and yellow currants, which to us was an agreeable state of affairs, for it was not every day that we came upon enjoyable fruit. In this little valley we came upon oaks again, which though small were the first we had seen.[9] This evening,

---

campment near a very small creek and a good spring, having traveled this afternoon six and three-quarters miles. . . . There is an abundance of grass here and the country appears to grow still richer as we proceed west, but very mountainous. There are many antelope on these mountains and the country is lovely enough but destitute of timber. About a quarter of a mile west from the camp is a cave in the rock about thirty feet long, fifteen feet wide and from four to six feet high [Cache Cave, first called by the Mormons "Redden's Cave"]. . . . [July 15] After traveling two miles we passed another spring of good water at the foot of a high hill a little to the right of the road. At half-past three we formed our encampment at the foot of some high red bluffs, having traveled four and a half miles . . . a beautiful spring of good, clear, cold water a little to the left of the road. . . . [July 16] At 8:45, we proceeded onward, passing through a narrow ravine between very high mountains. After traveling one and a quarter miles passed a deep ravine, where most of the teams had to double to get up. One half-mile farther, crossed the creek and found the crossing place very bad. . . . After passing this place, following the course of the creek, the mountains seem to increase in height, and come so near together in some places as to leave merely room enough for a crooked road. At half past twelve we halted to feed, having traveled six and three-quarters miles and are yet surrounded by high mountains.

This noon halt was at a point in Echo Canyon a little west of Castle Rock, about 2 miles below Lienhard's camp of July 30, and not far from Clyman's camp of June 4, 1846.

[9] There is some confusion in Lienhard's entry for this day and the next, and it is fortunate that we have the Jefferson map to straighten matters out; it is clear that Lienhard and Jefferson continued together until the afternoon of August 5, and journal and map are the more comprehensible for being studied together. Lienhard's apparent omission in this day's entry with respect to the distance traveled is apparent only; the 12 miles' travel down Echo Canyon he gives the following day, August 1, actually belongs to this day's entry, July 31. Evidence

as we were making our camp, crowded close to the bed of the brook
in a place where we found grass and water, Ripstein came back to us,
and just when we had given him up as wholly lost, for he had been
missing three days and two nights. He was at first quite incensed with
us, in view of the arrangements we had made for him to keep in
mind when he should turn toward camp. He had shot an antelope
and subsequently had carried it a considerable distance to where he
hoped to meet us; when however he did not find us, in the belief we
must already have gone far ahead, he proceeded rapidly on, leaving
the antelope behind and hastening forward until he came up with a
company far in advance of us, only to learn that we were still behind.

---

for this is found not only in Lienhard's own imperfect entry for July 31 but in
what the Mormon diaries have to say about the character of the vegetation in
lower Echo Canyon. Compare Clayton's description of the afternoon travel by
the Mormons on July 16, 1847:

> At 1:40, we proceeded onward and found the pass between the moun-
> tains growing narrower, until it seemed strange that a road could ever
> have been made through. We crossed [the] creek a number of times,
> and in several places found the crossing difficult. After proceeding a few
> miles, we saw patches of oak shrubbery though small in size. In the
> same place and for several miles there are many patches or groves of the
> wild currant, hop vines, alder and black birch. Willows are abundant
> and high. The currants are yet green and taste most like a gooseberry,
> thick rind and rather bitter. . . . The elder-berries, which are not very
> plentiful, are in bloom. In some places we had to pass close to the foot
> of high, perpendicular red mountains of rock supposed to be from six
> hundred to a thousand feet high. At a quarter to seven we formed our
> encampment, having traveled this afternoon nine and a half miles. . . .
> We are yet enclosed by high mountains on each side, and this is the first
> good camping place we have seen since noon, not for lack of grass or
> water, but on account of the narrow gap between the mountains. . . .
> There is a very singular echo in this ravine, the rattling of wagons re-
> sembles carpenters hammering at boards inside the highest rocks. . . .
> The echo, the high rocks on the north, high mountains on the south
> with the narrow ravine for a road, form a scenery at once romantic and
> more interesting than I have ever witnessed.

Clayton's mention of the acoustical characteristics of Echo Canyon had been
noted a year earlier by Jefferson, as is shown by the interesting name, "Echo
Defile," he applied to the canyon. Jefferson's map is not precise as to the campsite of July 31; one might even suppose it to be on the bank of the Weber below
the mouth of Echo Canyon. In the light of the information from Lienhard's
journal, however, it seems probable that this night's camp was very near that of
the Mormons a year later, about a mile above the mouth of the canyon. Although
possible, it is not very likely that Lienhard's company was spread out in the
canyon over a distance of a mile or two.

He then turned back again several miles along the road. The first night he attempted to spend under a rocky ledge, but the prairie wolves [coyotes] would not let him sleep; a small pack of these animals watched him incessantly, and when he rebelled and set off from the spot, they escorted him like a pack of dogs, only a few paces behind. He had shot a badger, but he had lost his knife while occupied with the antelope; accordingly it was not possible with anything he had at hand to cut off a piece to roast. He had therefore been obliged to fast until he fell in with the other company, when he was enabled to appease his hunger.[10]

On the 1st of August we took up our journey again, still through this narrow valley, which some had given the name Willow Canyon.[11] All along the brook we found many springs of water, so that the stream channel no longer remained dry as it had been farther back. The road was, however, if possible even worse than on the previous day; it had the same serpentine sinuosity, and often we were obliged to enter into alliance with the ax itself to carry the road through the densely grown wood.

In one place we found in bushes exceeding 8 to 12 feet in height the Juneberry [elderberry] tree (juni Beeren), extraordinarily full of the sweet, grape-like clusters of fruit. We halted a short time to gather of them, all helping themselves to hearts' content, for they were fully ripe and tasted amazingly good. We concluded that Master Bear must enjoy himself here also, from the evidence of the many broad

---

[10] This is the third tantalizing allusion Lienhard has made to a company traveling between his own and the Harlan-Young group. He has told us that 52 wagons were traveling in advance of his own party, but on the basis of information from the Mathers diary, this would seem to be too modest an estimate, as Mathers says that 57 wagons had reached the Bear River by July 25, two days before Lienhard arrived there. The Mathers diary is not very helpful on this point, but some of the rear wagons of the 57 may have made the second alternative road in the vicinity of the Bear. See Dale L. Morgan, ed., Overland in 1846 (Georgetown, Calif., 1963), 228, 415. Obviously it was with the Harlan "rear guard" that Hastings intended to spend the night on leaving Lienhard's party the evening of July 28. Ripstein's adventures in relation to the terrain are not quite clear, but presumably he had intended to meet his companions somewhere in upper Echo Canyon, had gone down the canyon in search of them, and on the second evening, after a night in the open, caught up with the wagons following the Harlan party, which by then probably had reached the valley of the Weber. Next day Ripstein turned back on the trail a mile or two and thus rejoined his own company.

[11] Evidently the name, "Willow Canyon," is owed to the Harlan-Young company. It did not appeal to Jefferson.

tracks in the here damp and somewhat softened ground, and the broken branches left dangling.

After proceeding for perhaps 12 miles[12] through various windings the ravine opened suddenly before us upon a valley with a beautiful little river of clear water flowing through it. This stream was known as the Weber River; it flows through a rather pretty little valley in a northeasterly [northwesterly] direction at the southeasterly foot of the high Wasatch Mountains,[13] which this valley enters from the Salt Lake. We followed down the windings of the little river, past high hill promontories which often looked like castle ruins. Thomen supposed Father Noah must have come this way with his Ark, and abandoned part of the same.[14] Traveling on about 5 miles farther along the banks of the Weber River, we camped on a high embankment near the river.[15] Some among us, desiring to bathe in the clear water,

---

[12] See note 9. It is probable that most of the terrain described, to this point, actually had been traversed the previous day. The entire distance traveled in Echo Canyon on the three days, July 30–August 1, could not have exceeded 20 miles.

[13] Variously spelled by Lienhard "Wahsatch," "Wassatch," and "Wasatch." This name, too, there seems reason to believe, is one he derived from a map in later years. Charles Preuss used the name "Wahsatch" (which Frémont picked up from Joe Walker in the spring of 1844 while traveling up through Utah), on his 1848 *Map of Oregon and Upper California.* but only applied it to that part of the Wasatch chain south of Utah Lake. It was not until after the Mormon entrance into Utah that the name began to be used for the mountains farther north.

[14] The earliest mention by any traveler of "the Witches," the monument-like forms eroded from pink conglomerate which are a striking feature of the Weber Valley below the mouth of Echo Canyon.

[15] Jefferson indicates that the whole day's travel was 11 miles. The night encampment was in the upper canyon of the Weber, probably about 2 miles below Devils Slide. Let us again turn to the Mormon journals for such light as they shed upon the route, resorting this time to the diary of Orson Pratt, who took the Mormon vanguard on while Brigham Young was ill. We will include Pratt's own account of Echo Canyon.

> July 13th . . . Those of the Twelve present directed me to take 23 wagons and 42 men, and proceed on the journey [from Cache Cave], and endeavor to find Mr. Reid's route across the mountains, for we had been informed that it would be impracticable to pass through the [Weber] kanyon on account of the depth and rapidity of the water. About 3 P.M. we started, and proceeded down the Red Fork [Echo Canyon] about 8 3/4 miles and encamped. At present there is not much water in this fork. . . .
>
> July 14th.—We resumed our journey. Traveled about 6 3/4 miles, and halted for noon. . . . In the afternoon travelled about 6 1/4 miles further,

discovered in the shallows an abundance of crayfish. At once we took ourselves, armed with forks, down into the waters and soon had a sufficient number of crayfish to provide us with the greater part of our evening meal.

On the slopes of the Wasatch Mountains rising above us grew some firs, a few groves of cedars, and sundry bushes. In the valley, on the other hand, willows and cottonwood trees were the principal

---

which brought us to the junction of Red and Weber's forks. Our journey down Red Fork has truly been very interesting and exceedingly picturesque. We have been shut up in a narrow valley from 10 to 20 rods wide, while upon each side the hills rise very abruptly from 800 to 1200 feet, and the most of the distance we have been walled in by vertical and overhanging precipices of red pudding-stone, and also red sandstone, dipping to the north-west in an angle of about 20 deg., (the valley of the Red Fork being about south-west.) These rocks were worked into many curious shapes, probably by the rains. The country here is very mountainous in every direction. Red Fork, towards the mouth, is a small stream about 8 feet across; it puts into Weber's Fork from the right bank. Weber's Fork is here about 70 feet wide, from 2 to 3 feet deep; a rapid current, stony bottom, consisting of boulders: water very clear; its course bearing west-northwest.... The road has been quite rough, crossing and re-crossing the stream a great many times. There is some willow and aspen in the valley and upon the side hills, and some scrubby cedar upon the hills and rocks as usual.
July 15th.—We resumed our journey down Weber's Fork, crossing on to the left bank. Travelled about 6 miles and encamped about one mile above the [Weber] kanyon, which at the entrance is impassable for wagons. The road, crossing the river to the right bank, makes a circuit of about 2 miles [through Croyden Valley], and enters the kanyon at the junction of a stream [Lost Creek, called by Jefferson "Berry Creek"] putting in from the right bank, about one-third as large as Weber's Fork. I rode on horseback, in company with Mr. [John] Brown, about 5 miles down from our encampment, and being convinced this was the 10 mile kanyon which had been spoken of, we returned to camp.
Pratt does not state precise mileages below the mouth of Echo, but this omission is repaired to some extent by William Clayton. On July 17 Clayton writes, "... the camp renewed the journey and one mile farther arrived at the Red fork of the Weber River [i.e., the Weber itself]. We also seem to have a wide space to travel through and now turn to the right in a western course, the ravine [Echo Canyon] having run mostly southwest.... The camp moved on and formed encampment on the banks of the river having traveled two and a half miles...." From this encampment, 1 1/2 miles below the mouth of Echo, Clayton proceeded on again July 19: "We found the road very rough on account of loose rocks and cobble stones. After traveling two and a quarter miles, we forded the river and found it about eighteen inches deep but proceeded without difficulty.... Three-quarters of a mile from the ford we found the place to make the cutoff...."

growing things; we also found some maples, oaks, and alders, the last over 20 feet high. In the valley there were a number of narrow places, which often forced us to cross from one side of the river to the other.[16]

On the 2nd day of August, we took up our journey on through the valley, now a little wider without the road being much better than on the previous day, for it proceeded through brush, across the bed of the river, and through a wood for a distance of 5 1/3 miles. Then the valley opened up again. We bore somewhat to the right and the river to our left, where two small brooks flowed into it. We proceeded from this place about 1 1/2 miles farther down the valley and then camped.[17] The mountains on both sides of us had a beautiful appearance. In consequence of the very long-continued dry weather, the thriving grasses in the gravelly soil were nearly all dry. Great smoke clouds were indicative of grass fires which probably originated through the negligence or thoughtlessness of careless travelers.

On the 3rd of August as we were making our way down along the river in a northerly [northwesterly] direction, and after we had traveled about 5 miles, we encountered Captain Hastings, who had returned to meet us. By his advice we halted here. He was of the opinion that we, like all the companies who had gone in advance of us, were taking the wrong road. He had advised the first companies that on arriving at the Weber River they should turn to the left which would bring them by a shorter route to the Salt Lake; this advice they had not followed, but trusting to their luck had taken the road down the river. We thereupon turned our wagons around and went back about 2 miles, where we encamped.[18] This day for a while was

---

[16] In addition to the two crossings of the Weber recorded by Pratt, Jefferson shows that the road went back and forth across the river six times this day and eight times the next before reaching the Morgan meadows.

[17] Again compare Jefferson, who estimates the total day's travel at 6 miles. The camp was in Morgan Valley on the north bank of the Weber River, perhaps a mile and a half northwest of present Morgan City. One of the brooks mentioned as flowing into the Weber is East Canyon Creek (Jefferson's "Magpie Creek"); the other doubtless is Center Creek, which now flows into the larger creek a few yards above its confluence with the Weber, but which as late as 1871, when the township surveys were made, flowed independently into the Weber some yards below the junction of the other two streams.

[18] This day's entry is one of the most important contributions of the Lienhard journal, and at the same time it clears up what has been a minor mystery of the Jefferson map, why Jefferson should have shown only 3 miles' travel for this day in the open Morgan Valley. It now becomes apparent that Lienhard and

Jefferson crossed to the south bank of the Weber below the confluence with East Canyon Creek, and continued on northwesterly to within about a mile of the site of Peterson. Here meeting Hastings, they backtracked 2 miles, encamping for the night perhaps on Smiths Creek.

Clearly, at the time they met Hastings, he was enroute up the Weber to leave the note at the first crossing of the Weber above Henefer which the Donner party would find there on the afternoon of the 6th (see the Reed journal, notes 9 and 11). We are now able to date this intervention by Hastings in the destinies of the Donner party, for whether he spent the night of the 3rd with Lienhard's party or continued on up the river, the note was left on August 4, some 48 hours before the Donner party found it alongside the trail. But it is even more interesting to learn from Lienhard that Hastings had never intended taking the wagons down the Weber River, that his intention from the beginning had been to take them across the mountains by the route he had traveled with Clyman in June. Hastings had been behind on the trail, working out the route from Bear River to Yellow Creek via Stagecoach Hollow and Coyote Canyon, at the crucial moment when Hudspeth came up the Weber to meet the Harlan-Young company and sell them on the river route. The result was a fundamental miscarriage of Hastings' plans. The difficulties the Harlan-Young wagons experienced in the lower canyon of the Weber thus were a contributing factor, not the primary cause, in Hastings' recommendation of the Big Mountain route to stragglers like the Donners who might be coming along behind.

We know from Bryant's entry of July 29 that the advance contingent of the Harlan-Young company had reached the Weber Valley by July 27, and it would seem that they finally got clear of Weber Canyon at present Uintah about August 4. This would square well with Jacob Wright Harlan's recollection (*California '46 to '88*, 43) which was that the company "worked six days building a road, and got through on the seventh day." The Samuel C. Young biographical sketch, *op. cit.*, says that "the male portion of these four companies [the advance contingent] spent four days clearing the boulders out of the way, and then they could make but one and a half miles per day." This information may or may not contradict that which we have from Jacob Harlan; the latter may refer to the entire canyon passage, the former only to the traverse of the lower canyon.

There is a further point of interest about the Harlan narrative, now that we can view it in the perspective afforded by the Lienhard account. By the time he set down his reminiscences, Harlan had come to labor under the delusion that the Reeds and Donners had been with the Harlan company all the way from Fort Bridger. He wrote:

> When we had come to within a half mile of the lake we halted at "Weber cañon," a pass which for about a half mile seemed impractica-ble. Our four head men held a council. Reid and Donner declared it to be impossible for us to get through. My uncle and old man [Edward G.] Pyle felt sure that we could; so there was a split. Reid and Donner turned, and trailed back for three days, and then crossed the mountains. We worked six days building a road, and got through on the seventh day.

It may well be that there was a big debate after Hastings caught up with the Harlan-Young company, and that the division of opinion as between the "new" and the "old" route is responsible for much of the confusing tradition that has

overcast, with a little rain, after which we again had warm sunshine.

On the 4th we remained in camp. A few of the company endeavored to seek out a better route but returned to camp without having effected their object.[19]

On August 5 we again set out, not however up the valley but down it, to where the so-called bad places of the Weber River commence. Kyburz, the Barbers, and we stopped and encamped, while the other part of our company made the passage of the dreaded places without any particular difficulty.[20] Instead of flowing to the north [northwest] as hitherto, the Weber River here had taken a westerly course; the worst place, properly speaking, was 5 miles long. The Weber River had broken through the steep, high Wasatch Mountains; it was a deep cleft through which the waters foamed and roared over the rocks.[21]

---

come down to us from descendants of the Harlan-Young party.

[19] Lienhard does not make it clear whether the scouts from his own party set out this morning or the previous afternoon, but it is obvious that the reconnaissance was made with Hastings as guide. It is unfortunate that we do not know just how much of the prospective route Hastings showed them, or why they decided against it. From the Jefferson map it is clear that a lingering doubt persisted in the party whether, after all, the route across the mountains was not best, for Jefferson shows "Reed's Road" over the mountains, and suggests, "It is perhaps better to take Reed's Road." What Jefferson depicts of the route, and his association of it with Reed's name, is clearly influenced by the events of four days later, when Reed overtook Hastings at Adobe Rock and induced Hastings to ride back and show him the recommended route.

Most gripping to the imagination, perhaps, is the different course history might have taken had Lienhard's company been persuaded by the alternative route across the mountains. Perhaps they would have been drawn down with the Donners in the tragic whirlpool of events. More probably the Donner party would have got across the Wasatch a week sooner, and all would have reached California in safety.

[20] As Jefferson shows, the company proceeded on through Morgan Valley, crossing back to the north bank of the Weber above Cottonwood Creek (Jefferson's "Raven Creek"), and commenced the passage of the lower canyon. Four of the wagons, belonging to the "five German boys," Kyburz, and the Barbers, encamped above Devils Gate, while the rest, numbering from 4 to 24, depending upon whose estimate one accepts as to the total strength of the company Hastings guided over his cutoff (see the Reed introduction, note 9), kept right on going. Jefferson traveled with the division of the party which went ahead, and his map shows that by nightfall they had succeeded in getting through the canyon.

[21] The lower canyon of the Weber, below Morgan Valley, as Jefferson feelingly remarks, was "a bad Canyon," made so principally by Devils Gate, approximately 3 miles above its mouth. Devils Gate was described by Lt. E. G. Beckwith on April 5, 1854, as a point at which "the river is narrowed to one half

On August 6 we ventured upon this furious passage, up to this point decidedly the wildest we had encountered, if not the most dangerous. We devoted the entire forenoon and until fully one o'clock in the afternoon to the task of getting our four wagons through. In places we unhitched from the wagon all the oxen except the wheel-yoke, then we tied one drove at both hind wheels, and the rest steadied the wagon; we then slid rapidly down into the foaming water, hitched the loose oxen again to the wagon and took it directly down the foaming riverbed, full of great boulders, on account of which the wagon quickly lurched from one side to the other; now we had to turn the wheels by the spokes, then again hold back with all the strength we had, lest it sweep upon a low lying rock and smash itself to pieces. In going back for each wagon we had to be very careful lest we lose our footing on the slippery rocks under the water and ourselves be swept down the rapid, foaming torrent.[22]

---

its usual width, having cut a passage 20 or 30 feet in depth through the solid rock, which on the north side overhangs the stream, at nearly a right angle."

[22] Lienhard and his fellow-travelers got their four wagons through the fearsome narrows at Devils Gate by descending in the bed of the river itself, an undertaking so hazardous that it is not surprising the Donner party decided against it. The alternative was even less attractive. Let W. W. Allen and R. B. Avery, in *The California Gold Book* (San Francisco, 1893), 62, 63, describe the tribulations of the Harlan-Young party here:

> The canyon is scarcely wide enough to accommodate the narrow river which traverses it, and there was no room for roads between its waters and the abrupt banks. In many places great boulders had been rolled by the mountain torrents and lodged together, forming an impassable way. . . . Three such obstacles were encountered, and only about a mile a day was averaged for more than a week. The sides of the mountains were covered by a dense growth of willows, never penetrated by white men. Three times spurs of the mountains had to be crossed by rigging the windlass on top, and lifting the wagons almost bodily. The banks were very steep, and covered with loose stones, so that a mountain sheep would have been troubled to keep its feet, much more an ox team drawing a heavily loaded wagon. On the 11th [i.e., 1st?] of August, while hoisting a yoke of oxen and a wagon up Weber mountain, the rope broke near the windlass. As many men as could surround the wagon were helping all they could by lifting at the wheels and sides. The footing was untenable and before the rope could be tied to anything, the men found they must abandon the wagon & oxen to destruction, or be dragged to death themselves. The faithful beasts seemed to comprehend their danger, and held their ground for a few seconds, and were then hurled over a precipice at least 75 feet high, and crushed in a tangled mass with the wagon on the rocks at the bottom of the canyon.

When I began the journey, I had three pairs of boots and one pair of shoes. Today I was given the last service by the one remaining pair of boots, for the heels near the foot had raised up sidewise and upside down. Henceforth I must manage to make my own footgear. When the first company came through, they of course found no road whatever, and it was only by much toil that they were enabled to get through; we had, in comparison, relatively little trouble.

After leaving to our right the Weber River, which empties itself in the Salt Lake not far from this place, we proceeded on south about 3 miles over good wild meadowland, the Wasatch Mountains now on our left, and encamped in a small grassy vale with a sufficiency of good water.[23] The weather was very warm.

On the 7th we reached the flat shore of the magnificent Salt Lake, the waters of which were clear as crystal, but as salty as the strongest salt brine. It is an immense expanse of water and presents to the eye in a northeasterly [northwesterly] direction nothing but sky and water. In it there are a few barren islands which have the appearance of having been wholly burnt over. The land extends from the mountains down to the lake in a splendid inclined plane broken only by the fresh water running down from ever-flowing springs above. The soil is a rich, deep black sand composition [loam] doubtless capable of producing good crops. The clear, sky-blue surface of the lake, the warm sunny air, the nearby high mountains, with the beautiful country at their foot through which we on a fine road were passing, made on my spirits an extraordinarily charming impression.[24] The whole day long I felt like singing and whistling; had there been a single family of white men to be found living here, I believe that I would have remained. Oh, how unfortunate that this beautiful country was uninhabited! I did not then foresee that within perhaps

---

[23] This night's camp probably was on Kays Creek, in a hollow some yards below present US 89, a mile south of the junction with the Hill Field road, State Route 193. The division of Lienhard's party with which Jefferson was traveling probably encamped 3 or 4 miles farther south, perhaps up on the bench east of Kaysville. Since Jefferson does not give the mileage between his camps of August 5 and 6 it is difficult to locate the latter camp precisely. Evidently he did not travel far this day; the reason why, it is hard to say.

[24] Lienhard was rounding Farmington Bay past Centerville and Bountiful— probably, from what he says about the luxuriantly growing bulrushes, nearer present I-15 than US 89. Other members of the year's immigration were similarly well impressed by the Great Salt Lake and its valley; see J. Quinn Thornton, *Oregon and California in 1848*, II, 99–100.

two or three weeks[25] of our passing, this solitude would be filled with hundreds of civilized men intending to remain, and yet it was so, the Mormons followed on our heels in the vain hope that here in this wilderness they would forever be permitted to live as they pleased. Since then hardly 29 years have passed, and the Mormons undoubtedly have understood for a long time that their cherished dream of independence is coming to an end.

Our road had taken us for the most part along the lakeshore through luxuriantly growing bulrushes. After traveling about 20 miles, I should say, we again pitched camp, having reached a small river, the Uta,[26] the water of which was a little warm, but otherwise of good quality. The grass was poor and fuel scarce.[27] The Wasatch Moun-

---

[25] A mistake; the Mormons arrived nearly a year later. In the next sentence Lienhard gives us a clue as to when this part of the manuscript was written, about 1874–75, further borne out by his remarks in note 26.

[26] Here Lienhard has written in the margin of his manuscript: "The Uta, which flows from the more elevated Uta Lake to the Salt Lake, is the present Jordan of the Mormons, in which the Mormons were baptized. We had bathed in the same, and relished it.—This was written about 16 years ago; it is now the end of December, 1890."

[27] For the location of Lienhard's camp this night, which was also the place where Jefferson had crossed the Jordan earlier in the day, we are indebted to the field note books of the Stansbury survey. In charge of the chain line which was ascending the Jordan River from its mouth, Albert Carrington recorded that his post 16 was "38 feet North of Hastings Trail." This was on the west bank of the Jordan some 2 1/2 miles northwest of Becks Hot Spring, at a peculiar hairpin bend in the river. Carrington did not show the actual "Hastings ford," but the existence of the crossing was incidentally remarked by Lt. John W. Gunnison on September 26, 1849: "Mr. Carrington carries River Survey to Hastings Ford." The hairpin bend referred to still existed at the time of the township surveys in 1856 and thus may be located with reference to modern maps: It was in Sec. 4, T. 1 N., R. 1 W. It is still depicted on the *Wasatch National Forest* map, being the southernmost "squiggle" in the river as it begins to flow more of a north course after bending northwest from the Hot Springs area. Actually, this hairpin bend no longer exists as such; the river appears to have returned to an old chan-nel Carrington noted in 1849, and flows north more directly than by this serpen-tine channel. To reach Lienhard's campsite one must drive west on Center Street in North Salt Lake to the Jordan and then hike northwest along the river bank some three-quarters of a mile.

That Jefferson crossed the river at the same point is shown by the fact that his map does not depict Hot Springs Lake, the Hot Springs, or the Warm Springs, as it undoubtedly would had he continued on Bryant's trail around "the point of the mountain" into Salt Lake Valley. Yet it is strange that Jefferson does not show the alternative road taken by some of the Harlan-Young wagons, which did in fact go on past the Hot Springs to cross the Jordan at the North Temple

tains were high. In several of the ravines we could see a few small conifers, but the country as a whole appeared to be scantily wooded.

On August 8 we left the Wasatch Mountains to our left or to our rear and set out in a southwesterly direction toward another reddish-brown mountain [the Oquirrh Mountains], which in the exceedingly bright and clear morning air appeared to be hardly 6 miles away,

---

ford. Presumably this latter was the route taken by the advance wagons, before those following behind found a feasible crossing 6 1/2 miles farther north.

As we are indebted to the Stansbury survey for what we know of the Lienhard-Jefferson crossing, so are we indebted to the Mormon diaries of 1847 for what we know of the Harlan-Young crossing. Upon their arrival in Salt Lake Valley, July 21–24, 1847, the Saints began to reconnoiter the surrounding territory, and on July 26 several of the brethren climbed Ensign Peak, which overlooks the valley at its north end. Coming back down, some of them, including William Clayton,

> descended on the northwest corner and found the descent very lengthy and difficult. . . . On arriving on the level again, we wound our way southward to meet the other brethren and after passing a little way saw one of the sulphur springs [Warm Springs] where a pretty large stream of sulphur water boils out of the rock at the foot of the mountain and thence branches out into several smaller streams for some distance till these enter a small lake [Warm Springs Lake, now vanished]. This water is about as warm as dishwater and very salty. . . . Elders Smith, Carrington and myself went lower down towards the lake in search of some fresh water to quench our thirst. We found a nice clear stream of cold water but a little way from the sulphur spring and having drunk of it, we concluded to go on and see the [Jordan] river which we had noticed from the mountain. We took nearly a west course and soon struck the old road made by emigrants last year. We found the land exceedingly rich all along, good grass and abundance of rushes. We found many wet places but no signs of swamps, nor danger of miring. After traveling about two miles, we arrived at the river having followed the road to the ford. This river is about five rods on an average, three and a half feet deep at the ford but in other places much deeper. The current is slow and the water of a dark lead color. The banks are about five feet high and the soil to the water level of a rich, black alluvial. There is no timber on the banks here and not many willow bushes. We went over the river and found the soil equally good on the other side.

Clayton thus had followed the Harlan-Young road of 1846 from a point below the Warm Springs to the North Temple crossing, his distances and the location of the road east of the Jordan being conclusive. The hot springs referred to were definitely Warm Springs, because after reaching the crossing of the Jordan, Clayton turned north again, going the entire 4 miles to Becks Hot Springs and Hot Springs Lake. He did not go north of this point, hence has nothing to say about the fork in the trail and the more northerly crossing we now know to have existed.

though before this day was over we could testify that it was fully twice that distance. Ten miles on across a plain brought us to a swampy section, where bulrushes and a little rank marsh grass grew, through which the road yet took us. The water was salty and unpalatable, so that the stock refused it.[28] Two miles farther on, we arrived at the foot

---

[28] This salt spring is north and a little east of present Magna. The road from the Jordan bent south around it and here it was subsequently joined by the Donner road; see the Reed journal, note 23. A Mormon diary of 1847 also refers to the junction of the two roads. In the journal he kept for George A. Smith, Albert Carrington wrote, describing a visit to Great Salt Lake on July 27, 1847:

> Pres. Brigham Young, the others of the Twelve, Albert Carrington and others, sixteen in number, started to explore, all on horseback, except the President and Elder Wilford Woodruff, who went in the latter's carriage. Crossed an outlet of Emigrant ford [i.e., crossed the Utah Outlet at Emigrant Ford]. When over the plain about 16 miles from camp they came to a fine large spring. Water cool but a little brackish. This spring is south-west from camp. Passed on south-west for about six miles, between high cliffs and the lake, passing three springs like the first mentioned and a point where Emigrant road [i.e., the Harlan road from the North Temple crossing] comes into Hastings' new route [i.e., the Donner road?], both of which were traveled for the first time with wagons last year. Halted and all went into bathe in Great Salt Lake. . . . Passed on same course about 3 miles to the mouth of a small valley [Tooele Valley] apparently dry. . . . Turned back to the first spring and camped.

The parallel entry Carrington wrote for the Amasa Lyman journal varies slightly from the above, and does not mention the road junction:

> Pres. Young, the 12 & A. Carrington & others, 16 in all, started to explore—crossed into outlet [footnote by Carrington: "Outlet of Eutah Lake"] at Emigrant ford, & in about 16 miles from camp, over the plain came to a large cool spring, water slightly brackish, rested—this spring is W by S from camp—passed on WSW about 6 miles between cliffs & lake, passing 3 springs like first, halted & all went in to bathe in the Lake. . . .

The rest of the Lyman journal is identical with the Smith journal. The language of the latter is such as to imply that the road junction was near Black Rock, where the party bathed in the lake; since the mention of the junction appears in one diary only, however, it is possible that Carrington put it in almost as an afterthought. In one respect both diaries are in error; it was nearer 11 miles than 16 from the Mormon camp to the first spring.

It remains unexplained why Jefferson did not show the alternative road by the North Temple crossing of the Jordan. Perhaps he saw the western junction and was content to describe it as what became "Reed's Road." In that case, the Harlan road and the later Donner road must have come together a little east of the point where the Lienhard-Jefferson road came in. Another mystery about the Jefferson map is the 32-mile drive his division of Lienhard's party made to reach

of the mountain, where a large, crystalline spring, somewhat warm and a little brackish, welled out of the ground. We halted here a short time, so that our stock might gain a little rest. Where the spring broke out of the ground, it formed a beautiful basin, in which, not even taking off our clothes, several of us bathed. In the vicinity of this spring stood an immense, isolated, rounded rock under which was a cave, and those going into it found a human skeleton.[29] During the forenoon's travel we had again caught up with the advance division of our company, and the reunited train continued their journey together.[30] We passed along the occasionally marshy shore at the south end of the Salt Lake and camped finally at a large spring at the foot of the mountains, the water of which was slightly brackish. An expanse of swampy meadowland here separated us from the lake. We must have made about 6 miles this afternoon.[31]

On August 9 we continued our journey westward, to round the south end of the lake. Ripstein, an American named Bunzel,[32] and I

---

the Oquirrhs. Unless they were making a determined effort to overtake the Har-lan-Young party, it would have been more reasonable for them to break their journey at the Jordan River on the night of August 7, as Lienhard did.

Perhaps it should be added that present Highway 186 west from the North Temple crossing of the Jordan follows the Harlan road only for a few yards. The 1846 road then angled south of west toward the Oquirrhs, as is shown by the map which accompanied the Stansbury *Report* and by the township surveys of 1856. Highway 186 on the other hand, today merges with I-80 and goes straight west on the route which came into use after Saltair was established in the 1890s; reaching the lake, it bends southwest to come into the original road just beyond Black Rock at Lake Point Junction.

[29] The cave Lienhard refers to may have been Deadman's Cave, in 1994 accessible from State Highway 201 near present Magna, a half mile from the site of Garfield, but it is possibly Black Rock Cave, which was much celebrated in pioneer days but is now buried under smelter tailings.

[30] Lienhard thus had again overtaken Jefferson. After the previous day's 32-mile drive, Jefferson's group probably did not move during the morning hours of the 8th. It seems likely that Jefferson's camp was near Deadman's Cave, the locality of Clyman's camp of June 1. If so, he did not choose to show the cave on his map.

[31] As the Jefferson map clearly shows, the night's camp was in Tooele Valley just beyond Adobe Rock, at the spring later employed for the Benson Mill. We know from James Frazier Reed's story that it was at this point and on this night that he overtook Lansford W. Hastings (see the Reed journal, note 9). Are we then to conclude that the entire Harlan-Young party was encamped this night at Adobe Rock? Or had some part of the company gone on to the springs at Grantsville?

[32] Lienhard does not identify "Bunzel," whose name he also spells

walked some distance ahead of our wagons and came to a place
where the road passed close to the lake.[33] The morning was so delightfully warm and the quick clear water, without any animal life, so
inviting that we soon resolved to take a salt water bath. The beach
glistened with the whitish-gray sand which covered it, and on the
shore we could see the still-fresh tracks of a bear, notwithstanding
which we soon had undressed and were going down into the salty
water. We had, however, to go out not less than a half mile before the
water reached our hips. Even here it was still so transparent that we
could see the bottom as if there were no water whatever above it, yet
so heavy that we could hardly tread upon the bottom with our feet; it
was here no trick at all to stand even on tiptoe. I confidently believe
that one who understood only a little of swimming could swim the
entire length of the 70-mile-long lake without the slightest danger of

---

"Buntsel," although a little further on he speaks of him as a "big, strong man"
regarded by the others as a little lazy, and perhaps a little timorous. Jacob Wright
Harlan speaks of a member of the 1846 immigration named Bonsell who later
had a ferry on the San Joaquin River and died of cholera in 1850; this fellow is
described as "a giant and as brave as a lion," in many ways a good man, but a terrible fellow when aroused. But we are given to understand that Harlan's
"Bonsell" had traveled the Fort Hall route rather than the Hastings Cutoff. See
Harlan, op. cit., 49, 141, 208.

[33] We may conclude from the Jefferson map that there was a considerable
difference of opinion among the companies as to the best route through Tooele
Valley to the springs at Grantsville. He shows an alternative route which diverged
from the road he himself traveled even before reaching Adobe Rock, probably in
the vicinity of present Lake Point Junction, and which by-passed Adobe Rock,
leaving it a mile or two to the left. West from Adobe Rock Jefferson depicts a
second, alternative road. This second fork in the trail was in the locality of present Mills Junction. One trail went nearly southwest, heading for the springs; and
this, as the township maps of 1856 make clear, was substantially the route of
present Highway 138. Lt. E. G. Beckwith, carrying on his reconnaissance of
Pacific railroad routes, traveled this road on May 7, 1854, and wrote, "For five or
six miles in crossing [Tooele Valley], our road lay along an old shore-line of the
lake, elevated some twenty feet above the general level of the valley. . . ." That
this was Lienhard's road is manifest; otherwise he could not have gone swimming in Great Salt Lake this day. Jefferson himself, however, took a route which
bent much more deeply to the south. The road shown on the map published with
the Stansbury Report would indicate that Jefferson's route was the one chiefly favored down to 1850, before Grantsville itself was settled. This road continued
south to what Stansbury called the Willow Springs, shown on the 1856 township
maps as the Bates Settlement, and now known as Erda, and then bent west and
somewhat north of west to come back into the other road at Grantsville. The
road Jefferson traveled was about 4 miles longer than the road which kept close
to the lake shore.

drowning. I was a poor swimmer, Ripstein none at all, and he could lay himself on his back, so that fully half of his body emerged above the clear salt brine. Had I not known that in ordinary water I sank lightly beneath the surface, I would have supposed that I had become an absolutely first-rate swimmer, for I could assume every conceivable position, without the least danger. I could in a sitting position swim on my side, swim on my back, and I believe one could make a competent somersault without special effort, for by giving only a slight push with the foot against the bottom, one could leap high up. Since my hair was thick, hanging down to my shoulders, when I lay on my back, I had to hold high a great part of my body before my head came under water. For learning to swim, no water in the whole world is so well adapted as the Salt Lake; here, at the mouth of an in-flowing fresh water stream where one could choose gradually lighter water, one could safely learn how to be a perfect swimmer. I swam nearly the whole distance back, yes, one could easily swim in water which was hardly more than 1 1/2 feet deep. Only a single feature had the swimming in this lake that was not conducive to pleasure; this consisted in the fact that when one got a little water in one's eye, it occasioned a severe burning pain; and after we reached the shore and dressed ourselves without first washing in un-salted water, being desirous of hastening on, we soon experienced an almost unbearable smarting or itching over the whole body where the salt water had filled up all the crevices of the skin with an all-enveloping deposit of salt.

Nearly the whole day the road led past the foot of the mountains close to the shore of the lake in a westerly direction; thereby we passed other large springs of water, of which most, however, were salty. At one of these springs, which was a little fresher, and where also we found grass for our cattle, we made our camp; the lake lay back from the road, separated from it by an expanse of marshland.[34]

On the morning of August 10 we found nearly exhausted, in one of the deep holes of spring water, an old ox belonging to Mr. Hapy [Hoppe]; he must have fallen in during the night and was unable to keep himself from being drowned, for he died soon after we helped him out.

We had reached a broad valley or cove, where there were many

---

[34] Lienhard could better have described his arrival, but this day's travel brought him to the abundant springs at Grantsville. The probabilities as to Lienhard's campsite are discussed in the Reed journal, notes 25 and 26.

deep but happily salt-free springs; we found, as well, much good grass, and a grove of trees was not lacking. Three [?] other companies were here in camp beside us, and since it was known that we would soon have hard work for our cattle, it was necessary to allow a thorough rest, that the cattle might be in very good condition. Hastings had ridden back to a company remaining behind, in case it should be necessary to point out the way; a few wanted to wait for his return before again taking up their journey. The rather high mountains surrounding the broad cove were but sparsely wooded; only a little brook [North Willow Creek] rising from several small springs carried some water toward the valley, which after reaching the valley soon exhausted itself in the sandy, even pebbly soil a half mile above our location, afterwards reappearing as deep springs here where the companies had been encamped.

Since we left Fort Bridger, where we encountered so many Indians, of the Sioux tribe I believe,[35] we had seen no more until yesterday; these last were dark, poorly clothed, not thin but undersized fellows, belonging to the Uta tribe. Those we came upon living here were the so-called Digger Indians, a tribe which had a reputation of being treacherous and cunning, and not averse to murdering white men when by craft they can do so without fear of punishment. "Digger" is the equivalent of the German "Gräber," and this name is applied to nearly all the tribes dwelling between this point and the settlements in California, because they all live on various roots which they dig with sharpened sticks. The Indians whom we met from here on called themselves Sho sha nee, or "Schoshanie," by which name only are they properly called. Of wild game we had seen for a long time nothing but occasional tracks, but these tracks gave evidence of the presence of bear, elk, deer, and the large mountain sheep, and showed that they at times frequented this region.

On August 11 we remained in camp resting. Two of the companies which had been encamped near us left this place to pursue their onward journey; in one of the other companies which was still encamped nearby, a man died who had been ill only a short time.[36]

---

[35] He had seen Sioux at Fort Laramie, but the Indians at Fort Bridger were Northern Shoshoni. The "Diggers" he describes, locally called Gosiutes, were Western Shoshoni. See Julian H. Steward, *Basin-Plateau Aboriginal Sociopolitical Groups* (Washington, 1938), Bureau of American Ethnology Bulletin 120, *passim*.

[36] It would seem that on the morning of August 11 all the wagons which had taken the Hastings Cutoff ahead of the Donner party were encamped together on the site of Grantsville, though it may be that some had already moved on around

On the 12th of August also we remained at the same place, having to wash and mend our shoes and clothing. Mr. Hastings had returned; he was of the opinion that we should give our cattle more opportunity to recruit.[37] The man who died yesterday in the company encamped nearby was buried today, whereupon they likewise left us to continue on their journey.

Again on the 13th we remained at the same camping place. Our stock, which at the time of our arrival had been badly worn down, had begun to recover their strength very satisfactorily; today it appeared as though they would commence a dance among themselves; they made all sorts of antic leaps, more in keeping with the demeanor of young goats than of old and large oxen. For our part, we had nothing against their being so light-hearted; on the contrary, we rejoiced in their revelry. The weather the last few days had been not unpleasant, although the sky was often cloudy.

On the 14th of August we at last went on again. At no other place, with the exception of the Platte, where we had to remain a few days for the purpose of obtaining buffalo meat, had we remained so long; we stayed here this length of time chiefly because our enfeebled cattle must soon undergo a long journey without grass and water, and

---

the Stansbury Mountains to Skull Valley. Lienhard's entry for August 11 provides a date and a place for the death of John Hargrave, the first overland immigrant for whom a grave was opened in Utah soil. According to Jacob Wright Harlan, *op. cit.*, 44, Hargrave was a brother-in-law of William Fowler, the latter being one of the principal personalities of the Harlan train, having gone to Oregon in 1843, to California next year, and in 1845 back to the States to bring his family out. Besides Hargrave's widow, who later married George Harlan, four children were left. His death is described in sentimental strain by W. W. Allen and R. B. Avery, *op. cit.*, 64, 65:

> John Hargrave had taken cold after a day of extra trying labor in the mountains, and it had fastened upon his system and developed into typhoid pneumonia. His sickness affected every member of the band. . . . He was too sick to travel, and no one thought of moving a rod until he was well again. The delay troubled them not a bit, but sorrow at the serious illness of Hargrave grieved every one of his comrades. From day to day he became worse, until at last he died, and a fearful gloom settled upon the camp. His grave was made on a knoll near the river Jordan [*sic*], and no one ever had a more sincere band of mourners to lay him away. His last resting place was a bower of flowers placed by loving hands.

For Hargrave's probable place of burial, see the Reed journal, notes 25 and 26.

[37] Hastings would appear to have separated from Reed on Big Mountain on the afternoon of the 10th, having gone that far on the trail to show Reed the route across the mountains. See the Reed journal, note 9.

their strength had to be renewed. Our road led along the base of the
mountains in a northerly direction a distance of ten or 12 miles, then
we bent again to the left around the point of the mountain, thus
leaving the Salt Lake to our right and gradually receding from it.
Along the way we came to more springs, passing them by because for
the most part the water was quite salty.

The bowels of the mountains which bound the lake on the south
most likely contain enormous deposits of rock salt, and the lake undoubtedly is composed in the main of salt. Since the lake has no
known outlet, the large quantity of water flowing down into it from the
rather sizable Bear River, the large Weber, and the perhaps nearly as
large Uta River must evaporate during the summer time. The salt
content of the many fairly large salty springs is likely to increase each
year, for the salt itself does not evaporate.

Late in the afternoon, in another cove of these mountains, we
came finally to another spring, the water of which, though somewhat
salty, we could drink, and which provided also sufficient grass for our
cattle.[38] John Barber brought us a scorpion about $2^{1/2}$ inches long,
without, however, knowing that he had such a thing. The insect was
dead; had it been alive, he would probably soon enough have
learned his mistake. John had supposed it to be a new species of
crayfish, for he had taken it out of a spring. I told him, however, that
had it been a live scorpion he would very soon have let it go. Thus
the catching of new crayfish appeared henceforth to have been
spoiled for him.[39]

Early on the 15th of August we arrived at the last fresh water
springs, of which there were several, and fortunately we found also a
great abundance of grass. Here again we overtook the last immigrant
company in advance of us, including the Harlans and Weimer, with
whom we had begun the journey from Indian Creek.[40]

On the next day, August 16, this company again started on. The

---

[38] At Burnt Spring in Skull Valley. Probably Jefferson had gone on ahead
with the first companies to pull west from the springs at Grantsville; otherwise
his map would have shown the grave of John Hargrave. His map is nonetheless
interesting, showing, in Skull Valley, even the "Rock Mound" which gave this
valley one of its early names, "Lone Rock Valley."

[39] Scorpions must have been abundant in Skull Valley this year. Clyman
made mention of them on May 30, and Jefferson saw fit to call the Cedar Mountains "Scorpion Mountain."

[40] Peter L. Wimmer's name Lienhard renders "Weimer," and this, Bancroft
says, was probably its original form.

first wagon was already in motion when from the hindmost wagon a
bundle of clothes was thrown out, belonging to the well-known, fat,
fair-haired Miss Lucinda. The owner of this bundle one would as little or even less want to keep in one's wagon as the bundle itself. The
bundle had flown from one of Mr. Harlan's wagons, into which Miss
Lucinda twice already had been admitted; they had again become
disgusted, and had probably thrown out the bundle of clothing as the
best means of getting rid of the ever eager-for-marriage Lucinda.
Had we not long been well-acquainted with the character of this
worthy individual, we would have regarded this action of the Harlans
as exceedingly heartless; as it was, some of us now considered that
although Mr. Hoppe had twice already put her out, she would never
have left the settlement except that he took her along, and thus he
was the one to take again into his wagon the bundle and the
speciously tearful Lucinda. There was a good deal of talking back
and forth, as everyone sought to impose the burden on someone else,
until at last we came generally to the opinion that as we could not
abandon this piece of human flesh in the wilderness, Mr. Hoppe's
family *must* take her in again, which view Hoppe unwillingly
accepted.[41]

We remained on the 16th of August here where the stock found
the abundant fresh grass as good as the excellent water. We ourselves
spent the time in preparing as well as possible for entering on the
morrow upon a long stretch of from 70 to 90 miles without grass and
water. With our pocket knives we cut as much grass as we could,
binding it in bundles to carry with us. Every receptacle that would
hold water was placed in readiness for our departure by being filled
with this indispensable fluid, and we would have been happy had we
possessed four times as much to take along.

The 17th of August dawned with our stock lying here and there
in the grass, contentedly chewing their cuds. The carefree time now
past, each of us was occupied loading into the wagons the prepared
grass and the small, water-filled receptacles, and that with all possible care, so that under no circumstances should any be lost. The
oxen we led once more to water, for now they could drink all they
might desire, but this would not be the case hereafter. It was 9
o'clock by the time we set off. Before us lay a broad salt plain or valley [Skull Valley], where grew only a very little thorny, stunted vegetation; indeed, the ground was often a salt crust. Our direction was

---

[41] Lucinda's case Lienhard takes up at length on August 20.

northwesterly, in a straight line to the mountain opposite [Cedar Mountains]. After a time the road began to ascend a hill, and about half-past 1 o'clock we reached a spring rather high on the mountain-side. We halted here solely that our stock might drink; however, the water, although attractive to look at, was quite salty and the stock were not yet thirsty enough to drink it. Similarly, the small supply of coarse grass in no wise served, for they were not hungry enough to eat it.[42]

According to report, the immigrants who had gone in advance of us had dug a well near the road on the west side of these hills, 15 or 20 miles from here. We decided among ourselves that four of us should go ahead until we came to the supposed well, and there await the arrival of our wagons. Big Bunzel, Zins, Thomen, and I were to search for the well, even though night should fall before we reached it.[43] The wagons were to continue on the way as long as possible, but if they met with some especial difficulty, they should wait for the next day. After a rest of 1 1/2 hours, we again set off on our journey, going ahead as above-mentioned, but without taking any firearms with us, each having only his walking stick. We traveled at first for several miles at the foot of a high range of hills [Cedar Mountains], proceeding along the lower slope in a northerly direction,[44] and came finally to the place where the road climbed upward over very steep hills [Hastings Pass]. We were sure that our wagons would camp here tonight, for in order to surmount the acclivity the teams would have to be at least doubled, if not trebled.

By the time we had attained this high summit and bent our steps toward the wide, desolate valley below, the great, dark-red disk of the sun already had reached the northwestern edge of a boundless flat plain lying before us, an oppressive solitude as silent as the grave. The soil was composed of sand and gravel, from which nothing but small, thorny shrubs, *greasewood*, perhaps 1 1/2 feet high, eked out a

---

[42] Redlum Spring. James Frazier Reed, on August 30, was even less impressed with it than Lienhard. Jefferson, who names the seep "Dell Spring," gives its distance from "Hope Wells" at Iosepa as 13 miles.

[43] Jefferson's map locates this "salt well" beyond Grayback Mountain, whereas Lienhard goes to hunt for it in the dry valley between the Cedars and Grayback. Drinkable water could perhaps have been found in the sand dunes west of Grayback by digging for it—but drinkable only by doing violence to the normal meaning of the word.

[44] The direction is arbitrarily translated as north, for Lienhard wrote "*nord-östlichen*" and then by a patent error struck out the *nord* instead of the *öst*.

miserable existence. Neither wolf nor antelope nor any other animal was to be seen or heard; however, lying scattered over the ground were the bones and gigantic horns of fallen mountain sheep and a few elk. The longer we continued on over the dusty, sandy road down toward the desolate plain, the darker it became. No sound was perceptible except our own muffled footfalls in the loose sand, which had been made unstable by the wagons and the hoofs of the livestock in advance of us. One behind the other, like so many recruits learning to march, we strode along without speaking. It was perhaps 10 o'clock when at last Bunzel suggested that we lie down by the side of the road, since under these conditions we could not expect to find the well. We scarcely replied to him but continued on as before. Bunzel was a big, strong man, but we all regarded him as lazy. He would not willingly stay behind by himself, so he followed along. After we had marched on perhaps another half hour, Bunzel broke the stillness of the night by saying that we must stop, for we had found no water and he was tired and sleepy, but we paid no more attention to him than before, so that at length he actually remained behind. The other three of us pursued our onward way until about midnight, when we too began to feel fatigued; to this time we had scarcely distinguished our sleepiness from the everlasting monotony of the darkness. We laid down on the gravel-strewn earth a few paces to the left of the road, but the night was quite chilly, and although previously we had run almost a sweat, we felt the cool night air not a little. Thomen had matches with him, and we attempted to gather a quantity of the half-dry bushes, *greasewood*, in the process injuring our hands to no small degree. We had no particular difficulty in kindling a fire, but it was of such a character that it soon went out, these plants not being woody enough to make a lasting fire. We dug holes in the sand and in these sought to shelter ourselves somewhat against the cold night air, in which, however, we scarcely succeeded. We made a fire again, and again laid down, until the gray light of day [August 18] appeared, when Bunzel once more caught up with us.

We had with us nothing either to eat or to drink, but the need to eat did not torment us especially. As the sun rose toward the zenith, however, its effects became ever more difficult to endure; there was then nothing which provided any shade at all, and if we threw ourselves on the ground, we felt the heat all the more, so that we longed for the return of the night.

Some 2 miles ahead of us we could see a rocky hill [Grayback Mountain] which rose about 70 feet above the plain, and over which the road led. Thomen, Zins, and Bunzel decided to go on that much further and there await the arrival of our wagons, while I preferred to wait where I was, that I might the sooner obtain water when the wagons should come.[45] Ever more insupportable grew my thirst and I scarcely turned my gaze from the place where I anticipated that the wagons must appear from the distant hill over which we had come last night. At length I saw a little dust arising, but it soon proved to be only a solitary horseman coming from that direction; on his reaching me, I found him to be a little old fellow from Baden, Müller, who was traveling with Hoppe.[46] He had come ahead on horseback with two small kegs and was to go on till he should reach fresh water, when he was to fill them and turn back again, Müller informed me that the company had remained overnight at the foot of the steep hill and had gotten over it early this morning only with considerable difficulty. He thought they must soon be seen coming down out of the hills, and rightly; there where I had seen the first dust cloud arising, another now ascended on high, and like a snake the wagons wound down into the plain. To me they seemed long in coming; however come they did, and I had quenched my thirst by the time we reached the rocky hill before us. At this hill we made a mid-day halt and rested for an hour. We gave each head of stock about a gallon of water, together with a little of the grass we had brought with us, of which, indeed, they ate, but more gladly would they have had additional water. It was probably fully 3 o'clock when we resumed our journey and proceeded down from the hill again into the plain, soon coming to a small Sahara desert. The wind blew strongly from the northeast and drove the whitish-yellow sand before it as our wagons wound their way among numerous sand hills from 10

---

[45] Lienhard waited for the wagons perhaps two miles beyond the point where the old "Hastings Road" crossed US 40-50 in the 1950s. A small monument, 35 road miles west of Grantsville on the line of the old highway, once marked the junction of highway and trail, but in 1994 nothing identifies where the trail crosses Interstate 80. The highway swings south around Grayback Mountain but the wagon road went directly across it. From this point the Hastings Road remains to the right of the highway, aiming for Pilot Peak, whereas US 40-50 had Wendover, at the south end of Silver Island, as its objective, as does I-80.

[46] Müller is not otherwise identified. A Franz and a Thomas Müller are found a little later at Sutter's Fort, and indeed are mentioned by Lienhard in that part of his narrative published by Mrs. Wilbur, but without anything to indicate that he had known them earlier. The former was a Swiss from Zollfinger, Canton of Aargau; the latter, a German, became Sutter's head gardener.

to 12 feet high; the air was darkened so that we could scarcely perceive the sun; one might have supposed that already twilight had come, although it was yet too early; this flying sand perhaps most resembled a very heavy snowstorm. Fortunately, this Sahara was not so great in extent as that of Africa; it could not have been more than 4 or 5 miles wide here where we crossed it.[47] When we had left it behind, the wind died away almost entirely.

We had now reached a totally barren plain where not the slightest sign of plant life was to be seen. In this heavy twilight it had become so dark that we could just make out the ground on which we were now traveling, a sand mixture infused with salt so as to form a grayish clay, which had a very considerable resemblance to the bottom of the salt lake itself. Either this locality at times stood under salt water, perhaps in the rainy season, or the plain had formerly been a part of the salt lake, or possibly it was here connected with it. On reaching this plain, we halted and again gave each head of cattle a little water and grass. Taking a little refreshment ourselves, we then recommenced our onward journey, hoping that by the next morning we would have arrived at the expectantly watched-for freshwater springs and their attendant good grass.

Zins and I remained with the wagon, while Ripstein, Diel, and Thomen went on ahead intending to go on until they should arrive at the freshwater springs. Step by step we continued over this gray waste in the increasing darkness of the night. Here and there the ground was a little soft, additional evidence that not long since water must have been standing here. We went on without ceasing until about 1 o'clock in the morning, when suddenly our three comrades spoke to us; a short distance from here they had come upon a man who had remained behind to take care of several wagons; from this man they had learned that the distance to the nearest freshwater springs and grass was at least 24 miles. We soon came up to the wagon in which this man was staying, and from him we learned that those ahead of us had left many wagons behind and driven the cattle ahead to the springs, there to recover strength, after which they would come back for the wagons. Up to this time our cattle appeared to be in passable condition; the night was cool, and the level plain excellent to travel on, with the exception of a few somewhat wet places. In the far-off it was gradually growing lighter; some distance to our right we could

---

[47] Compare Bryant's description of the area west of Grayback, in his journal for August 3.

perceive in the dawning light a chain of very steep-sloped mountains; a little to our left, almost in front of us, we could make out a few other mountain-tops [Silver Island] which rose almost perpendicularly from the gray, dead plain, and there we hoped to find the longed-for water. When the sun came up, slowly rising like a great, round, red disk from the apparently limitless plain that stretched before us, we had come to within a few miles of this last high mountain.[48] Up to this time we had passed 24 wagons which had been left behind;[49] now we made a halt. Our oxen all appeared to be suffering; the whole of their bowels appeared to cry out, an incessant rumbling which broke out from all; they were hollow-eyed, and it was most distressing to see the poor animals suffer thus. We could give them no more water, having only a little for ourselves, and the grass we gave them they would hardly touch. However, we could not remain here, we had to go on, and the poor cattle had to drag the wagons along behind them. Presently we came upon abandoned cattle, a few already dead, while others yet moved their ears; they could be saved only by others coming back bringing water for them.[50]

The lofty, precipitous mountains [Silver Island] rising from the plain now loomed up on our left as we approached their north end. On them, however, grew no vegetation; they appeared reddish-brown, as if burned; at the foot of these mountains it was perfectly dry, without a sign of moisture. In front of us, near these mountains, rose a pebbly knoll; surely we must now be near the water, so we hoped, but alas, when we reached the summit we saw, over a 10-mile-wide valley, through the bluish haze, another high mountain beyond [Pilot Peak], and we realized that we would have to reach this before we should have completed the crossing of the endless plain.

The valley between us and the haze-shrouded mountains in the distance looked like a wide, large lake, the apparent surface of which here and there mirrored a deceptive semblance of the mountains and hills; we knew, however, that this was only a mirage, having already

---

[48] Again Lienhard is somewhat arbitrarily translated. Although the sun rose behind him, his language, literally rendered, would be, "the sun came up, directly before us, slowly rising like a great, round, red disk from the apparently limitless plain."

[49] In other words, it had been necessary temporarily to abandon in the Salt Desert over a third of all the wagons comprising the Harlan-Young train.

[50] From various scraps of information Lienhard provides we may conclude that the Harlan-Young party crossed the Salt Desert during the three days August 16–18.

experienced several illusions of the kind. Straight through the seeming expanse of water, from the opposite shore, a black monster moved
toward us like a frightful, giant snake, in a long, sinuous line. We all
stared a long time at this puzzling apparition; it separated into detached parts, and we then supposed it must be a band of Indians.
However, as we traveled slowly down the hill to meet them, we realized that what we saw was neither a monstrous snake nor friendly
Indians, but a considerable number of men with oxen, a few mules,
and horses, who were going back into the barren desert to recover
their abandoned wagons.

We had taken but one short rest since sunrise, at which time we
drank the last of our warm water. Not only our cattle but all the
members of the company were now suffering from thirst. We found
the returning teamsters supplied with water, carried in small kegs on
the backs of some of the oxen or mules. At our request they willingly
gave each of us a drink, but they could spare none for our cattle and
we asked none for them. The sun shone burningly hot, as it did each
day when not obscured by clouds, and we were seriously afraid that
our cattle would not be able to get across this wide valley, for they
appeared to be suffering terribly.

Our wagon was the second in line, but our leading yoke of oxen
every instant were in danger of breaking their horns off in the wheels
of the wagons ahead of us, for they continually tried to pull up to it so
that they might remain a while in its shade, in this way continually
getting between the wheels. In an effort to avert this, Zins drove
while I walked ahead of them; soon, however, I received quite a
thrust from the horns, since each of the two foremost oxen sought to
profit by my small shadow, and to push the other away. Eager as I
was to alleviate as much as possible the sufferings of the poor devils,
in this way they very soon cured me of my enthusiasm for going
ahead of them.

In this valley there was a great quantity of the finest salt, often in
a 2-inch-thick crust. Here and there flowed, a few inches deep,
crystal-clear water which, however, was as salty as salt itself, and the
poor cattle, tormented by their dreadful thirst, tried constantly to
drink of it, only to shudder in consequence. Slowly we were nearing
the huge, common camping place where a small village of wagons
stood. To this point not a single head of our cattle had given out, and
we were coming ever closer to the green grass when suddenly first
one and then the other ox of our leading yoke fell, scarcely a quarter
of a mile from the grassy ground. Zins and I had considerable

difficulty getting them to their feet again, but after this was accomplished, we went slowly on until we arrived at the grass-covered ground, and scarcely had the oxen reached there than they began to run as rapidly as though they were not at all tired. On arriving at the lower end of this wagon village we stopped and freed the poor animals from their yokes. Fortunately the spring was so hedged about by the wagons that the cattle could not gain free access to it, and it was therefore necessary for them to satisfy their thirst slowly from the water that flowed over the ground and gathered in their own footprints. A full two hours passed before they seemed to get quite enough, after which their first need appeared to be rest.

The spring [Pilot Spring] was a fine one about 4 by 6 feet across, and from 4 to 5 feet deep, the water fresh and good, and entirely free from any saline or mineral taint. The Kollog [Kellogg] brothers had a fine, large, black hound which they had brought along with them to this point, and which probably was extremely thirsty by the time it arrived here; it had jumped into the spring, immersing itself and drinking, but when it came out upon the grass again, it had suddenly fallen down, and shortly afterward it died.[51]

---

[51] Some recollection of this sad happening was preserved in the Kellogg family. Frank E. Kellogg, *The Ancestors and Descendants of Florentine Erwin Kellogg* (Santa Barbara, 1907), 16, relates that the Kelloggs started to California with a "large and powerful Newfoundland dog (old Buck)," and that he "perished from thirst while crossing the 80 mile waterless desert a little west of the Great Salt Lake."

The "Kollog" brothers to whom Lienhard refers here and subsequently were Florentine Erwin, born at Batavia, New York, January 1, 1816, who died at Goleta, California, October 1, 1889, and his younger brother, Benjamin Franklin Ephraim, born in Illinois April 30, 1822, who died at Anaheim, California, December 16, 1890. According to the family tradition as published by the former's son, Florentine set out for California with his wife, Rebecca Jane Williams, and three small children, Angeline, Philander, and Jane. Their outfit consisted of "a two-horse carriage, two wagons loaded with provisions, tools and household goods, . . . five yoke of oxen, two yoke of cows, and three horses, two of which were exchanged for mules at Fort Bridger on the way. He and his family rode in the carriage, while he put the wagons in charge of his brother Frank, William McDonnell and John Spitler."

A letter written by the younger brother at the Upper Crossing of the Platte on July 5, 1846, has been deposited in typescript form in the Bancroft Library by Mrs. Irene D. Paden. This letter, among other interesting matters, mentions having encountered along the trail "brother Philander who had been out trapping in the mountains and caught about $700 worth of fur but unfortunately had 3 mules and 2 horses stolen by the Apaches and come up to the road to buy horses of the passing company." This third Kellogg brother, who was born at Batavia

Although Mr. Hoppe was not always our captain, our party was known as Hoppe's Company. We were told that the companies which had gone in advance of us had been generally of the opinion that our party would suffer most in crossing this long desert, to the point, perhaps, of perishing altogether. Here we were, however, the only company which had had to leave behind neither a wagon nor an animal, at which they were not a little amazed.[52]

The journey from the last good water to this point had taken from 9 o'clock in the morning of the 17th to about 4 o'clock in the afternoon of the 19th of August, and during this time only on the first night had the cattle actually enjoyed rest, without, even then, being freed from their yokes. Otherwise, all the stops we made put together could hardly have amounted to more than 4 hours, and apart from this it was continuous driving until our arrival at these springs. During that time, all the water we could give to each head of cattle could scarcely have exceeded $1\frac{1}{2}$ gallons. To be sure, we had spared our cattle as much as we could under the circumstances, but we had reason to congratulate ourselves that we had made this crossing without suffering the slightest loss.

In spite of long-sustained fatigue everyone was animated and happy; the young girls gathered together and sang, while the young Americans danced to the squeaky sounds which a man named Roadies[53] coaxed from his old fiddle, so that the dust eddied up in

---

June 17, 1810, did not go to California this year; he is said to have been killed accidentally by an Indian in 1848. He had figured in Lienhard's narrative at the crossing of the Platte, for Lienhard and some others hired his services as a buffalo hunter.

One additional detail concerning the Hastings Cutoff is furnished by the little work cited above, which says that the Kelloggs arrived in California with their teams "greatly reduced by reason of having to furnish a fellow emigrant by the name of Fowler with oxen, all of whose cattle had died on the 80 mile desert. Also their supply of food was almost entirely exhausted, owing to the fact that they had divided with others whose supplies had given out."

[52] It may be that Lienhard's company was the only ox-train that ever crossed the Salt Desert without losing an animal or having to go back into the desert. No other party accomplished this feat in 1846, and the swarming gold-seekers of 1850 did hardly better. Perhaps this explains Jefferson's otherwise incomprehensible advice that not more than 5 or 6 wagons should go in company in crossing the desert; if so, that in turn serves to indicate how many wagons here made up Lienhard's party.

[53] Lienhard's fiddler apparently was Thomas Rhoads, one of the numerous Mormons who looked Salt Lake Valley over before Brigham Young and the Pioneer party arrived. With his wife and 12 children, after reaching California,

clouds; in short, one might have supposed the whole journey completed.

On the 20th we of course remained here; again there was washing and mending to do while the cattle were given the rest and recuperation they so much needed. They seemed to relax very well indeed, except that the grass had become very short in consequence of the number of the cattle and the long stay here. Today two hunters came into our camp, Frenchmen if I am not mistaken, as also two or three Sho Shawnee Indians, with whom the hunters could carry on a somewhat halting conversation. As provision, the Indians carried with them in a leather bag a brownish mass which the hunters said was prepared from an edible root the Indians dug from the ground— the very same for which we called them Diggers (*Gräber*). One of these hunters, on leaving one of their camping places, had recently left behind a revolver which was found by a Shoshawnee. Not knowing whether the gun was loaded, or how to handle it, he had played with it aimlessly until suddenly, and to the great surprise of the Indian, the gun went off, thereby occasioning a slight injury. Thereafter the Indians had regarded the revolver as a mysterious object and went almost in fear of it, regarding the discharge of the same as a sign from the *Manito* (great spirit) that the object would bring nothing but harm should they keep it. They had very cautiously picked it up from the ground, and having observed which direction the hunters went, had concluded to carry this weird gun to them and hand it over, lest *Manito* take some other vengeful action. The hunters did not attempt to put an end to the superstition of the Indians; on the contrary, they sought to strengthen it yet further; to this state of affairs they owed it that they again had the revolver; such a firearm lost in the wilds is a loss that one cannot immediately replace.[54]

Rhoads settled on the Cosumnes River. His sons John and Daniel took an honorable part in the relief expeditions which brought the Donners out of the Sierra that winter. The sons remained in California, but the elder Rhoads, his wife having died, journeyed back to Utah in the summer of 1849 with some of the Saints who had come to California on the ship *Brooklyn*; J. Goldsborough Bruff met this little company of ten wagons on the Humboldt on September 5, 1849, and derived from Rhoads much information about the routes to and conditions in California. According to Bancroft's "Pioneer Register," Rhoads died in Utah in 1869 at the age of 77.

[54] It would be stretching coincidence beyond belief to suppose that Lienhard was not here describing the return of the "nine-shooter" rifle lost by Colonel Russell at Willow Creek, as described by Bryant under date of August 1. The "hunters" Lienhard mentions must have been Hudspeth and one or more com-

Today most of the wagons which had been left on the desert were brought into camp, and everyone was in good spirits. Stories were told, and there was singing and dancing. At one spot the young maidens had gathered together, and among them, like the devil among angels, Miss Lucinda also had taken her place, although, to be sure, without having been invited; we could easily enough see that Lucinda's presence among them was not very agreeable to the others. Such a thing, however, she would not perceive. The young men stood in a circle around the singing girls. Alfred, Lucinda's [former] ten-hour-husband, stood at my left close beside me, and like most of the rest of us was listening to the songs when all at once Lucinda hurled a short piece of wood at him—without, however, hitting him; the piece of wood grazed the hair of both of us. Had it actually struck Alfred, he might well have been injured, for Lucinda was a healthy specimen of two-legged animal. This new heroic deed of Lucinda's was too much for the people to stomach, and the elder Kellogg came up to Alfred to ask, "Are you going to let such behavior pass unnoticed?" In his simplicity, the young fellow answered that he was but a poor follower and did not know whether he even had a friend. Kellogg told him that we were all his friends, and he should, were he in Alfred's place, by no means permit the insulting behavior of this person to pass unnoticed. Although the girls had all moved away from her and all showed by their scornful glances the regard in which they held Lucinda, this in no way induced her to leave the place.

With respect to this person, I wish to have done with her, so I will here relate the rest of what I know about her. Lucinda had begun the journey with Hoppe's family, sought and found admission by the Harlans, and had from among them married the young fellow, Alfred, after failing of marriage with Zins, but during the night quarreled with him so that by the next morning they parted and would have absolutely nothing more to do with one another. She returned again to the Hoppes and cast an eye, if not two, on the large, good looking man, Mike, who drove the other wagon. He, however, no doubt to put an end to these pressing attentions, left Hoppe's employ

---

panions. If Lienhard has correctly placed the return of the rifle—if this did not happen back in Skull Valley—it follows that the Indians traveled more than a hundred miles, and across the Salt Desert at that, to propitiate the spirit watching over the gun. Lienhard's remarks about the "Manito" must be either an embellishment or a faulty understanding on the part of those who talked to the Indians, for the religious beliefs of the Shoshoni were animistic, not monotheistic.

the day after he shot the buffalo with my carbine. Hoppe had then written a letter purporting to be from Mike to Lucinda, which had allegedly been found on the road. Since Lucinda could not herself read the letter, Mr. Hoppe himself had the kindness to read it aloud in the presence of many belonging to the company. The letter consisted of an ardent declaration of love, such that the hearers, Lucinda excepted, had been much amused. Lucinda, however, hugged the excessive love letter to her breast after Hoppe handed it over, and had sighed, "Oh—my dear Mike, I wish you was here," etc. Miss Lucinda soon after returned to the Harlans again, with whom she remained till the beginning of the long desert known under the name, "the long trip" [i.e., "the long drive"]. Here, as already set forth, they had thrown her bundle of clothes out of the wagon as a means of ridding themselves of her, and only with great difficulty, by threatening him, almost, was Hoppe finally prevailed upon to take her again into his wagon. No sooner had we all arrived at this place where we, the Harlans, and the greater part of the whole company were gathered, than she again found shelter with the Harlans.

It is said that when Lucinda had hardly reached the first settlement in California she married a hefty young man; this fellow, however, soon turned sickly and died! In the autumn of 1847, while I was acting as superintendent at Sutter's Fort, I had the opportunity of seeing Lucinda again single, shortly after her "dear, dear husband" died and was buried. At the Fort, she felt most comforted when people said to her, "Lucinda, you are still very young and you will surely find another man." Her usual reply was, "Do you think so?" However, the people in the Fort did not well accord with her love's desire, for with the exception of a rather thin Irishman named Pray [Edmund Bray] nobody would have anything to do with her, and Bray himself shortly appeared to be doubtful whether upon taking her as his wife, he would be able to fulfill his duties as a husband. In view of such doubts it seemed that his first ardent desire to be married suddenly cooled and he decided that he preferred to continue a while longer in his proud bachelorship. At all events, Lucinda evidently at last became convinced that there was no fishing in the Fort. She left this region to rejoice with her presence Pueblo de San Jose (the village of the holy St. Joseph), which is situated near the southern end of the Bay of San Francisco. On arriving there, she reportedly put an end to her widowhood by marrying a sailor. This experiment, according to persons who knew and had seen her, she repeated three times within six weeks. It is well that I have no further particulars of Lucinda's history to relate, for it has been difficult enough to conclude this one story about her.[55]

On the afternoon of August 21, toward evening, we forsook this camping place, the grass having become scant, and went on 2 miles south, where water equally good, and grass undoubtedly better were to be found, although many others were there.[56]

On the 22nd we remained in camp here, since our cattle were in need of still more rest; moreover, we faced a long stretch of road on which we should find neither grass nor water. On this day I found two small scorpions. Around us there were many small springs, and as far as the water moistened the ground, the vegetation was green and beautiful; however, the water soon oozed away in the sandy ground, and beyond, all was the same everlasting dry monotony.

Again on the 23rd we remained here, yearning however to move on.[57] The weather was clear and quite warm; toward evening a warm

[55] A girl in her late twenties, Lucinda was first met by Lienhard as a servant of the Hoppes at the rendezvous west of Independence, Mo. Along the way, she was the victim of a practical joke at the hands of Zins, who induced her to believe that they were going to be married, to the point that she dressed in her best finery and appeared for the ceremony. After her arrival in California there are three references to her in the *New Helvetia Diary*. On August 20, 1847, the *Diary* records, "Th Green, Lucinda, Tucker etc. arrived." Next day, "Lucinda left for Bear Creek." And on September 21, "Lucinda the Widdow arrived." Edmund Bray, mentioned by Lienhard in this connection, who had come overland to California in 1844 with the Stephens-Townsend-Murphy party, during 1847 was an assistant overseer for Sutter.

[56] The first camp had been on the old Cummings Ranch, once the Pete McKellar property, and in 1994 the TL Bar Ranch; the spring to which Lienhard moved was that on the old Eugene Munsee homestead, once part of the Charles McKellar Ranch and now also part of the TL Bar. Note that Jefferson shows the change in camp, without dating the camp, or stating the mileage. A peculiarity of the Jefferson map is that it applies no name to the Pilot Range, and since it does not adequately depict the eastern slope of the range, gives the impression that "Bonark Wells" were located in the middle of a wide valley. The name, "Fire Mountain," which Jefferson applies to Silver Island is not inappropriate. His name for the Salt Desert, "Desert of Utariah," seems to be a coinage of his own, perhaps a combination of "Utah" and "pariah."

[57] Some of the Harlan-Young company already had begun to move on, but as yet we have no journal to describe the experiences of those breaking trail. In the *California Star*, February 13, 1847, George McKinstry, in criticizing the dilatory movements of the Donner party, remarked that the Donners should have been able to overtake the Harlan-Young train ahead, for the latter "were travelling slow, on account of being obliged to make an entire new rout for several hundred miles through heavy sage and over mountains, and delayed four days by the guides hunting out passes in the mountains."

west wind arose.

On August 24th we *five German Boys* broke camp, leaving the rest of the company behind. It appeared to us as if the zeal of our company to press on had relaxed. We still had a long and difficult drive before us, after which the cattle again would have to be allowed to recruit, hence no time should be wasted. Our way led at first in a southwesterly direction, through the salt plain, past several springs, some of which were salty and others fresh, with very little grass. After traveling perhaps 6 miles we climbed gradually through a gorge between rocky cliffs [Silver Zone Pass], a so-called *Gap*, whereby our course bent ever more to the west. On both sides of the gorge were high, overhanging rocks; in this gorge, so it was said, was a well which had been dug by immigrants who had passed through two years earlier, and this well we were obliged to reach this evening.[58] Although a pair of us were coming up the gorge ahead of the slowly moving wagons, too rapidly did the darkness of the night come over us to discover the indications of a spring. The oxen were tired and followed reluctantly in the track of those still in advance of us. At last we decided to wait until daylight. We fastened our cattle with a small chain in a hasty fashion to a wagon wheel, took a little to eat, and lay down to sleep, with the understanding that we would rise very early the next morning. Ripstein today felt quite unwell, having fever and no appetite; he was carried in the wagon.

On the next morning, the 25th, scarcely had the day begun to dawn than Father Thomen woke up his sleepy comrades in accordance with the agreement. The cold morning air felt only too agreeable, and we just then were quite willing to sleep on a while longer. But Father Thomen this morning was so ready with his heartfelt *Donner* and *Wetter* that I for one began to have a dislike for our wagon box and to rub my sleepy eyes. The creaking of the wagon box afforded sufficient evidence to Thomen that I had heard him. He left, but again his battery of *Donnerwetter* opened up, to such effect that Zins began to roundly abuse him and tell him it was wholly unnecessary under the circumstances to make so much noise. In my case, however, the result had been that my feet were now hanging down

---

[58] Lienhard obviously has reference to the Bidwell party, which in 1841 took the first wagons over the Toano Range through Silver Zone Pass, though John Bidwell's diary says nothing about digging for water in the pass. Lienhard's remarks about the distance traveled are somewhat misleading; it was perhaps 17 miles from his last camp to the summit of the pass. Clyman and Bryant of course crossed the Toanos some 20 miles farther south.

from the wagon and I was attempting to yawn myself awake. A few more *Donnerwetters* and I was on the ground supporting Father Thomen in his endeavor. Since Zins now found himself in the minority, he as well as Diel finally roused up.

We found in our vicinity a little bunchgrass, "*sagegrass*," which we cut and gave to our oxen, who greedily devoured it. With our breakfast we were soon enough finished, after which we yoked up and again proceeded slowly on down through the gorge. We had gone scarcely 100 yards before we actually found near the road a spring hole perhaps 12 feet deep. We stopped, naturally, and equipping myself with a bucket and a small receptacle I forced my way the few steps down to the water. The water was clear, cool, and pleasant to the taste. Of course we quenched our own thirst first and set aside a little to carry along with us, after which our oxen got about 2 gallons to the head. Though insufficient, this was for the animals some slight alleviation. Had hostile Indians come near us last night, they could hardly have found a better place to surprise and massacre us than from behind the various detached rocks around camp; it would not have been difficult for them to have trapped and gathered us up as into a sack.

We at last reached the end of the gorge, and from it emerged out upon the table land. Although this valley had no salt flats, the quality of the soil was in other respects the same, pebbly and sandy. On our right we came upon a great circle of interwoven cedar branches with a wide opening. The ground there was the same sort of dry soil as elsewhere, and what the purpose of this circle could be was to us at first an enigma. Later on, I learned from old hunters that in this circle the Indians caught the swift-footed antelope, and this was the way they went about it: Perceiving an antelope near this circle. a group of Indians would seek, by naturally drawing closer, to drive the animal into the entrance to the circle. The closer the animal approached the opening in the circle, the greater care the Indians took that it should escape neither to the side nor behind them. Finding itself approached ever nearer to the side and behind by the advancing Indians, the antelope would elect to flee into the wide opening before it rather than to accelerate its flight alongside the enemy. As soon as the antelope was actually inside the circle, the Indians looked on the hunt as a success. The best bowmen placed themselves on both sides of the opening in the cedar branches, while others formed a ring, part in and part outside the circle, and then began the true hunting. Seeing the enemy approaching from all directions, the antelope would be afraid of the cedar-circle, but would see the wide opening by which it entered and hope to escape the same way. Scarcely would it emerge, however, than it would be shot from both sides, the arrows entering the body with such great force that when it was not immediately killed, it could not flee much farther and soon would be brought down by the pursuing Indians.

The great, gray wolf catches the antelope in a very similar way, and perhaps the Indians have learned their cunning stratagem directly from the wolf. At all events. if I may be allowed a few more words, I shall demonstrate its intelligence and powers of calculation.

To catch a healthy antelope, at least four wolves must associate themselves, not that a single wolf is afraid, but because they know that the antelope is much swifter than they are. When this respectable company of four or more large wolves has assembled, they creep up in such a manner that they form a large circle, the antelope of course being in the middle between them. Naturally, they seek to take the antelope upon an open plain. Now they gradually approach it, so that when the antelope perceives one and seeks to turn in another direction, it see one there also, ahead and behind; suddenly, to its alarm, it perceives that wherever it turns, the frightful enemy comes ever nearer. In its agitation the antelope loses its presence of mind and seeks to break out of the wolf circle anywhere possible, but the wolves come on warily, and rapidly closer. The antelope becomes blind with fear and suddenly it is seized by one of the wolves; soon afterward, the one which but a short time before was so swift-footed will perhaps have been wholly devoured.[59]

We arrived at our new camping place about 11 o'clock in the morning, finding another company already encamped there.[60] At this place, two years earlier, an immigrant company had camped; apparently they had suffered the loss of the greater part of their stock along the way, for they had abandoned their wagons here, burying in the ground what they could not carry with them. After they left, the Indians had burned the wagons; the travelers in advance who had

---

[59] The version of Lienhard's narrative printed in Switzerland in 1898 at this point appropriately interjected, "*So horte man erzählen*" (So the story goes).

[60] It may be that Jefferson was with this company which had preceded Lienhard to the Big Springs at Johnson Ranch in Gosiute Valley, or Jefferson may have been one of those who came along behind Lienhard. All that is clear with respect to Jefferson's movements is that he traveled on from these springs, the "Relief Springs" of his map, on the 26th, one day ahead of Lienhard.

recently arrived here had found what was left of the wagons.[61] Ripstein today was quite ill; he had the true measles, which began to show on his skin. From our camp of last night we had traveled about 14 miles to this point. We had not found exactly a superabundance of grass here, but there was a tolerable supply, and the water was also good, so we decided to remain here the next day, August 26, and await the arrival of our company.

Although we caught sight of no Indians, during the night we could see their fires in the nearby mountains and hills; however, we were not molested in any way. Since our company had caught up with us again yesterday, we left our camp today together again.[62] Our road led us in a direction almost straight south. After traveling 14

---

[61] The Bidwell party of 1841 had in fact abandoned its last eight wagons at this point, journeying the rest of the way to California by horseback and afoot. After reaching California, John Bidwell sent east an abstract of his journal to be published for the information of other travelers. A copy of the printed diary, the only copy known to exist, is now in the Bancroft Library, brought to California in 1846 by George McKinstry. On the page where Bidwell describes the abandonment of the wagons, McKinstry scrawled a marginal note, unfortunately not dated: "We cooked our supper & breakfast with fires made from the remains of three wagons—McKinstry, Jr." The other five wagons presumably had been burned by the Indians. Jefferson takes note of Joseph Chiles' presence in the company which had left its wagons here by calling the locality "Chiles Cache."

[62] From this point on, a certain confusion attends Lienhard's dates. He has clearly said that the "five German boys" remained at the springs on the Johnson Ranch over the 26th, on which date those behind—probably referring to Kyburz, the Barbers, the Hoppes, and perhaps others—caught up with them. We are then justified in assuming that Lienhard broke camp again on the 27th. But as will be seen from the entry following, Lienhard has an additional entry for August 27, succeeded by entries for August 28–30. On the other hand, he has no entry at all for August 31. Did he fail to remember that August had 31 days, or by skipping a day, did he undertake to bring his diary in line with the calendar? This would offer an easy way out of our difficulties, by correcting his stated dates for August 27–30, except that his entries for August 27–28 would then describe two successive 14-mile journeys south down Gosiute Valley, whereas the distance to the springs at Flowery Lake, where the trail turned west across the Pequops, was only about half that distance—estimated by Jefferson at 15 miles. By way of compounding all these difficulties, Lienhard's travel later, as he proceeds south down Ruby Valley, is short by about one day's journey of the required distance to reach Hastings Pass. Is it possible that Lienhard scrambled either his diary of 1846 or the narrative based on his diary, by shifting to Gosiute Valley a day's travel which should properly have been placed in Ruby Valley? No other answer to the puzzle readily suggests itself. In the light of the above, however, we will conclude that Lienhard broke camp on the 27th, and that the present entry describes that day's travel.

miles, we reached a place where we found sufficient grass and water [Flowery Lake]. There was, on the other hand, no great abundance of firewood, but we managed with the pieces of wild sage at hand. The nature of the valley bottom is the same as hitherto.

On August 27th we left this camping place and proceeded about 14 miles across the valley bottom almost directly south, where we again made a halt at a spring of good water, in the vicinity of which there was also a sufficiency of grass. Wild game we frequently came upon; I saw today at least 40 antelope.[63]

On the 28th our road led almost wholly westerly across a depression in the mountain (*gap*) [Jasper Pass]. Emerging into a valley [Independence Valley] in all respects the same as the one we had left, we crossed it and after having traveled 14 miles once more camped at the foot of a mountain lying opposite, at a fresh water spring [Mound Springs] in the vicinity of which there was again a little grass. The nearby mountain [northern extension of Spruce Mountain] was smaller than the one [Pequop Mountains] we crossed today. The weather was clear, with a warm south wind at night. In this valley we today saw several sand-storms from 150 to 300 feet high, very rapidly turning or whirling about themselves, moving comparatively slowly as they moved along the valley from the south to the north.

On the 29th we resumed our journey directly up the mountain slope in a westerly direction, over a low place in the mountain, where a little water gave rise to some scattered grass, a few small cedars and several little white alder trees, and thence down into another dry valley [Clover Valley] across which the road led us to the mountainous region opposite [East Humboldt Mountains]. We found a spring at the foot of these mountains, and to the extent that the water moistened the ground, a scanty supply of grass. Of sage there was no lack. Our march this day again amounted to about 14 miles. [Not?] far off to the right from our camp, in several places, smoke mounted upward, evidence that Indians lived in this vicinity.[64] The weather was

---

[63] As seen by the previous note, either the travel here described is an inadvertent repetition of the actual travel of August 27, or experiences attributed to this day have strayed from their proper place—say, September 2.

[64] Lienhard has now reached the Warm Spring in Clover Valley, Jefferson's "Mill Spring." From the time he reached Flowery Lake, on the night of the 27th, his trail coincided with that of Clyman and Bryant. They had crossed the East Humboldt Range west of Lienhard's camp and gone to and from the Humboldt through Secret Pass, but the wagon trail Lienhard was following instead bent southwest into Ruby Valley to go down around the Rubies. The In-

the same as yesterday.

On August 30 we took up our journey again, starting off in a southwesterly direction. The low place where we crossed the mountains was rather steep. The valley [Ruby Valley] lying before us was again broad, in most respects resembling those crossed earlier. Our road during the day proceeded in a southwesterly direction across this flat valley; the mountains [Ruby Mountains] we were approaching rose from it high and precipitous. A large number of splendid, cold, freshwater springs broke out at the base of these mountains; we could perceive them at a distance, from the scattered timber which grew about them, and it did our eyes good to see the grass here growing. At one of these springs we encamped, finding there one of the companies which had gone in advance of us.[65]

The Indians here were not so shy as those in the vicinity of our previous encampment. Some 30 Sho shannees made their appearance at our camping place, of which two were old, exceedingly ugly squaws, and the others adult men, ranging in age from perhaps 18 to 50-odd years. The two eldest Indians were fat old fellows, one of

---

dian fires Lienhard noted were probably those of a band of Shoshoni who lived some miles farther north in Clover Valley; see Steward, op. cit., 145.

[65] Lienhard does not estimate this day's mileage, but Jefferson, now a day ahead, traveled 16 1/2 miles in going over this section of the trail, his camp probably on or near Thompson Creek. It will be observed that this campsite is the first Jefferson has dated since that of August 7, near Garfield, but thanks to Lienhard we can account for his movements with almost complete accuracy during the three weeks in which he has taken no account of the calendar. The trail Jefferson shows the road to have crossed enroute to this camp was an Indian trail making for the north end of Ruby Valley and Secret Pass, and it was substantially by this route that Lt. Beckwith in May, 1854, came back into the old Hastings Road, from which he had separated in Skull Valley to round the salt desert to the south. After the reconnaissance of Secret Pass described in the Bryant journal, note 72, Beckwith proceeded south through Ruby Valley by the Hastings Road as far as the west end of Hastings Pass, from which he struck off on his own into the mountainous country to the west, in preference to descending Huntington Creek to the Humboldt. It was Beckwith who gave name to the Franklin River, and the map produced by his topographer, E. W. Egloffstein, bestowed their present names upon Franklin Lake and Snow Water Lake, in Clover Valley to the north.

The *Wendover* and *Wells* quadrangles can be used to follow Lienhard and Jefferson from Pilot Peak to Clover Valley, and from this point on, in addition to the *Halleck* and *Jiggs* quadrangles, we have the *Humboldt National Forest* map (Ruby Division) and also one of the characteristically useful maps of the Wheeler Survey, *Atlas Sheet No. 19*. This latter map, based on field surveys of 1869 and 1872, is especially appropriate to these studies in that it depicts the Hastings road by name, clear around the Rubies, and on north down Huntington Valley.

whom had hair perfectly red, the only red-haired Indian I have seen. His hair, by the way, was coarse, but in his whole bearing and figure he was like the rest of his companions. A sour, doltish Englishman was smoking his clay pipe. The Indians gave him to understand by means of signs that they would find it most agreeable to be permitted a few puffs also. The Englishman, however, rejected their pleas, answering that these filthy Indians should not smoke from his pipe. Although the Indians did not understand his words, they recognized his forbidding mien as unfriendly to them, and we could immediately perceive an unpleasant expression on their dark faces.

The unfriendly behavior of the Englishman, however, was also disapproved by his fellow travelers; we regarded his action as rude, and under the circumstances, very unwise. While we were in the country of these Indians, it was to the interest of each of us to make them our friends, for through rude, hostile treatment we could soon transform these children of nature into bitter, treacherous enemies who could find many ways to injure us if they so desired. An elderly American woman, the mother of five grown children, who like her husband were members of the company encamped near us, sought to allay the angry feelings of the Indians. Quickly filling her own pipe with tobacco, she lighted it and handed it to one of the fat old Indians. He accepted it with every sign of the greatest satisfaction, took 10 or 12 large puffs, letting the smoke escape through his nose with obvious pleasure, and then gave it to his equally fat companion at his side. He, after having gratified himself similarly, handed it on to the next, and so it was repeated, without exception, until the last had had his turn. All were highly pleased over the signal favor which had been bestowed on them by the white man's squaw, and though earlier they had favored the unkind, rude Englishman with malignant, vengeful looks, the countenances they turned upon the woman without exception were friendly and smiling. Had the American woman stayed on here, the red-haired chief would perhaps out of sheer gratitude have raised her up to be the "Lady Chief."

The two old squaws were frightfully ugly, having only a small piece of animal skin around their loins, which barely covered their bodies. With their big, wrinkled, dirty bellies, they looked much like old sows which had just been wallowing in mud, although I do believe that a half-way respectable pig would have exceeded them in beauty. These Indian women were amazed at the soft, smooth, nearly white, yellow hair of an attractive 6-year-old boy. Their loud laughter was very like a high-pitched, many-sided, sonorous screaming which distorted their faces in a repulsive manner. They could hardly look enough at the boy; they must continually point at him; and their gabble with each other sounded much like that of a number of magpies when by chance a cat or a fox approaches. These squaws did not sit with the men but off by themselves. Of young Indians there was not a sign, which showed that the Indians were afraid the white men would carry them off; so that we could not so easily take them away, the children must have been hidden in a few coverts in the high, precipitous mountains near us, to remain while the whites stayed on. Probably the men would not have objected had the white men carried off the two old squaws, since they were permitted to visit the camp of the whites. A few of the men were adorned with a necklace of large bear claws, but otherwise they were almost wholly naked. In complexion they were as dark as the Sioux, but they were not so large and stately, more resembling the California Indians.[66]

On September 1 [August 31?] we remained here in camp.

On September 2 [1?] we traveled southward down this valley, not, however, making a very long day's journey.[67] The road led for the most part over a pretty, grassy, gradually flattening plain. Several large springs made fertile a considerable area; nevertheless, the large

---

[66] Ruby Valley had a relatively dense Shoshoni population, estimated by Steward at about 1 person to 2.8 square miles. They called themselves Wadadüka (*wada*, "rye grass seed," + *düka*, "eat"). Steward's list of bands, which he says is probably not complete, includes one of 13 families on the headwaters of the Franklin River, on the Ruby Valley side of Secret Pass; one of 16 families on the creek against the hills, west of the Neff Ranch; one in the flats near Overland; and a fourth, the largest of all, numbering some 20 to 40 families, at Medicine Spring, on the western slope of the "Cedar Mountains" east of Franklin Lake. Medicine Spring was preferred to the west side of Ruby Valley where Lienhard was passing because the Cedar Mountains were more productive of pine nuts than the Ruby Range. Steward, *op. cit.*, 144–52. Presumably Lienhard's visitors came from the first or second band above mentioned.

[67] In default of an estimate by Lienhard of the distance covered, we may assume that he traveled 9 1/2 miles to Jefferson's camp of August 30, which was probably on or near Overland Creek. For the day following, Jefferson shows a journey of 16 1/2 miles. As a comparable day's travel by Lienhard, we assign the 14 miles his narrative would have us believe he made on "August 27" to September 2 (see note 60 above). High-handed as this proceeding may be, it does establish some reasonable correspondence between Lienhard's dates and the calendar on the one hand, and his movements and the terrain on the other. We will assume, then, that after camping near Overland Creek September 1, he moved on September 2 south to about the locality of Indian Creek.

springs soon exhausted themselves after reaching the flat valley, so that close by we could see another waste of barren earth.

On September 3 we took up our journey on southward and made our camp near a rocky projection at the southerly end of the mountains, so to speak, in the middle of several large and magnificent springs of the best fresh water.[68] Were all these springs passed the last two days gathered together, they would form a not inconsiderable river, but here the water lost itself again in a scarcely half-mile-long stream. Several of the springs would have yielded water enough to drive a large mill. One of these springs, not far from our camping place, was particularly noteworthy. It formed a basin from 12 to 14 feet across and perhaps about as deep; it had the regular form of a stupendous, convex funnel. The water was crystal-clear; the sides were of an ash-gray color, and perhaps 5 or 6 feet beneath the surface, around the whole pool, there was a dark-colored band from 3/4 to 1 inch wide. From the bottom, exactly in the middle of the pool, the clear fluid welled upwards, driving small pieces of earth or mud a few feet high, which however, immediately sank back to the sides again. The basin was ringed around its entire circumference, the water flowing out only through a small opening in front. What made this spring even more interesting was that in it were perhaps a half

---

[68] On September 3 Lienhard possibly traveled about another 14 miles south to or a little short of the springs on the Toganini Ranch, where the famous Overland Ranch of the Overland Stage Company was established about 1864. The ranch had its genesis some five years earlier. George Chorpening, the mail contractor between California and Utah, had experienced so much difficulty getting through the winter mails by way of the Salt Lake Cutoff that in the fall of 1858 he undertook to lay out a new mail road which would go west from Camp Floyd to the southern tip of the Rubies, and thence use the original Hastings road across Hastings Pass, down Huntington Valley, and through the canyon of the South Fork to the Humboldt. The mails were packed over this route the last few months of 1858 and most of the following year, and the mail stages themselves were using the route when Horace Greeley made his celebrated *Overland Journey* in the summer of 1859. The name of Huntington Valley dates from this time, for Lot Huntington was Chorpening's superintendent on the west half of the route. However, in the summer of 1859 Captain James H. Simpson succeeded in looking out across the Great Basin to Carson Valley a new road which kept south of the Humboldt Valley the entire distance; Simpson's route veered southwest from the west end of Hastings Pass, and thus, when Chorpening and his successors, Russell, Majors, & Waddell, and later Ben Holladay, adopted the Simpson line for their own, even this last part of the Hastings Cutoff fell into disuse, the only point of contact being the few miles through Hastings Pass, thenceforward also known as "Overland Pass."

dozen small fish, from 4 to 5 inches long, which played in this natural aquarium.[69] Nowhere else, on the whole journey between Missouri and California, did we find so many beautiful springs, and such good water, as here.

In the evening, as dark was coming on, a few young Shoshanees came to our camp. We gave them a little food and signified to them that they should then leave our camp, which they willingly did.

On September 4 our way led past the above-mentioned rocky projection around to a southwesterly direction, whereby we came gradually if only slightly higher; there was again the same growth of small underbrush and sage, growing from the sandy, pebbly desert earth. Late in the afternoon we arrived at a small spring brook; with the good water there was also some grass, and we concluded to encamp here.[70] After we had made our camp, I went down the brook a short distance and there found in it a human skull—whether this skull originated from a white man or an Indian, there was no means of determining. I brought it back with me to camp, but as nobody seemed to be especially pleased over my find, I carried it back to where I had found it.

One of the company had shot a large, strong vulture still smelling of carrion—a so-called Turkey Buzzard—and brought it to camp. It had, however, so strong a stench that we quickly flung it away. It was soon disposed of a second time, by a few Indian children; seeing that

---

[69] There are a number of "fish springs" in the deserts of western Utah and eastern Nevada. A great curiosity to early travelers, they hark back to the lakes which overspread this region in the Quaternary period.

[70] Again we have trouble accounting for Lienhard's movements in relation to his chronology and the terrain. If he was correctly placed on the previous day in the vicinity of the Toganini Ranch, on this day he should have climbed up into Hastings Pass and descended its western slope to Huntington Creek, as Jefferson had done on September 2. By Lienhard's entry of the succeeding day, however, we have to suppose that this day's travel brought him only to a point somewhat short of the summit of Hastings Pass. This raises a serious difficulty: If Lienhard did not reach Huntington Valley until September 5, how is it possible that on the night of September 6th he was encamped at the head of the canyon of the South Fork? Jefferson, it will be noted, required three traveling days to get over this ground, and to his 46 1/2 miles must be added the 8 or 9 miles from the summit of Hastings Pass to his first camp on Huntington Creek. It is hardly conceivable that Lienhard and his companions, with their ox teams, made two successive drives of 28 miles on September 5 and 6. It may be that one day's entry somehow escaped the orderly progression of Lienhard's diary; if he crossed Hastings Pass on the morning of September 5, then he reached the head of South Fork Canyon on the night of September 7, not as the journal states, September 6.

the bird was left unemployed, one of them asked through signs whether they might be permitted to take it with them with a view to eating it. Naturally, we granted this request most willingly.

On September 5 we set out in the same direction as the previous day, but as we came higher up, the road veered around more to the right. Arriving at the summit of the pass [Hastings Pass] toward noon, we made a noon halt there where sundry springs broke out. Continuing on, we passed through an isolated forest of white alders and also, if I am not mistaken, a few cedars. The road wound first to the northwest and finally wholly to the north, now going steadily down into the valley [Huntington Valley]. Late in the afternoon, on reaching a place where we found sufficient grass and water, we camped again.[71] The high mountain, which for some days we had followed to the south, gone around, and finally climbed over, on its western side was not nearly so steep and precipitous as on its eastern, and must have been easy to climb, whereas the east side often rose nearly perpendicular. This range of mountains, and the three or four previously crossed, like the wide, flat, largely barren valleys lying between, extended nearly parallel with one another from north to south. The last range, I believe, is that called the Humboldt Mountains.[72]

September 6. Last night was the coldest we had up to this time; this morning the ground actually was a little frozen.[73] Still pursuing

---

[71] On Huntington Creek, probably some distance below Jefferson's camp of September 2, and perhaps in the vicinity of the present Sadler Ranch. The name Jefferson applies to Huntington Creek, "Glover Creek," is probably another mistake on the part of his engraver; "Clover Creek" would be more in keeping with Jefferson's taste in nomenclature. Be it noted, however, that Aquilla Glover, later prominent in the Donner relief, was an overland immigrant of this year, by what route is not known.

Jefferson's camp on Huntington Creek was probably about 6 miles south of the Sadler Ranch. He indicates that those ahead here had crossed the creek to go down its west bank, whereas he himself presumably crossed somewhere in the area of the Sadler Ranch.

[72] Evidence once more that Lienhard looked over a map of the area while writing his narrative. Frémont fixed the name "Humboldt Mountains" upon the Rubies, and this name has fought a stubborn battle for cartographical survival against the persistent local preference for "Ruby Mountains." The outcome has been something of a compromise; the main mountain mass is now called the Rubies, while that part of it north of Secret Pass is termed the East Humboldt Range.

[73] This meteorological report would be even more interesting if we could absolutely depend upon Lienhard's September dates. The Reed family, left without cattle on the Salt Desert, came close to freezing one night, but by our

our onward journey, we came continuously lower down the valley, entirely in a northerly direction. Below us in the valley a few Indians were encamped. One of them rose up by me with one hand held high over his head, shaking it like an enthusiastic preacher, beginning at the same time to speak—or preach—in a somewhat ceremonious tone. Since I could understand no syllable of what he said, I left him standing amid his companions and went on past them.[74]

Farther down the valley we came to a pretty little brook[75] which took its rise from the west side of these high, in-part-gone-round, in-part-climbed-over mountains. In such a case as this, a high country from which mountains rise higher still, it is probable that the heights are wholly covered with snow until late summer, to which circumstance the many large, cold springs owe their existence. The westerly slope appeared to us to be but sparsely wooded.

In the afternoon I followed the road not far from the right bank of the brook, again in a northwesterly direction, going along a couple of miles in advance of our company. On both sides rose small mountains, through which the road and the brook directly proceeded, the little valley becoming ever more narrow ahead. Often in the road I found fresh tracks of Indians, despite which I carried no firearms with me. The heat in this little valley was great; there was no breeze at all, so that the sun shone down with full power. As I approached the mountains ahead, I could see only a deep notch from which the rock rose sheer on either side; thither the stream course wound, and our road with it.

To the left, near the road and on the bank of the thus-far quietly

---

analysis of the Reed dates, that was the night of September 3. A cold front might have been moving slowly west, not reaching the area of Huntington Valley until 48 hours later, but if so it was running counter to the normal flow of air across Nevada, which is from west to east.

[74] The 900-square mile area of Huntington Valley supported a fairly high aboriginal population, about 1 person to 3.5 square miles; it provided access on the one hand to the fish of the Humboldt River, and on the other to the pine nuts on the western slope of the Rubies. Three villages or bands of Shoshoni have been located in the valley, one of 11 families 5 miles north of the old Huntington post office, another of 20 families in the vicinity of Lee, and a third of perhaps 10 families on upper Huntington Creek. There was also a considerable concentration on the Humboldt at the mouth of the South Fork, a favorite wintering ground. Steward, op. cit., 155–56.

[75] Probably Smith Creek, into which Huntington Creek flows—the "Grass Creek" of the Jefferson map. Jefferson also shows, without naming, the junction of the South Fork of the Humboldt proper with Smith Creek.

flowing, clear brook, not far from an immigrant, sat a dark Indian. I seated myself close to his left side and stroked his velvety back a few times, meanwhile exhibiting to him a friendly countenance and nodding approval to indicate my cordial feelings toward him. The Indian appeared to be neither frightened nor angry at my familiar behavior; on the contrary, he also nodded and smiled. We made no attempt to converse with one another through speech; instead we resorted to all manner of signs and gestures. Recalling what I had heard of the edible roots, I took my stick in my hand and made a motion with it, as if I wished to dig something from the ground. My gaze then left off roving over the ground, and exhibiting a small finger, I put it into my mouth and then moved my jaws as if I were eating, after which I put my walking stick into the hand of my dark friend. The Indian had understood me perfectly; he knew that I wanted him to dig a few roots for me. He immediately sprang from his seat, searched near the road on the ground about us, dug in a few places, and after a few moments returned with a couple of small, yellowish roots. I signified that he should first eat thereof, which he did at once, then I bit off a small piece and cautiously tasted it. The taste, much resembling that of a parsnip, pleased me, and I ate the rest of the small piece with relish.

The Indian regarded my confidence in him as complete, now that I had put into my mouth the rootlet he had dug. He took my stick from my hand, went quickly off again, and zealously dug still more roots. As soon as he had a small number, he pounced upon a few large grasshoppers and brought the whole back with him. One of the largest grasshoppers he pressed with its long, thrashing legs against a piece of root, opened his mouth, and made a movement with his jaws as if to eat, without, however, actually doing so. Then he offered me the grasshopper, together with the root, about as one would hand buttered bread to a child. The Indian appeared surprised that this time I would not accept the offering. By way of showing me that he expected me to do nothing at all strange, he now himself bit off a part of the upper body of the grasshopper, together with its head and a piece of root, and chewed this flesh and its garnishing in a lively manner, thus showing me that it tasted exceedingly good. Considering that he had in this way perfectly convinced me, he offered me yet again this rare dish. I was, however, in spite of his artful effort at persuasion, not at all encouraged to emulate his good example, and he turned upon me a look as though he half pitied me, and I should not be at all surprised if he thought that this was a most stupid person who did not have the least idea of what was good.

The rest of the roots I left for the others to taste, and Thomen, who came along about this time, gladly ate of them, so that once more the Indian busied himself roundabout, bringing back a moderate quantity of the roots. Not wanting to go farther down the gorge this evening, we decided to camp at this place. We *five German Boys*, as usual, had baked from bread-dough and fat three cakes apiece, which with a little buffalo meat, together with tea or coffee, was a meal that we repeated on the journey two or three times a day. We desired to take our supper in our tent, and had seated ourselves on the ground inside when the tent opened again and without ceremony in came our Indian friend. Seating himself beside Thomen and me, he thereby indicated that he too now was ready to eat. It was up to us to laugh and make the best of the situation. We each gave him half a cake, and meat, and coffee, and our comrades also each gave him a piece of their cake. Our evening meal thus became a little scanty, but it sufficed, and the Indian seemed satisfied with his new evening meal, going away well pleased. The enjoyment of unfamiliar raw vegetable was followed for Thomen and even more for me, by severe abdominal pains and—diarrhoea, the result being that often during the night I wished that I had never seen this Indian parsnip. Toward morning, however, all again became well.

On September 7 six or eight Indians came to our camp, among whom was my friend of the evening before; he came up just as we were about to leave the camping place. My root-friend had both of his hands completely full of roots, which he wanted to present to me. However, the pains and the running about which these had occasioned me last night had perfectly disgusted me with them. The brown fellow seemed not quite to understand why it was that I would have no more roots, when yesterday evening I had signified to him my desire to eat them. Only through signs could I make him understand, so I bent forward, holding my belly with both hands, and groaned as though I had severe abdominal pains; then I produced with my mouth certain sounds such as at times escape entirely different human organs, at the same time making a gesture with my hands toward my rear. The Indian understood me perfectly and a veritable storm of laughter burst from their throats. My friend laughed if possible hardest of all and tossed his roots on my back. We of course laughed with them and parted, after all, as good friends.

Scarcely 200 paces from our camping place, we entered the deep gorge through which the river cut its way, and through which our

road led. The mass of rock rose in several places nearly perpendicular, around which the stream twisted in several great bends, now to
the right, now to the left, the gorge becoming more contracted. Often
we believed the way completely obstructed until we closely approached the openings. In places we advanced through dense thickets principally made up of white alder and willows. If I remember
aright, the passage through this gorge (Echo Canyon?)[76] was six miles
long. Each moment we had to recross the stream, the water often
coming nearly as high as the wagon bed. As often there was a 3-, 4-,
or 5-foot drop from the bank down into the river bed, and it was just
as steep going out on the opposite side. In this way we had already
crossed the river to and fro 13 times when, late in the afternoon, we
arrived finally at the last crossing. Ripstein and Diel had gone ahead
without the least concern for the wagon or the company,
notwithstanding they had seen how difficult the road was.

Here, at the 14th and last crossing, the road on the right side was
ominously high, as also on the left. The stream was wide, and it
looked to us as if the water to our left were deep. The right ox of the
leading yoke was called Ben; he was a large, lean fellow with very
long horns, a little cross-eyed but for the rest a very good, obedient
animal; however, there were times when he would have his own way,
and thereby he displayed only too well his obstinate oxen nature. As
we approached this last crossing, our Ben seemed not well impressed
with the wide, deep-looking water to our left. He squinted and
blinked at it, as if he thought, "This brook is by no means empty;
herein go I not." More to the right the water was not so deep; it
flowed over a pebbly place, and we could easily see the bottom.
Ben's ox-understanding told him, probably, that an ox his size ran no
risk of drowning in water $1\frac{1}{2}$ feet deep. We no sooner commenced
the crossing than we found that Mr. Ben was not disposed to go
straight down into the water; he turned aside to the right (Gee). Zins,
who was driver today, fortunately stopped in time. Thomen remained
at the rear of the wagon to keep it from upsetting, for it had a heavy

---

[76] By the time Lienhard came to write his narrative, Echo Canyon had become one of the most talked-of sections along the line of the Union Pacific, hence
his effort here to identify it in relation to his own travels. This actually was the
canyon of the South Fork through the Elko Range, used by Chorpening's mail
stage in 1859, but no longer traversed by a road, the founding of Elko on the
Humboldt having pulled roads farther north. Lienhard's estimate of 6 miles for
the canyon was approximately correct. All travelers who went down it, in 1846 or
1850, made eloquent complaint of South Fork Canyon.

list to the left. I fastened a small piece of rope to Ben's right horn and sought through hard pulling to draw the stubborn old fellow to the left, while Zins cracked his whip and shouted "Oh haw," but Ben would Gee and our right wagon wheel rose still higher, as a result of which our wagon inclined yet more to the left. With some difficulty we managed to stop the oxen again. I now placed myself on the right side of the ox Ben and shouted "Oh Haw" while I sought with all my power to shove him to the left, but when all the oxen together began to pull again, I was brushed aside by the squint-eyed fellow as easily as if I had been only a child. Thomen and Zins shouted together, and over toppled our wagon into water 4 feet deep, the bows together with the covering under water and the wheels appearing there where the bows should have remained. The bows of course were broken, and all our belongings lay in the water. I thought that my fine, double-barreled gun must now be broken and my books ruined, but nevertheless said not a word. Zins also was quiet, though angry. Thomen however let loose a huge volley of *Donner und Wetter* g—d d—m, g—d d—m, a veritable giant avalanche of the strongest expressions of anger, which he varied with the question, "What shall we do now?"—a question he asked several times in succession. Our silence Thomen could not understand, and he continually repeated his question.

"We can't long remain here, and if we all abuse one another like sparrows or like Thomen we will get nowhere," I replied to the last of his what-shall-we-do-nows. "I know what we will have to do; we will have to unhitch the oxen, drive them to the little island yonder, come back and carry our belongings over there too, right the wagon, draw it over to our belongings, load them in, hitch up the oxen again, and again drive on."

Thomen at these words became so irritated that his *Donnerwetters* fell upon one another as thick as hailstones, succeeded with a whole stream of G—d d—m's. Zins broke out finally into laughter, which however did not serve to silence Thomen. Zins said, "Exactly as Lienhard has said, so must we do; if the three of us just stand here and abuse and scold as you are doing, our situation will never be mended." Thomen, who was not yet able to control himself, replied that he had been angered not so much by my words themselves as by the cold-blooded manner in which I spoke of our extremely precarious situation, as though it were nothing.—As I had proposed, so we did. There were, to be sure, a few more small *Donnerwetters*—, especially when Thomen and I lifted his bedding out of the water and a small river gushed out of it. For the rest, we soon completed our labor, hitched up the oxen again, and drove on, leaving the place just as the first of the wagons that were following us reached this last crossing. We had traveled on only a few feet when Ripstein and Diel came back; they had learned from a man on horseback who had passed us while our belongings lay in the water what had befallen us. They commenced to abuse us, but we gave it back to them with interest, calling them rotten, unfeeling fellows who would be well advised to keep their mouths shut, and they were finally glad when we stopped bawling them out. The damage we suffered was not great. The bows were broken. of course, the cover torn, and nearly everything more or less soaked; however, the gunpowder remained almost completely dry.

We found a place to camp immediately beyond the gorge,[77] where this stream joined Mary's [Humboldt] River, which was perhaps slightly larger than the river down which we had come. The wagons following us remained behind so long that we remarked jocularly among ourselves that several others must have upset their wagons in the same place, without, however, actually believing it. After a long while, they at last appeared, one after the other, and it turned out to be true—two other persons had upset their wagons in the same place, although in all the previous crossings only one such accident had occurred.

September 8 we made a day of preparation, our principal object being to dry out our things. In the nearby thicket I found a small bundle of Indian belongings hanging on a tree, among which was a bow shaped from two pieces of horn of a mountain sheep. I bound the things all together again and hung them up in the same place. In the afternoon several Shoshawnees came to our camp. One of them sought through signs, the sounds we made in driving our oxen,[78] to

---

[77] Jefferson's map shows that he himself camped at this point on the night of September 7, so that if Lienhard's dates are correct, the two left the Hastings Cutoff as they had entered upon it, together. But as we have seen in note 70, Lienhard's dates here are suspect. On setting off down the Humboldt on September 9 Lienhard apologizes for not being able, for a few days, to give exact details, a part of his memoranda being missing. Although this presumably would apply only to entries of September 9 and later, we cannot be fully satisfied as to the accuracy of his dates for some days before this time.

[78] The Indian vocabulary in the Humboldt Valley was rapidly enlarged by contact with white immigrants, for Shoshoni and Paiutes were soon referring to oxen as "whoa-haws," and to mules as "god-dams."

make us understand that from still another direction wagons were coming up [down] Mary's River. His information was correct, for here the road from Fort Hall joined that by way of Hastings Cutoff (which might much better be called *Hastings Longtripp*). How much we had profited by this cutoff we soon enough learned through a small company which had taken the Fort Hall road. They had left Fort Bridger 12 or 13 days after we did, and were now just as far advanced as we.[79]

---

[79] Hastings nevertheless preserved the respect and confidence of those who had followed him on his cutoff. He seems to have left the Harlan-Young train as soon as he reached the Humboldt—this had, indeed, as we have seen, been his intention from the beginning—and rode on ahead to California. The date of his arrival at Sutter's is not known, but Edwin Bryant encountered him in San Francisco October 18. After Lienhard reached California and joined Frémont's California Battalion, he was marched to San Jose, the volunteers from which place, he noted, included "the Mr. Hastings who showed us the cut-off that had seemed so interminable between Fort Bridger and Mary's River, and as all the emigrants knew and liked him, he was unanimously elected captain of our company." See Mrs. Wilbur's *A Pioneer at Sutter's Fort, 1846–1850*, 16.

—Harold Schindler photo

CACHE CAVE

—Harold Schindler photo

THE NEEDLES

—Harold Schindler photo

THE WITCHES

—Harold Schindler photo

ADOBE ROCK

THE JEFFERSON MAP

AMONG THE RECORDS that have preserved the story of the pioneering of the Hastings Cutoff for future generations, none exceeds and few match in interest the extraordinary *Map of the Emigrant Road from Independence, Mo., to St. Francisco, California,* which was published in New York in 1849 by T. H. Jefferson as the fruits of an 1846 journey to California by way of the Hastings Cutoff. So rare is this map—only three copies are known to exist—that its vital bearing on the Hastings Cutoff long escaped attention and has only come to be generally appreciated since the publication of George R. Stewart's book about the Donner party, *Ordeal by Hunger,* which appeared in 1936. In December, 1945, the California Historical Society reprinted 300 copies of the map and its brief *Accompaniment,* thus for the first time making it generally available to scholars. Not unnaturally, this edition itself promptly went out of print, and already copies have become difficult to find.

The strange thing about T. H. Jefferson is that down to this writing his map has been the sole evidence that such a person ever existed. His name is not mentioned in any of the known diaries or reminiscences of 1846; there appears to be no record of him in California; and although his map was published in New York City, from which it has been inferred he lived there, the only Thomas Jefferson the New York City directories list from 1842 is a colored porter, not the likeliest of candidates for the honor of having produced one of the great American maps.[1]

Dale Morgan's research in frontier newspapers identified Jefferson by name in the immigration of 1846, and confirmed New York as his place of residence, though whether city or state remains to be established. Fittingly enough, this shred of evidence comes from the Jefferson City, Mo., *Jefferson Inquirer,* of May 13, 1846, which paper quotes a late issue of the Independence *Western Expositor* as saying: "We notice among those going out, Col. Wm. H. Russell, Dr. Snyder, Mr. Grayson, Mr. McKinstry, Mr. Newton, and others from be-

---

[1] This man may not be such an unlikely candidate after all. Rush Spedden, "Who Was T. H. Jefferson?" *Overland Journal,* VIII, 3 (1990) makes a compelling argument that Thomas Hemings Jefferson, the son of Thomas Jefferson and his mistress, Sally Hemings, was the elusive mapmaker.

low,—Messrs. Lippincot[t] and Jefferson from New York,[2] and from about here, Ex-Gov. Boggs, Judge Morin, Rev. Mr. Dunleavy, and hosts of others." This allusion would indicate that Jefferson was regarded as among the notables of the year's immigration.

On March 15, 1849, the steamship *Crescent City* sailed for Chagres, and among her 838 passengers were "Mrs. Col. J. C. Fremont and child . . . C. D. Gibbs . . . [and] T. H. Jefferson."[3] Cartographer Charles D. Gibbes mapped much of the California gold region, publishing the *Map of San Joaquin River* in 1850 at San Francisco, and it would not be pushing coincidence to suggest that this T. H. Jefferson was our elusive overland mapmaker. Jefferson also appears on the passenger list of the *Oregon*, which arrived in San Francisco from Astoria, Oregon, on October 28, 1850. Some of the steamer's passengers were San Franciscans on a pleasure trip, leaving open the possibility that Jefferson resided in San Francisco. Yet apart from these mentions, Jefferson's *Map of the Emigrant Road* is still the sum total of our knowledge about him.

In the introduction he wrote for the California Historical Society's edition of Jefferson, George R. Stewart sums up all that can be deduced about the traveler whose remarkable map is provocative of so much curiosity about him:

> The *Accompaniment* tells much of the author's character, but little of his actual life. He had some familiarity with the city of St. Louis, but this may merely show that he outfitted there upon his way west. I would make a hesitant suggestion that he had had some sea-faring experience, for his diction has a nautical tang; he mentions, for instance, palm and pricker (sail-makers' implements), and ship bread. He recommends a spy-glass, and a sailor's sheath-knife instead of the common frontiersman's Bowie.
>
> In map and accompaniment alike his character stands out surely. He was accurate, but in a practical rather than a

---

[2] The association of Jefferson's name with that of Benjamin S. Lippincott might be taken to indicate that they traveled in company. That this was not the case, at least after the trans-plains journey began, is shown by the recurrence of Lippincott's name in several of the journals of the immigration, notably Edwin Bryant's, which place Lippincott in other places and at different times than are shown on the Jefferson map. Lippincott is understood to have reached California eventually by the Fort Hall route.

[3] *New York Herald*, March 16, 1849.

theoretical way. He was resourceful, and meticulous of detail. He must have kept an accurate daily journal or notes. He was independent of judgment. He took hardships as a matter of course. Yet he was withal a man of certain delicacies, despising the emigrants' doughy bread, and revolted by grease in cookery and sowbelly bacon. He was a water-drinker, mentioning whiskey only as an article of trade and allowing coffee and tea grudgingly.

Other conclusions reached by Dr. Stewart are not so well considered. In deciding that the map did not appear before the latter part of 1849, he was clearly mistaken, for J. Goldsborough Bruff carried a copy overland that year.[4]

Jefferson's map, according to the *Accompaniment* and the lithographed title which appears on its slip-case, was "published by the Author" and sold by Berford & Co., 2 Astor House, New York City, at $3 a copy—a high price for the time. It was lithographed by G. Snyder and engraved on stone by Ed. Herrlein. The map itself consists of four sheets, each 36.6 by 51.5 cm., and it has an 11-page printed *Accompaniment*, 13.5 by 9.5 cm. Of the complete work, two copies only are known, one in the Estelle Doheny Collection, St. John's Seminary, Camarillo, California, and one in the Philip Ashton Rollins Collection at Princeton University. However, a set of the maps, lacking the *Accompaniment*, is found in the Map Division of the Library of Congress, and photostats of these, supplied prior to the reprint by the California Historical Society, were of signal service to the researches set forth in these pages.

Only Part III of the Jefferson map, with an inset from Part IV to show the western junction of the Hastings Cutoff with the Fort Hall Road, is reproduced in the present volume. Consequently it is desirable to provide some account of the other sheets and their bearing on Jefferson's travels of 1846.

Part I explains that the map "represents the emigrant road from Independence, Mo., by the South Pass of the Rocky Mountains to California. The Author was one of a party of emigrants who travelled the road with waggons, in 1846. All the streams of water and springs upon the road are delineated, also daily distances, courses and camps, made by the party." As good as his word, Jefferson locates

---

[4] Georgia Willis Read and Ruth Gaines, eds., *Gold Rush, the Journals, Drawings, and Other Papers of J. Goldsborough Bruff,* xlix, 173, 550–51, 560–62.

and dates every campsite, so that—for the early part of his route, at least—it is possible to place him on each day of his journey. From the time he launched upon the Hastings Cutoff, his map is somewhat defective with respect to dates, but the Lienhard journal now enables us to clear up many ambiguities in this connection. Jefferson indicates with a heavy dotted line his own line of march, and with a lighter dotted line "the road travelled by some," the alternative routes being at times of critical importance. The first sheet of the map also contains a Table of Distances:

		Miles
From INDEPENDENCE MO. to KANSAS RIVER		98
"	KANSAS RIVER TO NEBRASKA RIVER	217
"	NEBRASKA R. to SCOTTS BLUFF	253
"	SCOTTS B to FORT LARAMIE	56
"	F. LARAMIE to ROCK INDEPENDENCE	156
"	R. INDEPENDENCE to SOUTH PASS (culminating ridge)	98
"	S. PASS to FORT BRIDGER	111
"	F BRIDGER to GREAT SALT LAKE (Utah River)	118 1/4
"	G S. LAKE to VALLEY OF FOUNTAINS	243
"	V. OF FOUNTAINS to MARY RIVER	118 1/2
"	MARY R. to SINK OF MARY R.	227
"	SINK OF M. R. to TRUCKEY PASS (summit of Californian Mo)	116 3/4
"	TRUCKEY P. to FIRST SETTLEMENT IN CALIFORNIA (Johnson's)	83 1/2
"	JOHNSON'S to FORT SUTTER	35 1/2
"	F. SUTTER to ST. FRANCISCO	207 1/2
	TOTAL from INDEPENDENCE to ST. FRANCISCO	2139

In dating his campsites, Jefferson undertook to make himself absolutely clear by double-dating them, e.g., his encampment at Indian Creek, on first setting out from Independence, is dated "11–12 May 1846," meaning that he reached this point on the night of May 11 and left there on the morning of May 12. This will be found characteristic of his campsites on the sheet of his map here reproduced. Ordinarily campsites between those which are dated can be assigned a date by simply counting them in sequence. Place names that Jefferson employs in some cases are those which were current on the trail in 1846; but often he seems to have applied rather unimaginative names of his own devising, as when he calls Sulphur Creek "Hare Creek" and East Canyon Creek "Magpie Creek." Few if any of these names have survived in Western nomenclature, and where they have, it is by reason of their obvious applicability rather than from any influence exerted by the Jefferson map.

Having sketched in some background, let us now take up Jefferson's travels as the four sheets of his map depict them. Clearly he left the frontier in the Morin-Harlan company, with which Lienhard at first traveled. On setting out, this company traveled in close proximity to the large Russell company, of which Edwin Bryant and James Frazier Reed were members, but began to pull ahead at the crossing of the Kaw. They were only one day ahead when they crossed the Big Blue River on May 25, but on the night of May 26, a few hours after the Russell company reached that river, a terrific storm blew up, rendering the Big Blue impassable for some days, so that the Harlan wagons gained a considerable head start which was never entirely overcome by the wagons behind. The Harlan group, as we have seen in connection with the Lienhard journal, split up into many fragments along the way, and the Harlans and Wimmers reached Fort Bridger fully as far in advance of Jefferson and Lienhard as they were themselves in advance of the Reed and Donner families. Since Lienhard's diary for the earlier part of his journey was lost, it is impossible to know how close together Jefferson and the "five German boys" traveled during their first weeks on the road, but the night Jefferson reached Fort Laramie, June 26, Lienhard was encamped 7 miles farther west. Thereafter now one and then the other took the lead. Jefferson left the Platte on July 7, a full two days ahead of Lienhard, but was some hours behind when both crossed South Pass ten days later. He overtook Lienhard again at the Green River on July 21, and the two, if not quite together, were traveling in very close proximity when they reached Fort Bridger on July 24.

From Fort Bridger west, Jefferson's travels as shown on his map and those of Lienhard as recorded in his journal are fully correlated in the notes to the Lienhard journal, hence it is unnecessary to treat here in detail Jefferson's experiences on the Hastings Cutoff. Nevertheless a few points about the map merit mention.

Certainly, one of these is the name "Echo Defile," which Jefferson applies to Echo Canyon a full year before the Mormon Pioneers fixed the name upon it. Farther along, Jefferson's use of the name "Gutter Defile" raises the question whether he had seen in the south wall of the Weber's upper canyon the twin limestone dikes which have since become famous as Devils Slide or whether he was referring to the then-striking character of Lost Creek at its confluence with the Weber. Below this area, Jefferson shows no fewer than 14 crossings of the Weber River above the Morgan meadows, an important comment on the road, for Jefferson was scrupulously accurate on such points. Eight more crossings of the river farther down would be a sufficient commentary on the difficulties at Devils Gate and below, even had Jefferson neglected to tell us that "Granite Canyon" was "a bad Canyon."

As we have observed in the Lienhard journal, Jefferson was in advance when he emerged from the canyons of the Weber, hence it is interesting that his campsite on the night of August 5 was at some springs at the mouth of Weber Canyon. These springs still flow. Two at the canyon mouth, presumably those shown by Jefferson, were sold by the owner, James Harbertson, to the U. S. government about 1920, and provided a considerable part of the water supply for the Ogden Arsenal and Hill Field. Three other springs lower down, which escaped Jefferson's notice, bubble up on present-day farms of the vicinity.

Jefferson's map of the Great Salt Lake area was clearly influenced by Frémont's maps of 1845 and 1848, but his striking originality and wealth of independent information is apparent even on cursory examination. He depicts the springs in the vicinity of Garfield (and the intersection of Reed's route at this point with the Hastings road), the marshy land bordering the lake farther south and west, and the rock formation in Tooele Valley which today we call Adobe Rock. Further, Jefferson shows the alternative route across the Stansbury Mountains which the Bryant-Russell party had taken, the numerous salt springs at the base of these mountains, and even the Lone Rock which rises so prominently at the north end of Skull Valley.

The formidable character of the Salt Desert is stressed on his map and insisted upon in his *Accompaniment*. In the latter he writes:

*Long drive, Desert of Utariah.—Distance.—*From Hope-Wells [Iosepa] to East side Scorpion Mt. [Cedar Mountains], 12 miles. Road good, a level plain. East to west side Scorpion Mt., 9 miles. Road, steep hills, some sideling, rather bad. West side Scorpion Mt., to Rock Ridge [Grayback Mountain] 14 miles. Road good, hard marly plain.

Rock Ridge to east side Fire Mt. [Silver Island], 32 miles.

Road a vast desert plain, good hard marl in places, deep sand
ridges in places, latter part damp or wet marl incrusted with
salt, into which the wheels cut and make hard pulling. From
east to west side Fire Mt., 8 miles. Road hilly, deep dust,
bunch grass in places, rather hard. From west side Fire Mt.
to Bonark Wells [Donner Spring at Pilot Peak], 8 miles. Road
a level plain of marl, damp, incrusted with fine table salt,
rather hard pulling. Total distance 83 miles. Dell [Redlum]
Spring affords a small supply of brackish water, cedar trees,
and some bunch grass; a good well could be made here. This
would reduce the drive to 70 miles.

Take in a supply of water and green grass at Hope-Wells.
Three or four gallons of water per ox is enough. Water is
more important than grass. Not more than five wagons
should start upon the drive in company. Travel night and
day; don't hurry the oxen; make a regular camp about every
20 miles. Remain at each camp two hours or more, and measure out the water to each ox in a basin. Unyoke at each
camp and leave the cattle loose. Keep strict guard over them,
and never for one moment allow them to leave your sight.
Adhere to these rules and you will go through safe. Scorpion
mountain affords cedar trees and some good bunch grass.

North-east of Hope-Wells, upon the mountain, about two
miles from the road, is situated Cedar spring. It affords an
abundant supply of delightful water, has cedar trees and
some bunch grass near it; a horse trail leads to it from Hast-
ings-Wells [Grantsville], over the mountain. If the Indians
catch an unarmed man alone, they will rob him.

The most curious aspect to this note is Jefferson's counsel, reit-
erated on the map, that in crossing the salt desert no more than five
wagons should go in company. Although founded on practical experience, the reason for this advice does not readily suggest itself, for it
might be supposed that larger groups would better be able to help
one another. It may be that larger numbers tended to impede and
delay, or in the miry sections turned the road into a morass for too
many wagons following too closely behind.

Jefferson dates no campsite between the north end of the
Oquirrh Mountains and Ruby Valley, his "Valley of Fountains."
Nothing could better illustrate the difficulties and the confusion oc-
casioned by the preparations for, the actual traverse of, and the recu-

peration from, the Salt Desert crossing. Only now that the Lienhard
journal has been brought to bear upon this part of the Jefferson map
is it possible to interpret it authoritatively.

The "Valley of Fountains" receives warm praise in Jefferson's
Accompaniment. It was, he said, "A large and fertile valley, abounding
in springs of pure water; soil black and rich, and covered with excellent grasses; a variety of timber in the vales of the mountain, also currants and service berries; game abundant, such as antelope, geese,
brant, cranes, plover, grouse, blue bird, robin, &c. The Digger Indians' 'bread root' is also found among the grass; it resembles a carrot.
The north part of the valley is best. Grain of all kind[s] could easily
be cultivated. This valley affords a good site for a settlement, or military provision post."

Part III of the Jefferson map just fails to show the junction of the
Hastings Cutoff with the Fort Hall Road, and accordingly we have inset a section from Part IV of the map, extended far enough west to
illustrate the last few entries of the Reed journal, i.e., to the vicinity of
present Winnemucca at the great bend of the Humboldt. The rest of
the fourth sheet of the Jefferson map though not here reproduced, is
quite as interesting as the record of the earlier stretches of the trail.
In locating "Truckey [Donner] Pass of California Mountain" Jefferson makes his only direct reference to the disaster which befell the
Donner party, remarking: "It was six miles east of the Truckey Pass
of the Cal. Mts that Reeds party in November encountered snow ten
feet deep and half the party perished. Emigrants who reach this
place by the first of October are safe. Those who come later and encounter snow, should at once retreat to Grass Valley [Truckee Meadows, present Reno] or the mouth of Truckey River and winter there
or to the southward on the streams of the eastern base of the Californian Mountains. The western descent of these mountains is the most
rugged and difficult of the whole journey."

Jefferson's map shows that after crossing "Truckey Pass" on October 7, he wound down the steep slope of the Sierra to arrive at
Johnson's Ranch October 20, the last date given for any map campsite. Presumably he reached Sutter's Fort about six days later. The
map shows that he continued on around San Francisco Bay to San
Jose and thence up the peninsula to San Francisco, from which
place sometime during 1847 or 1848, he must have returned home by

sea.[5] The fourth sheet of his map reflects the excitement prevailing at the time of its publication in that the legend, "Gold Region," is applied to the country north and south of the Feather River. The final sheet of Jefferson's map was reproduced by Carl I. Wheat in his *The Maps of the California Gold Region, 1848–1857* (San Francisco, 1942). Down to the publication of the present volume, Mr. Wheat's was the only separate reproduction of any sheet of the four comprising the Jefferson map.

The reprinting of Part III and a section from Part IV of the map in connection with this study of the Hastings Cutoff was greatly facilitated by the cordial cooperation of the California Historical Society, which generously proposed that the Utah State Historical Society make a lithographic reproduction from its own printing of the Doheny copy. Since this would afford a much clearer map than would be possible in reproducing the Library of Congress copy, the offer was gratefully accepted.

The Jefferson map, together with a modern map of the country traversed by the Hastings Cutoff, is contained in a pocket at the back of this volume.

---

[5] Jefferson's return east by sea is deduced from the fact that his map shows no first hand acquaintance with the Fort Hall variant of the California Trail. Had he gone east overland, he would unquestionably have accompanied one of the parties that went by that route.

JAMES FRAZIER REED and MARGARET KEYES REED

THE JOURNAL OF JAMES FRAZIER REED

July 31–October 4, 1846

INTRODUCTION

By FAR the most celebrated of the companies which traveled the Hastings Cutoff in the summer of 1846 is the Donner party. The horror and the drama of their plight when caught by snow in the Sierra Nevada, the relief efforts—at once heroic and grisly—carried on in their behalf, the spiritual and physical stresses to which they were subjected, the grim expedient to which so many of the survivors had to resort to preserve their lives—all these have made the ordeal of the Donner party one of the classic episodes of Western history.

These travelers came so close to escaping their hard fate—a difference of a few hours in reaching Donner Pass might have seen them through to safety—that no single day of their journey, from the time they left the main-traveled trail at Fort Bridger, goes unattended by history's remorseless "if." Had they made one decision instead of another, journeyed some one day instead of resting, taken this possible route instead of that ... how different their story. Our concern with them in their experiences upon the Hastings Cutoff is constantly attended by our painful consciousness of their eventual fate. But it is not simply their progress toward death that makes the day-to-day experiences of the Donner party so fascinating. The route over the Wasatch Mountains which the Donners pioneered for wagons became the Mormon Trail to Salt Lake Valley, and with the smallest of variations served for two decades as a principal highroad for transcontinental travel.

Only lately has it become possible, in the light of an actual daily journal kept by a member of the company, to deal definitively with the Donner party on the Hastings Cutoff and particularly on the important section of the trail between Fort Bridger and Salt Lake Valley. The journals of the Mormons who traveled the road next year have, before now, sufficed to identify most of the Donner route and to provide some insight into the trials that attended the opening of the new road, but the daily record that would fix their experiences in a chronology has been lacking. That diaries were kept by at least two members the party, Mrs. George Donner and John Denton, has long been known, but the first of these journals seems not to have survived that winter in the Sierra, and the second disappeared after it was brought into the settlements.[1] It was altogether unlooked for that a third diary should turn up among the papers of James Frazier Reed.

The journal in question, with others of Reed's papers, in 1946 came to the Sutter's Fort Historical Museum at Sacramento, as a bequest from Miss Martha Jane Lewis, daughter of that Martha Jane (Reed) Lewis, who is familiar in the annals of the Donner party as Patty Reed. Realizing the crucial significance for western history of the diary and the related papers, the curator of the museum, Mr. Carroll D. Hall, published than in an attractive limited edition under the title, *Donner Miscellany. 41 Diaries and Documents* (San Francisco: The Book Club of California, 1947). Mr. Hall has since made a photostatic copy of the journal available for study, consented to the republication of that part of it which pertains to the Hastings Cutoff, and cooperated in every way in this project to clarify phases of the Donner story until now only half understood. The Book Club of California joined with him in authorizing republication of so much of the Reed diary as was relevant to the present study.

This diary has some curious features. It was commenced, not by Reed himself, but by Hiram O. Miller, who in April, 1846, started from Springfield, Ill., in company with the Reed and Donner families. So much of the record as Miller himself set down is neither very interesting nor especially informative. On July 3, 1846, however, Miller left the wagon company to join the Bryant-Russell pack party, and he seems then to have given the journal to James Frazier Reed. From that date to its abrupt termination on October 4, Reed himself kept the little day-book. This he did in so odd a fashion, writing in the third-person even about himself, that at first glance one rejects Reed as the author. The handwriting being indisputable, and the

---

[1] John Denton's diary was recovered from his body after his death. The *California Star* of April 10, 1847, in printing a remarkable poem by Denton, a poem sometimes said to have been written as he lay dying in the snow, commented: "The following lines are from the journal of Mr. John Denton, one of the unfortunate emigrants who perished during the past winter in the California Mountains. . . . His journal was taken from his pocket and brought in. It is said to contain many interesting items in relation to the route from Missouri to the California Mountains, and a graphic description of the sufferings of the unfortunate party, of which he was a member. The journal will probably in a few weeks be placed in our hands." Unfortunately, this expectation was not fulfilled. As Denton was an Englishman, his diary may have been sent to relatives in his native land.

date of the diary's breaking off being so dramatically tied in with a crisis in Reed's affairs, it has to be concluded that Reed continued the journal simply as a record of the movements of the wagons with which he traveled, and not at all as a personal journal. The diary has some phrases to indicate that it was intended to be used by friends who might make the overland journey in later years, and this may have some bearing on its curious angle of view. The part of the diary here printed is a new transcription made direct from the original and varies in small particulars from the text as first published.

Before taking up the document which is made the basis of our account of the Donner party, let us review briefly the composition of the company.

The nucleus that started from Springfield, Illinois, in the spring of 1846, was made up of the families of James Frazier Reed and of George and Jacob Donner. Reed was born in Ireland, November 14, 1800, of noble Polish ancestry, the family name originally having been Reednoski. Emigrating to America in his youth, he lived for a time in Virginia and then came to Illinois, where he fought in the Black Hawk war, serving in the same company with Abraham Lincoln and James Clyman. Later he prospered as a manufacturer of cabinet furniture. In 1834 he married a young widow, Mrs. Margaret (Keyes) Backenstoe, whose baby daughter became the 13-year-old Virginia E. B. "Reed" who will figure in our narrative. Four other children had been born to the Reeds at the time they set out for California, and theirs was one of only two families to reach their destination without the loss of a single member.

George and Jacob Donner were brothers who had done well on their farms near Springfield. In middle age they succumbed to the wanderlust which at this period drew west so many of their kind. Including issue by previous marriages, there were five children in George Donner's family and seven in Jacob's. A young Englishman, John Denton, traveled with the former, and two teamsters, Noah James and Samuel Shoemaker, with the latter. Reed had a much more elaborate entourage, including four hired men—Milford ("Milt") Elliott, Walter Herron, James Smith, and Baylis Williams— and Baylis' sister Eliza, who came along as a servant. Others whom circumstance made members of the Donner company included Patrick Breen, his wife, and seven children; William H. Eddy, his wife, and two children; Lavina Murphy (whose name, according to researcher Kristin Johnson, was spelled "Levina" on most source documents), a widow said to have been a Mormon convert in Ten-

nessee,[2] with her five minor children, two grown daughters, their
husbands—William M. Foster and William M. Pike—and three
grandchildren; one Wolfinger and wife Doris; Lewis Keseberg, his
wife and two children, two other men, Charles or Karl Burger and
one Hardcoop, traveling in company with him; one Spitzer and his
partner, Joseph Reinhardt; and two young bachelors, Patrick Dolan
and Charles Tyler Stanton, who had attached themselves to the company enroute. Some of these may have joined the Donner party at
Fort Bridger, as was the case with William McCutchen, his wife and
child, and two herders, one Antonio and Jean Baptiste Trubode (or
Trudeau). Also at Fort Bridger Tamsen Donner compassionately
took in a waif, Luke Halloran, who was in the last stages of consumption and who was to die at the south end of Great Salt Lake. The
family of F. W. Graves, including his wife, eight minor children, an
older daughter, her husband Jay Fosdick, and a personable hired
man, John Snyder, overtook the Donner party after it began to cut its
way across the Wasatch. There were 29 able-bodied men, 15 years or
older, to share in the labor of hewing out the new road. In all, the

---

[2] The evidence that Mrs. Murphy was or at one time had been a Mormon
comes principally from Mormon sources. When members of the Mormon Battalion preparing to cross the Sierra Nevada to Utah reached Johnson's Ranch in
August, 1847, they talked with Mrs. Johnson, the former Mary Murphy—
"Murray," Tyler renders the name—daughter of Lavina Murphy. She told them
that her mother had lived in Nauvoo, and to obtain employment had moved
down to Warsaw and spent the winter of 1845–46 there. In the spring of 1846
one of the parties emigrating to Oregon or California offered to furnish passage
for herself and children on condition that she cook and wash for the party. She
accepted, as she understood that California was the final destination of the Saints,
and thought this a good opportunity to emigrate without being a burden to the
Mormon church. See Daniel Tyler, *A Concise History of the Mormon Battalion in
the Mexican War, 1846–1847* (Salt Lake City, 1881), 312, 313.

Prior to this time, the Mormon Pioneer party of 1847 was also given to understand that Lavina Murphy had been a Saint. When the westbound Mormons
met Miles Goodyear at the Bear River on July 10, 1847, and learned some details
of the Donner disaster, Wilford Woodruff recorded in his journal, "Mrs. L.
Murphy of Tennessee, whom I baptized while on a mission in that country, but
since apostatized and joined the mob, was in that company and died, or was
killed, and eaten. Her bones were sawed to pieces for her brains and marrow, and
then left strewn upon the ground." See Matthias P. Cowley, *Wilford Woodruff*
(Salt Lake City, 1909), 310. While on a mission to the southern states in 1836,
Woodruff recorded visiting Jeremiah B. Murphy of Dresden, Tennessee, in July,
and on August 6, 1836 reported baptizing "Brother & Sister Murphy." In his
journal for September, 1872, kept while on a visit to California by rail, Woodruff
again referred to the incident.

company numbered 87 persons, of whom only 47 would survive the journey.[3]

In after years, Reed wrote a brief reminiscent account of the journey to Fort Bridger. In this he said:

> I left Springfield Ill., with my family about the middle of April, 1846, George and Jacob Donner with their families accompanied me. We arrived at Independence, Mo., where I loaded two of my wagons with provisions, a third one being reserved for my family. Col. W. H. Russell's company had started from here before our arrival. We followed and overtook them in the Indian Territory. I made application for admission of myself and others into the company, and it was granted. We traveled on with the company as far as the Little Sandy, here [July 19, 1846] a separation took place. The majority of the members going to Oregon, and a few wagons, mine with them, going the Fort Bridger, Salt Lake Route to California. The day after our separation from the Russell company, we elected George Donner captain. From this time the company was known as "the Donner Company."[4]

The honor bestowed upon George Donner does not seem to have been in recognition of any particular qualities of leadership he possessed, being a tribute rather to his genial personality. Clearly the leading spirit in the company, with more drive and initiative than any of the others, Reed himself was disliked for his aristocratic bearing—the more obnoxious to many because he could hire his work done.

The Donner company reached Fort Bridger on July 27, 1846, and as they had driven their cattle hard during the two preceding weeks, they halted for several days to recruit. It would appear from

---

[3] See the complete roster in George R. Stewart, *Ordeal by Hunger* (New York, 1936), 299, 300. The total number of casualties, 42, includes two California Indians later drawn into the tragic current of events.

[4] *Pacific Rural Press*, March 25, 1871. A number of letters home, written along the way by the Reeds and the Donners, describe the first stage of the journey. See the Springfield *Sangamo Journal*, July 23, 30, 1846, the Southwest Museum's *The Masterkey* (May, 1944), 82, and Tamsen Donner's letter of May 11, 1846, in Morgan, ed., *Overland in 1846*, 526–27. These documents, like the opening pages of the Miller-Reed diary, here can be noted only in passing. The Bryant, Thornton, and McKinstry diaries contain much information on the Reeds and Donners to Fort Laramie and beyond.

Thornton's diary that they had already decided to take the new route south of Great Salt Lake when he parted from them at the intersection with the Greenwood Cutoff.[5] How long this decision may have been in the making, there is no way of knowing, though James Clyman remembered many years later that in returning to the States that spring he met his old comrade-in-arms at Fort Laramie, and that Reed was then much interested in the new route.

> I told him [Clyman says] to "take the regular wagon track [by way of Fort Hall] and never leave it—it is barely possible to get through if you follow it—and it may be impossible if you dont." Reed replied, "There is a nigher route, and it is of no use to take so much of a roundabout course." I admitted the fact, but told him about the great desert and the roughness of the Sierras, and that a straight route might turn out to be impracticable.
>
> The party when we separated took my trail by which I had come from California, south of Salt Lake, and struck the regular emigrant trail again on the Humboldt.[6]

Despite Clyman, it is not apparent why Reed should have been set on the new route so far east as Fort Laramie, for aside from the vague argument of the *Emigrants' Guide*[7] he had not at that time been exposed to Lansford W. Hastings' salesmanship; the open letter Hastings sent along the trail by the lone immigrant, Wales Bonney, did not fall into Reed's hands until some two weeks later. By whatever chain of circumstance, the Donner party did finally choose to take the new cutoff, and on July 31, 1846, 11 days after Hastings left Fort Bridger with the Harlan-Young train, the Donner wagons began creaking in his track.

As an appropriate introduction to Reed's journal, we print a letter Reed wrote at Fort Bridger, seemingly on the morning of his departure, setting forth as the diary does not the hopes he took with him west from the fort. This letter is now republished for the first time since it appeared in the columns of the *Sangamo Journal*, on November 5, 1846. It was the last letter Reed wrote home before creeping

---

[5] J. Quinn Thornton, *Oregon and California in 1848*, I, 142.

[6] Camp, ed., *James Clyman, American Frontiersman, 1792–1881*, 229.

[7] The Donner family carried George McKinstry's copy of this book, now one of the prized possessions of the Bancroft Library.

disaster enveloped him, and its mood of high elation is all the more poignant for that reason.

FROM A CALIFORNIA EMIGRANT

We have lying before us a letter from JAMES F. REED, late of Springfield, Ill., dated at "Fort Bridger, one hundred miles from the Eutaw or Great Salt Lake, July 31, 1846."

"We have arrived here safe [says Mr. Reed] with the loss of two yoke of my best oxen. They were poisoned by drinking water in a little creek called Dry Sandy, situated between the Green Spring [Pacific Spring] in the Pass of the Mountains, and Little Sandy. The water was standing in puddles.—Jacob Donner also lost two yoke, and George Donner a yoke and a half, all supposed from the same cause. I have replenished my stock by purchasing from Messrs. Vasques & Bridger, two very excellent and accommodating gentlemen, who are the proprietors of this trading post.—The new road, or Hastings' Cut-off, [this is manifestly Capt. Freemont's newly discovered route to California,] leaves the Fort Hall road here, and is said to be a savings of 350 or 400 miles in going to California, and a better route. There is, however, or thought to be, one stretch of 40 miles without water; but Hastings and his party, are out a-head examining for water, or for a route to avoid this stretch.[8] I think that they cannot avoid it, for it crosses an arm of the Eutaw Lake, now dry. Mr. Bridger, and other gentlemen here, who have trapped that country, say that the Lake has receded from the tract of country in question. There is plenty of grass which we can cut and put into the waggons for our cattle while crossing it.

"We are now only 100 miles from the Great Salt Lake by the new route,—in all 250 miles from California; while by way of Fort Hall it is 650 or 700 miles—making a great savings in favor of jaded oxen and dust. On the new route we will not have dust, as there are but 60 waggons ahead of us.[9] The rest of the Californians went the long

---

[8] See Edwin Bryant's journal for August 3, 1846.

[9] Reed was firmly persuaded of the fact that 60 wagons had preceded the Donners upon the cutoff. The same number is given in the Springfield *Illinois Journal*, December 9, 1847, on his authority, as also later in the diary itself. There is, however, a notable lack of agreement as to the number of these wagons. J. Quinn Thornton, *Oregon and California in 1848*, II, 97, on the basis of interviews with survivors of the Donner party in San Francisco in the fall of 1847, gives the

route—feeling afraid of Hastings' Cut-off. Mr. Bridger informs me that the route we design to take, is a fine level road, with a plenty of water and grass, with the exception before stated. It is estimated that 700 miles will take us to Capt. Sutter's Fort, which we hope to make in seven weeks from this day.

"I want you to inform the emigration that they can be supplied with fresh cattle by Messrs. Vasques & Bridger. They now have about 200 head of oxen, cows and young cattle, with a great many horses and mules; and they can be relied on for doing business honorably and fairly.[10] Mr. Bridger will go to St. Louis this fall and return with the emigration in the spring, and will be very useful as a pilot.[11] He will be found during winter in St. Louis at Mr. Robert Campbell's (merchant.) I must put you on your guard against two or three persons who have left California and Oregon for horse stealing and other crimes. Of course they dislike those countries. They are perfect vagabonds.[12]

"I have fine times in hunting grouse, antelope or mountain goat, which are plenty. Milford Elliott, James Smith and W. Herron, the

---

total as 66. George McKinstry, writing in the San Francisco *California Star*, February 13, 1847, is entitled to special credence and fixes the number at "some seventy-five." Edwin Bryant's figure, *What I Saw in California*, 250, is "about eighty." Jim Bridger told the Mormons in June, 1847, that there had been "nearly a hundred wagons gone on the Hastings route through Weber's Fork," though this included the Donner wagons, which according to the *California Star*, as above cited, totaled 23. After all this disagreement, the James Mathers diary appears to state that as of July 25 a total of 57 wagons had reached Bear River on the Hastings Cutoff. To this number must be added the wagons with which Lienhard traveled, which totaled not less than four and probably at least double that number.

[10] Reed wrote somewhat less cordially in the *Pacific Rural Press*, March 25, 1871, "Several friends of mine who had passed here with pack animals for California had left letters with Mr. Vasques—Mr. Bridger's partner—directing me to take the route by way of Fort Hall and by no means to go the Hastings cutoff. Vasques being interested in having the new route traveled, kept these letters. This was told me after my arrival in California." Compare Bryant's journal for July 18, 1846.

[11] If these were Bridger's plans as of this date, he was unable to carry them out, for on June 29, 1847, the Mormons met him at the Little Sandy, eastbound from his fort to Fort Laramie.

[12] This is possibly a reference to Joe Walker or those who had accompanied him and his horse-herd east from California during the spring. However, bad reports of California and Oregon were heard from nearly all of the year's eastbound companies.

young men who drive for me, are careful, first rate drivers,—which gives me time for hunting. We are beyond the range of buffalo.

"The independent trappers, who swarm here during the passing of the emigrants, are as great a set of sharks as ever disgraced humanity, with few exceptions. Let the emigrants avoid trading with them. Vasques & Bridger are the only fair traders in these parts.

"There are two gentlemen here—one of them an Englishman of the name of Wills, and the other a yankee named Miles[13]—who will

---

[13] Thus casually Reed seems to describe the true genesis of Miles Goodyear's post on the site of Ogden, about the date of which there has been much conjecture. The "Englishman of the name of Wills" had accompanied Edwin Bryant's party from Fort Laramie to Fort Bridger, and Bryant said of him: "Capt. Welles, as he informed us and as I was informed by others, had once held a commission in the British army. He was in the battles of Waterloo and New Orleans. He was a man of about sixty, vigorous and athletic, and his manners, address, and general intelligence, although clothed in the rude buckskin costume of the wilderness, confirmed the statements in regard to him, made by himself and others" (*What I Saw in California*, 119, 120). Miles Goodyear, whose given name was also his mountain name, was born in Connecticut in 1817, and journeyed to the mountains with Marcus Whitman's party in 1836. Trading out of Fort Hall, Fort Wintey, and Fort Bridger, he acquired a Ute wife and two children, and during the next seven years he appears frequently in the journals of overland travelers. In the summer of 1845 he made his first trip to the States in nine years, but returned to the mountains the same fall. Lienhard speaks of him, though not by name, at Fort Bridger under date of July 24, 1846:

As I was writing my diary in the evening, a red-haired mountaineer inquired whether I was writing a journal. When I replied in the affirmative, he remarked: "Then it is perhaps of interest to you to learn that at this place, in yonder willow thicket, 17 years ago, a man by the name of [Arthur?] Black was killed by a band of 50 Blackfeet Indians. For a long time he defended himself bravely and killed several of them and was wounded before they succeeded in overcoming him."

. . . The red-haired mountaineer lived near the fort and had taken a beautiful Indian woman as his wife, who just then was occupied in washing. He was the father of a boy, perhaps three years of age, who was practicing at shooting with a small bow and arrow. This man seemed to have definitely settled here; he owned a small flock of sheep, among which there were also two kids of tamed mountain sheep, they had rather sleek, grayish-blue hair and were as yet without horns, though born early this spring; they were already the tallest. He had acquired not only sheep but also a small herd of cattle, and we exchanged with him our two cows for two young oxen. We both gained by this transaction; for on account of the poor and dry grass, the cows had given us but little milk, we therefore preferred oxen, as they were better. On the other hand, for him the cows were preferable; he could hope

leave here in a few days to settle at some favorable point on the Salt Lake, which in a short time will be a fine place for emigrants to recruit their teams, by exchanging broken down oxen for good teams."

---

that with rest and good grass their milk would return, and also that in time to come they would bear calves.

It has been supposed that Miles Goodyear settled at the confluence of the Weber and Ogden rivers during the winter of 1844–45, but if so, it is strange that Reed speaks of the event as belonging to the future, and there is much more reason for the establishment of such a post after the Hastings Cutoff brought wagons to the valley of the Great Salt Lake. Wills, Welles, and Wells, as his name is variously rendered, was found by the Mormons at Goodyear's establishment in August, 1847, apparently having been left in charge while Goodyear went to southern California with a pack of hides. In the spring of 1847 Goodyear rode up through California, buying horses as he went, and by May 22 had reached Sutter's. The *New Helvetia Diary* noted his passage and the fact that he was going with a herd of horses "to the big salt lake, his new established trading post." With two Indian helpers and four immigrants who were returning to the States, Goodyear traveled east via the new cutoff, and had reached Bear River when the westbound Mormon pioneers, as we have seen in the Lienhard journal, note 6, encountered him on July 10, 1847. Goodyear sold out to the Mormons later that year, and died in California in 1849; see Charles Kelly and Maurice L. Howe, *Miles Goodyear* (Salt Lake City, 1937), and Dale L. Morgan, *The Great Salt Lake* (Indianapolis, 1947), 130–135, 147–149, 174, 175.

SIGNATURE OF MARGARET W. REED

—*Sutter's Fort Historical Museum*

EMPLOYMENT AGREEMENT

Between James F. Reed and Milford Elliott, his principal teamster,
illustrating the signatures of the two men.

THE REED JOURNAL

Frid. [July] 31 [1846] We Started this morning on the Cut off rout by the South of the Salt Lake. & 4 1/2 miles from the fort there is a beautiful Spring Called the Blue Spring as Cold as Ice   passed Several Springs and Encamped at the foot of the first steep hill going west making this day . . 12 [miles][1]

Sat. 1 Augt. 1846—left Camp this morning early and passed through Several Valleys well watered with plenty of grass, and encamped at the head of Iron Spring Vall[e]y making 15   15[2]

Sund 2   this morning left Camp late on acct of an ox being missing   Crossed over a high ridge or mountain with tolerable rough road an[d] encamped on Bear river making 16 on a little Creek abut 4 miles from Bear River   we ought to have turned to the righ[t] and reached Bear Riv[er] in one mile much better road said to be[3]

---

[1] Reed's language is somewhat ambiguous, in that the camp "at the foot of the first steep hill going west" could be at either the east or west foot of Bridger Bench. The distance traveled, 12 miles, would indicate that the latter was the case, and that the night's encampment was on the Muddy. The obvious is thus labored because of the difficulty raised by Reed's stated mileage next day. Had the camp been at the eastern foot of Bridger Bench, the Mormon noon halt of July 9, 1847, the day's travel from the Donner camp half a mile below Fort Bridger could not have exceeded 8 miles, yet their encampment was an estimated 7 1/2 miles beyond the first spring Reed mentions. Compare the Lienhard Journal, note 3.

[2] This day's travel brought them to the springs in Pioneer Hollow where the Mormons made their noon halt on July 10, 1847, a measured distance of 9 miles which makes Reed's estimate unaccountable, assuming that the company started this morning from the Muddy.

[3] To the crossing of Sulphur Creek, 9 miles from the previous night's encampment, the company's route was identical with the Mormon afternoon journey of July 10, 1847, as described in the Lienhard journal, note 3. But whereas the Mormons turned west down Sulphur Creek, as Lienhard had done and as Reed here suggests his party should have done, the Donners went on by Hastings' original road to strike the Bear higher up. This was the same route by which Joe Walker had guided the Chiles wagons to the Bear in August, 1843. The road, from where it forded Sulphur Creek, proceeded south along Hilliard Flat, gradually inclining to the west, and crossed over a low ridge to the Bear Valley proper in the S. W. quarter of Sec. 18 and the N. W. quarter of Sec. 30, T. 13 N., R. 119 W. The road is clearly shown on the Veatch map and on Sheet 7 of the *Plan of Bear River Damsites*; it was also noted by Captain J. H. Simpson when in 1858 he reconnoitered a military road from Camp Floyd to Fort Bridger by way of Chalk Creek. See his *Preliminary Map of Routes Reconnoitered and*

Mon 3[4] left our encampmt and traveled a tolerable rough Road Crossing Several very high hills and encamped at the head of a larger Vall[e]y with a fine little running Stream passing by the edge of of [sic] our Camp[5] Cattle plenty of grass Count[r]y appear more hale

---

Opened in the Territory of Utah . . . in the Fall of 1858. The point where the old road comes down to the meadows bordering Mill Creek was pointed out to me in August, 1948, by Mr. Alex Jamison, whose Arrow Ranch is situated here. Mr. Jamison, who had lived on this ranch 26 years, said that no evidence of roads remains in the flat haylands of the Bear River bottoms, but that years ago he had observed old wagon tracks descending the long slope some three-quarters of a mile southeast of his ranch buildings.

The celebrated Tar Spring, later known as the Brigham Young Oil Well, lay a little to the left of the southern road, a mile and a half south of its junction with the road down Sulphur Creek. Reed estimated the total distance from the fork in the road to his encampment on Bear River (here possibly meaning the easterly fork, Mill Creek) at 4 miles. By Mormon estimate it was a little farther, for Albert Carrington writes in the Lyman journal under date of July 11, 1847, "G. Brown and [Sterling] Driggs took Jake & Lyon & rode on the southern road to Bear river about 5 miles gone 4 or 5 hours." The Mormons understood that the Donner party had taken this southern road, for as they set out on the other one William Clayton wrote "There is scarcely any wagon track to be seen on the northern road, only a few wagons of Hasting's company having come this route; the balance went the other road and many of them perished in the snow; it being late in the season and much time was lost quarreling who would improve the roads, etc." Actually the Donners lost little if any time through taking the southern road to the head of Echo Canyon.

[4] It may be that some member of the party turned back this day to Fort Bridger, for C. T. Stanton inexplicably contrived to send home a last communication from this point. In a letter now in the Bancroft Library, written to George McKinstry and dated "Brooklyn (long Island) Feby 14, 1848," Philip Stanton mentions having received long and interesting letters from his brother Charles, dispatched at every opportunity, and "forming a complete journal of the incidents," until the company "had passed the Rocky Mountains, and had reached the Bear river valley, the 3rd of August. . . . His last letter was received, I think, in October 1846 . . . the last words . . . [said] that the company took a new route down the Bear river valley, not traveled before that season, and he might not write to us again until he got to California."

[5] West of the Bear River, the southern road taken by the Donner party may be approximately followed today as far as Yellow Creek, 2 miles west of the so-called "Chalk Creek crossing" of the Bear, by the present improved road which makes for Coalville; after leaving the Bear, it surmounts a low ridge and descends to Yellow Creek. It seems likely that the road of 1846 then turned sharply northwest down this creek, following it as far as its elbow bend just inside the present Utah state line, after which it climbed the ridge to the west, and somewhere up on the divide above Cache Cave reunited with the later road taken by Lienhard and the Mormons. One cannot well descend the narrow upper course of Yellow Creek today by car and must be content to approximate the

west[6]   Made this day 16

Tues 4 this day left our encampment about 2 oclock   Made this day about 8   Our encamp was this day in red Run Valley [three words interlineated:] fork of weaver[7]

Wed 5 Started early and traveled the whole day in Red Run Valley and encampe below its enterens [?] into Weavers Creek 15[8]

Donner trail by a more circuitous route to the west, continuing on the Coalville road to cross another divide into a wide basin which is the head of one of the branches of Chalk Creek. Here leaving the Coalville road, one may follow a lateral road running to the north which climbs up on the plateau west of Yellow Creek and parallels its course until the valley of Yellow opens out widely at its elbow bend. The distance by car speedometer from the Bear River to the big bend of Yellow Creek is 15 1/2 miles. It is barely possible that the road thus described is the veritable trail of 1846, adopted by Hastings to avoid the narrow, perhaps brush-choked bottoms, of Yellow Creek. The available evidence does not suffice to establish that the road the Donners followed was one or the other of these.

Reed's description of his place of encampment may be compared with the Mormon accounts of their night halt on July 12 a year later; this was, so Clayton writes, "near a very small creek and a good spring," and is located by Erastus Snow at "the head of a broad and beautiful opening of the Valley where two small springs run in it," with "excellent spring water; Deep black soil and the best feed for our stock we have had on our route." Since the question must be raised whether Reed did not encamp back on Yellow Creek at its bend, we may note that he speaks of having crossed "several" very high hills during the day, while his "fine little running Stream" hardly suggests Yellow Creek. See Lienhard's entries for July 28–30, and compare the diaries of 1847.

[6] The Mormon journals are in entire agreement with Reed as to the improved aspect of the country west of Bear River. Erastus Snow writes on July 12, 1847, "There has been a very evident improvement in the soil production and general appearance of the country since we left Fort Bridger, but more particularly since we crossed Bear River. The mountain Sage has, in a great measure, given place to grass and a variety of Prairie flowers and shrub cedars upon the sides of the hills." Similar comments are found in the other diaries.

[7] "Red Run Valley" is of course Echo Canyon. The company probably encamped 3 or 4 miles below present Castle Rock.

[8] If this day's entry is to be taken at face value, the Donner party encamped for the night on the Weber a mile or so below the mouth of Echo Canyon. But the entry for August 6 gives 10 miles as the full day's travel, impossible without moving on down several miles into the upper canyon of the Weber. As the Mormons logged the road in 1847, it was 3 3/4 miles from the mouth of Echo to where the river was crossed to its south bank. Three-quarters of a mile farther on, the Mormons turned away from this road to follow the Donner track southwest up Main Canyon, but it is probable that on first reaching this point, the Reed-Donner party continued on a little farther, say a mile and a half, to where the Hastings' road recrossed to the north bank of the Weber preparatory to swinging over into Croyden Valley. The maximum distance the Donners could

Thur 6 left our encamp. about ten oclock and encamp above the Cannon   here we turn to the left hand & Cross the Mountain instead of the cann[o]n which is impassible although 60 waggons passed through.[9] this day made 10

---

have covered on August 6 would have been some 6 miles. Thus there is an irreconcilable discrepancy between the language of August 5 and the mileage of August 6.

[9] Here the journal must be supplemented from two other accounts by Reed. The first is the narrative published in the Springfield *Illinois Journal,* December 9, 1847, "prepared for the press by Mr. J. H. Merryman, from notes written by Mr. J. F. Reed," and declared to be an abstract of his journal:

He [Reed] says that his misfortunes commenced on leaving Fort Bridger, which place he left on the 31st of August [July], 1846, in company with eighty-one [!] others. Nothing of note occurred until the 6th of September [August], when they had reached within a few miles of Weaver Canon, where they found a note from a Mr. Hastings, who was twenty miles in advance of them, with sixty wagons, saying that if they would send for him he would put them upon a new route, which would avoid the *Canon* and lessen the distance to the great Salt Lake several miles. Here the company halted, and appointed three persons, who should overtake Mr. Hastings and engage him to guide them through the new route, which was promptly done. Mr. Hastings gave them directions concerning this road, and they [the Donner party] immediately recommenced their journey.

In later years Reed published in the *Pacific Rural Press,* March 25, 1871, a more extended account of this episode, our chief source of information about it:

Leaving Fort Bridger, we unfortunately took the new route, traveling on without incident of note, until we arrived at the head of Weber canyon. A short distance before reaching this place, we found a letter sticking in the top of a sage brush. It was from Hastings. He stated that if we would send a messenger after him he would return and pilot us through a route much shorter and better than the canyon. A meeting of the company was held, when it was resolved to send Messrs. Mc-Cutcheon, Stanton and myself to Mr. Hastings; also we were at the same time to examine the canyon and report at short notice. We overtook Mr. Hastings at a place we called Black Rock [probably Adobe Rock], south end of Salt Lake, leaving McCutcheon and Stanton here, their horses having failed. I obtained a fresh horse from the company Hastings was piloting, and started on my return to our company, with Mr. Hastings. When we arrived at about the place where Salt Lake City is built, Mr. Hastings, finding the distance greater than anticipated by him, stated that he would be compelled to return the next morning to his company. We camped this evening in a canyon. Next morning ascending to the summit of the mountain where we could overlook a portion of the country that lay between us and the head of the canyon, where the Donner party were camped. After he gave me the direction, Mr. Hastings and I separated. He returned to the companies he had left

Frid 7. in Camp on weaver at the mouth of Canon[10]
Sat 8 Still in Camp

---

the morning previous, I proceeding on eastward. After descending to what may be called the table land, I took an Indian trail and blazed the route where it was necessary that the road should be made, if the company so directed when they heard the report. When McCutcheon, Stanton and myself got through Weber canyon on our way to overtake Mr. Hastings, our conclusions were that many of the wagons would be destroyed in attempting to get through the canyon. Mr. Stanton and McCutcheon were to return to our company as fast as their horses would stand it, they having nearly given out. I reached the company in the evening and reported to them the conclusions in regard to Weber canyon, at the same time stating that the route that I had blazed that day was fair, but would take considerable labor in clearing and digging. They agreed with unanimous voice to take that route if I would direct them in the road making, they working faithfully until it was completed.

On the basis of this narrative, which appears to be entirely trustworthy, and the dates which come to us from the other documents, we may conclude that Reed and his two companions left the company encamped on the site of Henefer on the morning of August 7, 1846, and overtook Hastings at Adobe Rock in Tooele Valley on the night of August 8, a ride so long and exhausting that it is no wonder their horses gave out. Next morning Hastings turned back with Reed, and they encamped that night, as Reed says, in a canyon above Salt Lake City, probably where Clyman had encamped on June 2. The following morning, August 10, Hastings continued as far as the summit of Big Mountain to point out the way. The only difficulty about this interpretation is that Reed speaks of "descending to what may be called the table land," from the elevated point to which Hastings had taken him. Properly speaking, there is no table land east of the pass over Big Mountain; note, however, that Parley P. Pratt in July, 1848, applied the phrase to canyon terrain a few miles to the south (see p. 255). Over and against any objections to Big Mountain on this score, it must be agreed that no other height answers the requirements of Reed's summit "where we could overlook a portion of the country that lay between us and the head of the canyon, where the Donner party were encamped." Perhaps Reed and Hastings, like Orson Pratt and John Brown a year later, climbed not only the Big Mountain pass but Big Mountain itself north of the pass, the "table land" being the long slope immediately east of the pass. Reed could have mistaken the trail at several points had Hastings left him earlier, but from Big Mountain Hastings could point out Little Emigration Canyon, at the head of which they stood, and tell Reed to follow that ravine down into East Canyon, descend that canyon 7 or 8 miles to where it closed up in rugged narrows, turn right up a ravine, and from its head follow down a canyon which would bring him directly to his wagons. From Big Mountain Reed could not possibly have mistaken the trail. Nor did he.

[10] It is one of the peculiarities of the journal that, kept by Reed, it devotes itself for four days, not to Reed's strenuous exertions in quest of information, but to placid notations that the company remained in camp.

Sond 9 Still in Camp

Mo 10 Still in Campe   James F. Reed this evening returned he and two others having been sent by the Caravan to examine the Canon and proceed after Mr Hastings, who left a Note on the on the [*sic*] road that if we Came after him he would return and Pilot us through his new and direct rout to the South end of the Salt Lake[11] Reed having examined the new rout entirely and reported in favour, which induced the Compa[n]y to proceed

Tues 11 left Camp and took the new rout with Reed a Pilot he having examined the mountains and vallies from the south end of the Lake   this day made 5[12]

---

[11] Something more should be said concerning the letter Hastings left at the crossing of the Weber. As we have seen from Lienhard's journal, note 18, Hastings probably had posted his notice by the side of the trail on August 4, two days before the Donners arrived there. J. Quinn Thornton, *op. cit.*, II, 97, 98, says that Hastings' letter was found by the company

at the first crossing of Weber river, placed in the split of a stick, in such a situation as to call their attention to it. In this letter they were in-formed that the road down Weber river, over which the sixty-six wag-ons led by Lansford W. Hastings had passed, had been found to be a very bad one, and expressing fears that their sixty-six wagons could not be gotten through the cañon leading into the valley of the Great Salt Lake, then in sight; and advising them to remain in camp until he could return to them, for the purpose of showing them a better road than that through the cañon of Weber river which here breaks through the moun-tains. . . . In this letter, Hastings had indicated another road which he affirmed was much better; and by pursuing which they would avoid the cañon. Messrs. Reed, Stanton, and Pike then went forward, for the purpose of exploring the contemplated new route.

Thornton says that Stanton and Pike accompanied Reed on the ride to overtake Hastings. Reed, as quoted in note 9, declares that it was McCutchen rather than Pike who made the journey, but this probably confuses the subse-quent mission of McCutchen with Stanton to seek help from Sutter; McKinstry, in the *California Star*, February 13, 1847, says specifically that the Donners "sent on three men, (Messrs. Reed, Stanton and Pike) to the first company, (with which I was then travelling in company,) to request Mr. Hastings to go back and show them the pack trail from the Red Fork of Weber River to the Lake. Mr. H. went back and showed them the trail, and then returned to our company, all of which time we remained in camp, waiting for Mr. Hastings to show us the rout."

[12] Again the Mormon diaries are helpful in detailing "Mr. Reid's route across the mountains." In the Lienhard journal, note 8, we have followed Orson Pratt on July 15, 1847, as he reached the second crossing of the Weber on the Hastings road and followed it around through Croyden Valley to convince him-self that he had arrived at the famous "kanyon." Pratt writes further of the search prosecuted for "Reid's route":

Wed, 12 left Camp late and encampe on Bosman Creek on New rout   made 2 [the numeral 3 over written with 2]¹³

. . . In the meantime Mr. [Stephen] Markham, with one or two others, had gone up the river on the right bank, in search of Reid's trail across the mountains, leading down to the south-eastern shores of the Salt Lake. Mr. [John] Brown and I also went in search, travelling along the bluffs on the south. We soon struck the trail, although so dimly seen that it only now and then could be discerned; only a few wagons having passed here one year ago, and the grass having grown up, leaving scarcely a trace. I followed this trail about 6 miles up a ravine [Main Canyon], to where it attained the dividing ridge leading down into another ravine, in a southerly direction. . . .

[July 16, 1847] . . . We concluded to send Mr. [Porter] Rockwell back, to report to the other portion of the pioneers that we had found the new route, &c., which we had anticipated would be troublesome to find. We resumed our journey up a small stream on Reid's route [Main Canyon], sending in advance of the wagons a small company of about a dozen with spades, axes, &c., to make the road passable, which required considerable labour. We travelled about 6 miles, and, crossing the ridge, began to descend another ravine [Dixie Hollow]. . . .

The Donner encampment of August 11 was probably over the "Hogsback," at the head springs in Dixie Hollow where Clyman had camped on June 3, or possibly farther down Dixie Hollow, Reed's estimates of mileage in mountain traveling being what they are. Reed gives the distance as 5 miles for the whole day's travel; the Mormon roadometer next year logged the road from the turnoff on the Hastings road to the Hogsback as 5 3/4 miles.

¹³ Reed's estimates of distances this day, and for the whole route across the mountains, in fact, are astonishingly low; generally speaking, they should be doubled to conform to the facts of the terrain; compare the *Fort Douglas* quadrangle. The journal gives us to understand that on the second day's journey, August 12, the company reached "Bosman [East Canyon] Creek" in 2 miles' travel. Again let us take up the Mormon journals to see what this involved. We resume with Orson Pratt's diary entry of July 16, 1847, at the head of Main Canyon where we broke off in note 12:

. . . crossing the ridge, [we] began to descend another ravine [Dixie Hollow]. Travelled down about 2 1/2 miles, which took about 4 hour's labour, and encamped for the night. . . . After we had encamped Mr. [Elijah] Newman and myself walked down the ravine to examine the road. We found that Mr. Reid's company last season had spent several hour's labour in spading, &c., but finding it almost impracticable for wagons, they had turned up a ravine, at the mouth of which we had encamped, and taken a little more circuitous route over the hills.

July 17th . . . Early this morning I started out alone, and on foot, to examine the country back, to see if there was not a more practicable route for the companies in the rear than the one we had come. I was soon satisfied that we had taken the best and only practicable route . . . I returned to camp and counselled the company not to go any farther

Thur 13 Mad[e] a New Road by Cutting Willow Trees &
[encamped?] on Basman Creek   2 [again the numeral 3 is overwrit-
ten with 2][14]

---

until they had spent several hour's labour on the road over which we
passed yesterday afternoon; and all who were able to work laboured
about two-thirds of the day upon the same. . . .

Even more helpful is William Clayton's description of this section of the
trail, from the Hogsback down into East Canyon:

. . . arrived [July 19] on the summit of the dividing ridge and put a
guide board up, "80 miles to Fort Bridger" . . . . The descent is not
very steep but exceedingly dangerous to wagons being mostly on the
side hill over large cobble stones, causing the wagons to slide very
badly. . . . At two o'clock, we halted beside a small creek [Dixie Creek]
to water teams. . . . at 3:35 we started forward, the road turning suddenly to the right for about three-quarters of a mile and then a southwest course again. Here we ascend a very long steep hill for nearly a
mile, then descend by a very crooked road. I think a better road might
be made here and this high hill avoided and save a mile's travel. After
traveling a little over three miles, we crossed a creek [East Canyon
Creek] about a rod wide and eighteen inches deep, pretty steep going
down but good going out. . . .

To interpret: Reed had found it impossible to take the Donner wagons down
Dixie Hollow southwest to the floor of East Canyon without an inordinate
amount of work cutting out brush, hence had pulled up a ravine to the northwest
and detoured the bottoms, coming down into East Canyon about a half mile below the mouth of Dixie Hollow. It was many years before a road was cut all the
way through Dixie Hollow, and the pioneer wagon road of 1846–47 is still clearly
distinguishable on the *Fort Douglas* quadrangle. The Donners, and the Mormons
after them, reached the floor of East Canyon about half a mile above what Erastus Snow calls its "tremendous impassable Canyon."

The Mormon description of the route is borne out by Thornton in accurate
detail, but an ambiguity in his language, or more properly a misunderstanding on
his part at the time he interviewed the survivors in San Francisco, has led to the
supposition that three rather than two days were required to reach East Canyon.
He writes (p. 98): "On the second day after resuming their journey [August 12]
they came to a grove of willows and quaking asp, through which their way led.
Here they were compelled to open a road, which occupied one day [i.e., most of
that day, August 12]. They again continued their journey, and passing over some
very difficult bluffs, entered a hollow [East Canyon] leading into the Utah River
valley. . . ." (This and all subsequent citations to Thornton's book refer to Vol. II.)

[14] That Reed, for both this and the previous day, estimated the distance
traveled at 3 miles and then scaled down the figure to 2 makes it seem likely that
he neglected his journal and brought it up to date by writing the entries for a
number of days at one time. For August 13–14 Reed shows only 3 miles' total
travel up East Canyon, but the Mormon journals conclusively establish that the
whole distance was 8 miles (which determines also that Little Emigration rather
than Little Dutch Canyon was the lateral ravine up which the road went to the

Frid 14 Still on Basman Creek and proceeded up the Creek about one mile and Turned to the right hand up a narrow valley to Reeds Gap and encamped about one mile from the mouth making this day 2 [Written in margin:] Spring of water[15]

Sat. 15 in Camp all hands Cutting and op[e]ning a road through the Gap.

Son 16 Still Cl[e]earing and making Road in *Reeds Gap.*[16]

Big Mountain summit). Orson Pratt wrote on July 17, after reaching East Canyon: "We followed the dimly traced wagon tracks up this stream for 8 miles, crossing the same 13 times. The bottoms of this creek are thickly covered with willows, from 5 to 15 rods wide, making an immense labour in cutting a road through for the emigrants last season. We still found the road almost impassable, and requiring much labour."

Thornton well describes the same portion of the road, saying (pp. 98–99) that after the Donners reached East Canyon "they were under the necessity of cutting [their way through] eight miles of very thick timber and close-tangled underbrush," a difficult labor which "occupied eight days." This last is an evident misunderstanding on Thornton's part; Reed's journal makes it clear that the eight days apply not to the passage up East Canyon but to the whole period from the time the wagons left the site of Henefer to the time they descended the western slope of Big Mountain to reach the "prairillon" of Mountain Dell.

[15] Reed would place the Donner camp about a mile above the mouth of Little Emigration Canyon. The Mormons next year chiefly remarked a spring 2 miles higher up. William Clayton writes on July 21, 1847:

> ... the road turns to the right leaving the [East Canyon] creek and ascending the mountains gradually. Much time was necessarily spent cutting down stumps, heaving out rocks and leveling the road. It is an exceedingly rough place. There are several springs at the foot of the mountain and one a mile from the top which runs above the ground a little distance, then sinks under again. The last half mile of the ascent is very steep and the nearer the top the steeper it grows. There is considerable timber up this gap but mostly destroyed by fire.

In his *Latter-Day Saints' Emigrants' Guide* (St. Louis, 1848), 19, Clayton notes, with respect to this section of the trail, "You will probably find water in several places, but it is uncertain where, as it runs but a little way in a place, and then sinks in the earth."

[16] Thornton, our most credible authority, says (p. 99) that it was on the sixth day of cutting out the road that the Graves family, with their three wagons, overtook the Donner party, the last addition to the company. On the theory set forth in note 14 above, the Graveses overtook the others on this day, August 16, at their camp a mile up Little Emigration Canyon, and thus added three more hands to the last day's work on the road. W. C. Graves, writing in the Healdsburg, Calif., *Russian River Flag*, April 26, 1877, implies that the family overtook the Donners immediately after Reed's return over the mountains, but there are so many inaccuracies in the Graves narrative that it is entitled to no credence on this score.

Mon 17 Still in Camp and all hands working on the road which we finished and returned to Campe

Tus 18 this Morning all started to Cross the Mountain which is a Natural easey pass with a little more work and encamped making this day—5[17] J F Reed Brok[e] an axletree[18]

Wed 19 this day we lay in Camp in a neat little valley   fine water and good grass   the hands ware this [day?] on the other on West Side of Small mountain,[19] in a small Valley [Emigration Canyon]

---

[17] "On the ninth [eighth] day," as Thornton writes (p. 99), "they left their encampment, and traveled into an opening which they supposed led out into the Utah River valley." In other words, the wagons were taken up Little Emigration Canyon to "Reed's Gap," the pass over Big Mountain, down its western slope to Mountain Dell Canyon, and on down that canyon to the upper reaches of the valley today overspread in considerable measure by the waters of Mountain Dell Reservoir. The distance covered more nearly approximated 8 than the 5 miles estimated by Reed.

[18] Reed's narrative of 1871 would place this mishap back at the camp in Little Emigration Canyon. Thornton, on the other hand, says (p. 102) that it happened at the south shore of Great Salt Lake; he writes: "Here Mr. Reed broke an axletree and they had to go a distance of fifteen miles to obtain timber to repair it. By working all night, Mr. Eddy and Samuel Shoemaker completed the repair for Mr. Reed." The west slope of Big Mountain has such a breakneck character that it is wholly plausible to suppose the mishap happened as one of Reed's wagons was descending it, yet Thornton's detail of having to go 15 miles for timber is good supporting evidence for the story he tells.

[19] Not the least interesting feature of this entry is that so early as 1846 Little Mountain was designated as the "small mountain." Reed's diary says nothing of an attempt to get down through Parleys Canyon, up which Hastings had traveled with Clyman on June 2–3, and again with Reed on August 9–10. Thornton indicates why. "Here," he writes (p. 99), "Messrs. Stanton and Pike, who had been lost from the time Mr. Reed had gone forward with them to explore, were found by the party they had sent to hunt for them. These men reported the impracticability of passing down the valley in which they then were, and they advised their companions to pass over a low range of hills into a neighboring valley. This they did."

When Orson Pratt, accompanied by John Brown, reconnoitered the road for the Mormon Pioneers, on July 19, 1847, he described it from East Canyon in these terms:

[we] ascertained that the road left [East] Kanyon Creek near the place where we stopped the day before, and run along in a ravine to the west [Little Emigration Canyon]. We ascended this ravine gradually for 4 miles, when we came to the dividing ridge [Big Mountain] . . . the descent is very rapid at first. We travelled down several miles and found that the small stream we were descending [Mountain Dell Creek, called by the Mormons Browns Creek] passed through a very high mountain [the gorge of Parleys below the present Mountain Dell Reservoir],

Clearing a road to the Vall[e]y of the Lake   We have to Cross the
outlett [Jordan River] of the Utah Lake on this Rout Nearr the Salt
Lake

Thus 20 Still in Camp and hands Clearing road

Frid 21 this day we left camp and [this word crossed out]
Crossed the Small mountain and encapd in the vally running into the
Utah outlett making this day 4[20]

Sat 22 this day we passed through the mountains and encampd
in the Utah [Salt Lake] Valley making this day 2[21]

---

where we judged it impossible for wagons to pass; and after searching
awhile, we found that the wagon trail ascended quite abruptly for about
$1^1/2$ miles, and passed over a mountain [Little Mountain], and down
into another narrow valley [Emigration Canyon], and thus avoided the
kanyon. . . .

[20] As they had done at the base of Big Mountain, the company remained in
camp until the whole road had been made, then moved up over Little Mountain
and down into Emigration Canyon. Thornton says (p. 99) that the Donners here
"worked five days in cutting through the timber." In this he is mistaken, but
William Clayton remarks, under date of July 22, 1847, "It is evident that the
emigrants who passed this way last year must have spent a great deal of time
cutting a road through the thickly set timber and heavy brush wood." Reed's
estimate of the distance traveled this day is too low. The party probably camped
about $4^1/2$ miles down Emigration Canyon, just above Donner Hill.

[21] Illustrating the extent to which the extraordinary had become the com-
monplace, Reed's diary entirely passes over the difficulties the Donner party had
to contend with in emerging from Emigration Canyon out upon the table land
overlooking Salt Lake Valley. At its mouth, Emigration Canyon in 1846 was
much obstructed by an abutment from the south wall, which forced the creek
through a narrow opening thickly overgrown with willows. "The cañon being
impracticable as a wagon way," Thornton writes, "they doubled teams and got
their wagons to the top of the hill, from which there was a gradual descent into
the valley." More graphically, Virginia Reed Murphy relates in her "Across the
Plains in the Donner Party," *Century Magazine*, July, 1891, p. 418, "we reached
the end of the cañon where it looked as though our wagons would have to be
abandoned. It seemed impossible for the oxen to pull them up the steep hill and
the bluffs beyond, but we doubled teams and the work was, at last, accomplished,
almost every yoke in the train being required to pull up each wagon."

More illuminating still are the Mormon journals in their simple description
of the terrain. Orson Pratt discovered, on July 21, 1847, that "the wagons last
season had passed over an exceedingly steep and dangerous hill. Mr. [Erastus]
Snow and myself ascended this hill, from the top of which a broad open valley,
about 20 miles wide and 30 long, lay stretched out before us. . . . we could not
refrain from a shout of joy which almost involuntarily escaped from our lips the
moment this grand and lovely scenery was within our view." Erastus Snow described the ground in similar terms, saying that he and Pratt made their way
"down the Valley [Emigration Canyon] six or seven miles, and came to a small

Son 23 left Camp late this day on acct. of having to find a good road or pass through the Swamps of the utah outlet   finally succeeded in and encamped on the East Bank of Utah outlett making 5[22]

---

canyon just above where the creek opens into the Valley of the Utah outlet—To avoid this canyon the old Pack Trail crosses the creek and leads up an exceedingly steep hill onto a Butte that commands the vallies, and a view of the Salt Lake."

Here, for a few rods at the mouth of Emigration Canyon, in an effort to avoid this steep and dangerous grade up the south wall of the canyon, the Mormon Pioneers made their only independent contribution to the "Mormon Trail." The way of it is described by William Clayton on July 22, 1847:

> After traveling one and three-quarters miles [down Emigration Canyon], we found the road crossing the creek again to the south [misprinted "north" in the published journal] side and then ascending up a very steep, high hill. It is so very steep as to be almost impossible for heavy wagons to ascend and so narrow that the least accident might precipitate a wagon down a bank three or four hundred feet,—in which case it would certainly be dashed to pieces. Colonel Markham and another man went over the hill and returned up the canyon to see if a road cannot be cut through and avoid this hill. . . . Brother Markham says a good road can soon be made down the canyon by digging a little and cutting through the bushes some ten or fifteen rods. A number of men went to work immediately to make the road which will be much better than to attempt crossing the hill and will be sooner done. . . . After spending about four hours' labor the brethren succeeded in cutting a pretty good road along the creek and the wagons proceeded on, taking near a southwest course.

The Mormon wagons, in short, kept down the gulch of Emigration to a point immediately above the present Hogle Zoo, then to avoid a marsh in the bottoms, pulled up on the benchland to the south, roughly paralleling the present Wasatch Boulevard but a few yards below it, to arrive at the bench at the intersection of Wasatch Boulevard and Michigan Avenue, the northeast extremity of the present Bonneville Golf Course. From this point they wound down the sloping plateau to camp on Parleys Creek, in the vicinity of present 5th East and 17th South streets. This, it should be noted, was also the route of Brigham Young two days later. The "This Is the Place Monument" north of the gulch of Emigration serves to commemorate imposingly the historic circumstance of the Mormon arrival in Salt Lake Valley, but is not to be taken as marking the site where Brigham Young got his first sweeping view of the future home of the Saints.

[22] Where in Salt Lake Valley the Donners encamped after getting clear of the mountains the previous afternoon it is hard to say, but perhaps on Parleys Creek in the vicinity of present 11th East and 21st South streets. Until recently it has been conjectured that the Mormons followed the Donner track all the way from the mouth of Emigration Canyon to the floor of Salt Lake Valley, but in the light of what we now know about the Donners, having crossed the Jordan some 4 miles south of the North Temple ford, it must be supposed that the trails parted on the benchland in the vicinity of present Downington Avenue and 15th East

Mo 24 left our Camp and Crossed the plain to a spring at a point of the Lake mountain [Oquirrh Mountains] and 1½ miles from the road traveled by the people who passed the Cannon[23] 12 [Written in margin:] Brackish Water [Written in margin still later:] It took 18 days to gett 30 miles[24]

Street, the Donner road from this point swinging to the southwest, the Mormon road more to the west. Although some Mormon records speak of having made "an entire new route through the Kanyon," this must be understood as applying only to the road cut around "Donner Hill," in the mouth of Emigration Canyon.

To judge from Reed's entry for August 23, the wagons he was guiding had considerable difficulty in getting through the Mill Creek morass to their night encampment on the east bank of the Jordan, a little south of present 27th South Street.

[23] The encampment of August 24 was in the vicinity of Garfield, probably where Clyman camped on June 1. Reed's language with respect to "the road traveled by the people who passed the Cannon" is not in itself wholly clear, but a study of the township surveys of 1856 and the map published with the Stansbury report makes it evident that the road from the North Temple crossing of the Jordan, angling rather south of west across Salt Lake Valley, intersected the Reed road at present Magna, near the junction of present State Highway 201 and I-80. Reed therefore is to be understood as saying he camped 1½ miles west of the road junction. Reed's narrative of 1871 backs up his diary of 1846 about the place the Donner road came into the Hastings' road: "We progressed our way and crossed the outlet of the Utah, now called Jordan, a little below the location of Salt Lake City. From this camp in a day's travel we made connection with the trail of the companies that Hastings was piloting through his cutoff. We then followed his road around the lake without incident worthy of notice until reaching a swampy section of country [Grantsville] west of Black Rock [Adobe Rock?], the name we gave it. . . ." Compare the Jefferson map and the Lienhard journal, note 31.

[24] Reed's 18 days evidently comprise the period August 7–24, including the four days the company lay by in Weber Canyon. The mileages stated add up to 39 rather than to 30. Reed supplied the same figures for the account published in the *Illinois Journal*. December 9, 1847: "After traveling eighteen days they accomplished the distance of thirty miles, with great labor and exertion, being obliged to cut the whole road through a forest of pine and aspen." George McKinstry, writing in the *California Star* of February 13, 1847, reports Reed told him a few weeks later that the Donner party "were sixteen days making the road, as the men would not work one quarter of their time." Apparently this was the source of Clayton's remark of July 22, 1847, "It is reported that they [the Donners] spent sixteen days in making a road through from Weber River which is thirty-five miles but as the men did not work a quarter of their time much less would have sufficed. However, it has taken us over three days after the road is made although a great many hours have been spent in improving it." Thornton wrote in 1849 (p. 99) that the Donners were "occupied thirty days in traveling forty miles," and in the course of time Reed was subjected to much criticism over the choice of route, so that in 1871 he protested, "I here state that the num-

Tues 25 left Camp early this morning intending if possible to make the *Lower Wells*[25] being fair water 20 which we made [Two words written in margin:] fair water and in the evening a Gentleman by the name of *Luke Halloran,* died of Consumption having been brough[t] from Bridgers Fort by George Donner a distance 151 miles we made him a Coffin and Burried him at the up[p]er wells at the forks of the road in a beautiful place.[26]

---

ber of days we were detained in road-making was not the cause by any means, of the company remaining in the mountains during the following winter." It must at any rate be said that the four days lost while encamped in Weber Canyon would have been gone beyond recovery regardless of the decision the company made when Reed came back to them on August 10.

[25] It is notably difficult to establish just what Reed means by "the Lower Wells." His mileages are not reliable enough that one can depend on them, and as we have seen in consideration of Lienhard's journal, note 28, there were two alternative roads Reed might have taken west of Adobe Rock. Assuming that he kept to the shorter road closest to the lake, 20 miles would have brought him, from the area of Garfield, to the center of Grantsville. Going the other way, Clyman estimated this distance at 20 miles, but we cannot prove that they took precisely the same routes through Tooele Valley. It may be that the "Lower Wells" were those situated in Section 28, T. 2 S., R. 5 W., and Reed's campsite of this night about half a mile west and three-quarters of a mile north of the point where the modern highway, State Route 138, changes from a southwest to a west course to enter Grantsville.

On the following day the Donner party moved on 2 miles to what Reed calls the "Upper Wells." It may be that these are the springs Lienhard describes under date of August 11, which he declares to be situated half a mile from where North Willow Creek sank into the earth; this hypothesis seems the more likely in that John Hargrave appears to have died there. These "wells" broke out, as shown by the 1856 survey of T. 2 S., R. 6 W., along the line between Sections 25 and 36, some 2 1/2 miles west of the springs I conjecture above to be the "Lower Wells," a half mile north and a half mile east of where State Route 138 turns from west to northwest on leaving Grantsville today.

Reed speaks of an unspecified number of Lower Wells and ten Upper Wells. Thornton (p. 103) calls the whole area "Twenty Wells," and says the name was suggested "by the circumstance of there being at this place that number of natural wells, filled to the very surface of the earth with the purest cold water. They [the immigrants] sounded some of them with lines of more than seventy feet, without finding bottom. They varied from six inches to nine feet in diameter. None of them overflowed; and what is most extraordinary, the ground was dry and hard near the very edge of the water, and upon taking water out, the wells would instantly fill again."

[26] Thornton closely corroborates Reed's account by saying (p. 102) that on this day, "About 4 o'clock, P.M., Mr. Hallerin, from St. Joseph, died of consumption, in Mrs. George Donner's wagon. About 8 o'clock, this wagon (which had stopped) came up, with the dead body of their fellow traveler."

Wed 26 left Camp late and proceed[d] to the upper wells   One of them delightful water being entirely fresh   the rest in No. about 10 all Brackish   this day Buried Mr Luke Halloran hauling him in his Coffin this distan[ce] 2 which we only mad[e] and Buried heem as above Stated at the forks of the [road] One Turning directly South to Camp the other West or onward.[27]

Thur 27 left early this day and went west for half the day at the foot of the Lake [Stansbury] Mountains the latter $1/2$ the day our Course S. W. to a No. of Brackish Wells making 16 *miserable water*[28]

In his account of 1871 Reed wrote: "We . . . followed his [Hastings'] road around the Lake without incident worthy of notice until reaching a swampy section of country west of Black Rock. . . . Here we lost a few days on the score of humanity. One of our company, a Mr. Halloran being in a dying condition from consumption. We could not make regular drives owing to his situation. He was under the care of Mr. George Donner, and made himself known to me as a Master Mason. In a few days he died." Thornton adds (p. 103) that Halloran "gave his property, some $1500, to Mr. George Donner." Halloran having died at the same place as John Hargrave, next day, as Thornton says (p. 103), the company buried him "at the side of an emigrant who had died in the advance company."

After many years of uncertainty as to where Hargrave and Halloran are buried, the educated guesses of historians ranging from the Jordan River to Adobe Rock, the approximate location of the two graves in Grantsville is now fixed on the mutually supporting authority of the Lienhard and Reed journals, and a historical marker can now be erected to commemorate the burial place of the first two overland immigrants to be committed to Utah soil. To locate the graves exactly, however, is another matter. Reed says Halloran was buried "at the forks of the road," and explains that one road turned "directly South to Camp the other West or onward." But what does he mean by "directly South to Camp"? If his own camp, which would be most logical, are we to assume that the road west from the "Lower Wells" passed the area of the "Upper Wells" below or north of the "Upper Wells," and that a road branched off a few hundred yards south to the camp ground—this road perhaps also being the western terminus of the road through Tooele Valley Jefferson traveled? If so, further researches as to the exact location of the graves must be prosecuted a little north of the area tentatively identified in the previous note as the location of the "Upper Wells." See also pp. xiv–xv.

[27] The fact that Reed twice related the circumstance of the burial would indicate that his journal was kept somewhat spasmodically, and that in bringing it up to date, he repeated himself. Of the events of the 26th Thornton says simply (p. 103), "The day . . . was spent, with the exception of a change of camp, in committing the body of their friend to the dust."

[28] Normally the first camp made after leaving the area of Grantsville was at Burnt Spring in Skull Valley, distant about 19 or 20 miles. Reed's distance, 16 miles, might be merely a faulty estimate, but if so, next day he overestimates the distance to the fresh water at Iosepa by about 3 miles. Any errors in the estimates

Frid 28 left Camp and glad to do, so, in hopes of finding fresh water on our way but without Success untill evening when it was time to Camp Came to a No of delightful fresh water wells[29]   this Camp is at the Most Suthern point of the Salt Lake   20 miles North west[30] we Commence the long drive   We are taking in water, Grass, and wood for the various requirements.[31] 12

Sat 29 in Camp wooding watering and laying in a Supply of grass for our oxen and horses, to pass the long drive which Commence about [ ] miles   we have one encampment between but neither grass wood or water of sufficient quallety or quantity to be procured   water [One word written in margin:] *sulphur* Brackish, grass short and no wood—

Son 30 made this day—12 to a Sulpher Spring [Redlum Spring] in the mountain which ought to be avoidid   water not good for Cattle,

---

cancel out if Burnt Spring was the intermediate point. It may be that he did not actually make it to Burnt Spring on the 27th and stopped at a saline spring short of it; but as against this, he relates having traveled a southwest course—that is, into Skull Valley—the latter part of the day.

[29] At Iosepa, the name of which is reminiscent of a Hawaiian colony once established in Skull Valley.

[30] Here and in his entry for August 30 Reed seems to regard the marshes at the north end of Skull Valley as a southern arm of Great Salt Lake.

[31] At Iosepa, Thornton says (p. 103), the company "found a letter from Lansford W. Hastings, informing them that it would occupy two days and nights of hard driving to reach the next water and grass." Eliza P. Donner Houghton, who was only four years old at the time, but who perhaps draws upon the recollections of the older children, writes in *The Expedition of the Donner Party and Its Tragic Fate* (Chicago, 1911), 39–40:

> Close by the largest well stood a rueful spectacle,—a bewildering guide board, flecked with bits of white paper, showing that the notice or message which had recently been pasted and tacked thereon had since been stripped off in irregular bits. In surprise and consternation, the emigrants gazed at its blank face, then toward the dreary waste beyond. Presently my mother [Tamsen Donner] knelt before it and began searching for fragments of paper, which she believed crows had wantonly pecked off and dropped to the ground.
>
> Spurred by her zeal, others also were soon on their knees, scratching among the grasses and sifting the loose soil through their fingers. What they found, they brought to her and after the search ended she took the guide board, laid it across her lap, and thoughtfully began fitting the ragged edges of paper together and matching the scraps to marks on the board. The tedious process was watched with spellbound interest by the anxious group around her. The writing was that of Hastings, and her patchwork brought out the following words: "2 days—2 nights—hard driving—cross—desert—reach water."

emigrants Should keep on the edge of the lake and avoid the mountain entirely[32]   here Commenced the long drive through the Salt
dessert.[33]

EXTRACT FROM JAMES FRAZIER REED'S NARRATIVE OF 1871, DESCRIBING THE CROSSING OF THE SALT DESERT

We started to cross the desert traveling day and night only stopping to feed and water our teams as long as water and grass lasted.
We must have made at least two-thirds of the way across when a great
portion of the cattle showed signs of giving out. Here the company
requested me to ride on and find the water and report.[34]   Before

---

[32] Reed seems to be recommending that instead of watering at Redlum
Spring and crossing the Cedar Mountains by Hastings Pass, immigrants should
keep to the base of the Cedars and continue north to Low Pass (through which
I-80 runs today). As such a course would have added measurably to the length of
the "dry drive," the immigrants much preferred the steep pull up over Hastings
Pass.

Reed's language may also be interpreted as meaning that the immigrants
should not have penetrated south into Skull Valley at all, instead making straight
for Low Pass as soon as they rounded the Stansbury Mountains, the course taken
by the U.S. highway today. What has been developed concerning the marshy
character of the north end of Skull Valley in 1846 makes it doubtful that Reed
had this in mind; and if he did, the idea was impracticable since on such a route
no water was available between the springs at Grantsville and those at Pilot Peak.

[33] Reed's journal being quite literally without words to picture the hardships
of the desert crossing, a long extract is here inserted in the text from his narrative
in the *Pacific Rural Press*, March 25, 1871. Thornton, who is usually reliable as to
facts though hardly ever as to dates, says (pp. 103–104) that the traverse of the
Salt Desert began about daylight on September 9 and continued without ceasing
until 10 A.M. of September 12, when William Eddy and some others reached the
springs at Pilot Peak, Eddy's wagon having been left 20 miles out. In so saying,
Thornton does not distinguish between the preliminary movement of the wagons
to Redlum Spring and the subsequent crossing of the Salt Desert proper. If
Thornton's dates are translated, the desert crossing required from August 31 to
September 2 for the advance contingent of the Donner party.

[34] In his introductory remarks to this narrative, Reed declared that if he had
to live through the experience of 1846 again, this was one of only two things he
would do otherwise than he had done, "leaving my family and wagons in the
desert to hunt water to gratify the desire of a number of the company, when
there was a plain road traveled by companies before us." In her letter of May 16,
1847, recounting to her cousin Mary Gillespie her family's fearful experiences,
13-year-old Virginia Reed mentioned her stepfather's departure on this mission:
"We traveld day and night and at noon next day papa went on to see if he Coud
find Water, he had not gone long till some of the oxen give out and we had to
leve the Wagons and take the oxen to Water   Walter Herren & Bailos staid with

leaving I requested my principal teamster [Milford Elliott], that when my cattle became so exhausted that they could not proceed further with the wagons, to turn them out and drive them on the road after me until they reached the water, but the teamster misunderstanding unyoked them when they first showed symptoms of giving out, starting on with them for the water.

I found the water about twenty miles from where I left the company and started on my return.[35] About eleven o'clock at night [September 2] I met my teamster with all my cattle and horses. I cautioned them particularly to keep the cattle on the road, for that as soon as they would scent the water they would break for it.[36] I proceeded on and reached my family and wagons.[37] Some time after leaving the men one of the horses gave out and while they were striving to get it along, the cattle scented the water and started for it. And when they started with the horses, the cattle were out of sight, they could not find them or their trail, they told me afterward. They supposing the cattle would find water, went on to camp. The next morning they could not be found, and they never were, the Indians getting them, except one ox and one cow. Losing nine yoke of cattle here was the first of my sad misfortunes. I stayed with my family and wagons the next day, expecting every hour the return of some of my young men with water, and the information of the arrival of the cattle at the water. Owing to the mistake of the teamsters in turning the cattle out so soon, the other wagons had drove miles past mine and

---

us and the other boys Milt. Elliot & J Smith went on with the cattel to water papa was coming back to us with Water and met the men thay was about 10 miles from water papa said thay would get to water that night, and the next day to bring the cattel back for the Wagons and bring some Water." Quoted from a photostat of the original letter in the Southwest Museum. Before it was mailed, an older person—from the handwriting, Reed himself—made some corrections and additions, which makes it all the more valuable as a source document. The letter is usually known from the freely edited version first printed in the Springfield *Illinois Journal*, December 16, 1847.

[35] According to Thornton (p. 104), Reed reached the water at Pilot Peak just at dark, telling Eddy that his wagons and those of the Donners were 40 miles back. He rested an hour and then set out into the desert again, accompanied for 5 miles by Eddy, who carried a bucket of water to resuscitate an ox left by the way.

[36] As Thornton tells it: "Mr. Reed met the drivers ten miles from the spring, coming forward with the cattle. He continued on, and the drivers came into camp about midnight, having lost all of Mr. Reed's team after passing him." See also Virginia Reed's account, in note 34.

[37] Virginia Reed's letter says he got back to the family "about daylight next morning," i.e., September 3.

dropped their wagons along the road, as their cattle gave out, and some few of them reaching water with their wagons. Receiving no information and the water being nearly exhausted, in the evening [September 3] I started on foot with my family to reach the water. In the course of the night the children became exhausted. I stopped, spread a blanket and laid them down covering them with shawls. In a short time a cold hurricane commenced blowing; the children soon complained of the cold. Having four [five] dogs with us, I had them lie down with the children outside the covers. They were then kept warm. Mrs. Reed and myself sitting to the windward helped shelter them from the storm. Very soon one of the dogs jumped up and started out barking, the others following, making an attack on something approaching us. Very soon I got sight of an animal making directly for us; the dogs seizing it changed its course, and when passing I discovered it to be one of my young steers. Incautiously stating that it was mad, in a moment my wife and children started to their feet, scattering like quail, and it was some minutes before I could quiet camp; there was no more complaining of being tired or sleepy the balance of the night. We arrived about daylight [September 4] at the wagons of Jacob Donner, and the next in advance of me, whose cattle having given out, had been driven to water. Here I first learned of the loss of my cattle, it being the second day after they had started for the water. Leaving my family with Mrs. Donner, I reached the encampment. Many of the people were out hunting cattle, some of them had got their teams together and were going back into the desert for their wagons. Among them Mr. Jacob Donner, who kindly brought my family along with his own to the encampment.[38]

---

[38] Compare the 13-year-old Virginia's account with that of her stepfather. After mentioning Reed's return to his family and the fact that the hired man, Walter Herron, took Reed's horse and went on to water, she writes:

We waited thare thinking thay would come   we waited till night and We thought we would start and walk to Mr Donners wagons that night distant 10 miles   we took what little water we had and some bread and started   papa caried Thomos and all the rest of us walk   we got to Donner and thay were all a sleep so we laid down on the ground we spread one shawl down we laid down on it and spred another over us and then put the dogs on top Tyler, Barney, Trailor Tracker & little Cash   it was the couldes night you ever saw for the season   the wind blew very hard and if it haden not been for the dogs we would have Frosen   as soon as it was day we went to Mrs Donners   she said we could not walk to the Water and if we staid we could ride in thare wagons to the spring so papa went on to the water to see why thay did not

THE REED JOURNAL RESUMES

Mon [August] 31 in dessert

) drive of sixty miles 60

Tusdy Sepr 1 in dessert

Wed 2 in d[itt]o Cattl got in   Reeds Cattl lost this night[39]

Thusdy 3 in d[itt]o   Some teams got in [last five words crossed out]

Fridy 4 in d[itt]o [these two words crossed out]   lost Reeds Cattle 9 Yok[e] by Not driving them Carefule to water as directed by Reed— the rest of teams getting in and resting, Cattle all nearly given out [Six words written in margin:] Hunting Cattl 3 or 4 days

Sat 5 Still in Camp in the west Side of the Salt Dessert

---

bring the cattle   when he got thare thare was but one ox and one cow thare   none of the rest had got to Water   Mr Donner came out that night with his cattel and braught his wagons and all of us in

In this letter, Virginia says nothing of the stampede to which Reed refers; however, in her (probably ghostwritten) article in *Century Magazine*, p. 417, she says:

Can I ever forget that night in the desert, when we walked mile after mile in the darkness, every step seeming to be the very last we could take! Suddenly all fatigue was banished by fear; through the night came a swift rushing sound of one of the young steers crazed by thirst and apparently bent upon our destruction. My father, holding his youngest child in his arms and keeping us all close behind him, drew his pistol, but finally the maddened beast turned and dashed off into the darkness. Dragging ourselves along about ten miles, we reached the wagon of Jacob Donner. The family were all asleep, so we children lay down on the ground. A bitter wind swept over the desert, chilling us through and through. We crept closer together, and, when we complained of the cold, papa placed all five of our dogs around us, and only for the warmth of these faithful creatures we should doubtless have perished.

These three accounts have small discrepancies as to sequence, but they agree impressively as to the events.

[39] This date squares with the chronology employed in editing Reed's reminiscent narrative. Note, however, that Virginia's letter of 1847, as quoted in note 34, says that Reed first left his family after traveling a day and a night, i.e., September 3. The demoralizing character of the whole experience in the Salt Desert is in no way better summed up than by Reed's difficulties in trying to get even the bare bones of the story set down in his journal afterwards.

Thornton's history of these events is if not confused at any rate confusing. Picking up his narrative from where we left it in note 36, we find him to say: "The Messrs. Donner got to water, with a part of their teams, at about 2 o'clock, A.M., of September 13th [3rd]. Mr. Eddy started back at daylight on the morning of the 13th [3rd], and at dawn of day on the 14th [4th], he brought up Mrs. Reed and children and his wagon."

Send 6 Started for Reeds waggon lying in the Salt Plains 28 miles from Camp   Cached 2 waggs and other effects[40]

---

[40] Thornton continues his account, "On the afternoon of the 14th. they started back with Mr. Reed and Mr. Graves, for the wagons of the Messrs. Donner and Reed: and brought them up with horses and mules, on the evening of the 15th." By our adjustment of Thornton's dates, his 14th and 15th would properly be September 4 and 5. But the diary dates these events for two days later.
Reed's narrative of 1871 says further:

We remained here [at Pilot Peak] for days hunting cattle, some of the party finding all, others a portion, all having enough to haul their wagons except myself. On the next day, or day following, while I was out hunting my cattle, two Indians came to the camp, and by signs gave the company to understand that there were so many head of cattle out, corroborating the number still missing; many of the people became tender footed at the Indians coming into camp, thinking that they were spies. Wanted to get clear of them as soon as possible. My wife requested that the Indians should be detained until my return, but unfortunately before returning, they had left. The next morning, in company with young Mr. Graves—he kindly volunteering—I started in the direction the Indians had taken; after hunting this day and the following, remaining out during the night, we returned unsuccessful, not finding a trace of the cattle. I now gave up all hope of finding them and turned my attention to making arrangements for proceeding on my journey. In the desert were my eight [three] wagons; all the team remaining was an ox and a cow. There was no alternative but to leave everything but provisions, bedding and clothing. These were placed in the wagon that had been used for my family. I made a cache of everything else. Members of the company kindly furnishing team to haul the wagon to camp. I divided my provisions with those who were nearly out, and indeed some of them were in need. I had now to make arrangement for sufficient team to haul that one wagon; one of the company kindly loaned me a yoke of cattle, and with the ox and cow I had, made two yoke. We remained at this camp from first to last, if my memory is right, seven days.

Some odds and ends of information with respect to the salvage operations and the caching of some of the wagons and property are provided by Thornton and Virginia Reed. The former writes (p. 105), "On this drive thirty-six head of working cattle were lost, and the oxen that survived were greatly injured. One of Mr. Reed's wagons was brought to camp; and two, with all they contained, were buried in the plain. George Donner lost one wagon. Kiesburg also lost a wagon." In her straightforward way, the 13-year-old Virginia Reed wrote in 1847 while the memory was still fresh, "We staid thare [at Pilot Peak] a week and hunted for our cattel and could not find them   the Indians had taken them so some of the companie took thare oxens and went out and brout in one Wagon and cashed the other tow and a grate many things all but What we could put in one wagon   We had to divied our provisions with the Company to get them to cary it   We got three yoak of cattel with our ox and cow & we went on that way." In later years,

Mon 7 Cam[e] in to Camp in the Night and the waggon Came in on Tuesdy morng

Tuesdy 8 Still fixing and resting Cattle

Weds 9 Mr Graves Mr Pike & Mr Brin loaned 2 Yoke of Cattle to J F Reed with one Yok[e] he had to bring his family waggon along

Thrs 10 left Camp and proceeded about [this word crossed out] up the lake bed   7[41]

---

in her *Century Magazine* account, she added, "Some of the company went back with papa and assisted him in cacheing everything that could not be packed in one wagon. A cache was made by digging a hole in the ground, in which a box or the bed of a wagon was placed. Articles to be buried were packed into this box, covered with boards, and the earth thrown in upon them, and thus they were hidden from sight. Our provisions were divided among the company."

[41] Compare Lienhard's entry for August 21. Thornton's version (pp. 106–108) of this day's travel is:

Having yoked some loose cows, as a team for Mr. Reed, they broke up their camp on the morning of September 16th, and resumed their toilsome journey. . . . On this day they traveled six miles, encountering a very severe snow storm. About 3 o'clock, P.M., they met Milton Elliot and William Graves, returning from a fruitless drive to find some cattle that had got off. They informed them that they were then in the immediate vicinity of a spring, at which commenced another dry drive of forty miles. They encamped for the night, and at dawn of day of September 17th, they resumed their journey, and at 4 o'clock, A.M., of the 18th they arrived at water and grass, some of their cattle having perished, and the teams which survived being in a very enfeebled condition.

Apparently it was on this day, September 10, that Charles T. Stanton and William McCutchen left the company to ride ahead to Sutter's and bring back a fresh supply of provisions. Thornton (pp. 119–120) says that "on the day they broke up their encampment on the Salt Lake, they dispatched Messrs. Stanton and McCutcheon to go to Capt. Sutter's Fort for relief." Virginia Reed's *Century Magazine* account (which seems to have been influenced throughout by Thornton) relates: "Before leaving the desert camp, an inventory of provisions on hand was taken, and it was found that the supply was not sufficient to last us through to California, and as if to render the situation more terrible, a storm came on during the night and the hill-tops became white with snow. Some one must go on to Sutter's Fort after provisions. A call was made for volunteers. C. T. Stanton and Wm. McClutchem bravely offered their services and started on bearing letters from the company to Captain Sutter asking for relief." The remarks by McKinstry in the *California Star*, February 13, 1847, are to the same effect: "After crossing the long drive of 75 miles without water or grass, and suffering much from loss of oxen, they sent on two men (M[ess]rs. Stanton and Mc-Cutcher.) They left the company recruiting on the second long drive of 35 miles, and came in to Capt. J. A. Sutter's Fort, and asked for assistance. . . ." The account in the Springfield *Illinois Journal*, December 9, 1847, based on information

Frid 11 left the Onfortunate lake and mad[e] in the night and day– about 23   Encamped in a valley wher[e] the[re] is fine grass & water[42]

Sat 12[43]

Sond 13 left Camp and proceeded south in the Vally to fine sp[r]ing or Basin of water and grass—difficult for Teams   Made this day 13[44]

Mo 14 [this date written over the word "Sunday"] left the Basin Camp or Mad Woman Camp as all the women in Camp ware mad

---

supplied by Reed, says simply: "When within nine hundred miles of the California settlements they discovered that their stock of provisions was insufficient to last them until they had traveled that distance; therefore, they appointed two persons, Messrs. C. F. Stanton, of Chicago, and William McClutchem, of Clay county, Mo., who should proceed with all possible haste to Fort Sacramento, owned by Capt. Sutter, procure supplies, and return as soon as possible. They accordingly started on their errand, and although having a thousand miles to go, they calculated that they would return in a short time."

Stanton actually did get back across the Sierra with supplies, meeting the company on the Truckee about October 19. This effort at succor cost him and the two Indians Sutter sent with him their lives, for all three subsequently died in the snow. McCutchen, too ill to return with Stanton, joined with Reed in the urgent relief expeditions organized later in the winter.

[42] Thornton's version of the journey around the shoulder of Pilot Peak, on across the Toano Range by Silver Zone Pass, and down to the water at the Johnson Ranch is quoted in the note above. It was at this campsite, it will be remembered, that the Bidwell-Bartleson party abandoned their wagons in 1841, the "Chiles Cache" of the Jefferson map. Although Reed's diary is silent on the point, Thornton declares (p. 107) that "Here the most of the little property which Mr. Reed still had, was buried, or *cached*, together with that of others. . . . Mr. Eddy, proposed putting his team to Mr. Reed's wagon, and letting Mr. Pike have his wagon, so that the three families could be taken on. This was done. They remained in camp during the day of the 18th to complete these arrangements, and to recruit their exhausted cattle."

[43] Bringing his diary up to date, Reed began to write the events of Sunday, the 13th, under date of Saturday, the 12th, then realized his mistake and corrected the date, leaving the 12th without an entry. Thornton's account, as quoted in note 42, makes it evident that after reaching the springs on the Johnson Ranch just before dawn on the 12th, the company spent that day recuperating from the last of the "dry drives" on the Hastings Cutoff.

[44] The day's journey was south to Flowery Lake. The route from here on to the Humboldt, as indeed from the time the Donner party reached the south shore of Great Salt Lake, is that described in the notes to Lienhard's journal. It will be seen that the speculation, e.g., by George R. Stewart in *Ordeal by Hunger*, as to whether the Donners shortened the Hastings route in eastern Nevada is now disproved. The error has arisen from Thornton's account, which is defective for this part of the journey. See note 47.

THE JOURNAL OF JAMES FRAZIER REED 231

with anger and mad[e] this d[a]y to the Two mound Springs 14 [this figure written over an apparent 13][45]

Tus 15 left the 2 mound Sp[r]ings and Crossed the mountain as usual and Camped in the West Side of a Vally and made this day about 14[46]

Wed 16 left Camp Early this morig   Crossed flat mount[ai]n or Hills and encamped on the east sid[e] of a Rug[g]ed Mountain [Ruby Mountains]   plenty of grass & water   18[47]   here Geo Donner lost little gray & his Cream Col. Mare Margrat—[48]

Th 17 made this day South in the Mineral Vally about 16[49]

---

[45] In view of Reed's remark about the temper of the women, Edwin Bryant's account on August 7 of a serious altercation between two members of his own party at precisely the same place is a curious coincidence. The day's journey was across the Pequop Mountains via Jasper Pass to Mound Springs.

[46] During the day the party climbed over the northern extension of Spruce Mountain for a night encampment at Warm Spring in Clover Valley.

[47] Thornton somehow dropped from his narrative the events of September 13–15, improving his chronology at the expense of his geography, but his account (p. 108) of this day's travel from the Warm Spring over into Ruby Valley is in full accord with that of the diary:

> Early on the morning of Sept. 19th, the emigrants broke up their encampment, and passing over a low range of mountains, came down into the head of a most beautiful and fertile valley. They gave to it the name of the valley of the Fifty Springs, the name being suggested by that number being here found. They encamped by one of them, situated in the centre of a cone about ten feet high. The water rose to the top, but did not flow over. Many of the springs were hot, some warm, and many cool, and slightly acid. They saw hundreds of Indians, who were friendly, and seemed never before to have seen a white man. Here were great numbers of antelopes and Rocky Mountain sheep, which they had no difficulty in killing. This valley is destitute of timber, and is about fifteen miles wide.

The encampment on the night of September 16, if Reed's estimate of mileage be accepted, was probably on or near Thompson Creek, some 10 miles north of the old Ruby Valley post office. (In 1994, the Ruby Valley community post office is located some 25 miles north of the old "Rock House" post office.)

[48] Presumably they were stolen by the Indians. The immigrants of 1846, in contrast to those of 1850, were not bothered much by the Indians while on the Hastings Cutoff, although Bryant on August 8, just as he reached the Humboldt Valley, recorded an attempt to steal his mules.

[49] Reed's name for Ruby Valley is not readily explainable, unless suggested by the mineral water in many of the hot springs. During the mid-1850s the Mormons gave the valley its present name after finding some garnets, but this does not explain "Mineral Valley." The day's journey brought them to a point perhaps 4 miles south of the old Ruby Valley post office.

Thornton's parallel account (p. 108) for this and the following two days'

Frid 18 this day lay in Camp

Sat 19 this day mad[e] in Mineral Vally 16 and encamped at a large Spring breaking out of from the and part of large Rock Stream la[r]ge enough to turn one pr [pair] Stone   passed in the evening about 10 Spring Branches Springs Rising about 300 Yds above where we Crossed[50]

Son 20 this day made 10 up the Mineral Vally   passed last evening and this day 42 Beautiful Springs of fresh water[51]

384 Miles from Bridger

Mon 21 Made 4 miles in Mineral Vally due South   turned to the west 4 miles through a flat in the mountain [Hastings or Overland Pass] thence W N W 7 miles in another vally [Huntington Valley] and encamped on a smal[l] but handsome littl[e] Branch or Creek [Huntington Creek] making in all 15 miles[52]

Tues 22 Made this day nearly due North in Sinking Creek Val[le]y about ten miles owing to water   10[53]

---

travel (he takes no account of the day spent resting, and thus brings his chronology yet closer to actuality) reads: "Early on the morning of the 20th, they continued their journey, and traveling about fifteen miles down the valley in a southerly direction, encamped at night near good grass and water. They proceeded down this valley three days, making about fifty miles of travel. The valley, however, still continued to extend south, beyond the reach of their vision, and presenting the same general appearance."

[50] For an account of Cave Creek see the WPA Writers' Project's *Nevada: A Guide to the Silver State* (Portland, 1940), 163. It is curious that Jefferson and Reed, traveling in 1846, noted the existence of Cave Spring, while no mention of it is made in any of the journals of 1850. This spring, the night encampment, is located 19 1/2 miles south of the old Ruby Valley post office and lies at the base of 11,000-ft. Pearl Peak.

[51] This last camp in Ruby Valley was probably in the vicinity of the Davis Ranch. See the *Jiggs* quadrangle.

[52] Compare the Jefferson map and the *Jiggs* quadrangle. Reed's encampment of September 21 was probably identical with Jefferson's of September 2, on Huntington Creek some 9 miles south of the Sadler Ranch. Thornton's contribution (p. 109) this day is: "On the morning of September 23d, they left the valley of the Fifty Springs, and crossing over a low range of mountains, came into a valley of great beauty and fertility. Crossing this valley, which was here seven miles wide and finding water, they again encamped. In all these valleys there are no springs on their eastern sides. The water being uniformly found breaking out at the foot of the mountains, upon the western side."

[53] Reed does not say whether he crossed to the west bank of Huntington Creek or, like Jefferson when faced with the same choice, remained on the east bank for some miles. The name he applies to Huntington Creek commemorates its tendency to flow underground; from a point about a mile south of the Sadler

Wed 23 Made this day owing to water about Twelve 12 miles Still in Sinking Creek Valley—[54]

Thrs 24 this day North west we mad[e] down Sinking Creek valley about 16 [this figure written over an apparent 17] and encamped at the foot of a Red earth hill   good grass and water   wood plenty in the vallies Such as sage greace wood & cedar [?] 16—[55]

Frid 25 September This day we made about Sixteen miles 16 for six miles a very rough Cannon a perfect Snake trail   encamped in the Cannon about 2 miles from its mout[h][56]

Sat 26 this day made 2 miles in the Cannon and traveleed to the Junction of Marys River   in all about 8[57]

Ranch, over a stretch of almost 15 miles, Huntington Creek flows beneath the surface more often than not. Reed's night encampment was probably made where the stream first disappears. Thornton remarks (p. 109): "They had been traveling in a southerly direction for many days, but on the morning of the 24th, they commenced traveling due north. This they continued to do three days, following the tracks of the wagons in advance. They then turned a little west of north, and traveled two days, so that in nine days' travel they made but thirty miles westward."

[54] The night encampment was perhaps 6 miles south of the confluence of Huntington and Smith creeks, about 3 miles southwest of Jiggs.

[55] This night the company camped in the vicinity of the confluence of Smith Creek and the South Fork of the Humboldt. Thornton's version (p. 109) runs: "On the night of the 28th, they encamped at the head of a cañon leading into the valley of Mary's or Ogden's river. Here they saw large bodies of Indians in a state of perfect nudity. They hovered around in the vicinity, but did not come into camp."

[56] Of this encampment in South Fork Canyon Thornton writes (p. 109): "On the morning of the 29th, they entered the cañon, and traveling about eight miles, found, at 11 o'clock, P.M., a place sufficiently large to admit of an encampment out of the water."

[57] Thus the Donner party came back into the established California Trail at present Moleen, Nevada. As Thornton writes (p. 109), "On the 20th [sic] they pursued their way down the cañon, and after traveling eight miles, came out into the valley of Mary's river, at night, and encamped on the bank of the stream, having struck the road leading from Fort Hall. Here some Indians came into camp and informed them by signs, that they were yet distant about two hundred miles from the sinks of that river."

At the time of leaving Fort Bridger, the Donners were 5 days behind Lienhard, whose little group otherwise was the last to take the Hastings Cutoff. On arriving at the Weber River, they were only 4 days behind. But by the time they reached the springs at present Grantsville, they were 15 days in the rear. They had picked up a day when they set out into the Salt Desert, but so devastating was the crossing of the desert that on leaving Pilot Peak the Donners had fallen a full 18 days behind. They had made up only one day of that arrears when they

Marys River

Sond 27 Came through a Short Cannon and encamped above the first Creek (after the Cannon) on Marys River   6[58]

Mond 28 this day after leaving Camp about 4 miles   J F Reed found Hot Springs   one as hot as boiling water   left the River Crossed over the Mounta[in] to the west Side of a Can[n]. and encamp in Vally   12[59]

---

reached the Humboldt, from which point their weakened cattle fell ever farther behind. Lienhard crossed the culminating ridge of the Sierra on October 4, Jefferson 3 days later. The Donner party reached Donner Lake, just under the divide, on October 31. That was, for nearly half of them, the difference between life and death.

Stories that have become current in the literature of the Donner party declare that when they came back into the regular trail, they found notices posted at the junction by friends from whom they had parted at Fort Bridger, advising that they had passed on weeks before. It is possible that such notices were posted somewhere along the trail, but hardly at the point where the Hastings Cutoff came into it, for the place of junction was not known until the Harlan-Young wagons emerged there. Until that moment, passersby would have assumed that the intersection was higher up on the Humboldt, where Clyman and Hastings had diverged from the Fort Hall road in May.

Properly speaking, our concern with the Donner party ends here, with their arrival in the Humboldt Valley. There are only seven more entries in the diary, however, and in the interests of laying to rest the folklore which has attached to Gravelly Ford, this annotation is carried on to the end of the diary.

[58] After making their way through Moleen Canyon, shown on the Jefferson map as "Wall Defile," the company encamped for the night apparently on Susie Creek, that being the first stream below the canyon. However, as Jefferson shows only one stream here, "Robin Creek," and as Maggie Creek enters the Humboldt only a mile below, there is a bare possibility that Reed had reference to the latter. Thornton's version of the day's travel (p. 110) is: "On the morning of October 1st, they resumed their journey, and traveled along the usual route down Ogden's river and encamped that evening at some hot springs, at the foot of a high range of hills."

To follow the progress of the Donners down the Humboldt Valley see the maps and text of the U. S. Geological Survey's Bulletin 612, *Guidebook of the Western United States, Part B. The Overland Route* (Washington, 1915), 163–178.

[59] The road here left the river, Palisade Canyon being impassable for any but railroad builders, and like I-80 today, climbed the hills to the north. Note that the diary slightly corrects Thornton, as quoted in note 58, concerning the hot springs and the relation of the camp to them. The night encampment was at present Emigrant Springs, which Jefferson did not neglect to note on his map. Thornton's account (p. 110) combines the events of this day and the next:

On the morning of the 2d, they commenced passing over these hills. About 11 o'clock, an Indian, who spoke a little English, came to them, to whom they gave the name of Thursday, on account of their

Tus 29 This day 11 o.clock left Camp and went about 8 mil[e]s to the river a gain   2 graves   had 2 oxen taken by 2 Indians that Cam[e] with us all day[60]

Wed 30 left Camp about 10 o clock and made this day 12 miles down the River[61]

Thurs Oct 1 left Camp and made 15 miles down the River   encamped on a Rich bottom   this night Mr Graves, lost a fine mare by the Indians[62]

---

believing that to be the day; although at the time, they were inclined to believe that they had lost one day in their calculation of time [!]. About 4 o'clock, P.M., another came to them, who also spoke a little English. . . . They traveled all that day, and at dark encamped at a spring about half way down the side of the mountain. A fire broke out in the grass, soon after the camp fires had been kindled, which would have consumed three of the wagons, but for the assistance of these two Indians. The Indians were fed, and after the evening meal they lay down by one of the fires, but rose in the night, stealing a fine shirt and a yoke of oxen from Mr. Graves.

[60] By this day's travel the company returned to the Humboldt at Gravelly Ford, near present Beowawe. For years oral and printed folklore has made Gravelly Ford the scene of the tragic encounter between James Frazier Reed and John Snyder, and "the Donner graves" (in the plural) have been pointed out here to visitors. Even before the Reed diary appeared, however, George R. Stewart had correctly concluded on the basis of the available evidence that the tragedy occurred farther along the trail. Since there is no reason to doubt the date assigned to that sad event (October 5), and since that date fits perfectly into the pattern of the diary, we can hope that the Gravelly Ford story will now cease to trouble the history of the Donner party.

Reed's detail concerning the loss of the oxen to the Indians, while it slightly corrects Thornton's account quoted in note 59, serves to emphasize how remarkably Thornton managed to reconstruct the movements of the Donner party in the absence of a diary.

[61] This night's encampment was evidently on the Humboldt 8 or 9 miles east of Argenta Station on the Southern Pacific Railroad. The events of the day disappear from Thornton's narrative. The several days thus dropped have gradually adjusted his chronology so that it will coincide with that of the diary for the critical date, October 5.

[62] The day's travel brought Reed out from between Shoshone Mesa and Shoshone Range into the wide plain through which the Humboldt meanders below Argenta. His encampment this night was probably about equidistant from present Battle Mountain and Argenta; and the Jefferson map would indicate that it was on the north bank of the river, near the crossing of a hairpin bend in the Humboldt. Thornton says only (pp. 110–111), "On the evening of October 5th [*sic*], the emigrants again encamped on Ogden's river, after a hard and exhausting drive. During the night the Indians stole a horse from Mr. Graves."

With respect to his father's losses, W. C. Graves writes in the *Russian River*

Fridy [Oct. 2] Still down the River   made to day 12 miles[63]
Sat 3 left Camp early   made this day 10 miles[64]
Son 4 Still—[65]

[Here the diary closes. In the end pages are some calculations, appended to this chapter, evidently based on the mileages in the diary.]

EPILOGUE

Virginia E. B. Reed to her cousin Mary Gillespie
Napa Valley, California, May 16, 1847.

. . . . o my Dear Cousin you dont [k]now what trubel is yet   a many a time we had on the last thing a cooking and did not [k]now wher the next would come from but there was awl wais some way provided   there was 15 in the cabon we was in and half of us had to lay a bed all the time   thare was 10 starved to death while we ware there   we was hadley abel to walk   we lived on litle cash a week and after Mr Breen would cook his meat and boil the bones   Two or three times we would take the bones and boil them 3 or 4 days at a

---

Flag, April 26, 1877: ". . . we had no more trouble till we got to Gravelly Ford, on the Humboldt, where the Indians stole two of father's oxen and in two days after they stole a horse. . . ." This is in exact accord with the diary.

[63] For this and the remaining entries in the diary, compare the *Sonoma Range* quadrangle. Reed evidently encamped this night about midway between Stonehouse and Battle Mountain, but on the north bank of the Humboldt.

[64] The last complete entry in the diary brings Reed to a point on the south bank of the Humboldt very near present Stonehouse.

[65] That Reed was interrupted in the middle of this entry and never completed it, is one of the fascinating features of the diary. It seems likely that on October 4 the detachment of the company with which Reed was traveling moved down the river from 10 to 15 miles to encamp for the night in the vicinity of Redhouse. Next day, while engaged in the toilsome traverse of Emigrant Pass between the Osgood Mountains and the Sonoma range—Jefferson's "Pauta Pass"—Reed fell into the altercation with the Graves' hired man, John Snyder, which ended with Snyder's death and Reed's expulsion from the company. Unable to protect his family by staying with them, Reed went on ahead to seek from Sutter provisions and fresh livestock to bring them through. His diary stayed behind with his family, no one having the heart to carry it on in his absence, and when the snows closed the passes of the Sierra before he could return, it remained in the camp at Donner Lake—brought in at last with his children, in one of the major relief efforts Reed engineered. After a hundred years, the diary has come forth to add its contribution to the Donner story.

time   Mama went down to the other cabin and got half a hide   carried it in snow up to her wast   it snowed and would cover the cabin all over so we could not get out for 2 or 3 days at a time   we would have to cut pieces of the loges in sied to make fire with. I coud hardly eat the hides   Pa stated out to us with provisions on the first of November and Came into the Great California Mountain, about 80 miles and in one of the Severest Storms Known for Years past, A raining in the Valley and a Hurrican of snow in the mountains   it Came so deep that the horses & mules Swamped So they could not go on any more   he cash his provision and went back on the other side of the bay to get a compana of men and the San Wakien got so hye he could not crose   well thay Made up a Compana at Suters Fort and sent out   we had not ate any thing for 3 days & we had onely a half a hide and we was out on top of the cabin and we seen the party a coming

O my Dear Cousin you dont [k]now how glad i was, we run and met them   one of them we knew   we had traveled with them on the road   thay staid thare 3 days to recruet a little so we could go   thare was 20 started all of us started and went a piece and [8-year-old] Martha and [3-year-old] Thomas giv out and the men had to take them back   one of the party [Aquilla Glover] said he was a Mason and pledged his faith that if we did not meet pa in time he would come and save his children ma and Eliza James & I come on and o Mary that was the hades thing yet to come on and leiv them thar . . . did not now but what thay would starve to Death   Martha said well ma if you never see me a gain do the best you can   the men said thay could hadly stand it   it maid them all cry but they said it was better for all of us to go on for if we was to go back we would eat that much more from them   thay gave them a littel meat and flore and took them back and we come on   we went over great hye mountain as steap as stair steps in snow up to our knees   litle James walk the [w]hole way over all the mountain in snow up to his waist. . . . when we had traveld 5 days travel we met Pa with 13 men going to the cabins   o Mary you do not nou how glad we was to see him   we had not seen him for 5 months   we thought we woul never see him again he heard we was coming and he made some seet cakes the night before at his Camp to give us and the other Children withe us   he said he would see Martha and Thomas the next day   he went in tow day what took us 5 days   when pa went to the Cabins some of the compana was eating those that Died but Thomas & Martha had not ate any   Pa and the men started with 12 people   Hiram O Miller Car-

ried Thomas and Pa caried Martha and thay were caught in a Snow
Storm which lasted two days & nights and they had to stop   Two
days it stormd so thay could not go and the Fishers took their
provision and thay weer 4 days without any thing   Pa and Hiram and
and all the men started [with] one of Donner boys Pa a carring
Martha Hiram caring Thomas and the snow was up to thare wast and
it a snowing so thay could hadly see the way   thay [w]raped the
children up and never took them out for 4 days & thay had nothing to
eat in all that time   Thomas asked for somthing to eat once   Those
that thay brought from the cabins some of them was not able to come
from the Starved Camp as it is called, and som would not come
Thare was 3 died and the rest eat them   thay was 10 days without
any thing to eat but the Dead   Pa braught Thom and paty on to
where we was   none of the men Pa had with him ware able to go
back for Some people Still at the Cabins, there feet was froze very
bad so thare was a nother Compana went and braught them all in
thay are all in from the Mountains now. . . . O Mary I have not wrote
you half of the truble we have had but I hav Wrote you anuf to let
you [k]now what truble is but thank god and [we were] the onely
family that did not eat human flesh   we have left every thing but i
dont cair for that we have got through with our lives but Dont let this
letter dishaten anybody   never take no cutofs and hury along as fast
as you can

Mileage figures appended to James Frazier Reed's journal.

5		12	43	480
6		15		By 80
5		16		Upset [?]80
11		16		1 BB1 [?] 80
12		8		
20		15		
2		10—		
16	Brack water	5		
12	to fresh spr	2		
12	to Sulphur do	2		
60	Salt plain	2		
30	Desert drive	5		
———		4		
191		2		
		5		
27		———		
120		119==		
———		12	1 encampm [?]	
147		20	lower wells	
550		2	upper wells	
———		16	on south of Lake	
400		12	to South end Lake	
		18	to long Drive	
		40	long Drive	
		———		
		239		
		550		
		191		
		———		
		359		

— *Sutter's Fort Historical Museum*

TWO PAGES FROM THE REED DIARY

Showing entries for August 17–23, 1846, covering the route of the Donner party from Little Emigration Canyon to the Jordan River.

THE HASTINGS MAP AND WAYBILLS

BEFORE THE MORMON pioneers of 1847 left Fort Bridger, the Saints had the benefit of Lansford W. Hastings' own directions— given by him to Samuel Brannan and Charles C. Smith in California early in 1847, before Brannan and Smith set out overland to find the Mormon Pioneer company. Brannan met his brethren at Green River on June 30, but it was not until July 8, at Fort Bridger, that Thomas Bullock, "Clerk of the Camp of Israel," wrote in the official journal, "made a copy of Hastings directions from Bridgers Fort to the Settlements in California also a map of the route—returning the originals to brother Brannan." Bullock's remark prompted Dale L. Morgan and J. Roderic Korns to look for the Hastings material, and they noted in *West from Fort Bridger,* "This waybill and map have been searched for in the archives of the (LDS) Historian's Office without success."

By 1976, the archives had catalogued Hastings' instructions, and in July, 1991, LDS archivist Michael N. Landon brought the waybill and map to the attention of researchers. The file contains a single sheet of instructions in Hastings' handwriting measuring 31.5 by 21 cm., and Bullock's copy of the map, labeled "Hastings Map," which shares the page with "Miles Goodier's Map," dated July 12, 1847. The text of the Brannan waybill described how to cross the Ruby Mountains and the road from the Great Salt Lake to Fort Bridger thusly:

> The road via the Salt Lake intersects the old road, on Mary's River about 230 M. above the sink. Leaving the old road at this point you continue up the South fork of Mary's river about 20 M. to a point where the road bears almost directly south. At this point or near this, you will observe an opening, or gaps in the mountain at the east, through which you will pass instead of continuing around the point of the mountain at the south. By this course you will save fifty or sixty-M.
>
> When you pass the south [end] of the Salt Lake, you will take the right hand road leading directly east, over the mountain instead of bearing to the North up Weber's River.
>
> After crossing Weber's River (the 1st river of any importance after passing the Salt Lake) you will continue up a

small fork of that River coming in from the East. When you leave this fork be sure to take the left hand road, as it is much the nearest and best.

Be sure to Examine the mountain laying at the north, about midway of the "long drive."

/s/ L. W. Hastings[1]

The instructions provide several insights into Hastings' knowledge of the trail. They clearly describe how to find "an opening, or gaps in the mountain at the east" to cross the Ruby Mountains through present Harrison Pass, thus avoiding some 60 miles of the wagon road Hastings used in 1846. The waybill, however, supplied no information about the difficult country of eastern Nevada and did not even mention the Salt Desert.

From the Great Salt Lake, the waybill told how to locate the "right hand road leading directly east," the trail the Donner-Reed party used to cross the Wasatch. Once in the mountains, Hastings recommended following Echo Canyon, "the nearest and best" route to the high plains of present Wyoming. One of the mysteries of the waybill is its reference to "the mountain laying at the north" in the last paragraph.

Brannan did not take Hastings Cutoff, and a letter written at Fort Hall on June 18, 1847, provides a possible explanation. Brannan wrote that he and his three companions were not "able to travel the regular route due to the high waters."[2] If Brannan assumed the Hastings Cutoff was now the "regular route," the floodwaters of May on the South Fork of the Humboldt spared Brannan a dangerous—and possibly fatal—crossing of the Hastings Cutoff.

Although Brannan failed to follow Hastings instructions, Captain James Brown's party of Mormon Battalion veterans returning from California in the fall of 1847 followed Hastings' directions precisely.

In July, 1993, researcher Robert K. Hoshide located a *second* Hastings waybill in the Thomas Bullock papers at the LDS Archives. Bullock described this as a "copy of the Route, as made out by Mr. Hastings, and given to Mr Smith"—a reference to Brannan's companion, Charles C. Smith, an 1845 Oregon emigrant and distant relative of Joseph Smith. The Hastings-Smith waybill provides a possible explanation for the lack of detail in the Brannan waybill: the Smith

---

[1] Lansford Warren Hastings, "Instructions, 1847," LDS Archives.
[2] *L. D. S. Millennial Star*, IX (October 15, 1847).

waybill gives point-to-point instructions, suggesting the two documents were meant to supplement each other.

ROUTE FROM MR. JOHNSON'S SETTLEMENT—CALIFORNIA TO BRIDGER'S FORT, AS PER MR. HASTINGS ACCOUNT

From Johnson's to Bear River Valley, 60 miles—thence to Trucker's Lake, on the other side of the mountains 40—thence down Trucky River 60—thence to the sink of Mary's River 40—thence up and along Mary's River, 250—to the forks of the Road—thence taking the right hand road, up the South Fork of Mary's River 15—Thence up a branch of the South Fork 8—thence to a sink of a small creek 7—thence up the said creek to the point where the road leaves it 5 miles—thence through a pass in the mountain 12—thence along the foot of the mountain passing numerous springs 30, to a point where the road leaves the foot of the mountain—thence 20 miles over the plain and hills to a Spring—thence 10 miles to a Spring—thence 9 miles to a Spring—thence 12 miles to a Spring—thence 25 miles to a Spring—thence 4 or 5 miles along the foot of the mountain, passing several Springs to a Spring, and a large encampment, at the west side of a Salt Plain—thence over the Salt Plain 55 miles to a Spring—thence 6 miles to a Spring—thence along and around the foot of the mountain passing numerous Springs on the West side 20 miles to a Spring on the East side—Thence keeping [to] the right hand road, along the foot of the mountain passing several Springs. Then bearing to the left, across the plain 20 miles, to the point of the mountain at the Salt Lake. Thence passing several Springs, and keeping [to] the right hand road, 12 miles to the Eutaw Outlet—Thence over the mountains 12 miles. Thence down a small Creek, and bearing to the right over the hills 15 miles to Weber's River—Thence up Weber River 7 miles—Thence up the Red Fork 40 miles—Thence keeping to the left hand road 25 miles to Bear River—Thence 25 miles to Bridger's Fort, on Black's Fork of Green River.[3]
//exd.//

---

[3] Thomas Bullock Journal Sketches, LDS Archives. For a copy of Bullock's holographic transcription and a line-by-line analysis by a leading expert on the Hastings Cutoff, see Roy D. Tea, "The Hastings-Smith Waybill," *Crossroads*, V (Winter, 1994).

The above is a copy of the Route, as made out by Mr. Hastings, and given to Mr Smith—from Johnson's Settlement, Upper California to Bridger's Fort—obtained by me, from Mr. Smith, this 8 July 1847

Thomas Bullock.
Clerk of the Pioneer C⁰. of L. D. Saints

From "the Forks of the road" west of present Elko, Nevada, the Smith waybill describes ascending the South Fork of the Humboldt to Huntington and Smith creeks. At the west entrance of the "pass in the mountain," modern Harrison Pass, the waybill parted with Hastings' wagon road, which continued south to Hastings Pass. The trail followed the eastern side of the Ruby Mountains north for 22 miles and then passed, in succession, Sulphur Springs, Warm Spring, Mound Springs, and Flowery Lake Springs. Hastings provided no directions in his waybill, but here the trail turned abruptly north, to reach Big Springs at Johnson Ranch, where the Bidwell-Bartleson company abandoned its wagons in 1841. After a "long drive" of "25 (actually, 28) miles to a Spring," the road reached Halls Spring at the foot of Pilot Peak, and then proceeded "4 or 5 miles along the foot of the mountain" to the encampment at Pilot or Donner Spring on the TL Bar Ranch, now restored and marked by the efforts of the Utah Crossroads chapter of the Oregon-California Trails Association.

One of the most significant pieces of information the waybill provides is Hastings' estimate that it was "over the Salt Plain 55 miles to a Spring." Hastings consistently misrepresented the distance of the waterless crossing to the emigrants of 1846—as Virginia Reed commented, "Haistings said it was 40 but i think it was 80 miles." Roy D. Tea's detailed measurement of distances using U.S.G.S. quadrangles shows Hastings' estimates are erratic, but they are closer to the mark than previously supposed. The waybill's estimate of 55 miles to cross the Salt Desert compares with a map-measured reading of 67 miles between Donner and Redlum springs.

The waybill proceeds 12 miles across Skull Valley to "Hope Wells" at Iosepa, rounding the Stansbury Mountains at Timpie Point to reach a spring located near the modern lime plant in Tooele Valley. The "several Springs" were in and near the present town of Grantsville, site of Jefferson's "Hastings Wells" and known to other emigrants as Twenty Wells. (These were also James Reed's Upper and Lower Wells).

From "the point of the mountain at the Salt Lake," Hastings directed Brannan and Smith to keep to "the right hand road," apparently "Reeds Road"—the Donner Trail—across the "Eutaw Outlet" (the Jordan River) to Emigration Canyon; the "left-hand road" would be the route the 1846 wagon companies followed from Weber Canyon.

To cross "over the mountains," the Smith waybill describes either the trail up Emigration Canyon and over Little Mountain— "Reeds Road"—or the pack trail up Parley's Canyon to Mountain Dell Hastings had followed in the spring of 1846. Both routes converged before crossing Big Mountain to East Canyon. Hastings' directions then follow the "small Creek" of East Canyon to the present reservoir and over Hogsback Ridge to the Weber River and the site of the town of Henefer.

At 40 miles, Hastings dramatically overestimated the approximate distance of 24 miles required to traverse Echo Canyon, which Orson Pratt also called "Red Fork" in 1847. The "left hand road" to Bear River is probably the Lienhard-Mormon cutoff to Coyote Creek, while the right-hand road would be the trail south up Yellow Creek that Hastings, the Harlan-Young company, and the Donner-Reed party followed over to Bear River and down to Sulphur Creek in 1846. Hastings' final directions underestimate the distance to Bridger's Fort.

Hastings' map—or, more precisely, Bullock's copy of Hastings' map—shows the country between the Great Salt Lake and Green River, including the Snake River and "Eutaw" Lake. Assuming this copy accurately represents the original, the map reveals deficiencies in Hastings' geographical knowledge. For example, it shows Bear River heading directly for the Great Salt Lake after parting with the emigrant road to the Snake River; since Hastings had seen the Bear at Soda Springs in 1842 and 1845, this seems a curious mistake and may be Bullock's error. The map gives a good account of the main rivers of the area, listing, east to west, the Sandy (noted twice, presumably to account for the Little and Big Sandy) flowing into Green River; a generally accurate representation of "Black's Fork," showing "Ham's Fork" and "Muddy River" as its tributaries; the abbreviated Bear River; "Weber's River," with a much elongated main branch and a short fork showing Echo Creek that may be labeled "Red Fork"; and finally, the Jordan River, shown as the "E. Outlet" of "Eutaw Lake." To the north, a dotted line depicting the emigrant road to Fort Hall runs to the Snake River. To the south, looped lines

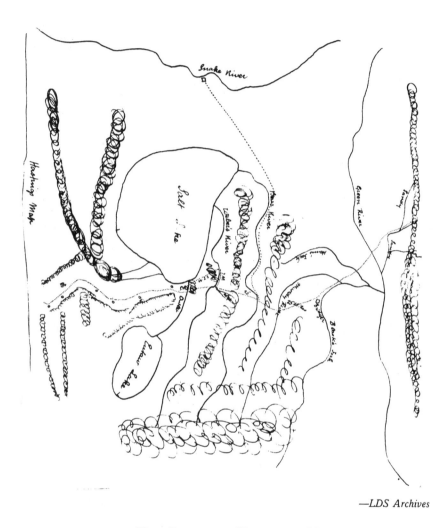

THE BULLOCK-HASTINGS MAP

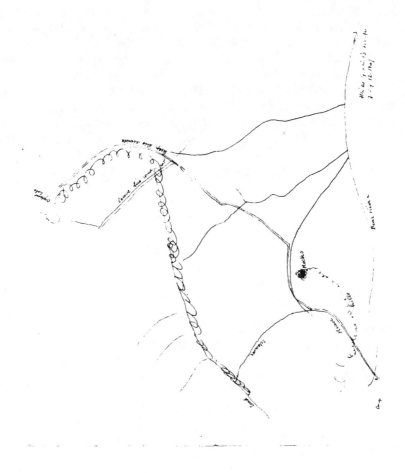

THE BULLOCK-GOODYEAR MAP

portray a mountain range running east-west, a fair if slightly mis-
placed representation of the Uintas. Hastings Cutoff is shown as a
dotted line; on the line approaching the Salt Lake from the west, the
map shows springs or campsites as circles in Skull and Tooele valleys
and depicts both the Hastings road to Weber Canyon and the Donner-Reed trail to Emigration Canyon.

On Saturday evening, July 10, 1847, Miles Goodyear rode into
the Mormon camp two miles east of Bear River. A veteran mountaineer, Goodyear was at Sutter's Fort on May 22, 1847 when the *New
Helvetia Diary* noted "Myers" was "going with a band of horses to the
big salt lake, his new established trading post." Goodyear and seven
companions "Started for home" on June 2, driving the horses over
the Sierra, up the Humboldt, and across the Salt Desert to Fort
Buenaventura, the trading post he had established in 1846 at the site
of Ogden. Thomas Bullock reported Goodyear "has made a map of
the route & gave it to the brethren—" As already noted, the Mormons
concluded Weber Canyon was too difficult for wagons. William
Clayton revealed their suspicions of Goodyear's information when he
noted in his journal, "we have an idea he is anxious to have us make
a road to his place through selfish motives."

The Goodyear-Bullock map is even more primitive and symbolic
than the Hastings map. It is a very simple sketch of the country between Bear River and "Ogdens Hole," and its single purpose was to
direct the Mormons to the Weber Canyon trail from their camp near
Bear River. It shows a double line marked "Road" running through
and past a looped line labeled "hills" and "Rocks." A line breaks off
the road to become the "Weaver"—the Weber River—which curves
into a second looped line. The latter would seem to represent a ridge
of mountains, but it is labeled "load," presumably to be read as
"road." Neither line makes much sense in terms of the area's actual
topography. The original double-line of the "Road" continues from
the "Weaver" to a parting of the ways, presumably at the site of
Henefer. The road going to the left is labeled "leave this road" and
may be the Donner-Reed trail over Big Mountain, while a second
line—"keep this divide"—runs to "Ogdens hole." This is not the site
in Ogden Valley that now bears the name, but is probably the location near present Mountain Green in Morgan Valley where American trappers confronted a Hudson's Bay Company party under Peter
Skene Ogden in May 1825. The line on Goodyear's map likely represents the road down Weber Canyon to Goodyear's fort.

The directions Lansford W. Hastings gave to Brannan and Smith show the young promoter continued to believe in and tout his cutoff after 1846. In Hastings' opinion, "the cause of this loss of life and property, and of this intense suffering among the emigrants, ought to be immediately removed." The cause was the unimproved trail, and "to make the route intirely [sic] direct from the South Pass to the California mountains, it is only necessary to make some slight improvements upon it, via the south side of the Salt Lake. This route when thus improved, and when water is found upon what is called the 'long drive,' is far preferable to any with which I am acquainted."[4]

To this day, no one has found a reliable water supply of any kind on the Salt Desert crossing.

Although it saw some use in the Gold Rush, Hastings' Road fell quickly into disrepute: Brigham Young warned Mormon Battalion veterans, "Some few have passed by a new route to California called the Hastings cut-off by the south border of the Salt Lake, but it is not a safe route on account of the long drive without water, and it is not wisdom for you to come that way."[5] On April 1, 1848, the *California Star* carried this warning to emigrants:

> THE OLD ROAD—We cannot too strongly urge upon Emigrants the importance of keeping the well defined *"old road"* to California. Their safety, and that of their property, depends upon this. Parties that have followed this road have reached this country without difficulty. Last season, all succeeded in bringing their wagons in. The last companies arrived at the first settlements before the middle of October. It is not deemed safe to be on the mountains later than the last of that month.
>
> The fate of those who deviated from the old road to try *"short cuts,"* so alluring to way-worn travellers, is a sufficient warning. The horrible sufferings of those who were overtaken by the winter snows on the California mountains in 1846, are enough to appal the stoutest heart.

---

[4] The *California Star*, February 27, 1847, attributes this article to "Paisano," but historians since Josiah Royce have identified Hastings as the author. Paisano commented, "persons who cross the mountains for the purpose of guiding the emigrants merely for the very trifling salaries . . . have not time, while acting as guides, to examine the extensive country through which they pass."

[5] Journal History of the Church, LDS Archives, August 7, 1847, hereafter cited as Journal History. Young probably received this information from Miles Goodyear.

In taking leave of the companies that followed Lansford Hastings across his problematic cutoff in 1846, we should note his later career. Having arrived in California four months after its conquest by the American Navy and John C. Frémont, Hastings saw his opulent dreams of an independent republic collapse in the face of events driven by the American declaration of war against Mexico in May, 1846. Hastings served as a captain in Frémont's California Battalion, elected, as Heinrich Lienhard noted, by many of the same emigrants he had led to California. He played no role in the rescue of the Donner party and left no account of his feelings concerning their fate, though when the young George Donner arrived in San Francisco next spring, Hastings bought clothes for the orphan.

Hastings dreamed of empire to his last days, but failure dogged him. He founded the town of Montezuma on Suisun Bay, which failed to thrive despite the gold rush. Settling in Sacramento, Hastings served as a judge and was elected a delegate to the California Constitutional Convention, where his geographical expertise helped establish the border along the crest of the Sierra. Hastings married Charlotte Toler at Sutter's Fort in 1848 and went into business at Coloma with John A. Sutter, who remembered, "The store made money, but I lost. Hastings was a bad man." Hastings' subsequent career in Sacramento was lackluster, and in 1857 he secured the position of postmaster of Arizona City in New Mexico Territory for his work in James Buchanan's presidential campaign.

Hastings' life disintegrated into comic opera. In 1861, he wrote to Brigham Young proposing to supply the Mormon settlements via the Colorado River. During the Civil War, he was commissioned a major in the Confederate Army as part of a wild scheme to conquer New Mexico Territory and southern California. With the South's defeat, Hastings tried to establish a confederate colony in Brazil, and wrote an *Emigrant's Guide to Brazil* to promote the effort. He died on board ship for Brazil between 1868 and 1870, a figure of mystery and romance to the end.

THE GOLDEN PASS ROAD

1848–1850

IN FOLLOWING THE Hastings-Donner trail west from Fort Bridger in July, 1847, the Mormon Pioneers were grateful to find a beaten track already existing across the mountains to the valley of the Great Salt Lake. Reconnaissance made it clear the Donners had found the best if not the only route for crossing the Wasatch along the general line they adopted.

Even so, the Pioneer trail was a difficult, not to say desperate, proposition. It required the crossing of two steep and dangerous heights, and travel in the narrow, crooked canyon bottoms was almost as hard on wagons and animals as the ascent and descent of the two mountains. In East Canyon the road crossed and recrossed the stream 13 times in 8 miles; after surmounting Big Mountain, it lurched back and forth across Mountain Dell Creek 12 times in the space of 5 miles, "all bad crossing places"; and after struggling over Little Mountain, it snaked across Emigration Canyon Creek 19 times in 5 miles before emerging into Salt Lake Valley.[1] He who could find a route which on the one hand would keep out of the bed of the lower Weber River—the original Hastings route—and on the other would evade the stiff grades and serpentine canyons of the Donner route would earn the thanks of the Mormon community and all the Saints yet to reach the valley.

Doubtless there was some preliminary examination of the canyons opening out upon Salt Lake Valley, if only by hunters seeking to augment the precarious food supply, that first winter after the founding of Great Salt Lake City. The first attempt at a formal reconnaissance, however, was by Parley P. Pratt in late June, 1848. Elder brother of Orson Pratt, who had led the vanguard of the Mormon Pioneers across the mountains the previous summer, Parley had reached the valley in the early fall of 1847 with the large "second company" which had followed in the path of the Pioneers. With the

---

[1] Compare Clayton's journal entries for July 19–22, 1847, and his *Latter-Day Saints' Emigrants' Guide*, 19–20. The number of crossings of Mountain Dell Creek does not appear from the Mormon journals but is mentioned by a California immigrant, Beeson Townsend, on August 7, 1849; see Dale L. Morgan, "Letters by Forty-Niners," *Western Humanities Review*, III (April 1949), 112. As late as 1860 the road up East Canyon still crossed the creek 13 times; see Richard F. Burton, *The City of the Saints* (London, 1861), 235.

PARLEY PARKER PRATT

SAMUEL J. HENSLEY

sanction of the High Council, the governing authority of the tiny
Mormon settlement, Pratt left Great Salt Lake City on a tour of exploration June 28, 1848, accompanied by a Brother Workman.[2] According to Pratt's official report made two days later, he and Workman set
out up Emigration Canyon, following the established road as far as
Mountain Dell, beyond Little Mountain.[3]

> After crossing the north fork of Canyon creek [Mountain
> Dell Creek], we took up the south fork [Parleys] of the same
> traveling nearly due east. This seemed to lead more south-
> ward and to head in very lofty mountains, densely covered
> with forests of fir trees [Lambs Canyon]. We followed up a
> small branch which came in from the east which I call mid-
> dle fork.

> The country was good for pasturage, well watered and
> consisting of hills and vallies covered with timbers. There
> was a very good passage for a wagon road, the ascent to the
> summit being very gradual.

Having reached the head of Parleys by a route which, from
Mountain Dell, is that of I-80 today, the two men descended "by a
very gradual and easy passage, among groves of fir, pine and aspen,
mixed with open country, for a mile or two, when we found ourselves
on a main branch of the Weber river, and 16 miles from the city."
They had reached upper East Canyon Creek at present Gorgoza.
Following the stream up several miles, they arrived at what has ever
since been known as Parleys Park, "a beautiful meadow, or park,
nearly circular, averaging 3 miles in length and 2 miles in width, and
comprising some three or four thousand acres of excellent land,
clothed with grass and interspersed with wild flax and strawberry
vines." Large groves of aspen stood here and there in the broad valley, and the surrounding mountains were well grown with fir and aspen. Ten lovely, clear streams combined in this park to form "the
west branch of the Weber river." Continuing their journey east, Pratt
and Workman passed over a gentle divide to another little park
through which flowed what Pratt somewhat inadequately called the
"eastern fork" of the Weber—present Silver Creek. It impressed him

---

[2] Probably Jacob Lindsay Workman, but possibly his son, Jacob R.
[3] The terrain figuring in the history of the Golden Pass Road has been
mapped by the U. S. Geological Survey; see the *Salt Lake City, Fort Douglas,*
and *Coalville* quadrangles.

that the divide between the two expanses of meadowland was simply "a few hundred yards of sage desert."

Having thus had a preliminary look at the country, Pratt turned back to Great Salt Lake City to recommend that the High Council appoint a committee of two or three persons to make a more thorough exploration. His report concluded:

> These parks are from 20 to 25 miles from our city; a good road may be made the entire distance, without any mountains or canyons to pass, except this first canyon through which [Parleys] Canyon creek enters our valley.... I would further state to your honorable body that I believe a wagon road may be made in that direction, so as to intersect the present emigrant road in the neighborhood of Bear River, and be much nearer while at the same time it avoids all the mountains and canyons....[4]

Impressed with Pratt's communication, the High Council appointed John Van Cott and Daniel Spencer to accompany him on a more extended reconnaissance. The three men left the city on July 3, 1848, and returned home three days later to report as follows:

> Great Salt Lake City, July 8, 1848.
> President Smith and the Council:
> Gentlemen: The undersigned being appointed by your honorable body as a committee to explore a new road from this place towards Ft. Bridger beg leave to submit the following report:
> Left the city on the morning of the third inst. proceeded up Canyon creek to the junctions of its two principal forks [Mountain Dell and Parleys] at the eastern foot of the first mountain [Little Mountain]. Found the Canyon extremely rugged, narrow and brushy and about 4 or 5 miles through it.[5]
> We are of the opinion that a good wagon road can be made through it at a cost of about 800 dollars and thus dis-

---

[4] Parley P. Pratt to Pres. John Smith and Council, Great Salt Lake City, June 30, 1848, original letter in the LDS Archives.

[5] Compare James Clyman's description of June 3, 1846. On this second exploration, Pratt set out up what was then called Big Kanyon, but now bears his own name. On the first reconnaissance, he had gone by way of Emigration Canyon.

pense with the mountain over which the road now runs.

Passing up a fine table land or inclined plain[6] for about two miles on the south side of the south fork of Canyon creek we crossed it and took up a trail branch eastward two or three miles more to the summit of a Divide between east and west Canyon creek, the one putting in to the Weaver river and the other into this valley.

This is an easy pass, scarcely worthy to be called a hill and is about 15 miles from town or answering to the second mountain [Big Mountain] on the road.

Thence two miles down a forest and meadow or inclined plain, interspersed with pine, fir, aspen and open ground, we came to east canyon creek. Thence up that creek three miles south east to Parley's park. Thence eastward three miles over meadow and sage plains to a small stream which we named Silver creek. Thence the new road will pass down said creek, 5 miles through a Canyon of willows and hills down two miles more through an open valley, to the Weaver river. Thence down the open valley of that river 10 miles to the junction of the Old road.

This road is thirty miles from our city to the Weaver and forty miles to the junction of the old road where it leaves Cave [Echo] canyon and comes to the Weaver. The whole forty miles is cut through a mountain or a hill that is unworthy the mention in so rough a country. It is a direct course, or nearly so and winds its way through three principal ranges of mountains, over which the old road runs. And we know it to be the only practical pass to be found for a good road from our city to the Weaver river.

It passes through some of the finest country in the world, and abounds in fine streams, beautiful grassy meadows and a full supply of timber, to accommodate emigration or settlement.

Before finding this pass we were driven south and East about 30 miles by a range of mountains [the West Hills] before we could reach the Weaver.[7] We were on the Great stream [Provo River] which puts into the Utah Lake. Passed

---

[6] See the James Frazier Reed journal, note 9.

[7] They followed the route of US 40 as far as present Hailstone and then turned up the Provo River, anticipating the route of US 189.

up its valley eastward for many miles. It is well wooded and as large as the Weaver.

The valley of this river, and that of the Weaver connect in a singular manner, forming an easy pass from the Weaver to the Utah Lake.

At the junction of these two streams or rather the junction of the valleys through which they ran, we found a beautiful park 10 miles long and 3 broad. Embracing some thousands of acres of land well watered and well supplied with timber, grass and free stone.[8]

The Weaver issues from a high range of mountains [Uinta Mountains] eastward of this park, and sweeps through it in a south western direction, lined with a majestic forest of cotton woods.

We camped on its banks after being drenched with the rain on Tuesday the 4th of July.

Wednesday the 5th. Passed up its Canyon eastward for two or three miles between rugged mountains, and then abandoned any further progress because of the thickets of willows and the steep hill sides, and returned down the Weaver.

It is about thirty miles down the stream to the old road from where it breaks from the mountains. And the whole distance is bounded on the east by a lofty range of mountains which separate the Weaver from Bear river.

If there is a pass to be found south of Cave Canyon it is the pass where the Weaver breaks from this range of mountains, for there is no other.[9] We think that a pass may be found in that direction at some future day.

We passed down the open valley of the Weaver nearly 30 miles and returning up the same some ten miles. Encamped for the night near the mouth of Silver creek which here enters the Weaver. We had seen its head branches before.

Thursday the 6th, passed up the Canyon of Silver Creek

---

[8] Kamas Prairie. In geologically recent times the Weber and Provo rivers met here and flowed as one stream down Provo Canyon; later the Weber found an independent channel by which to escape from the mountains.

[9] Curiously, Pratt and his associates were so little impressed as not even to mention Chalk Creek Canyon, the first major opening in the mountain wall south of Echo, and the only one up which a usable road to Bear River has ever been made.

and home where we arrived at sundown weary and worn, and some of us without shoes, and nearly without pantaloons. The Canyon having robbed us of these in a great measure, and of much of our flesh and skin, the first morning of our ride.

We would suggest to the Council that as many hands as possible be raised forthwith with axes, shovels, spades, etc., and that the road be diverted from the other side of the first canyon or mountain to the Weaver which will not cost more than $500 and that the big canyon be put off till after harvest. Should companies arrive they can then repose a day or two in the parks within 15 or 20 miles of us, or they can come within ten miles. We can then join with them and open the canyon, or pass them over the mountain as is thought best. A messenger should also be sent to [Fort] Bridger, or to meet any camp this side of Bridger with instructions to the first companies to leave the old road as soon as they reach the Weaver, and take up that stream ten miles: in the meantime sending into town for a pilot. We have the honor to subscribe ourselves your obedient servants and brethren

> Parley P. Pratt
> John Van Cott
> Daniel Spencer[10]

Pratt's explorations suggested the long-range possibility of finding a new route that would intersect the established immigrant road at Bear River, Fort Bridger, or even farther east. More immediately to the point, his actual investigation seemed to establish that the immigration could be diverted from the Pioneer road at the mouth of Echo Canyon and conducted by a new and superior route into Salt Lake Valley. As late as mid-August it was supposed that the 1848 Mormon immigration would be able to come in by the new route. A letter of August 9, written from the valley to the westbound companies, announces: "We are making a new road for you as far as the Weber which will shun the mountains. When you arrive at Weber you will turn up the river about ten miles, then up a canyon about eight miles

---

[10] Original letter on file at the LDS Archives. For copies of this letter and others preserved by the Mormon church I am indebted to my old friend the late Alvin F. Smith, who as church librarian made me unfailingly welcome in visits I made to the historian's office over a period of many years. I am saddened by his passing, which occurred in Salt Lake City on January 4, 1948.

into a beautiful valley in the tops of the mountains, called Antelope
or Parleys Park, then up a plain. Ascending a little, then down a hollow and canyon about 20 miles, following Big Canyon creek to the
valley and fort."[11]

Fair as was this promise, it could not be redeemed, neither in
1848 nor in 1849. It was 1850 before the new route was opened to
travel. Clearly the proposed road ran into unanticipated difficulties—
and at its eastern end, for the heavy labor required to work a road
through the rugged gorge of lower Parleys Canyon need not have prevented bringing in the immigration to the eastern foot of Little
Mountain by way of Silver Creek, Parleys Park, and upper Parleys
Canyon. It would seem that Silver Creek Canyon was the stumbling
block, for Pratt never did get his road through this canyon; when
finally completed, the Golden Pass Road was carried through the
West Hills by way of Threemile Canyon, the next canyon to the
south.

The reasons for the change of route become evident from some
notations in the journal of Captain J. H. Simpson, who reconnoitered
Silver Creek Canyon on August 29, 1858, ten years later. The first
mile or so, as he rode down the canyon, Simpson was disposed to
think that a road could be made "with some little side cutting." But
through the remaining 5 3/4 miles he found "the canon quite narrow,
side hills close to stream which is full of Beaver dams, forcing us
along left slope up bank, along an Indian Trail—The route is
scarcely admissible for packs, & is entirely out of the question as a
wagon route—The labor to make it would be immense, & the greater
part of it is rocky." In his journal next day he added, "It would be a
difficult route for pack mules in the winter on account of the very
steep sidling rocky places, over which the trail goes."[12]

Despite the blighting of his first hopes, Parley P. Pratt retained

---

[11] John L. and A. B. Smith to George A. Smith, Great Salt Lake City,
August 9, 1848, quoted in LDS Journal History for this date. Also see Lorenzo
D. Young's journal for August 19, 1848, in the *Utah Historical Quarterly*, XIV
(1946).

[12] J. H. Simpson, manuscript journals in the records of the War Department, Corps of Topographical Engineers, National Archives, Washington, D.C.
I am indebted to Dale L. Morgan for a transcript of this journal, kept while
Simpson was exploring a military road from Camp Floyd to Fort Bridger Also
see Simpson's instructive *Preliminary Map of Routes Reconnoitered and Opened in
the Territory of Utah . . . in the Fall of 1858*. For the country between Fort
Bridger and the valleys lying west of the Wasatch, this map is far more
illuminating than the one that accompanies his published report of 1876.

his faith in the route he had explored, and after the Forty-Niners commenced to pour into Great Salt Lake City in June, 1849, he undertook to build it himself as a toll road. His *Autobiography* relates:

> I commenced in July [1849] to work a road up the rugged Kanyon of Big Kanyon Creek. I had the previous year (1848) explored the Kanyon for that purpose, and also a beautiful park, and passes from Salt Lake City to Weber River eastward, in a more southern and less rugged route than the pioneer entrance to the valley. . . . I soon had so far completed my road as to be able to obtain a large amount of fuel and timber. In November I ceased operations in the Kanyon and broke up my mountain camp and returned to the city.[13]

It would seem that Pratt's road, while under construction, was a topic of much speculation in Great Salt Lake City. There is an odd allusion to it in a letter of July 8, 1849, by John B. Hazlip, a New Yorker enroute to the gold fields: "The city of the Lake has appropriated $5,000 for the purpose of making a good road from the city to the North Fork of the Platte river, which will be the means of turning a great number of the emigrants in this direction." A second letter by a California immigrant, written in October, remarks more accurately that the Mormons were "making a road through the mountains from the Webber to this place."[14] The following spring, as early as possible, Pratt resumed his road-building, and he describes its completion in this language:

> Some time in this month [March, 1850] I again commenced work on my road in Big Kanyon Creek, and in getting out timber and wood from the same. I continued this operation during the remainder of the season—obtaining much building and fencing timber and a large quantity of poles. In July I had so far completed my road as to open it for the California emigration. The amount of toll taken this first season was about one thousand five hundred dollars.[15]

Utah's first newspaper began publication just in time to herald

---

[13] Parley P. Pratt, *Autobiography of Parley Parker Pratt* (New York, 1874), 407. Although it was not published until 18 years latter, Pratt had written this autobiography by 1856.

[14] Dale L. Morgan, "Letters by Forty-Niners," 100, 116.

[15] Parley P. Pratt, *op. cit.*, 413.

the opening of the new route. The third number of the *Deseret News*, June 29, 1850, featured the following advertisement:

THE GOLDEN PASS!
OR,
NEW ROAD THROUGH THE MOUNTAINS

Travellers between the States and California, are respectfully informed that a new road will be opened on and after the 4th of July, between the Weber River and Great Salt Lake Valley—distance about 40 miles: avoiding the two great mountains, and most of the Kanyons so troublesome on the old route.

The road is somewhat rough and unfinished; but is being made better every day. Several thousand dollars are already expended by the proprietor, who only solicits the patronage of the public, at the moderate charge of

50 cents per conveyance drawn by one animal.
75 cents per conveyance drawn by two animals.
10 cents per each additional draught, pack, or saddle animal.
5 cents per head for loose stock.
1 cent per head for sheep.

The foregoing prices will average about one dollar per wagon. This route lies up the valley of the Weber River some 15 or 18 miles, open, smooth, and grassy; thence, through a dry hollow, and over an abrupt range of hills, some 3 miles; thence, through well watered, grassy, and beautiful plains and meadows, 3 miles; thence, down the open and grassy valley of a stream 3 miles; thence, 2 miles up a smooth ascent, through meadows, and table lands of pine, fir, and aspen forests, to the summit of a mountain; thence, 6 miles down a gradual descent of table land to the head of the Great Kanyon; thence, through a rough road with grass and fuel abundant, 6 miles to the valley; entering which, thousands of acres of fresh feed cover the table lands at the foot of the hills and mountains, where teams can recruit, while all the principal flouring mills are in the same vicinity.

If a road worked by the most persevering industry, an open country, good feed and fuel, beautifully romantic and sublime scenery, are any inducement, take the new road, and thus encourage public improvement.

G. S. L. City. June 22, 1850

P. P. Pratt,

Proprietor

The *Deseret News* gave its warm—or at any rate lukewarm—approbation to this new variety of home industry by remarking, "The Golden Pass, advertised on our first page, is a matter of interest. Whatever difficulties travellers may meet with, on the new, they will be sure to avoid some very bad places, by leaving the old route, from the Weber to this place. Those only can know the difference, who travel both routes."

The name given to the new road neither Pratt nor anyone else ever explained, perhaps because it was regarded as self-evident. Doubtless it was suggested by the golden-colored rock outcropping on the north wall of Parleys Canyon at its mouth; and doubtless, also, the magic significance attaching to the word "gold" for all California-bound immigrants made the name seem a happy inspiration.

Pratt opened his road on schedule, for on July 6 the *Deseret News* commented, "'The Gold Pass' has been travelled, the travellers inform us, tis a pretty good road."

The first company through on the new route consisted of ten men calling themselves "the Newark Rangers," from Kendall County, Illinois. The *Deseret News* of July 20, 1850, published a letter signed by these men, Martial, Fielding, and Clark Heavenhill, Julius Tremain, Henry Verbeck, O. G. Wood, Evan Griffith, John Harrison, Philip Haden, and Stephen S. Benalleck. The letter is mainly laudatory of the Mormon achievement in making the desert to "rejoice, and blossom as the rose," but in signing their names, the men declare that they comprise "the first company to follow Mr. P. P. Pratt, through the Golden Pass or new road through the mountains, from the Weber river to this valley where we arrived on the 4th of July and left the 15th for the Gold regions without a sick man or horse." They add graciously, "The Golden pass is good, for a new road."

How large a proportion of the 1850 immigration by way of Great Salt Lake City used the new road in preference to the old is difficult to determine. In his *Autobiography* Pratt says his receipts the first year amounted to about $1,500, and since his advertisement estimated that the toll would average about a dollar per wagon, some

6,000 immigrants may be estimated to have passed over the new
route, figuring four persons to the wagon. However, a part of Pratt's
tolls would have come from Mormon settlers getting out timber and
building stone from the canyons. Accounts of travel over the new
route are found in a number of the published and unpublished journals kept by immigrants of 1850, although a still larger number of diaries could be cited of those who stayed with the old route over Big
and Little mountains. Upon those who did take Pratt's route, the
rugged gorge of lower Parleys Canyon made the greatest impression;
it was the wildest terrain they had seen since leaving the Missouri
River.[16]

Except for the Mormon trains, which in any event seem to have
preferred the older trail, the first year's immigration had largely
ceased by the time Captain Howard Stansbury, his exploration of
Great Salt Lake completed, set out for home late in August, 1850.
The journals kept by himself, Lieutenant John W. Gunnison, and
Albert Carrington afford an interesting and exact account of the
Golden Pass Road, and extracts are printed below to document the
route.

But first we have to consider the untimely decease of this venture
which had promised so well. The first season would appear to have
been entirely successful, with no suspicion at its close that the
Golden Pass Road would not continue in use indefinitely. When,
early in 1851, Joseph Cain and Arieh C. Brower published their now
excessively rare *Mormon waybill, to the gold mines,*[17] their little book
became the first and last "emigrant's guide" to give space to Pratt's

---

[16] Among overland travelers who describe Pratt's route are Franklin
Langworthy, *Scenery of the Plains, Mountains and Mines; or a Diary Kept Upon
the Overland Route to California, by Way of the Great Salt Lake ...*
(Ogdensburgh, N. Y., 1855); Madison B. Moorman, *The Journals of Madison
Berryman Moorman* (San Francisco, 1948); Henry S. Bloom, diary serialized in
the Kankakee, Ill., *Daily Republic,* May 27–July 3, 1931, typewritten transcripts
in the California State Library and the Utah State Historical Society; Charles
Kelly, ed., "The Journal of Robert Chalmers," *Utah Historical Quarterly,* XX
(January 1952); and John R. Shinn, manuscript diary in the Bancroft Library.
Curious to note, all of these men except Langworthy tried the Hastings Cutoff
this year. Probably twice as many diaries can be cited of 1850 immigrants who
kept to the pioneer road in preference to Pratt's route.
[17] Printed by W. Richards at "G. S. L. City, Deseret, 1851," in 40 pp. Of
this guidebook, which was first advertised for sale in the *Deseret News,* February
22, 1851, copies survive in the Coe Collection at Yale University and at the
Daughters of Utah Pioneers Museum in Salt Lake City.

road. Their account of the route thus has considerable historical interest. Having brought the immigrant down Echo Canyon to the Weber River, they pause to explain, "Here the road forks, the left hand road goes around the mountains, and the right hand road passes over two high mountains, the road very rough," after which they take up Pratt's road in detail:

Left Hand Road.

To the crossing of Weber, good ford, even at the highest stages of water, good grass, wood and water,	5 [miles]
From the crossing of Weber river to Dry hollow [Rockport], no camping place,	10
From Dry hollow to [upper] Silver creek, good grass, sage and water,	6
Thence through a smooth, grassy and well watered country,	8
Thence to the head of the Great Kanyon [Mountain Dell], grass, wood, and water,	6
Thence down the kanyon to the valley, good feed, wood, and water,	6
Thence to Gov. Young's grist mill,	2
Thence to Great Salt Lake City,	5

By this account, the distance from the mouth of Echo Canyon to Great Salt Lake City was 48 miles, 2 1/2 miles longer than the old route. Actually, measured by roadometer the new road was a full 9 miles longer.

For all the pains that had been expended upon the Golden Pass Road, it fell almost instantaneously into disuse, and as a continuous whole the road had only this one year's existence. Several causes seem to have contributed to this end. Perhaps as important as any was that Parley P. Pratt, early in 1851, sold his interest in the road to finance a mission for his church to Chile. This information comes to us from the journal of Martha Spence Heywood, who notes that at a meeting in Great Salt Lake City on April 13, 1851, Brigham Young spoke about "Parley P's canyon which right he sold out to several individuals for his benefit to provide for his expedition," the Saints being told that "such individual rights ought not to be interfered with."[18]

---

[18] Juanita Brooks, ed., *Not by Bread Alone: The Journal of Martha Spence Heywood, 1850–1856* (Salt Lake City, 1978), 56–57. Pratt left Great Salt Lake

Although no one else ever took quite so much interest in the route, Pratt's sale of his rights does not in itself account for its ceasing to be used. The cost of maintenance may have been high, especially in the canyons. The additional 9 miles' travel it imposed was a disadvantage, certainly. Sales resistance may well have developed to a toll-road maintained alongside a free road—and one not only free but shorter, even if more difficult. From some combination of these causes, the Golden Pass Road fell into desuetude.

Over the next ten years some stretches of it may have seen service, but Captain Simpson's journal of 1858 indicates that the traffic had not been heavy. On August 28 of that year he wrote of crossing Parleys Park and getting into "the old Pioneer road to Salt Lake—or Parleys Park road—the same which turns up the Weber, instead of down from mouth of Echo Canon. . . . we took this tolerably plain wagon road for a distance of 2¾ miles, which brought us to the crossing of Silver Creek." From the men employed at lumbering in Parleys Park he learned that the mail, "when in the winter it could not be carried by the Big Mountain, has been carried over the old Weber route . . . and in one or more instances when the snow was such as to prevent the mail carrier from getting over the divide between Silver creek & Weber River, he has gone down successfully Silver Creek junction with Weber River." But next day, in the Weber Valley, he recorded that, "the old wagon road," while still perceptible, showed signs "of having been but little traveled recently."[19]

In the course of time, Pratt's vision was justified. In 1862 the Overland Stage began using lower Parleys in preference to Emigration Canyon, and that same year a toll road was worked down Silver Creek Canyon. The Mormon immigration of 1862 and subsequent years came this way in preference to the old road over Big and Little mountains.[20] With some small variations, the mainline highway from

---

City on his mission March 16, 1851, hence had been gone nearly a month at the time of this journal entry.

[19] See note 12, and Tullidge, *Tullidge's Histories*, II, 126–127, for details of Daniel H. Wells' work in the autumn of 1860 on a wagon road in Silver Creek for use by mail coaches.

[20] John D. T. McAllister, of whose diary the Henry E. Huntington Library has a photostat copy, documents the use of the new route this fall. Coming home from a mission to Great Britain, he described the last few miles of his journey as follows:

Tuesday [September] 30th. we Started at 6 & ½ o'clock   crossed "Yellow Creek"   2 miles brought us to the Summit of Ridge   4 miles to "Cache Cave" head of Echo creek   2 miles brought us to "Echo

Salt Lake City to Wyoming today is the route of which, in that long ago July of 1848, the travel-worn but exultant Parley P. Pratt, John Van Cott, and Daniel Spencer rode home to apprise the Saints.

JOURNALS OF THE STANSBURY PARTY ON THE GOLDEN PASS ROAD 1850[21]

Wednesday, August 28. [*Gunnison:*] Leave Salt Lake City and start Odometer from Adobie Hall at 00.00 & take [road] South to Big Field S. of City plot—[i.e., to 9th South Street] then toward Emigration Kanyon to top of table[land], then along base of mts [11th East Street], crossing Emigration creek which runs S. W. from its Kanyon to bottom & encamp at Golden Pass or Big Kanyon creek. There is nothing at the mouth of this kanyon to hinder an easy grade into the valley. . . . 8.59 [miles][22]

Kanyon"   travaled 3 miles down Echo & nooned two hours. then travaled 7 miles   met Several Brethren from the valey & Camped with them. in the evening all who wanted enjoyed a dance. . . .

Wednesday Oct. 1st. Settled up with the Company P. M. by invitation I accompanied Bro J. W. Young to the City. we left Camp at 1. o'clock 11 miles brought us to the "Mouth of Echo," 3 mile to "Grass Creek," 3 miles to "Chalk Creek"   took Supper at Bro "Ira Eldredges"   from Chalk Creek to mouth of "Silver Creek" 9 miles, we campd just before reaching Silver Creek with Pres Young Coal teems, 26 miles this afternoon

Thursday 2nd Oct   we started early & drove to Wm Kimballs for Breakfast   he resided 10 miles from Mouth of Silver Creek. Stoped one hour & again Started; 6 miles we reached the Summit, 13 miles down hill, brought us to the mouth of Parleys Kanyon; 6 miles more we reached the City, (35 miles this day). . . .

[21] Extracts from these journals, by courtesy of Dale L. Morgan, are derived from the originals in the National Archives. Carrington seems to have kept a personal journal parallel with his official journal, and this, as published in *Heart Throbs of the West* (Salt Lake City, 1947), VIII, 77–132, may be read in comparison. In editing the extracts from these journals, information is also drawn from the odometer record kept by Carrington and printed in Appendix A of Stansbury's *Exploration and Survey of the Valley of the Great Salt Lake of Utah* . . . (Philadelphia, 1852), 278–79.

[22] The entrance to the Golden Pass Road is shown on the township survey of 1856. From what is now 11th East and 21st South streets, the road proceeded east to the locality of present 15th East, and then bent southeasterly toward the gulch of Parleys, dropping down into it just above present 21st East Street, although in 1850 the trail may have run straight up the ravine from 11th East. Camp No. 1 of the Stansbury party was some rods higher up, perhaps in the vicinity of the one-time Brigham Young mill near 23rd East Street.

[*Stansbury:*] . . . finished all our arrangements settled up every thing, & two hours by sun left the Salt Lake City for home. . . . Found the Camp in a deep ravine at the mouth of Pratts Kanyon. Arrived there by dark. . . .

Thursday, August 29. [*Gunnison:*] Move from camp at 9 oclock— the arranging of packs taking some time which would usually be devoted to travelling—& delay by narrow road also where pass wagon by two mules. Pass up rather narrow ravine about ³/₄ mile to P. P. Pratts toll house²³—The toll per wagon of 2 horses—75 cts & 20 cts per additional pair & 10 cts for pack or riding animals & 5 cts for loose animals. Paid six dollars toll the whole being passed in lump. [7.05 miles]

[*Stansbury:*] Morning fine & cool. A train of three mormon wagons just arrived from the States encamped near us. Off by 9 oclock Followed up Pratts golden pass all day. The ascent is not as steep as I expected, although the road is very crooked. The valley is very narrow scarcely affording room for a turbulent little mountain stream which comes rushing down & winding its sinuous course at the base of the mountains on either side Thro' a growth of cedar, oaks maple service berry, quaking asp, & bitter cottonwood & willows with a gurgling mu[r]muring sound, which after the dead silence of the sand flats of the lakes, & the barren flatness of the sage plains was peculiarly pleasant & refreshing. Had to unload the wagon thrice & take out a part of the team a dozen times on account of the crookedness of the road. The rock is sandstone, intermingled with limestone. The sandstone much stained occasionally with iron. I observed a fine view of the wild hops Rose bushes also abounded near to top of the pass.²⁴ The valley is very narrow & will require much grading & expensive side cutting & walling beside several inclined planes to render it at all fit for a rail road. A good wagon road however can be made at a moderate expense. The difficulty is that no expense will keep the valley from filling with snow during the winter which will effectually block up the pass for 6 months of the year. . . .

Friday, August 30. [*Stansbury:*] Morning quite cool. Great coat comfortable. The old road by emigration kanyon is about ¹/₂ mile to

---

²³ The journals do not locate the toll-house precisely, but there is little doubt that it was situated half a mile below the geological formation at the mouth of the canyon which is known as Suicide Rock. A spring up a ravine to the north here would have supplied water for the toll-house and its watering trough.

²⁴ By "top of the pass" Stansbury has reference to the steep grade I-80 climbs today just below the dam in Parleys.

west [i.e., 1¹/2 miles to north].²⁵ Old Caroline one of our most faithful mules & who had gone thro' all our hardest trips, gave out yesterday & this morning, finding it impossible to get her any farther, gave her into possession of Mr Haikes an inhabitant of the City with instructions to put her into the hands of the Presᵗ Young, so that if she was fit to go thro with the wagon with our goods to the States he might take her thro, if not the man was to retain her for himself. The road this morning continued up the same creek as yesterday to a point where it forked, one kanyon coming down from the S. E. & the other bearing off more to the N N W [i.e., E. N E.].²⁶ The road follows up the latter to a divide descending which we struck upon a branch of East Kanyon Creek or Bauchemins a branch of the Weber.²⁷ Here an observation was taken for latitude. Following down the valley of this little stream stopped to noon near its mouth.²⁸ The vallies of both these streams are from two to three miles broad. Scrub oak, & quaking asp are the predominant growth. Near the summit several very fine large pines (3 leaved) were growing as yet undisturbed by the Emigration. The road continues up the valley of Bauchemins cr[eek] crossing several small affluents until it comes to a main fork coming in from the right.²⁹ This stream which is about 6 ft wide & two deep heads in a range of hills three miles to the S W³⁰ whence it issues with a beautifully clear & quick current crossing the valley & discharging into Bochmans cr which flows at the foot of the northern ridge to the W & N W, into the Weber   Where it issues from the hills is a broad level prair[i]e skirted with trees³¹ & two miles N E [S. E.?]

---

²⁵ The previous night's camp had been at the confluence of Mountain Dell and Parleys creeks. The site is now under the waters of Mountain Dell Reservoir, a little below the junction of I-80 with State Route 65, the "Little Mountain loop road."

²⁶ Compare Pratt's reports of two years before. The canyon trending southeast is Lambs Canyon, the other Parleys proper.

²⁷ The branch flows out of what is locally called Tollgate Canyon but has the map name Peterson Draw.

²⁸ Present Gorgoza, which is almost universally misspelled Gorgorza.

²⁹ Snyders Creek, which flows north through the west end of Parleys Park. A few miles east of present Kimball Junction, US 40 veers south and thus parts company with the Golden Pass Road. I-80 follows the original road nearly to Silver Creek.

³⁰ The hills in which Park City is situated.

³¹ Parleys Park. No longer a tiny farming community, Snyderville is located at the west edge of the park, 2 miles south of where Stansbury wrote down these notations.

a trail passes over the hills to the Proveaux 6 or 8 miles dist[ant].[32]
Odom[ete]r 43.36. Crossing this prairie & heading a noble spring[33] on
our left, we crossed the Bauchemins Creek, here about 20 ft wide & 2
ft deep with a rapid current & beautifully clear cold water[34] we
followed up a dry branch for about 2 miles ... & encamped upon a
little spring branch with plenty of fine grass for the horses about 1
mile from Silver cr[eek].[35] The country begins to be flatter & the
valley much wider   The ascent for the last few miles is quite gentle
& the land excellent, wheat & grass could be raised to any extent on
the prair[i]e which extends to our left all the way from Bauchemins
Creek to Camp.

[*Gunnison:*] It is about 1½ miles N. to the old Road where it rises
over the last Mtn; for which see "guide book."[36] E. about 2.05 miles
cross creek ... & ascend mt:—a small Ravine on left ... ¼ m. to
turn. Now turn E. N. E.—about 1½ m. cross the rivulet & have a
kanyon on Rt. over wedge ¼ cross & follow rivulet—short & bad
turns & some mud holes—up to its head & by an ascent of steep
grade ½ m. long reach the "Divide"—Latitude-40-44 51.2—3.43
ms. ... Odometer—21.04—the zero at camp No. 2. Sighting back for
general direction by Pack Needle Ford reading to ½ m of Bauchmin cr[eek] E. N. E. 3.64 ms. Then S. E. in general direction of valley in Mts—Noon & read odo[meter]s on a small branch of Bkme cr
[Beauchemin Creek]:—Odo[meter]s 35.01. Start 3¼ at 3½ a smart
creek fr. S. W.—at 3.52 a large branch fr. South odo[meter]s 43.36 &
at 420 47.13 cross main stream of B. cr. & travel E. N. E. (Note we
have on the South & Rt a beautiful rich meadow covered with grass
about 3 ms. in diameter—It is nearly circular. at 4.45 2 fine cool

---

[32] Once again, a reminder that Indian trails preceded virtually all of our
modern highways, in this case US 40.

[33] Deep mining at Park City, and the driving of drain tunnels, has so disturbed the flow of underground water in Parleys Park that this "noble spring,"
like others mentioned by Gunnison, no longer rises on what is now the Bittner
Ranch.

[34] Present Kimball Creek. East Canyon Creek is formed by the various
small runs which flow into Parleys Park, and particularly by the union of Snyders
and Kimball creeks.

[35] The night encampment was near Silver Creek Junction, a few hundred
yards north of where US 40 leaves I-80.

[36] Referring to the account of the original road provided by William Clayton
in his *Latter-Day Saints' Emigrants' Guide,* a copy of which Stansbury carried.
Gunnison's further entries for this day may be read in the light of the notes
provided for Stansbury's journal.

springs to South of crossing—Still N. 60 E.—at 5 another cool stream from a spring 300 feet above road crossing Odo[meter]s- 54.67 & at camp No. 3. Day's work—14.23 [miles]

Saturday, August 31. [*Stansbury:*] Left Camp about 8, the main train following the road under Mr Carrington with orders to encamp on the Weber whilst Mr G, Archambault & self started to cross over to the Proveaux to examine a prairie called Camache prair[i]e, thro which it is said a level route can be obtained from the Weber to the Proveaux. . . .[37]

[*Carrington:*] cloudy & cool—Capt[n] S & Lieut G went off road on S side to reconnoitre—took camp across Silver Creek[38] road good— grass plenty—to top of hill[39] to 1st water E side of hill[40] down a spring run ravine into Weber bottom[41] & down Weber on west side to near mouth of sil[r] creek[42] still down same side of Weber to ford[43] a very sideling pt just as you near the ford, needs gradeing—across ford

---

[37] Both Stansbury and Gunnison have long accounts of this reconnaissance, not here quoted, since our interest centers upon the Golden Pass Road.

[38] By the odometer record it was .95 miles from the previous night's camp to the ford, and in it Carrington remarks further, "In East Park; creek 30 by 2 feet, well grassed and willows, as in west, or Parley's Park. Good ford." The crossing of Silver Creek was several hundred yards south of where I-80 reaches the bank of the stream today; the road of 1850 separated from the modern highways about half a mile back.

[39] For many years I used the old Golden Pass Road as a short cut to the valley of the Weber when going fishing, but gave it up because dangerous washes have developed along its course. The road is shown on the *Coalville* quadrangle. At first angling E. S. E. up the west slope of the West Hills, a distance of 1.67 miles by Carrington's odometer record, it then turns at right angles to descend Threemile Canyon in a generally northeasterly direction.

[40] By the odometer record, 2.22 miles from the divide above mentioned.

[41] Threemile Canyon. It opens upon the valley of the Weber at present Rockport. Carrington does not give the distance down it, apparently about 2 miles from its head spring.

[42] To present Wanship, the total distance to this point from the spring in Threemile Canyon given by Carrington as 6.01 miles. The Golden Pass Road from Rockport to Wanship is followed today by US 189.

[43] US 189 joins I-80 near Wanship, but Pratt's original road is still employed as a county road which keeps to the west or left bank of the Weber until it reaches a point just south of present Coalville. Carrington gives the distance from the crossing of Silver Creek to what he calls "Weber ford, upper or Golden Pass ford," as 8.25 miles. As the road now runs, the distance is 5.8 miles, the river being bridged perhaps 1.75 miles above the site of the old ford. Fenced and grass-seeded hay fields at this point have eradicated all signs of the original road. Concerning the ford itself, Carrington says in the odometer record, "This is an excellent crossing, and fordable during the whole season of traveling."

& made camp No 4 in bottom[44].... sprinkling most of the p. m.—
rock noticed on route & each side, mostly a light gray fine grit
sandstone, dip about 30°, to the N 40°, & 45° & 60° W—some
pudding stone & some earthy red sandstone—from dark till 10 p. m.
rained most of the time quite fast with much thunder & lightning—
the Capt[n] & Lieut G arrived in camp at 9 3/4 a.m. [P.M.]

Sunday, September 1. [*Stansbury:*] Morning clear & fine. Engaged in drying up after last nights storm. . . .

[*Carrington:*] Clear & plsnt—laid by—many good places for farms
in Weber R bottom—

Monday, September 2. [*Stansbury:*] Last night was quite cold &
at sunrise therm[r] stood at 33° with a heavy white frost. The horses
took a stampede last night probably being frightened by a wolf & this
morning were very wild difficult to catch, so that it was 9 oclock before the train got off. The cattle evinced an obstinate disposition to
run back & it was with no little trouble that they were prevented from
doing so. The road follows N. down the Valley of the Weber for a
mile when we cross Morins Creek a small affluent.[45] & a short distance farther on another small stream[46] for which the mountaineers
have no name, it not being deemed worthy of notice by them as no
beaver had ever been found in its waters. Still following the bottom &
occasionally mounting a high wash bank of the river, at 5 miles we
cross the Red Fork or Echo Creek,[47] about 150 ft above its junction
with the Weber which is here a clear rapid stream about 100 ft wide
& 2 1/2 in the deepest part. The creek breaks thro a bluff of conglomerate & pebbles 150 ft high cemented by lime & agglutinated red
sandstone, with occasional layers of stone firm enough for building
purposes, but for the most part the conglomerate is of too friable a
texture for any useful purpose. It is very highly colored with oxide of

---

[44] At the outskirts of modern Coalville.

[45] Carrington's odometer record here remarks what none of the journals do,
"A trail leads off from this creek to a crossing of Bear River." Thus was anticipated Simpson's road of 1858 up Chalk Creek. The name Stansbury applied to
this stream is another of the trappers' names now disused, Archambault being his
source of information.

[46] Grass Creek. After crossing to the right bank of the Weber at Coalville,
Stansbury continued along the line of I-80, though the Echo Reservoir has
pushed the modern highway higher up on the hillside between Coalville and the
mouth of Echo Canyon.

[47] The odometer record gives the total distance from Great Salt Lake City to
this junction as 54.60 miles, which included the 8.59 miles from the city to
Stansbury's first camp in the gully of Parleys below the canyon proper.

iron. Here the old & new roads fork the one going by Emigration &
the other thro' Big or Pratts Kanyon. On the left of the road to this
point the bottom of the Weber is covered with willows, cottonwood &
grass which affords good feed for stock. At the junction observations
were taken for the latitude. Ther[mometer] 80. From this point the
old road follows up the Valley of Red Fork. . . .

[*Gunnison*:] Leave camp at 9-40 N 22W to Morin Creek .85 mile
fr. E. S. E. at 9-52 then W 58 (5 & ?) W to Red fork—4.77   Small
creek muddy at 10.35 fr S. E. & mtn in front—at 11-05 strike Red fork
& old road—Set Draper [theodolite] & read back along Weber opening to Morin creek S 58 E and North 68 W along old road 3 ms—then
the road bears more Westerly & crosses R[iver] at 4 ms to South
passing over a high ridge & then down to E. Kanyon creek &c [the
word "Bauchemin" interlineated above "E. Kanyon"]—N.32 E is up
Red Fork. . . .

[*Carrington*:] clear cool—slight frost—down Weber River in right
hand bottom to Morin's Creek N 22—00W m .85, 30 ft x 1¹/₂—to old
road near mouth of Red Fork, N 58—00 W (a small stream) 4.77 m—
up Red Fork, N 32 00 E, crossing Fork several times. . . .

Having brought the Stansbury party back into the original road at
the mouth of Echo Canyon, we need not follow them farther on their
journey. However, in view of the question raised by Pratt's first exploration of whether a route from the Bear could be found south of
Echo Canyon, it will be useful to summarize the conclusions of
Stansbury and his aides. The Stansbury and Gunnison reconnaissance on August 31 had the possibilities of this alternate road very
much in mind. Their route very largely was that of Pratt, Van Cott,
and Spencer on July 4, 1848, except that they did not go all the way
south to the Provo. Instead, some 2 miles north of the Provo, they
turned east up the slope of the West Hills, and on the far side descended City Creek into Kamas Prairie, or Rhodes Valley, as it is
sometimes now called.

After observing with approval the prairie between the Weber and
Provo rivers, the connection "as perfect as I ever saw," Stansbury
questioned his guide about the country to the east in which these
rivers rose. "Bear river," he then wrote in his journal, "is said by Archambault to take its rise in the same mountain with the Weber &
Provaux. If so, & they can be connected near their sources, the rail-

road should follow down the Provaux into the Utah Valley. The kanyon through which the little river descends into that valley is said to be sufficiently wide for this purpose, & is not therefore liable to the objections which can be urged against both Pratts, Emigration, & Weber Kanyons."

After rejoining Carrington and the wagons, Stansbury, as we have seen from his journal, continued up Echo Canyon. On September 3, as he was approaching the point where the road left Echo Creek to pull over toward Cache Cave, Stansbury noted that ravines heading to the south made it "highly probable that a pass may be obtained by means of one of these vallies over to some of the head branches of the Weber, or the river itself before passing thro Camache Prair[i]e. It is well worth a thorough examination, as success w^d give an almost level & very direct route thro the Timpanogas to the Utah valley." He also permitted himself to speculate whether a suitable route down the upper Weber above Kamas Prairie could be found by following Yellow Creek to its head and then striking over the divide.

In part for its bearing on these larger questions respecting a "direct route," and in part for what it has to say about the Golden Pass Road, a letter written by Albert Carrington before going on east with Stansbury from Fort Bridger is printed to round out the documentary history of the short-lived cutoff:[48]

Fort Bridger Septr   1850

President Brigham Young, Dear Sir,

We arrived at this place on the 5th & immediately the same afternoon began to prepare for packing—We traveled by the way of the Golden Pass & made the distance from the city to where we came into the old road at the mouth of Red Fork 54 1/2 miles being 10 miles further than the old road; but with the same amount of labor expended, at the present condition of each road, as near as I can learn of the condition of the old road from those who have come through on it with the relief teams, the new road can be made much the best for heavy loads, & is very much the best grassed; & should the new road be worked down Silver Creek, as it ought by all means, if it *should continue to be used*, it would not probably be over about 4 miles the longest.

---

[48] This letter, in the LDS Archives, I quote by courtesy of A. William Lund, assistant historian, and the late Alvin F. Smith, librarian.

THE GOLDEN PASS ROAD

Captn Stansbury has altered his views as to going the
Arkansas route to the Missouri, & Bridger is to go with him to
the east base of the Black Hills [Laramie Mountains], crossing Green River near where our old road leaves it to cross
this way onto Black's Fork, and then Easterly, passing in the
neighborhood of the Medicine Bow Mountains, & onto the
Republican Fork & down the Kansas, or on the dividing
ridge between the Kansas & Platte—

In connection with above items, I thought it might be
well to offer my opinions as to our best route from the City to
Bethlehem, before much more labor was expended on the
last half of Parley's road or any other going East—

From what I have seen previously & this time & from
what I have read and heard, in case Fort Bridger is to be
made a point in our road, I should proceed on Parley's road
until you reach the Park on the main branch of East Kanyon
(maybe making a few alterations) or to the valley of Silver
Creek, from there through a portion of the Camassia or Ka-
mass Prairie (this is that section of land where Br. Parley said
the Provo could be turned into the Weber, & very correctly)
then to mouth of Weber River upper cañon, then by the
nearest feasible tributary to the Weber that will lead across to
Bear River & from Bear River across a rolling & table land
country to Fort Bridger, a country well watered & abundantly
grassed, and which embraces & opens into coal formation of
Bear River Mtn or Basin Rim, & the sulphur & tar springs
coal, & will probably be a nearer route to Fort Bridger than
the present one by at least 10 miles, if we allow for the same
amount of windings & ups & downs, which I do not think can
be near so much, especially the ups & downs.

Another consideration, is, that the Kamas Prairie will accommodate a large settlement of stock & dairy farmers, and
very likely wheat, oats, barley, &c can be raised there in great
abundance, as the soil is very rich & well watered & lies ad-
mirably for irrigation, should it be needed—

And still another reason, (perhaps,) is the accommoda-
tion it will afford to all of our i[m]]migrations that purpose
settling in Utah & the valleys south as they can easily pass
down the Provo from K Prairie, saveing themselves much
travel—

The Provo runs nearly S W from K Prairie to Utah Valley—

Captn S & Lieut G visited the Prairie, while I took the camp onto Weber River, & they told me that the broad leaved grass in the neighborhood of all the little streams wandering through the Prairie was nearly up to their horses' breasts: they also visited the tar spring, while I visited the sulphur spring & its coal bed,[49] & Lieut G noticed the same breaking down or low depression in the Basin Rim, to the south, that we noted in 1847, making a nearly level country from the table south of Fort Bridger to Bear River, & agreeing with the statements of Bridger & Vasquez to us since our arrival here about the route from this point to Kamas Prairie—

The coal at the sulphur spring does not crop out sufficiently for me to determine its depth & breadth, without much boreing of the surface, but judgeing from the sandstone dikes on either side & the clay between, I should say this bed would be 150 feet wide by height or depth unknown—This coal as far as I am able to judge from surface specimens, is bituminous & of the kind known in England as the Cherry coal; it burns with a bright yellow flame & leaves no residuum except a light ash like wood coal—It is possible, that owing to heavy immigration to our valley, both our own, & to the coast for gold, a new route would be an advantage, if only for grass, & I would suggest a route may be found either from this Fort, or from Bear River by the route above described, leaveing this Fort on the North, and crossing Green River somewhere between where our old road leaves it & Brown's Hole, & across the tributaries of Green River that rise in the table land south of the South Pass, & passing on in the neighborhood of the Medicine Bow Mtns on the North end of the North Park, & onto the head waters of the South Fork of the Platte & down it & down the main Platte to its mouth, or, onto the head waters of the Republican Fork down it until a point is reached that would be feasible for crossing over to the Main Platte & then down it, to its mouth; the present presumption is, that the route named is very practicable, with plenty of grass, water, & fuel, much nearer than our old

---

[49] In the same sentence Carrington has jumped from a discussion of Kamas Prairie to the valley of Sulphur Creek, just east of the Bear River.

route, & by opening another, will divide immigration in such a manner that all would be better accommodated. Should this presumption prove correct as we go through, & I am liberated [from duty with Stansbury] early enough, I would willingly pilot up any of our trains next season, in case you may deem it politic; in case you should, I shall expect to be notified to that effect, either at St. Louis or Washington.

In case any of the above suggestions are of any benefit, I shall be pleased, if they are not, I hope there is no harm done.

Brother Brigham, I feel *in a manner* alone, & not alone, & feel to ask it, as a great favor, that you will bless me, & sustain me by your prayers, that I may acquit myself wisely & efficiently and do good.

From Yours in the new & everlasting covenant
Albert Carrington.

The views about the overland route which Carrington voices in this letter have been very largely borne out, as will be apparent to everyone who has driven over I-80 east to the Missouri River. But west of Fort Bridger the hope that a superior new road would be found, south of the old one, turned out to be vain, notwithstanding the use of Simpson's Chalk Creek—Weber River—Kamas Prairie—Provo River route during Camp Floyd's heyday. Modern highway builders have kept to the north of the old trail as far as the head of Echo Canyon. From this point the mainline highways through the Wasatch Mountains today follow the westbound route pioneered by Lansford W. Hastings and Parley P. Pratt.[50]

---

[50] For additional information on Pratt's road, see W. W. Phelps' letter of October 3, 1855, in the *Deseret News*, October 24, 1855.

THE TWIN SISTERS

The southern gate of the City of Rocks showing a part of the
California Trail near its junction with the Salt Lake Cutoff.

THE SALT LAKE CUTOFF

IN THE PERSPECTIVE of history, a road north around Great Salt Lake became inevitable from the hour the Mormons entered the valley of the Great Salt Lake. The development of population concentrations in Oregon and Utah sooner or later must have required a road to connect them by the most direct possible route. Interstate 84 and US 30S, the so-called "Snowville Cutoff," reflect in our own day the historical pressures that began to build up in 1847.

In the beginning, however, the pioneering of what became known as the "Salt Lake Cutoff," the "Salt Lake Road," and the "Deep Creek Cutoff" owed nothing to the existence of Oregon. Islanded as they were in the immense distances of the Far West, the Utah and Oregon communities did not for many years begin to exert any real gravitational attraction upon each other. The wagon road north around the lake came into existence, rather, as a direct consequence of the shortcomings of the Hastings Cutoff as a means of access to the California Trail from the valley of the Great Salt Lake.

The valleys which open out upon the northern shores of the salt lake had reëchoed to the sound of horses' hoofs from the time the mountain men first penetrated to this area. Peter Skene Ogden, after his discovery of the Humboldt River in the winter of 1828–29, came east as far as the Bear and Portneuf rivers, and, following Indian trails through the snow, very largely anticipated the subsequent cutoff. More to the south, the Bidwell party a dozen years later took wagons around the lake, but although their route in good time commended itself in part to railroad builders, it never appealed to other California immigrants. At the time the Hastings Cutoff was tried and found wanting, the potentialities of the country north of Great Salt Lake for a wagon road were an exciting unknown.

The first wagon tracks north from Goodyear's fort were made in March, 1848, by Hazen Kimball, James Pollock, and Joshua Terry, who took two wagons to Fort Hall. Not all the Saints who reached Salt Lake Valley in the fall of 1847 were pleased with the designated gathering place, and within a few days several of them, including Hazen Kimball, took their wagons north to Goodyear's fort. The annoyed authorities presiding over the Mormon settlement promptly sent the marshal to order them back. The dissidents took their time about returning, and made no bones about their displeasure. Eventually all left the valley, some going to California by the southern route, some returning to the States, and some, like Kimball, going north to Fort Hall and thence to California by the Humboldt route.

A number of references to Kimball appear in the Mormon annals, and since he made the first known wagon track between the valley of the Great Salt Lake and Fort Hall, it will be well to quote them. The 35-year-old Kimball, accompanied by his wife, Deirdra, 28, and children Helen, 5, and George, 4, had been captain of the Third Ten in Jedediah Grant's overland company. The authorities in Salt Lake Valley wrote Brigham Young on March 6, 1848 (a letter quoted in the LDS Journal History): "A Mr. Pollock, who was cut off the Church on the road and Hazen Kimball with their families left a few days ago intending to intersect [Joseph R.] Walker's company somewhere on Bear river, south of Fort Hall and go to California." Apparently Kimball failed to find Walker and went on to Fort Hall, whence, later this year, he accompanied James Clyman's immigrant company the rest of the way to California. Henry W. Bigler met Clyman's company at the Sink of the Humboldt on August 15, and wrote in his journal, "I met with one man Bro. Hazen Kimball that wintered thare [at Salt Lake] last winter but left in March and went to fort hall and cum on with the emegration   he was dissatisfide with the situation of that place and with the people and left   he said they was sowing wheat all last fall and all winter [and] that they had put in a 8 thousand achors. . . ."[1]

To these scattered references from the Mormon annals, Dale L. Morgan added Kimball's own account, in the form of a letter.[2] Writing from San Francisco on December 7, 1848, Kimball said in part:

> I arrived in Salt Lake Valley on the 3d of October, 1847, and remained there during the winter. On the 2d of March, I left in company with one team for Fort Hall—a distance of 200 miles—where a wagon had never been before without a guide without difficulty. On the 15th of July I left Fort Hall with 25 wagons and 34 men, emigrants from the States, for California. We had very good luck—came over the Sierra

---

[1] This text and subsequent quotations of Henry Bigler's journal are from the Utah Historical Records Survey typescript of Bigler's daybook, made by Jessie E. Empey under the direction of Juanita Brooks, copy at the Utah State Historical Society.

[2] *Warsaw* [Ill.] *Signal*, April 7, 1849.

Nevada by a new route, one the Mormons opened this fall on their way in to the Salt Lake. The road is very good—much better than the old one, it is said by those who have travelled both.

Parley P. Pratt rebaptized Kimball in California in 1851, and Bancroft reported he was living in San Francisco in 1883, a member of the Society of California Pioneers.

Apparently in going north to Fort Hall, Kimball kept to the east bank of the Bear until he reached a point near Deweyville, then crossed it to go on up the Malad. This was the same road Stansbury traveled to Fort Hall in September, 1849. With little variation, both Kimball and Stansbury followed the route Frémont had taken, northbound with his howitzer, in 1843.

Kimball was not the only Mormon with the Clyman company. Addison Pratt recorded that the immigrants he encountered at the Sink were accompanied by "some brethren from Salt Lake." When he finally reached Salt Lake Valley, Pratt found his family "in a house with Sister Rogers, whose husband we had met at the sink of Mary's river, on the road to California."[3] This was Mary M. Rogers, wife of Isaac Rogers, a friend of Parley Pratt and recent resident of New Jersey.[4]

Azariah Smith's August 26 journal entry, made 11 days after the meeting with Kimball, described an encounter with a Mormon, probably traveling with the Peter Lassen company: "Today we met an imigration Company, and there was one man with them belonging to the Church, from Salt Lake Vally, and he said that there was the best of grain there, and that corn grew fine; and all sorts of garden Sauce done well. And he calls it five hundred miles from here to the

---

[3] S. George Ellsworth, ed., *The Journals of Addison Pratt* (Salt Lake City, 1990), 350, 358.

[4] At Fort Hall on July 11, 1848, Rogers wrote his son, "I came to Fort Hall in April. Mr. Walker did not go. I have had to wait till now; it is 200 miles from the valley. I start for the Bay of Francisco to-morrow or next day to get some goods I sent around by ship." Rogers journeyed to California to recover freight he had shipped on the *Brooklyn* with Samuel Brannan. "Mr. Walker" is probably Henson Walker, an 1847 Mormon emigrant, but may be mountain man Joseph R. Walker, who accompanied Joseph Chiles to California later that summer. In an undated letter, probably written in October, 1848, Rogers reports receiving a letter from his wife dated July 23, 1848, that was probably carried west by the Hensley party. See Isaac Rogers to Lester P. Rogers, LDS Archives. Isaac Rogers died in Sacramento in April, 1849; his widow married Thomas Rhoads.

Salt Lake settlement."[5] Ephraim Green's journal explicitly identifies this man as "mr. riter [who] gives a verry faverable report of the country." This was Levi E. Riter, who was bound for San Francisco to collect freight he had sent around Cape Horn in the *Brooklyn* with Samuel Brannan.[6]

This leaves the backslider Pollock and Joshua Terry to be accounted for. James Pollock, an Irishman born in Tyrone, was accompanied on the journey to Fort Hall by his wife, Priscilla, 19, and his children, Clarinda, Thomas, and Utah-born John J.[7]

Joshua Terry remembered that he left Salt Lake Valley "because I was starved out," and told this story in 1907:

> When the winter of 1847 came on, I had one peck of wheat to live on till the next harvest, and I started to go to California to see if I could not get along better through the winter there. I never got to California. Instead, I was turned out of doors to drift without even my peck of wheat or a gun, and only a little powder and lead, and a fire flint. James Pollack engaged me to drive to California. We started, he agreeing to furnish my board in return for my work in driving his team. We got as far as Fort Hall and then he wanted me to herd his cattle as well as drive, and I told him whenever he was ready to roll west, I was ready to drive, but when he wanted his cattle tended that was not my work. He told me I would either herd cattle or never go a day's journey farther with him.[8]

---

[5] David L. Bigler, ed., *The Gold Discovery Journal of Azariah Smith* (Salt Lake City, 1990), 139.

[6] See Will Bagley, ed., *A Road from El Dorado: The 1848 Trail Journal of Ephraim Green* (Salt Lake City, 1991), 31. In 1917, W. W. Riter wrote an account of his father's journey, published in Kate B. Carter, ed., *Heart Throbs of the West* (Salt Lake City, 1939–1951), VII, 402–408. Other quotations from the Green, Pratt, and Smith journals are from the published editions and can be located by reference to their date.

[7] The LDS Journal History lists the Pollocks as members of the Asa Barton company of ten in the 1847 emigration. James Pollock was born in Tyrone, Ireland, on September 14, 1813, and "was one of the first and most esteemed settlers in the Cosumnes Valley." Pollock died February 28, 1878, and is buried in the Slough House cemetery. See Norma B. Ricketts, *Historic Cosumnes and the Slough House Pioneer Cemetery* (Salt Lake City, 1978), 67.

[8] *Deseret Evening News*, August 3, 1907, 26.

Terry went on to spend the spring with Peg-Leg Smith and Jim Bridger.

These events set the stage for the opening of the Salt Lake Cutoff in the summer of 1848. By one of the ironies history occasionally permits itself, the slim biography of the man who made the effective discovery of the Salt Lake Cutoff route for overland travel is without reference to the feat. And Utah has repaid its debt to him shabbily by corrupting his name upon its map. A poor memorial is better than none, and the "Hansel" Mountains, Peak, Spring, and Valley have preserved down through the generations, after a fashion, the memory of Samuel J. Hensley. But our maps should now be corrected.[9]

Born in Kentucky in 1816, Hensley seems to have been at one time a trapper, and to have spent some years in New Mexico. He traveled to California with the Chiles party of 1843 and entered Sutter's employ, serving him in many positions of responsibility. In 1846 he took a prominent part in the Bear Flag Revolt, and became an officer in Frémont's California Battalion. After the serious falling out between Kearny and Frémont which led to the latter's being ordered to Washington and arrested, Hensley journeyed back to the States with Commodore R. F. Stockton's party. He testified in the celebrated court-martial of November, 1847–January, 1848, and then set out for California again, this return trip being the one which figures so large in the history of the Salt Lake Cutoff. After reaching California he tried mining for a while, opened a store in Sacramento, and eventually became president of the California Steam Navigation Company. He lived for many years at San Jose, but died at Warm Springs, Alameda County, on January 7, 1866. Bancroft says of Hensley that his record was that "of an honest and successful man of business, of strong will and well-balanced mind, generous, temperate, and brave."[10] We now have to add to his biography the chapter that has so long been wanting.

If Hensley himself left any account of his association with the Salt Lake Cutoff, nothing is known of it. Except for entries in the overland journal of Richard Martin May, the Mormon annals have

---

[9] On July 10, 1951, following the publication of *West from Fort Bridger*, Dale Morgan wrote A. R. Mortensen proposing that the Utah State Historical Society "request an official ruling from the U. S. Board on Geographical Names by which this change in name, or spelling, shall be approved and thereafter used on the map of Utah." See Morgan to Mortensen, Dale L. Morgan Papers, Utah State Historical Society. As of 1994, however, the name Hansel persists.

[10] H. H. Bancroft, *History of California*, III, 781.

preserved what little information we have, at the same time pointing
up the direct relationship between the difficulties of the Hastings
Cutoff and the pioneering of the Salt Lake Road.

The record begins with a letter of August 9, 1848, written by the
Mormon authorities in Great Salt Lake City to Brigham Young, then
enroute to the mountains for the second and last time. Amid many
odds and ends of local news the letter tucked in a stray sentence of
great interest to us now: "Ten of the U. S. Troops under Capt.
Hensley lately arrived in our valley on their way to California; they
tried the Hastings route, but the desert was so miry from heavy rains
that they have returned and gone on by way of Fort Hall."[11]

Casual as it is, this remark omits a great deal that we would like
to know—when Hensley arrived from the States, how far out on the
Salt Desert he got before turning back, when he returned to the
Mormon city, and when he set off for the north—to Fort Hall as he
supposed at the time, but actually to pioneer the new road north of
the lake. The letter was perhaps erroneous in one respect; the men
with him were more probably discharged troops than U. S. soldiers.

On August 17, 1848, overlander Richard Martin May met Hensley at Goose Creek and noted "that there was good mountaineers &
energetic men in that Little band." May's description of these adventures is the closest we can come to Hensley's own story.

> Major Hensley who Left us at independence rock with
> the Mule Train overtook us to day. He intinded to pass to
> Fort Bridger & Thence South of Salt lake intending to follow
> [the Hastings Cutoff] Trail. He passed on without difficulty
> untill he Reached the South western portion of the Lake and
> Traveled Several Miles upon an incrustation of Salt and un-
> fortunately for the Major and his Train (10 in number) There
> fell a heavy rain which So weakened the incrustation that
> they were verry near perishing in the mire. They were under
> the necessity of Cutting Loose the packs to Save the animals.
> in this way they lost their provision or nearly So with part of
> their clothing   They were 48 hours without food or water and
> hard at work most of the time to Save the Property   They
> then retraced their Steps to the Mormon City and there re-

---

[11] Parley P. Pratt, John Taylor, and John Smith to Brigham Young, Great
Salt Lake City, August 9, 1848, quoted in LDS Journal History for this date.

plenished their Larder[12]

Hensley is next heard from ten days later, far down the Humboldt Valley. On August 27, 1848, a company of discharged Mormon Battalion members under the leadership of Samuel Thompson was encamped on the Humboldt. These men had wintered in California, helped build Sutter's historic mill on the South Fork of the American River, and participated in the discovery of gold, and were now enroute to join their brethren in Salt Lake Valley. Henry W. Bigler of the Thompson company brings Hensley back into focus for us:

> Sun [August] 27th   lade by   plenty of good grass   at 3 oclock the camp cum to gether at Br. Pratts waggon and had a prair meeting, just as meeting was over we was met by Capt. S. Hinsley [and] a packing company of 10 men   we got a way bill of our Road from here to salt lake and not [to] go by Ft Hall and save a bout 8 or 10 days travel. we learn from Mr. Hinsley that it is not more than a bout 380 miles to the lake [and] to take a serten cut off which we are sure to find with plenty of wood and water and grass [by] a route that he cum but waggons have never went there before   a good waggon rout   he got defeated in attempting to go Haistings cut off and turned back and found this knew rout of 70 miles saveing a bout 150 or 200 m.

This encounter was fully as important for the history of the new cutoff as the actual exploration of the route, for if Hensley first used the Salt Lake Cutoff as an integral part of the overland trail to California, it was they who converted it into a wagon road. In passing, let us note that this was not the only contribution of these Battalion men to the history of the California Trail. In crossing the Sierra they had pioneered a new road over Carson Pass and down the Carson River, from that time to the present one of the highroads into California and more traveled by the Forty-Niners than the famous Truckee route.

Important as their contribution to the Salt Lake Cutoff was to be, the Battalion boys actually marked out this route in a mood of frustration, for they were advised of a way yet "nearer," and would have taken it had they been able to find it. On the evening of August 29,

---

[12] Devere Helfrich and Trudy Ackerman, eds., *The Schreek of Wagons: A Sketch of a Migrating Family to Callifornia by Richard Martin May* (Hopkinton, Mass., 1993), 86.

two days after the encounter with Hensley, they fell in with a company of 48 wagons that had come by way of Fort Hall, guided by those inveterate overland travelers, Joseph C. Chiles and Joseph Reddeford Walker. As Bigler tells the tale, "a party of imegrants has roled in sight and will camp about a mile a bove us on the River We[dnesday] 30th   Met the emegrants   Bought some Baken and Buffalow meet and got a way bill of Capt. Childs still nearer a Rout than Hinsleys."[13]

Eager to reach their families in Salt Lake Valley at the earliest possible moment, the Battalion boys decided to take the Chiles road. This route is not described in any of the journals, but it seems obvious that the "waybill" Chiles provided was designed to take them over the Bidwell route of 1841. It also seems obvious that the waybill was insufficiently clear in describing the proper place to diverge from the Fort Hall Road, for on September 5, while encamped not far from the mouth of Secret Creek, where Clyman had left and Bryant had regained the Fort Hall Road, Bigler wrote in his diary:

> Tu. 5 cool and frosty   at 8 we le[f]t camp [and] went a bout 2 m[iles] and found that 1 horse & a mule was missing it was thought best to camp here and hunt for the horse and mule and send 4 men a head to ascertain if possible whare we are to leave this road to go Childses cut off and meet us day after-to-morrow. in the evening the Boys Returned with the mule and horse, the mule was shot through the thigh by the indians. Lieutenant Thompson lost a horse [that] eat something that gave him the scours so badly that he was left this morning
>
> Wed. 6th at 8 we was on the march   had a good road but little dust   went 20 miles and found a note left by the 4 men for us to camp here. good grass and water some sage hens was kild
>
> Thur 7th at 8 we was on the march   went a bout 2 miles and entered a canion which is a bout 3 or 4 m through and the Road in places bad in this canion   we crost the creek ten

---

[13] The Mormons first encountered the Chiles party on August 29, and apparently did some trading with them on the following morning. Azariah Smith noted on August 29, "this evening another train of wagons came in sight over the hills." Ephraim Green recorded the next day, "Last night thare was a company of emgrants came in of thirty six waggons   the captain of the company was mr waker   we had to in quire about the rout and give directions about ours."

times verry bad fording   past through a bout 2 or 3 miles and
met our 4 men and encampted here, at the head of Marys
River whare it cums out of the ground [as] cool good water
in a fiew rods it becume quite a running stream 3 or 4 yards
wide and deep   here we caught some fine trout. beautiful
country here surrounded with low mountains   plenty of grass
in the valley   today we come ten miles   in the evening we
had a report from the 4 men and a councel [was] held [to
decide] what to do   they Reported that acording to Mr.
Childs map this must be the place to turn off but they had
been 10 miles a head   2 of them got sick and they turned
back without finding water   it was voted [that] we not give it
up that we start out 5 men in the morning with plenty of
water to hunt a camping place and the camp Roll out as far
as the top of the mountain which is a bout 6 miles whare
thare is several springs and thare wait until they could se[e] a
signal which the pilots was to make by making a smoke

Bigler's journal does not specifically describe the terrain, but
compare Azariah Smith:

> Wednesday Sept the [6th.] Today we travailed eighteen
> miles, when we came to the head of [the] Canion, where the
> Pilots left a paper for us to stop and encamp.
> Thursday Sept the 7th. Today we travailed through the
> canion about twelve miles, when we encamped. The Pilots
> are here, and say that they did not see any place, that they
> thought a prop[er] place for turning across for Bear River.
> Friday Sept the 8th. Last night at a me[e]ting, to decide
> which way to go, there was some disputeing, but finally we
> concluded to take Mr. Childs,es cut o[ff]   Accordingly today
> we went up on the hill, about eight miles, [sending] the Pilots
> ahead to find water, and if they found water they [were] to
> raise a smoke, for us to come to[o] and just at night s[ome] of
> them came back not finding any water, but Brother S[ly] and
> Diamond went another way, and have not got back.

To interpret: On September 5 the four scouts went on up Bishops
Creek through Emigration Canyon, the gorge by which it passes
through the Snake Mountains. The main company followed next day,
encamping that night 10 miles below the head of Bishops Creek. On
September 7 they went on to the springs where the road left the creek

to cross over into Thousand Springs Valley, and learned that their scouts, casting about widely from this point, had found neither Chiles' cutoff nor any promise of a good route by which to strike off in the direction of Great Salt Lake. There would have been no wagon trace to mark the Bidwell route of 1841, even had they not come too far east in search of it, and it is not surprising that the "Chiles Cutoff" totally defeated them.[14] Returning at last to the Fort Hall Road, they resigned themselves to the necessity of following it to where Hensley's Cutoff began. Since the place of junction was at City of Rocks, Bigler was well within the facts in saying that "from the chart" it should be easy to find the turn-off.

On September 10 the Battalion boys (with whom traveled one non-Mormon, James Diamond) crossed the Humboldt divide into Thousand Springs Valley, and on September 12 reached Goose Creek. For two days they followed the Fort Hall Road down this stream, and then left the creek, still following the traveled road, to strike over to City of Rocks. For the better understanding of their route and experiences, we will print the whole available record of their travels, from the day they left Goose Creek to the day of their arrival in Great Salt Lake City.

(In planning the revision of *West from Fort Bridger*, Dale Morgan hoped to replace the version of Henry Bigler's journal he had taken from the *Utah Historical Quarterly* with the text of Bigler's daybook copied by Jessie E. Empey of the WPA Federal Writers' Project Utah Historical Records Survey. So this chapter now includes both Bigler's daybook [noted as *"Bigler WPA"*] and the *Utah Historical Quarterly* version of his revised journal [noted as *"Bigler UHQ"*] published in the original edition.[15] Extracts from the Ephraim Green, Addison Pratt, and Azariah Smith journals have been taken from the previously cited published editions, with the kind permission of editors Will Bagley, S. George Ellsworth, and David L. Bigler and of the University of Utah Press. The diaries of Jonathan Holmes and Samuel Rogers are available at the LDS Archives.)

---

[14] So singular is this affair of the "Chiles Cutoff" that I may be permitted a speculation. In 1841 the Bidwell party, before bending its course south down the east base of the Pilot Range, had sent two scouts, John Bartleson and Charles Hopper, to look out a westerly route to the Humboldt. These scouts reported adversely, and the more southerly route was then adopted. Is it possible that Chiles' recommendations for a cutoff reflected the abortive reconnaissance of 1841?

[15] For discussions of the many variants of Bigler's journal, see Erwin G. Gudde, *Bigler's Chronicle of the West* (Berkeley, 1962), 1–7, and Kenneth N.

JOURNALS OF THE SALT LAKE CUTOFF 1848

Thursday, September 14. [*Bigler WPA:*]—Clear while at Breakfast an indian cam in camp having a mule he wished to swap for a horse one of the men Mr. [James S.] Brown give him a trade. it is said by some emegrants if a person loses a horse [that] strays a way from the camp and if the indians find it they will fetch it to camp for the owner at 8 we was on the march continued down the creek 6 miles and the road lead in to the mountain Climb the mountain nearly to the top and campt a good spring on Running Branch food good but not plenty wood plenty made today 12 miles this last end of the Road steep after dark our gides Returned with the news that they had found the cut off about 8 miles further on this old road.

[*Bigler UHQ:*]—While at breakfast this morning an Indian came in with a mule to swap for a horse, no doubt but the mule was a stolen one from some emegrant. Mr. Brown gave the indian a trade made 12 m. & campt in the mountain[16] At dusk our pilots that had went a head in the morning returned and reported they had found Capt. Henslys Cutoff about 8 m. [a]head.

[*Green:*]—today I went ahed in company with sidney willes and captain [Samuel] thompson we had a verry hard days ride we roa[d] about fifty milds to the casier we went back to the camp rather late we traveld 14 milds today and campt at a beautiful spring and very good grass

[*Holmes:*]—Made another move traveled 15 miles & Campt

[*Pratt:*]—About noon we left the creek and ascended some of the worst hills between the Sierra Nevada and Salt Lake, and camped in the mountains near some cold springs.

[*Rogers:*]—We traveled 8 miles down the stream when we left it and traveled 7 miles over a verry rough road. camped after sun set.

Owens, "The Mormon-Carson Emigrant Trail in Western History," *Montana,* XLII (Winter, 1992), 26–27.

[16] Leaving Goose Creek at the point where that stream bends sharply north toward the Snake, the Fort Hall Road ascended a nearly dry run locally called Birch Creek and then climbed up the Goose Creek-Raft River divide over what is now called Granite Mountain. The night's camp was probably at the spring in Granite Pass now called Granite Spring. When I first went over this ground with Charles Kelly in 1936, a mining company kept the old road open, but by 1945 it had become substantially if not wholly impassable for travel by automobile, with road and bridges both washed out.

[*Smith:*]—This morning the Pilots went ahead to find the Cut off; and we travailed seven miles down the Creek, and then left it and travailed three miles, when we came to a Spring, where we were to stop, til the Pilots came; and we stop[p]ed there two or three hours, when Brother Thompson came, and said that there was a place about four miles ahead that would do the camp. So we hitched up and started, but haveing some very bad hills to come up, we did not get encamped till just dark. Brother [James C.] Sly came after a little haveing found the turn off place.

Friday, September 15. [*Bigler WPA:*]—set of[f] this morning in good spirits   every person was in a fine humor   we left the old road a bout 8 miles from camp, in a chain of low mountains near 2 high Rocks on our left which Brother Pratt named the Twinsisters   from this place our course is east through sage Bruch and over some stone Granite   at 3 we campt on Casier Creek   made today 13 miles plenty of wood and water   poor grass

[*Bigler UHQ:*]—Set off this morning in good spirits   everyone seemed to feel fine and after makeing a bout 8 m. we came into a chain of low mountains and nearby on our left was 2 towering rocks near each other which Mr. A. Pratt named the "Twin Sisters," since known by travelers as the "City of Rocks,"[17] as there are several masses piled up all around in the same neighborhood   here we left the fort hall road on our left[18] takeing a course directly east through sage brush and over rocks and boulders and campted on Cashier Creek[19] makeing today about 13 miles.

---

[17] Bigler's manuscript at the Bancroft Library is not the original diary but a copy of it he made for H. H. Bancroft. Here and in a few other places later interpolations in the original record will be observed.

[18] The Salt Lake Cutoff left the Fort Hall Road about a mile south of where the road emerged from the southern gate of the "City of Rocks." Irene D. Paden, *The Wake of the Prairie Schooner*, 307, 375, has asserted that the place of separation—or junction—was in Junction Valley, but in this she is mistaken. Junction Valley lies west of the fork in the trail, separated from it by a gentle divide. The name of this valley may have arisen from roads built many years later to connect with the Central Pacific at Lucin.

Between Junction Valley and the southern gate of City of Rocks much of the California Trail has been washed out, though it can still be identified. Automobiles can parallel the old trail by a road that runs about a mile north of it but now and then touches and runs concurrent with the trail.

[19] This name for the Raft River, and its several dozen variants, derives from the French *cajeux*, long ago applied by French peasants to small rafts. Clearly, it is a translation of the name of Raft River, applied during the era of the North West Company in the Snake Country, 1818–1821. See Dale L. Morgan, ed., *The*

[*Green:*]—we started very erly to day we traveld ten milds on the old road we then struck off of the old road and traveld fore milds and struck the cosery we traveld about 16 milds to day to night I am on gard again

[*Holmes:*]—Started this morning [and] traveled 8 miles on the old road & then turned for Hensleys Cut off traveled 8 miles on it & come of Casey Crick

[*Pratt:*]—We left Fort Hall road, at the Rock Gemini, and made a waggon road from here to Salt Lake. That night we camped on the headwater of Cassier Creek. This also discharges its waters into some of the larger tributaries of the Columbia.

[*Rogers:*]—We traveled 8 miles on the road We then left it striking for Bear river the same way that Mr. Haisten [Hensley] came from Salt Lake City we traveled 6 miles since we left the road.

[*Smith:*]—Today we travailed seven miles, then left the old road, and travailed two miles further and camped on the Cajvese (Casver,) a french name.[20]

Saturday, September 16. [*Bigler WPA:*]—Continued down Casier ten miles and encampted wood and water good and plenty, grass only midlin, we was met on the Road by a party of indians 11 on horse back, Snakes, or in their own tunge, Shoshoneys, had a good road.

[*Bigler UHQ:*]—Continued down this stream ten miles and Campt.[21] We were met by 11 indians of the Snake nation on horse

---

Overland Diary of James A. Pritchard (Denver, 1959), 161–62. In 1832, Nathaniel Wyeth employed two of the many variant spellings, "Casu" and "Ocassia." By modern usage the name Cassia is still locally pronounced *cashu* and is restricted to an affluent of the Raft River that rises in the City of Rocks and flows into the Raft a little south of Malta, Idaho.

[20] Bigler's estimate of the day's travel was closest. It was about 8 miles from their previous night's camp to the fork in the trail, and another 5 miles straight east brought them to the Raft River, here flowing about N. N. E. For this and each succeeding day's journey to September 21, compare the illuminating *Atlas Sheet No. 41A*, published by the Wheeler Survey in 1880. The *Oakley* and *Grouse Creek* quadrangles depict this country, and the *Sawtooth National Forest* map is helpful.

[21] Bigler's language is not to be taken literally; the road did not keep to the actual bank of the Raft. The river makes a wide bend to the north only to be forced south again by an obstructing ridge. The pass around the south end of that ridge is also the pass around the north end of a spur of the Raft River Mountains, and constitutes the "notch in the mountains" to which Azariah Smith's account refers. The road, from the first crossing of the Raft, took a slightly north of east course for this notch, the Raft River Narrows, in the passage of which it had to

back.

[*Green:*]—we traveld to day 10 milds   crost the river three tims
hear we leav the river

[*Holmes:*]—Moved again   traveled 12 miles down Casey to the
turning off place & Campt. road good land good Grass & water
plenty.

[*Pratt:*]—We traveled down and camped again on the Casier.
Here the stream was large and afforded plenty of trout.

[*Rogers:*]—We traveled 10 miles   crost a stream on the way
camped on its bank.

[*Smith:*]—We travailed ten miles in an easterly direction, and encamped again on the Cajvese, in a notch in the mountains. We saw
several Indians on horseback.

Sunday, September 17. [*Bigler WPA:*]—traveled 11 miles and
encampt on the side of the mountain to our right on a small creek or
branch which is nearly dry   plenty of wood   food good but not
plenty for our camp, this morning we left Casier at our camp   it soon
turns and runs to the north   the road was good except sum gravel
and sage   the country is poor [with] no timber but willow and Cedar
on the Mountains   last night the gard lost Brother Greens watch case
and was not found.

[*Bigler UHQ:*]—Last night one of the guard lost a silver case from
off a valuable Silver watch belonging to Mr. E. Green   how that was
done the guard could not tell and remains to this day a mystery! At
this camp we left the Cashier it turning and running north while our
course was east over and through sage brush for ten or 12 m. and
campt on the side of a mountain where there was plenty of Cedar
timber.[22]

[*Green:*]—traveld 12 milds to day and campt at a beautiful spring
at the foot of the mountain

[*Holmes:*]—Moved again traveled 10 miles & found water & Grass
& Campt.

[*Pratt:*]—We left this stream and followed a packtrail that led
through an ascending valley and camped towards evening on a

---

cross the river twice. Many journals of later travelers describe these crossings as
difficult, because of the steep banks.

[22] Addison Pratt's account is much the best for this day's travel, making it
certain that the night encampment was on present Clear Creek (the "Rock
Creek" and "Stony Creek" of later diarists), a little south of Naf, Idaho. From
the site of Strevell, the Salt Lake Cutoff closely parallels US 30S, but lies from 1
to 3 miles south of the highway most of the way to Snowville.

mountain stream that ran down and sank near where we stopped. But I could see by the course of the dry bed of it below us, that in winter or spring it communicated with Cassia, and of course I concluded there must be trout in it higher up where there was a running stream. After our camping affairs were arranged, I took my rifle, and steered off towards the head of the stream and soon obtained a goodly string and returned to camp with my fish, to the astonishment of all hands, and they gave it as a general opinion, that I could catch a mess of trout, if I could only find rainwater standing in a cow track.

[*Rogers*:]—We crost the stream, traveled 10 miles, camped some bearch gro here.

[*Smith*:]—We travailed ten miles farther, in an easterly direction, and encamped by a Spring, at the point of a Mountain.

Monday, September 18. [*Bigler WPA*:] Monday evening we campt on evening we encampted on the same side of the Mountain we campted on a Sunday night.[23]

[*Green*:]—we traveld to day about 10 milds and campt at a beautiful spring at the foot of the mountain and a plenty of grass hear we saw salt lake for the first time at a distance of about twenty milds thare was a plenty of seders hear

[*Holmes*:]—Started this morning traveled 10 miles & Campt

[*Pratt*:]—We continued on a circuitous route the next day and camped at night on a mountain side at a spring in sight of Salt Lake, but on the opposite side from the city.

[*Rogers*:]—We traveled 10 miles, camped on the side of a mountain we are now with in site of Salt Lake. This morning we left the waters of the Columbia.

[*Smith*:]—Today we travailed eleven miles through a pass of the Mountains, and encamped on the side of a Mountain, in sight of Salt Lake.

Tuesday, September 19. [*Bigler WPA*:]—went 20 miles a cross a sage plain and campt on deep creek plenty of grass and water from

---

[23] This entry was actually made on September 23, when Bigler noted, "I have made a mistake a bout last Mondays travel." The error persisted in later versions of his journal; here his entries have been placed under their proper date.

This day's travel was along the base of the Raft River Mountains, the night camp being made at Emigrant Spring, which breaks out at the eastern-most extremity of these mountains. Several other springs break out along the line of travel, including Cedar Springs, which furnished water for the Cedar Creek Ranch, 4 miles southeast of Strevell. Emigrant Spring lies 2 miles south of Cedar Springs.

our camp this morning we could see a lake a bout 20 or 30 miles off supposed by the most of the camp to be salt lake   at this camp I think gold could be found. 11 indians has cum in camp on horse back to trade and will camp with us.

[*Bigler UHQ*:]—This morning we could see as we supposed Salt Lake off to the South east of our camp some 20 or 30 miles—To day we made some 20 miles east and campt on Deep Creek. Here a lot of natives came in on horse back to trade and will camp with us.[24]

[*Green*:]—we traveld today 16 milds and campt on the creek that is cald deep crick in a beautiful valley   thare is plenty of grass and water hear to nig[ht] I am on gard to night

[*Holmes*:]—Moved again traveled 16 miles & Come to deep Creek & Campt

[*Pratt*:]—We descended the mountain at a regular slope and crossed a large dry sage plain, in the center of it we found a large cold spring, about noon.[25] At night we camped on Deep Creek. All the streams we crossed from here to the city discharged their waters

---

[24] Between the eastern end of the Raft River Mountains and Snowville, US 30S runs an east and west course, parallel with the Utah-Idaho line, across the wide sage plain of lower Curlew Valley. The immigrant road of 1848 and later years, considered from the point of view of one going east, runs slightly north of east between Emigrant Spring and the Sink of Deep Creek, nearly parallel to the modern highway, but about 2 miles south of it.

The area once called "the Sink of Deep Creek" is now the Rose Ranch.

[25] Pilot Springs, now Pilot Reservoir, 5 3/4 miles east of Emigrant Spring, and directly on the line of travel between that point and the Sink of Deep Creek. From this circumstance, doubtless, its name originated. Joseph Cain and Arieh C. Brower, in their *Mormon way-bill, to the gold mines*, 6, speak of "the Pilot springs," as "2 lone springs in a desert place." They are sometimes referred to in overland journals as "Double Springs."

Soon after the Salt Lake Cutoff came into use, a subsidiary cutoff was employed between Pilot Springs and Clear Creek. It was thus described by Cain and Brower in 1851: "From Pilot springs to Stony creek,—about 4 miles from the springs bear to the right; the main road leads to some springs [Emigrant Spring] on the mountain side, which is about 6 miles further; you will intersect the main road about three miles from where you leave it, have a better road, and a much shorter one." The alternative roads are mentioned in many of the diaries by this route, and are also depicted on the Wheeler Survey's *Atlas Sheet No. 41A*. The longer road around by way of Emigrant Spring provided grass and other camping facilities, which was not the case with the cutoff to the north. Cain and Brower's estimate of distances here is misleading, the fork in the trail being about a mile and a half west of Pilot Springs, and the whole distance to Emigrant Spring less than 6 miles. The cutoff came back into the main trail 6 1/2 miles east of Clear Creek and was generally thought to save between 2 and 3 miles' travel.

into Salt Lake.

[*Rogers*:]—We traveled 18 miles, during the time we past a spring in the valey and crost Deep creek camped. a number of Indians came in to camp they stayed all night.

[*Smith*:]—Today we travailed fifteen miles across a plain and en-camped on deep Creek, having been named that by Mr. Hensly as where he crossed it, it was so deep that he had to make a bridge.[26]

Wednesday, September 20. [*Bigler WPA*:]—traveled 18 miles and encampt [with] plenty of grass & water   good road except a fiew sage brush in the way.

[*Bigler UHQ*:]—made a bout 18 or 20 m.

[*Green*:]—we have traveld east and south east to day too a spring in the mountains whare we campt for the night after a march of about 13 milds   we campt at a beautiful spring and good grass [with] aplenty of seeder wood

[*Holmes*:]—Started this morning traveled 14 miles & found water & a Butiful Camping Ground & Campt.

[*Pratt*:]—We continued our route over hills · and vallies and camped at a cold spring that is in a deep valley between two high mountains,[27] and notwithstanding the spring affords a large stream, it sinks in the valley not more than a quarter of a mile from its source. Here we lost an old cow that had been much trouble to us to drive on account of her being a slow traveler. What become of her, we could never find out. We hunted near a half day for her.

[*Rogers*:]—We traveled 14 miles. camped at a spring between two mountains.

[*Smith*:]—Today we travailed five miles up the creek,[28] and then left it, and travailed ten miles further and encamped by a Spring in

---

[26] Although this entry explains the origin of the name of Deep Creek, it is certainly extraordinary to find a party unencumbered with wagons reduced to bridging a desert creek. Materials for making a bridge would have been hard to find, sagebrush not being well adapted to the purpose.

[27] Hansel Spring Valley, lying between the Hansel Mountains and the North Promontory Range. The immigrant road closely hugged the southern base of the pass through the Hansel Mountains, whereas I-84 swings over its open expanse perhaps a quarter of a mile farther north. Hansel Spring is not seen from the present highway.

[28] Since the Cutoff proceeded along the north bank of Deep Creek about 6 miles, this entry might indicate that the previous night's camp was about a mile above the Sink. The creek was crossed at its great bend, roughly 2 miles south-west of present Snowville. In ascending Deep Creek, the immigrant road still kept from a mile to 2 miles south of the line of I-84.

the Mountains.

Thursday, September 21. [*Bigler WPA:*]—Lost one cow last night, traveled 13 miles and encampted by a spring   the water Brackish   poor food

[*Bigler UHQ:*]—Lost a cow last night what became of her we could not tell—made a bout 12 m. and campt by a spring of brackish water and poor feed.[29]

[*Green:*]—Thursday, the 21   today this morning we started again the same as usal   traveld over the hills to a spring whare we campt for the night   we traveld 12 milds to day and campt for the night

[*Holmes:*]—Made another Start this morning traveled 12 miles & come to water & Campt.

[*Pratt:*]—We continued our route over an uneven country well grassed and but little sage brush. We camped at night in a valley where there were a number of warm springs, they came out and formed a large stream. The water has a brackish sulphery taste and smell, and was the only bad water we camped on between the sink of Mary's River and Salt Lake.

[*Rogers:*]—We traveled 12 miles, camped. the water is brackish since we camped. we seteled the Canon Accounts. we paid 192 Dollars for the work of Browett,[30] which makes the whole cost 512 Dollars. I paid J[acob]. M[ica] Truman two Dollars and fifty cents for

---

[29] Blue Springs, located at the northwest corner of a prominent, isolated mountain standing in the floor of Blue Creek Valley, and situated about $2^{1}/_{2}$ miles south of the old Blue Creek post office. Now dammed, in the 1940s the main spring was circular in shape, 10 or 12 feet in diameter, and gave forth a good-sized stream. Although not of first quality, the water was sufficiently good that nearby farmers trucked it away by the barrelful. Most diarists speak of Blue Springs as providing the worst water along the line of the Salt Lake Cutoff. The quality of the various springs seems not to have been constant, for Hansel Spring and Pilot Springs were sometimes reported as brackish or sulfur-tainted.

It would appear from the *Mormon way-bill* that westbound travelers had some small choice of routes in traveling the stretch between Blue Springs and Hansel Spring. The authors advise, "From Blue springs to Hensell's spring take the right hand road from the Blue springs." I have not settled the facts about these alternative roads to my entire satisfaction, but I would hazard the suggestion that the right-hand road proceeded, like the present gravel road, north up Blue Creek Valley to the vicinity of present I-84, and then turned west, while the left-hand road may have cut across the hypotenuse of the triangle thus formed, rejoining the other road somewhere below the pass by which the North Promontory Range was crossed.

[30] Daniel Browett was killed at Tragedy Springs in the Sierra Nevada while scouting the road the company opened across Carson Pass.

breaking my horse.

Friday, September 22. [*Bigler WPA*:]—Rained some traveled 18 and campt on Mudy Creek plenty of fish here the boys catch them fast good road nice country we are now in sight of Bare River all hands is merry and full of talk and sing we have the promise of a good song to morrow night composed by Br. Denit.

[*Bigler UHQ*:]—Rained in the night made to day a bout 18 m. and campt on the "Melad"[31] here the boys Ketchd fish allmost as fast as they threw their hooks in We are now in Sight of Beare River and the whole camp is all life talking and Singing and to morrow night the camp has the promise of a new Song to be composed for the occasion by Mr. Daniel Denit

[*Green*:]—we traveld too day 20 milds and campt on moody creek this was averry dark and rany night and no wood of any acount I am ongard to night

---

[31] For the route east of Blue Springs, see the Wheeler Survey's *Atlas Sheet No. 41B*, the *Cache National Forest* map, and the *Tremonton* quadrangle as the best available maps. In crossing the Blue Spring Hills over Rattlesnake Pass, the road of 1848 was substantially that of Interstate 84, though the present highway, in descending toward Tremonton, takes a more direct course than the winding road which preceded the modern graded highways. Just at the mouth of the canyon, a warm spring breaks out, sometimes called "Mountain Spring," or "Blind Spring," not mentioned by the diarists of 1848. Its waters were potable if not very palatable, and occasionally were used by later travelers. From the vicinity of Tremonton, practically all traces of the original Salt Lake Cutoff have been plowed under, and modern roads east and south of that point follow section lines. The road of 1848 and later seems to have continued southeast after leaving the mountains, bypassing the site of Tremonton a little to the south and west, to strike the Malad River about 3 miles farther down. The township surveys of 1856 show that the Malad was bridged in Section 26, T. 11 N., R. 3 W., and it is a fair presumption that the road during the eight years preceding reached the stream near this point. The January 16, 1856, *Deseret News* reported the Legislative Assembly placed control of the Malad bridge under Brigham and Joseph Young for "the next three years."

On reaching the west bank of the Malad, the Battalion company crossed the first wagon tracks they had met with since leaving City of Rocks, though it would doubtless have required prolonged search to find any trace of them. The Bidwell party of 1841, on emerging from Cache Valley, after much trouble had succeeded in crossing the Malad at Rocky Ford above present Plymouth and had then descended the west bank of this stream to below the site of Corinne. Two years later, while Fremont was southbound with his howitzer enroute to Great Salt Lake, he came down the eastern bank of the Malad but eventually crossed to the west bank just above the point where the Malad flowed into the Bear. The trace of the carriage which bore the howitzer of course would have been far more obscure than that left by the nine wagons of the Bidwell company.

[*Holmes:*]—Started this morning traveled 20 miles & Come to Muddy Crick & Campt. had some rain.

[*Pratt:*]—We came in sight of Salt Lake again, and a smart day's travel brought us to [Malad] Creek, this was the worst creek to cross of any we found on the road, on account of its banks being muddy and the water near up to the waggon beds. Ours got over safe, but some others filled with water or capsized. We found an abundance of fish in it called chubs. The circumstances that gave the creek that name are these. Some years ago some Canadian French camped on it, to catch beaver of which there was an abundance at that time, and their general food is willow, but as there is none of that on that stream, the beavers lived on the roots of a vegitable called wild parsnips or meadow fennel, and it possesses some poisonous qualities, but it does not affect the beaver. But when the hunters ate of their flesh it made them all sick and they gave the creek that name.[32]

[*Rogers:*]—We traveled 23 miles. camped on the bank of mud creek. the day has been cloudy and rainey.

[*Smith:*]—Yesterday we travailed fourteen miles and encamped on the head of a Stream of poor water. Today we travailed twenty three miles, and encamped on a small Stream about a mile from Bear river, where we caught plenty of fish.

Saturday, September 23. [*Bigler WPA:*]—traveled about 7 miles and encampted on the east side of Bare River   the crossing of mudy creek was bad   broke one waggin crossing   the crossing of Bare River was good   after we had campt we had a fine shower of rain and a bout dusk it becum clear, every man brought in his tithing of wood for a good fire to hear the new song after prairs   we had a number of good songs sung and we had quite a good time in passing off the evening. we are with in 40 miles of Capt. Browns, and a bout 70 miles from the city

---

[32] It would be interesting to know where Addison Pratt derived his information about the Malad, which faithfully reflects the lore of the mountain men, except for the mention of "Canadian French." Warren A. Ferris, in giving an account in 1830 of the Malad (present Big Wood) River of central Idaho and the unfortunate experience of trappers who fed upon the beaver frequenting its waters, added, "There is a small stream flowing into the Big Lake, the beaver taken from which, produce the same effect. It is the universal belief among hunters, that the beaver in these two streams feed upon some root or plant peculiar to the locality, which gives their flesh the strange quality of causing such indisposition. This is the only mode in which I ever heard the phenomena attempted to be explained, and it is more probably correct." Paul C. Phillips, ed., *Life in the Rocky Mountains* (Denver, 1940), 66–67.

[*Bigler UHQ:*]—This morning in crossing the Melad we broke down a wagon   the crossing was very bad the stream was narrow and not very deep but the bottom very soft and muddy   in comeing out on the opposite side passing on for 6 or 7 miles we came to Bear River the fording of which was good[33]   in consequence of breaking down we made but a short drive and campt on the east side of bear river— just as we went into Camp a shower of rain was upon us but it soon held up when almost every man brought in an armful of wood to have one common fire around which we were to have some singing, after Supper and prayrs the Camp just enjoyed themselves Singing Songs, telling "yarns," Cracking jokes on each other &c &c.

[*Green:*]—we crost the c[r]ick and the river and traveld 6 milds and campt at a spring   thare was plenty of feed and water and wood

[*Holmes:*]—We crossed the Crick this morning & went on to Bare River. it is a fine river [and] a good ford. traveled 6 miles & come to water & Campt. past through a fine country. Some rain. Soil Good grass good.

[*Pratt:*]—This is but three miles from Bear River, the largest stream between Sutter's Fort and Salt Lake City. The next day we cross'd it, and found the water at a low stage and the crossing good. The bed of the river is about fifty yards wide, and the banks high, and in the spring of the year it is a formidable stream, and a verry strong current.

After crossing we traveled six miles down the river and camped at some springs, here we found the grass green and fresh, and the cattle ate till it seemed as if they would burst, we saw no green grass after we left Truckee and notwithstanding the grass is dry and yellow, there is no rain during the summer season and it is full of nutrement, and our cattle kept fat. We had a snow storm about the first of September near the head of Mary's River and frosty nights. But while here we had a fine shower, and from the appearance of the grass it is a common thing here all summer long, and Bear River Valley is a beautiful one, and verry wide and affords an immense quantity of grass.

We now began to feel as if we were nearing home fast. Some Indians came to us here and appeared verry friendly. (I should have mentioned while at Deep Creek some fifteen or twenty of them came

---

[33] The Bear was probably forded a little below present Honeyville; it is likely the company proceeded diagonally southeast across the approximately 3-mile-wide tongue of land between the two rivers.

to us and camped with us over night and sold us some buckskins, &c.)

[*Rogers*:]—We dug down the bank of the creek, forded it pased on to Bear river, forded the same, past on 4 miles making 5 miles in all. I paid 150 Dollars to be given to the widow Browett [wife of the scout killed at Tragedy Springs]. we had a shower.

[*Smith*:]—We crossed the stream which was very bad, and one wagon got broke, but we fixed it up and travailed about four miles and encamped. There are old wagon tracks here that lead to Salt Lake Settlements.[34]

Sunday, September 24. [*Bigler WPA*:]—traveled 18 miles   good road   some of our calves is getting verry tired traveling

[*Bigler UHQ*:]—made only a few miles owing to many of our Calves being so tender footed.[35]

[*Green*:]—we traveld 18 milds to day and campt

[*Holmes*:]—Started again traveled 18 miles & Campt   a fine valey Sunday. [*End of journal.*]

[*Pratt*:]—We left here and pass'd down the valley leaving a high range of mountains on our left and Bear River and Salt Lake on our right, cross'd a rappid and clear stream of cold water called I believe Cottonwood Creek and camped at some of those deep wells.[36] Some of our cattle fell in them, but we got them out without harm.

[*Rogers*:]—We traveled 18 miles, camped. we past a warm spring.

[*Smith*:]—We travailed eighteen miles down Bear Vally.

Monday, September 25. [*Bigler WPA*:]—Traveled 15 m and encampted on Ogdens creek near Capt. Browns   some bad road   broke 3 waggons today.

[*Bigler UHQ*:]—We reached Ogden City.[37] Here lives Captain

---

[34] These wagon tracks, made by Hazen Kimball and company, would have been better described as leading "from" the Great Salt Lake settlements.

[35] Bigler's transcription error for this date has led to much confusion, but Bigler's daybook and the other journals confirm that the party traveled 18 miles.

[36] Pratt's stream was Box Elder Creek, and the night's encampment was at present Brigham City.

[37] The name "Ogden City," which Bigler applies to Brown's establishment, is one of his interpolations, as the name did not come into use until a year later. As Pratt observes, this had been Miles Goodyear's post, the imminent founding of which James Frazier Reed had recorded two years before (see the Reed journal, note 6). Their hard experience with "old settlers" in Missouri and Illinois had given the Mormons a strong desire to be the "old settlers" of this new country, and from the beginning they were anxious to buy Goodyear out. The necessity had become the more obvious in the light of their experience with Hazen

James Brown and a few of the Saints, who bid us welcome, and let us have all the melons and young corn we wanted, which to us was a treat.

[*Green*:]—we travled to day 18 milds and campt at Capatin Browns ranch yesterday we traveld by several hot springs and several today this is a beautiful vally

[*Pratt*:]—A smart day's drive from here brought us acrost Ogden's Creek. This and Weber's Creek form a junction just before they fall into Salt Lake, and in their fork is situated Gudger's [Goodyear's] Fort, and is 40 miles from Salt Lake City. This situation was bought by James Brown, Esqr., after his return from the [Mexican] war as he was one of the captains in the Mormon Battalion. He also bought cattle, goats and hogs with it and was now keeping a dairy. We bought cheese of them at twenty cents per pound. Ten cents per pound was the price before we came along, but they supposed that we had been drawn through the gold mines with our hides greased and that a perfect shell of gold had grown over us about two inches thick, and for us to pay a double price for a thing was only relieving us of our burthens. Captain Brown was gone to Salt Lake City, himself, but had a large family living there at the fort. We staid here one day and recruited our teams as we had drove hard for sevral days before.

[*Rogers*:]—We traveled 16 miles on the way we past a warm spring. we past some houses, camped one half mile from Captain [James] Brown's. the Cannon wagon broke down.

[*Smith*:]—We travailed twenty miles and encamped by Captain Browns, and bought some cheese

---

Kimball, for Goodyear's post could become a gathering place for all the dissatisfied spirits of the Mormon community. Early in November, 1847, an effort was made to find funds to buy Goodyear's fort, but without success. The arrival of Captain James Brown from California (by way of the Hastings route) on November 16, 1847, was providential in that he brought with him some $5,000 owing the Sick Detachment of the Mormon Battalion. Goodyear agreed to sell for $1,950 in gold, and the property changed hands on November 25, 1847. The authorities in Salt Lake Valley, in their letter of March 6, 1848, informed Brigham Young of this happy result, and added that "Captain Brown and his family with Bro. Chilton, Mr. [Lewis B.] Myers, Mr. [George] Thurlkill and their families have moved to the Goodyear Place." Brown had been in possession of the premises about nine months when the Battalion company arrived. (This James Brown should not be confused with his nephew, James S. Brown, a witness to the discovery of gold at Sutter's Mill and a member of the Thompson company.)

Tuesday, September 26. [*Bigler WPA:*]—Lade by and mended our waggons and eat Roasen ears [roasting ears of corn] and melons we feel that we are almost home   some is going to stop here   it is said to be only 25 m to the city. the campt is in fine spirits, shaving and washing, dressing and mending waggons   every person buisy and in the best of homor   here I believe some person stole my spir [*End of journal*]

[*Bigler UHQ:*]—We lay by to repair wagons that broke down yesterday. Every body in camp busy washing, shaving, cutting hair, changing clothes, etc. Some of the camp will remain here as they have friends and relatives living here, while the rest of us will proceed to Salt Lake City.

[*Green:*]—we ramind in camp today to mend some waggons & brother homes and brother thompson went to the sitty

[*Pratt:*]—I inquired here after my family but could get no news of their arrival, but several of the brethren that heard of their families being at the city left us here on horseback and tried to pursuade me to go with them, but I told them No!! for I had got so habituated to disappointments during the five years past, that I would not run the hazard, for if I went down there and found they had not arrived, my anticipations would be at an end, but if I staid where I was, I should have the pleasure of hoping that I might find them there when I arrived. So they went away and left me.[38]

[*Rogers:*]—AM we sent back for the Cannon. I gave Bro [Ephraim] Green one Dollar to make up the loss of his watch case. I paid [Richard] Bush $1.43 for Coffee and chease.

[*Smith:*]—Today we bought some mellons, grean cor[n] &c. as we are laying by, for yesterday the cannons was left back about ten miles, and today we sent back and brought them up.[39]

Wednesday, September 27. [*Green:*]—this morning we [s]tarted again the same as usial   past the river and traveld on   to day we

---

[38] Pratt had been separated from his family since June 1843, while serving a mission for his church in the Society Islands. The story, from the point of view of his wife, is told in the "Journal of Louisa Barnes Pratt," *Heart Throbs of the West*, VIII, 189–400. In his own journal Pratt has a rather affecting account of his reunion with his wife and children on reaching Great Salt Lake City, but it is too long for me to quote. Addison Pratt, it is interesting to note, despite his name, was not related to the brothers Parley P. and Orson Pratt who have figured so prominently in these pages.

[39] Two small cannon had been purchased from Sutter before leaving California and were carried the whole way.

traveld 16 milds and campt on hurd creek whare we campt for the night [*End of journal.*]

[*Pratt:*]—Another day's travel from here brought us to Herd Creek. When we were about half way we met a waggon, and a young man was with it by the name of James Park, who told me that my family were at the city, that they had arrived the week before with a large emigration company that came in from Winter Quarters. I asked him if he was sure of it? He said he was, for he was one of the company that were sent back from the city to meet and assist the emigration, and it fell to his lot to drive my family's team for them into the city, and that they were all alive and in good health. At this news my heart was filled with gratitude for his preserving care over us during this our long separation. I now traveled on with some courage, and soon after met Capt. Brown, whom I was glad to see, as he was an old acquaintance. He told me he had seen my family while at the city &c, and after passing some jokes (for which he is celebrated) I passed along and we went into camp at Br. Hates, who was herding cattle in company with some others, at Herd Creek, about twenty miles from Salt Lake forts.[40] He told me he was herding a yoke of oxen that belonged to my wife and we left some of our spare cattle there.

[*Rogers:*]—We left the loose horses and cattle at this place in the care of Truman and Brown to be herded at one cent per head a day we then traveled 18 miles, camped.

[*Smith:*]—We left the most of the Cavia [horse herd] to be herded, and I took my horse, but left my Mule and Ma[re] with the herd. After travailing about eighteen miles we encamped.

Thursday, September 28. [*Bigler UHQ:*]—We arrived in Salt Lake City on Thursday the 28th, early in the afternoon and were received with open arms by friends and dear relatives, and the Saints in general.

[*Rogers:*]—We drove in to the Great Salt Lake City it being 18 miles but I found not my relatives, onley Washington I toock up my lodgin with Sister Mary Smith.

[*Smith:*]—I rode ahead and about two oclo[ck] arrived at Salt Lake City; and after riding about considerable found Father, Mother,

---

[40] Herd Creek is present Farmington Creek, where Hector Haight as an outgrowth of his herding enterprise became one of the first settlers. His "hotel" at "Blooming Grove" is mentioned in many later journals, and was duly advertised in the *Mormon way-bill, to the gold mines.*

Sisters and brother; and they were all w[ell]. They were liveing four miles from the city, on the place where [he] put in his crop, such as Wheat, Corn, Peas, Beans and other gar[den] Sauce, but the crickets ate up or spoiled the most of it. But [he] has saved twelve bushel of Wheat, and has got some corn, Bea[ns], Peas, Mellons &c. growing.

[*Pratt:*]—The next morning after the teams were ready I with some others mounted our horses, and started ahead, Br. Haight accompanying us. As we drew near the forts, we began to meet our friends coming out to meet us. Br. Haight told me he knew the house my family lived in and would conduct me there. We found them in the South Fort, in a house with Sister Rogers, whose husband we had met at the sink of Mary's River, on the road to California. . . . In the evening our wagons arrived. . . .

———————

The route of the Salt Lake Cutoff, which we have followed in such meticulous detail, during later years varied in hardly the smallest particulars from the track left by the wagons of 1848. The only real difference from one year to the next consisted in where the Bear was crossed. Since the crossing varied not only from year to year but from season to season, according to the amount of water flowing in the river, no effort will be made here to distinguish between the ferries and fords of the Bear. It is worth remarking, however, that none of these, before the building of the Pacific Railroad in 1869, carried a road across the Bear below the mouth of the Malad. Although such a crossing might now seem to have been desirable, to avoid the infinitely laborious passage of the narrow but high-banked and miry-bottomed Malad, it was not practicable because of the sloughs and marshes which beset the lower course of the Bear.[41] It was necessary to go up almost as far as present Honeyville, well beyond Box Elder Lake, to reach the Bear on reasonably firm ground. The subsequent ferry at Bear River City marked the extreme lower limit of the

———————

[41] The desirability of a crossing at or below the site of Corinne was recognized in the years of immigrant travel as well as now, for in a letter to the War Department from Benicia, Calif., August 25, 1855, Captain Rufus Ingalls wrote as the fruits of his travel through this area with Steptoe's command during the summer, "The road should cross Bear river *below* the confluence of the Malad. Had we crossed there, more than 20 miles traveling could have been avoided." See the "Report of the Secretary of War" for 1855, in *House Executive Document No. 1*, 34 Congress, 1st session, Vol. I, Part 2 (Serial 841), 162. But what was abstractly desirable was not physically practicable.

immigrant crossings, which otherwise extended all the way up to present Deweyville and for travel directly north into Idaho, higher still.

It is no part of my purpose to detail travel on the Salt Lake Cutoff after 1848, but a little attention should be given to use of the new road by the Forty-Niners, which permanently established it at the expense of the Hastings Cutoff. The first gold-seekers, we are given to understand, led by Captain G. W. Paul, reached Salt Lake Valley on June 16, 1849.[42] Three days later Eliza R. Snow noted in her diary, "People with pack animals arrive from the States going to California. They expect wagons in 2 or 3 days."[43] Next day Alexander Neibaur re-

---

[42] A letter from Brigham Young, Heber C. Kimball, and Willard Richards to Orson Hyde and the church in Pottawattamie County, Iowa, under date of July 20, 1849, relates: "On the 16th of June, the gold diggers began to arrive here on their way to the gold regions of California. . . ." *L. D. S. Millennial Star*, XI (November 15, 1849), 337. This letter does not name Paul, but A. W. Babbitt, who had reached Great Salt Lake Valley on July 1 and who returned east with the mail, on his arrival back in the States wrote a letter to the *St. Louis Union* in which he reported, "When I arrived at the Great Salt Lake, I found I was not ahead of the emigration. I was informed that Capt. Paul's company arrived there on the 16th day of June, with a company of pack mules. . . ." *Ibid.*, XI (December 1, 1849), 366. Captain Paul is readily identified, since the St. Louis *Missouri Republican*, April 12, 1849, describes him as "Lieut. G. W. Paul from St. Louis," also naming the other nine men composing his company. On April 23 the *Republican* mentions Paul's as one of only two companies reported to have left Independence.

A knotty problem, however, is that William G. Johnston, whose diary, *Experiences of a Forty-Niner* (Pittsburgh, 1892), is an eminently responsible record, gives us reason to think that Captain Paul did not go by way of Great Salt Lake City at all. After various earlier mentions of him, Johnston writes at Fort Bridger under date of June 17, 1849, "We learned at the fort that Captain Paul, who is in the lead of all emigrant parties, is but thirty-six hours in advance of us. He did not take the route via Sublette's cut-off, but coming hither by the old and more familiar way, followed from this point the Oregon trail, going northward via Fort Hall" (p. 166). Subsequently, on reaching City of Rocks via Great Salt Lake City on July 2, Johnston notes his surprise in meeting travelers by the Fort Hall road, saying that his party had been flattering themselves "that with the exception of Captain Paul's pack train—and even this a matter of doubt—we were in the lead of all emigrants" (p. 200). Eleven days later, while on the Humboldt, Johnston overtook an ox train that had come by the Sublette Cutoff, members of which told him "that at Fort Hall they were six days ahead of Captain Paul's pack train, and that it was now but one day in advance" (p. 266). It is difficult to imagine that Paul went first to Great Salt Lake City and then to Fort Hall.

[43] LeRoi G. Snow, ed., "Pioneer Diary of Eliza R. Snow," *Improvement Era*, XLVII (April, 1944), 241.

corded, "A company of 35 men from Ohio bound for California arrived in Great Salt Lake City."[44] We have no first-hand accounts by members of any of these pack parties, but it is hardly to be doubted that they used the Salt Lake Cutoff in continuing their journey. The Hastings Cutoff by this time had a thoroughly bad reputation, and although it was used by a few companies late in the summer of 1849, the big news in Salt Lake Valley this summer was that a respectable road, having water and grass at reasonable intervals, had been found north of the lake. Nothing more was needed to start the immigration flowing over the Salt Lake Cutoff.

Perhaps the earliest Forty-Niners to take wagons over the new route were the companies with which William Kelly and William G. Johnston traveled. Kelly's account of his experiences is a mixture of fact and unabashed celebration of William Kelly, and his dates west of Fort Laramie are not as firm as could be desired, but he obviously reached the Mormon city on Friday, June 22. While his party was yet in the mountains east of the city, they fell in with a few Saints who were getting out timber, and these men, Kelly says, furnished him with "an introduction to some relatives of theirs who had just returned from California by the north end of Salt Lake, and would give us all particulars about the mines, and the nature of the new route first discovered by them from Salt Lake valley to that country, which alone was practicable for wagons." Kelly's party remained in Great Salt Lake City over Sunday, June 24, and he goes on to say:

I got every information I believe they [the Mormons] possessed relative to the new route to California; but to make assurance doubly sure, I was anxious to procure a guide who had travelled over the line, and engaged a man, with the consent and approval of my party. However, when it came to the ears of the rulers they forbade his leaving; for I believe they are apprehensive that the golden inducements of that rich country might empty the valley of its population if they came to be particularly disseminated; a reason, too, why they deprecate the traveling of emigrants to their city, which they say (and, I believe, with truth) is two hundred miles of a round.

---

[44] Quoted in LDS Journal History, June 20, 1849. The entries in the Snow and Neibaur journals are the earliest known references in personal diaries to overland arrivals. Perhaps a diary will yet be found with something to say about the company which reached Great Salt Lake City on June 16.

On June 25 Kelly's company resumed their journey north around the lake, their trials and tribulations a tale that loses nothing in the telling, for the impression Kelly was concerned to make was that his party was the first to reach California with wagons, and he gives one to think he was traveling an untrodden wilderness most of the way. However, he names July 3 as the date of his arrival at the junction with the Fort Hall Road, and there is no reason to question the accuracy of this date.[45]

Much more reassuring is William G. Johnston's narrative. His party, numbering 31 persons and five wagons, reached Great Salt Lake City just after sunrise on Saturday, June 23, 1849, having camped the previous night on the bench 4 miles above the city. Notwithstanding Kelly's story, Johnston's party soon arranged with a Mr. Sly—who had traveled the route the previous fall[46]—Sly's father-in-law, and an unnamed young Mormon, to accompany them as guides. Johnston, like Kelly, left Great Salt Lake City on June 25, and he recognizably describes the march north to Bear River, across this stream and the Malad, and on to the junction of the roads at City of Rocks, which point they reached about noon on July 2. Johnston's account stands up well under study, and it is quite possible that his company was first among the Forty-Niners to take wagons west over the Salt Lake Cutoff. He makes no claim to this effect, but up to the time of reaching City of Rocks he seems to have labored under the impression that his party was ahead of all others on the trail.[47]

From June, 1849, the Salt Lake Cutoff could be regarded as permanently established. Although the Hastings Cutoff enjoyed a brief vogue in the summer of 1850, when perhaps five or six hundred immigrants gave it a final trial, the superiority of the Salt Lake Cutoff to the Hastings Cutoff was evident. For a decade it stood as almost the only avenue of travel west from Great Salt Lake City. In 1859 Captain J. H. Simpson explored a new road across the Great Basin to Carson Valley, one which kept south of the Salt Desert and the Humboldt alike, and this became the line of the Overland Stage and the Pony Express, also seeing a little travel by overland immigrants. Not until the completion of the Pacific Railroad in 1869, however, did

---

[45] William Kelly, *An Excursion to California over the Prairie, Rocky Mountains, and Great Sierra Nevada*, I, 223, 231, 234–56.

[46] This of course was James C. Sly, whose name recurs in the 1848 journals we have quoted. Johnston gives a considerable account of him, *op. cit.*, 183–84.

[47] *Ibid.*, 192–99.

the Salt Lake Cutoff fall into desuetude. Responding to the pull of the railroad, the wagon road to Wells, Nevada, from that time diverged from the old Salt Lake Cutoff at the Sink of Deep Creek, bending south around the Raft River Mountains through Park Valley, down to Bovine, and thence on to Wells, closely paralleling the steel rails. Still later, the building of US 40 across the Salt Desert made both of the old California roads north of Great Salt Lake obsolete. Its original function gone, the Salt Lake Cutoff continued in use as a route to Oregon and western Idaho, though west of Strevell the original trail was little used, travelers instead turning north down the wide Raft River Valley to the Snake.[48] After large-scale reclamation of the Snake plain began, this road carried a steadily increasing volume of traffic, and with the coming of the automobile and modern highways it was transformed into the arterial route we travel today as US 30S and Interstate 84.

---

[48]For additional information, see L. A. Fleming and A. R. Standing, "The Road to 'Fortune': The Salt Lake Cutoff," *Utah Historical Quarterly*, XXXIII (Summer, 1965). The authors' interpretation of mileages and descriptions "differs a little from *West from Fort Bridger*."

INDEX

Adobe Rock (Black Rock): 83; Reed
overtakes Hastings at, 142n19; Jeffer-
son camp near, 148n31, 149n33;
mentioned, 192, 221n25; gravesite?,
221n26
Adobie Hall: 265
Alfred, [   ]: Lucinda's ten-hour hus-
band, 164
Allen, W. W. and R. B. Avery: on desert
crossing, 122; on Harlan-Young in
Weber Canyon, 143n22; on John
Hargrave death, 151n36
Altamont: site of, 64n15, 129n4
American River: 23
Andrus, Manomas (Gibson): Aunt
Nome, mentioned, xxvi
Antelope Creek: 63n12; Edwin Bryant
describes, 127n3; Pratt describes,
128n4; see Pioneer Hollow
Antelope Island: in Great Salt Lake, 8–
9; Frémont describes visit, 8–9;
named by Frémont, 9; good grass,
water, timber, game, 9n14
Antelope Valley: 18
Antelope: large numbers seen, 63; W.
B. Brown shoots three, 65; men-
tioned, 68, 171n63
Applegate Cutoff: 7
Applegate, Jesse: locates cutoff, 7
Arbuckle, Clyde: San Jose historian,
15n6
Archambault (Archambeau), Auguste:
scouts Salt Desert, 10, 11; men-
tioned, 12, 13; guides Stansbury
across Salt Desert, 16n27, 17; tells
Stansbury of Frémont, 35n15; men-
tioned, 269, 270n45, 271
Argenta Station, Southern Pacific Rail-
road: 235n61
Arkansas River: 8
Artifacts: sent to Sutter's Fort Museum,
xiv
Ashley, Otis: 19n31
Ashley, William H.: fur trapper, 3;
overtakes party of mountaineers,
3n1; takes wheeled cannon across
South Pass, 4
Aspen Mountain: Clayton describes,
128n4
Aspen Tunnel: 63n11, 64n14

Astoria, Ore.: 188
Atkinson, Gen. Henry: 3
Avery, R. B.: see W. W. Allen

Babbitt, Almon W.: Mentions first gold-
seekers, 303n42
Bannock River: 5
Barber, John (Jr.?): 123, 142n20
Barber, John: Kyburz's father-in-law,
123, 142n20; catches scorpion, 153
Barber, Samuel: 123, 142n20
Barker, A. J.: 132n7
Bartleson, John: scouts, 286n14
Bartleson-Bidwell party: see Bidwell-
Bartleson party
Basin Spring: 132n7
Basman Creek: 215–16, see also Beau-
chemin's Creek and East Canyon
Creek
Bates Settlement (Erda): 149n33
Bauchemins: 267, 268, 271 see Beau-
chemins
Bauchmin's Fork: see Beauchemin's
Creek
Bear Lake: and Jedediah S. Smith, 3
Bear River Divide: 63n11
Bear River Valley: mentioned, 4, 6, 46,
47, 131
Bear River: 46, 64; camp on, 128; emp-
ties into Great Salt Lake, 131; men-
tioned, 132n7, 140n18, 153, 208,
209n5, 254, 256, 273
Beauchemin's Creek: in Hudson's Bay
Company correspondence as early as
1845, 42n33; early name for East
Canyon Creek, 42n33
Beauchemin's (Bauchmin's, Bossman's)
Fork: 42n33
Beauchemin, Jean Baptiste: Hudson's
Bay Company employee, 42n33
Becks Hot Spring: 145n27
Beckwith, Lt. E. G.: reconnoiters
Weber Canyon, 70n29; describes
Secret Pass obstacles, 108n73; on
Devils Gate, 142n21; names
Franklin River, 172n65
Benalleck, Stephen S.: Newark Rangers
member, 261
Bent's Fort: 8
Beowawe: 235n60

pher, gives name to Clover Valley,
172n65
Eight-Mile (Sulphur) Spring: in Skull
Valley, 36n21
Eldredge, Ira: 264n20
Elephant's Statue: named, 67
Elko (Nev.): Clyman-Hastings party
reach, 29
Elliott, Milford (Milt): teamster, 199,
204; unyoked oxen, 225; mentioned,
229n41
Emigrant Pass: site of Reed-Snyder ar-
gument, 236n65
Emigrant Springs: 234n59, two miles
south of Cedar Spring, 291n23,
292n24
Emigration Canyon (Nev.): 285
Emigration Canyon: 32n3, 217, 218n20,
218n21, 245, 248, 251, 264, 265, 272
Ensign Peak: Salt Lake Valley, several
Mormons climb, 145n27
Eutaw Lake (Utah Lake): 203
Eutaw Outlet (Jordan River): 243, 245
Eutaw (Uinta) Mountains: 44
Evanston (Wyo.): Clyman in vicinity of,
44n23; Bryant near site of, 64n17
Ewing, Robert: mentioned, 52

Fairmont Park: 40n28
Farmington Bay: 79, 144n24
Farmington: 79
Farnham, Thomas J.: mentioned by
Hastings, 25
Father Noah's Ark: see Witches
Favour, Alpheus H.: Old Bill Williams
biographer, examines Williams' ac-
count records, 17n29
Ferguson, J. C.: in Bryant-Russell
party, 60n6; leaves party, 89, 90
Ferris, Warren A.: relates naming of
Malad, 296n32
Fever: prevails among emigrants, fre-
quently fatal, 65
Fire Mountain: see Silver Island
Fish springs: 176
Fishing: Bryant catches trout, 60; Miller
and salmon-trout, 76; apparatus in
great demand, 76–77
Fitzpatrick, Thomas (Broken Hand):
Clyman comrade, 28
Five German boys: in Lienhard party,
123; had one wagon, 123; Bancroft
on, 123n14; trade cows to Miles
Goodyear, 124; mentioned, 142n20,

176n52; break camp, 167, 170n62;
eat baked bread dough, 180; dissen-
sion at canyon crossing, 183; and
Jefferson, 191
Floating Island: in Great Salt Desert,
14; mentioned, 96
Flowery Lake: 15n24, 18, 34n13, 35n15,
106; springs at, 170n62, 171, 244;
Donner-Reed party reaches, 230n44
Fort Bernard: Clyman at, 115n8
Fort Boise: first wheeled vehicle at, 4;
Chiles pack party at, 6
Fort Bridger (Britcher, fort Pritcher,
Bridgers Trading house): 28; and
Clyman, 39n28; Hastings and
Clyman at, 46, 48; Col. Russell party
at, 51; described as a miserable pen,
52; and two or three miserable log-
cabins, 55; location of, 55; Hastings
wagon train departs, 77, 89, 184; two
roads lead west from, 127; Mormons
near, 127n3; mentioned, 197, 209n4,
233n57; Mormons at, 241; men-
tioned, 273
Fort Hall: trading post (Hudson's Bay
Company), 26, 28, 29, 32, original
wagon trail to, 32n3; mentioned, 51,
55, 58, 127, 184, 188n2, 195n5, 203,
277, 287n16.
Fort Laramie: Clyman party at, 47;
Russell at, 50; mentioned, 55
Fosdick, Jay: 200
Foster, William M.: 200
Fowler, Mrs. Malinda (Harlan): wife of
William Fowler, 122
Fowler, William: loses oxen, 122;
brother-in-law of John Hargrave,
151n36
Francis Creek: erroneously identified on
Bryant-Russell trail, 66n20, men-
tioned, 67n21
Franklin Lake: 18, 33n6, 174n66
Franklin River: 33n6, 108; named,
172n65
Frazier, [   ]: mentioned, 76
Frémont Island: in Great Salt Lake, 5
Frémont, John Charles: explorer, takes
howitzer, 5; Third Expedition of, 7;
borrows incidents for Memoirs, 8n12;
camps at site of Salt Lake City, 8;
describes Antelope Island visit, 8–9;
names Antelope Island, 9; and Utah
Indian (Wanship's son?), 9n14;
crosses Salt Desert, 10; loses a few

Goodyear's road, 132n7; vetoes the road, 132n7

Lone Rock Spring: 36n20, 87n57

Lone Rock Valley (Rock Mound): 153n38; in Skull Valley, 192

Long, Dr. T. Pope: on Hastings, 49; mentions U.S.-Mexico War, 50; mentioned, 77n40, 115n6

Lost Creek (Berry Creek, North Fork of Weber, Pumbar's Fork): 43n37; and James Hudspeth, 59n3, 65n18, 67n21, 69n25–27; Low Pass: north end of Cedar Mountains, 37n22, 224n32

Lowe Peak (Oquirrh range): 38n26

Lower Wells: 221, attempt to identify, 221n25

[   ], Lucinda: Hoppe maidservant, 124; the well-known, fat, fair-haired Miss, 154; Lienhard describes, 154; behavior of, 164–66; husband dies, 165; marries sailor, 165

Lund, William A.: LDS historian, xxv, 21, 272n48

Lyman, Amasa: journal, 127n1

Mad Woman Camp (Basin Camp): 230

Maggie Creek: 234n58

Magna: salt spring near, 147n28, 148n29; Donner-Reed camp at, 220n23

Magnuson, Mrs. E. J.: Lienhard grand-daughter, 118, 122

Mail route: Camp Floyd to the Rubies, 175n68

Main Canyon (Little East Canyon): 42n36; and Hudspeth, 70n28; and Hogsback, 73n24, 213n12

Malad River: 4, 5, 279, 295, 296n32

Malan, Kent: tracks Bryant-Russell party, 65n18

Malheur River: 6

Maly, Mrs. Charles A.: see Rowena Korns

Margrat: George Donner's cream-col-ored mare stolen, 231

Markham, Stephen: Mormon, searches for trail, 213n12

Marsh, John: 24

Martin, Thomas S.: and manuscript narrative of Frémont Third Expedi-tion, 8n13

Marys River: and Clyman-Hastings party, 29, 31n2, 32n3; mentioned, 33,

89, 121, 183, 233n57, 234, 243, 297; see also Humboldt River, Ogden's River

Mathers, Carolan: 19n31

Mathers, James: member of Harlan-Young company, 19n31; journal published, 19n31; 57 wagons on Hastings Cutoff, 130n5; mentioned, 124, 137n10, 203 n9

Maxwell, Lucien: scouts Salt Desert, 10, 12

May, Richard Martin: overland journal of, mentions Hensley, 281–83; *The Schreek of Wagons: A Sketch of a Migrating Family to Callifornia*, cited, 282–83

McAllister, John D. T.: describes route down Silver Creek Canyon, 264n20

McBride, John R.: describes Hastings, Hudspeth, and vaquero, 47, 48

McClary, James: in Bryant-Russell party, 60n6; stricken with fever, 65, 98; and Bryant find spring, 103; kills duck, 106

McCutchen (McClutchem, Mc-Cutcheon, McCutcher), William: in Donner party, 200; overtakes Hast-ings, 211n9; rides on to Sutter's fort, 229n41

McCutchen, John: in Young party, 115

McCutcheon: see McCutchen, William

McDonnell, William: teamster, 161n51

McKellar, Charles: rancher, 166n56

McKellar, Pete: Pilot Peak rancher, aids in search for relics, xiv; property owner, 166n56

McKinstry, George Jr.: unpublished journal, mentioned, 114; criticizes Donner party, 166n57; mentioned, 187; *Emigrants' Guide* owned by, in Bancroft Library, 202n7; receives Stanton letter, 209n4; in *California Star*, 213n11; on Stanton and Mc-Cutchen, 229n41

McMonagill (William McDonald?): in Young party, 115

Medicine Bow Mountains: 273, 274

Medicine Butte: unmistakable land-mark, 64n17

Medicine Spring: Indians at, 174n66

Meek, Joe: mountaineer, 4

Melad (Malad): Battalion boys fish, 295; 295n31; fishing in, 296; named for tainted beaver, 296

Pratt, Addison: encounters Isaac Rogers at Humboldt Sink, 279; diary quoted: 286–301; names Twin Sisters, 288; fishes for trout, 291; relates naming of Malad River, 296n32; family background, 300n38

Pratt, Orson: 41n32; journal, 127n1, 134n8; describes Red Fork, 138n15; climbs Big Mountain Pass, 211n9; cited, 213n12, 214n13, 215n14; describes Little Mountain, 217n19; cited, 218n21, 245, younger brother of Parley P. Pratt, 251

Pratt, Parley Parker: Mormon apostle, elder brother of Orson Pratt, 251; on tour of exploration, 252; official report quoted, 253; believes in Golden Pass route, 258–59, 275; *Autobiography* of, 259; quoted, 261; sells canyon rights to finance mission, 263

Preuss, Charles: cartographer, maps Frémont's Third Expedition, 8, 17; deficiencies of map, 18n30; mentioned, 34n14, 138n13

Promontory Mountains: 4

Proveaux (Provo) River: 268, 269, 272, 274

Provo (Provaux, Proveaux, Eutaw) River: and Frémont expedition, 8

Pumbar's Fork: named for Louis Pombert, 59n3, 67n21; see Lost Creek

Pyle, (Edward G.): votes for Weber Canyon passage, 140n18

Raft River Mountains: 4, 291n23; 292n24

Raft River: 7, 20, 287n16

Rattlesnake Pass: 295n31

Reading, Pierson B.: diary of, 6; joins Chiles, 6n10

Red Butte Canyon: 39n28

Red Buttes: 47

Red Chimney Fork: see Trail Creek Canyon

Red Fork: Pratt describes, 138n15, 243, 270; see Echo Canyon

Red Mineral Spring: extreme redness of soil, 128n4

Red Run Valley: fork of the Weaver (Weber); in Echo Canyon, 210n7

Red sandstone: impassable barrier, 64n14

Redden's Cave: see Cache Cave

Redhouse: 236n65

Redlum Spring (Dell Springs, Sulphur Spring): 14, 16n27, 17, 36n19, 36n20, 37n22; 87n58, 87n59, 155n42; a Sulphur Spring, 223, 224n32, 244

Reed, James Frazier (Reednoski, Reid): journal found, 19; overtakes Hastings at Adobe Rock, 148n31, 191; diary discovered, 198; partially written by Hiram O. Miller, 198; biographical sketch of, 199; in Black Hawk war with Clyman, 199; furniture manufacturer, 199; married Margaret Keyes Backenstoe, 199; writes reminiscent accounts, 201; sets out to overtake Hastings, 211n9; breaks axletree, 217; letter in *Sangamo Journal*, 203–06; two oxen poisoned, 203; on number of wagons on the trail, 203n9; critical of Louis Vasquez, 204n10; says Bridger is his pilot, 204; mentions Robert Campbell, 204; warns of horse thieves, 204; returns with Hastings, 211n9; oxen lost in desert, 225n36; caches abandoned wagons, 228; borrows animals from company, 228n40; describes Salt Desert crossing, 224–226; his afterthoughts, 224n34; hardships of desert, 226; cattle lost, 227; left Basin camp or Mad Woman Camp, 230; notes Cave Spring, 232n50; finds Hot Springs, 234, 234n58, 234n59; and John Snyder death, 235n60, 236n65; expelled from company, 236n65; mileage figures, 239

Reed, Mrs. Margaret Keyes Backenstoe: 199

Reed, Virginia E. B.: letter of, 49n5; (Virginia Reed Murphy), 199; describes Emigration Canyon passage, 218n21; author of *Across the Plains in the Donner Party*, quoted, 218n21; writes to cousin, 224n34; letters in *Illinois Journal*, 224n34; hardships of desert crossing, 226n38; attacked by thirst-crazed steer, 226n38; letter to Mary Gillespie, 236–38

Reeds Gap: 216, 217n17

Reed Journal: irreconcilable discrepancy in mileage, 210n8; abstract appears in *Illinois Journal*, 211n9, 220n24

Reeds Road: 142n19, 245

Reinhardt, Joseph: 200

Relief Springs: mentioned, 169n60

235n60, 235n62
Thousand Springs Valley: 286
Threemile Canyon: 258, 269n41
Timpanogos: 272
Timpie Point: 14, 244
TL Bar Ranch: 98n64, 244
Toano Range: 15n24, 18; mentioned, 34,
    34n14, 35n15, 102, 105, 167n58,
    230n42
Toganini Ranch: site of Overland Stage
    Ranch, established ca. 1864, 175n68
Toler, Charlotte: married to Lansford
    W. Hastings, 250
Tollgate Canyon (Peterson Draw):
    267n27
Tollhouse: Parley P. Pratt's, 266; loca-
    tion, 266n23
Tooele Valley: Bryant reaches, 83;
    Mormon party reaches, 147n28; Jef-
    ferson camp in, 148n31; Beckwith
    on, 149n33; mentioned, 192, 221n25,
    244
Townsend, Beeson: mentions numerous
    crossings of Mountain Dell Creek,
    251n1
Tracks: by wheeled vehicle, 3
Trade: with emigrants, importance of,
    58; with Indians, 71, 72; Bryant
    trades darning needles for grasshop-
    per "fruit-cake," 81, 124
Traders: described, 58
Trail Creek Canyon: Bryant-Russell
    party descend, 65n18; rough going,
    66n19; described, 67; Red Chimney
    Fork, 67n21, 69n25
Trails: parted on benchland, 219n22
Tremain, Julius: Newark Rangers, 261
Tremonton: 295n31
Trubode, Antonio (Trudeau): 200
Trubode, Jean Baptist (Trudeau): 200
Truckee River: 23
Trucker's (Truckee) Lake: 243
Trucky (Truckee) River: 243
Truman, Jacob Mica: breaks horse, 294
Twenty Wells: see Grantsville
Twin Sisters (Twinsisters): in City of
    Rocks, 288; named by Addison Pratt,
    288

Uinta Mountains: 58, 62, 131, 248, 256
Union Pacific: mentioned, 63n12, 70n29
Upper Wells: Donner camp at, 221n25
Uta river: see Jordan River
Utah Outlet: see Jordan River

Utah Valley: and Frémont Expedition,
    8
Utah (Uta, Eutaw) Lake: Clyman com-
    ment on, 38; empties into Great Salt
    Lake, 82; Lienhard mentions,
    145n26; mentioned, 218, 255, 256

Valley of Fifty Springs (Ruby Valley):
    232n52
Valley of Fountains (Ruby Valley): 193;
    described, 194
Van Cott, John: on exploration commit-
    tee, 254, 265
Van Gordan, Ira: member Harlan
    company, 113
Van Gordan, John: member Harland
    party, 113
Vasquez, Louis: Bridger's partner,
    mentioned, 52; Reed critical of,
    204n10
Vasquez & Bridger: trading post propri-
    etors, 203; Reed praises, 205
Veatch, A. C.: *Areal Geology of a Portion
    of Southwestern Wyoming with Special
    Reference to Coal and Oil*, cited,
    44n44, 62n9, 132n7, 208n3
Verbeck, Henry: Newark Rangers
    member, 261
Victory Highway: xiv

Wadaduka: Ruby Valley Indian name,
    174n66
Walker, Henson: 279n4
Walker, Joseph Reddeford: moun-
    taineer, 5; guides Chiles' wagons, 6ff;
    mentioned, 12, 138n13, 204n12; has
    low opinion of Salt Desert route: 17;
    leads Frémont detachment, 23; to
    meet Frémont, 24; W. E. Taylor
    mentions, 47n2; carries letter to St.
    Louis, Mo., 50; Bryant describes, 58;
    with horse herd, 58; Chiles party
    guide, 61n8; and salt plain water
    holes, 89; guided Frémont party, 89;
    mentioned as guide, 102; guides
    Chiles wagons, 208n3, 278
Walker-Chiles party: see also Chiles
    party; trail followed by Talbot, 61n8
Walker Lake: Frémont rendezvous, 18,
    23, 31n2; mentioned, 34n10
Wall Defile: 234n58 see Moleen Canyon
Walnut Creek: 31n2
Wanship (Ute Indian): son of, 9n14
Wanship: town of, 269n42, 269n43